Streamer Fly Tying and Fishing

Books by Joseph D. Bates, Jr.

Spinning for American Game Fish

Trout Waters and How to Fish Them

Streamer Fly Fishing
in Fresh and Salt Water

Spinning for Fresh Water Game Fish

Spinning for Salt Water Game Fish

The Outdoor Cook's Bible

Streamer Fly Tying and Fishing

Elementary Fishing

Atlantic Salmon Flies and Fishing
(with a subscribed limited edition of 600 copies)

Reading the Water

Fishing

How to Find Fish and Make Them Strike

The Atlantic Salmon Treasury *(editor)*

Streamers and Bucktails: The Big Fish Flies

Fishing *(revised, enlarged edition)*

The Art of the Atlantic Salmon Fly

Streamer Fly Tying and Fishing

Books by Joseph D. Bates, Jr.

Spinning for American Game Fish

Trout Waters and How to Fish Them

Streamer Fly Fishing
in Fresh and Salt Water

Spinning for Fresh Water Game Fish

Spinning for Salt Water Game Fish

The Outdoor Cook's Bible

Streamer Fly Tying and Fishing

Elementary Fishing

Atlantic Salmon Flies and Fishing
(with a subscribed limited edition of 600 copies)

Reading the Water

Fishing

How to Find Fish and Make Them Strike

The Atlantic Salmon Treasury *(editor)*

Streamers and Bucktails: The Big Fish Flies

Fishing *(revised, enlarged edition)*

The Art of the Atlantic Salmon Fly

Streamer Fly Tying and Fishing

Joseph D. Bates, Jr.

Frontispiece and line drawings by Milton C. Weiler
Original color plates by Walter Whittum, Inc.

*With new material presented by Pamela Bates Richards
and new color plates photographed by Michael D. Radencich*

STACKPOLE BOOKS

Copyright © 1950 and 1966 by Joseph D. Bates, Jr.
Copyright © 1995 by Pamela Bates Richards
New color plates copyright © 1995 by Michael D. Radencich
New illustrations copyright © 1995 by the estate of Milton C. Weiler

Published by
STACKPOLE BOOKS
5067 Ritter Road
Mechanicsburg, PA 17055

All rights reserved, including the right to reproduce this book or portions thereof in any form or by any means, electronic or mechanical, including photocopying, recording, or by any information storage and retrieval system, without permission in writing from the publisher. All inquiries should be addressed to Stackpole Books, 5067 Ritter Road, Mechanicsburg, PA 17055.

Printed in the United States of America

10 9 8 7 6 5 4 3 2 1

First edition

Cover illustration by Milton C. Weiler

Library of Congress Cataloging-in-Publication Data
Bates, Joseph D., 1903–
    Streamer fly tying & fishing / Joseph D. Bates, Jr. ; foreword by Keith Fulsher.
    p.   cm.
    Originally published: Harrisburg, Pa. : Stackpole Books, 1950. With a new pref.
    Includes index.
    ISBN 0-8117-1702-X
    1. Flies, Artificial. 2. Fly casting. I. Title. II. Title: Streamer fly tying and fishing.
SH451.B287   1995
799.1'755—dc20   94-44618
                                                                                 CIP

To
My Wife
HELEN ELLIS BATES
—With Devotion

The Author Expresses His Appreciation
to The Anglers and Fly Dressers
Who Have Added Their Knowledge and Skill
to This Book, including:

A. I. Alexander, III, Francis Ames, Dan Bailey, A. W. Ballou, Ray Bergman, Kenneth J. Botty, Joe Brooks, Jr., Edgar Burke, Robert H. Cavanagh, Jr., Herman Christian, Eugene V. Connett, Paul Cook, Robert Coulson, Lee Davis, Gordon Dean, Maury Delman, Jim Deren, Frank Dufresne, Dick Eastman, Bill Edson, Art Flick, C. L. Franklin, Keith C. Fulsher, Arthur W. Fusco, Don Gapen, Harold Gibbs, Larry Green, Elizabeth Greig, B. A. Gulline, Don Harger, Austin S. Hogan, Herbert Howard, John Alden Knight, Paul Kukonen, Earl Leitz, Gene Letourneau, Bill Lohrer, Stuart Longendyke, Hal Lyman, Ed Materne, Robert McCafferty, Al McClane, John McDonald, Arthur Mills, Jr., Chief Needahbeh, Lew Oatman, Charles Ortloff, Zell Parkhurst, Roy Patrick, Gardner and Lisle Percy, S. L. Perinchief, C. Jim Pray, Bert Quimby, Warren Raymond, Fred Reed, Bill Reynolds, Homer Rhode, Jr., O. H. P. Rodman, Alex Rogan, E. W. Rogers, E. H. Rosborough, Hubert Sanborn, Hagen R. Sands, Ray Salminen, Peter J. Schwab, Don Shiner, S. R. Slaymaker, II, Harold Smedley, Roy Steenrod, Carrie Stevens, Joseph S. Stickney, Robert Stone, Paul Stroud, H. G. Tapply, Benn Treadwell, Ted Trueblood, Bill and Morrie Upperman, Jim Warner, Oscar Weber, Herbert Welch, Don E. West, Charlie Wetzel, E. C. Wotruba, Lee Wulff and Paul Young

Additional Acknowledgments

Personally and on behalf of the author, I also would like to express my most sincere appreciation to the following individuals and organizations. Their assistance and contributions have been invaluable to this new edition.

The American Museum of Fly Fishing, Captain Jimmie Albright, Carolyn Capstick Meehan, Carrie, Chris and Eric Capstick, Bill Catherwood, Bob Cavanagh, Bruce DeMustchine, Keith Fulsher, Robert Hilyard, Alanna and Don Johnson, Jerry King, Jacquline Knight, Nick Lyons, Dixon Merkt, Ted Niemeyer, Don Palmer, Dorothy Porter and the estate of the Reverend Robie M. Brown, The Rangeley Lakes Region Historical Society, William Shattuck, John Swan, the estate of Milton C. Weiler—and of course the team: Michael Radencich, Bob Warren, Peter Castagnetti, and Mark Waslick.

Pamela Bates Richards

Thomas Capstick, Jr.
1931–1981

Before his fiftieth year had ended and moments after shooting a wild goose, Tom Capstick died. Tom possessed an infectious and remarkable zeal for living. He was a man of wit, humor, compassion, and commitment.

The collection of trout and streamer flies he acquired during his abbreviated life is testimony to his dedication to the world of angling. Had he lived longer, perhaps that collection would have been part of his own book.

Many of the streamer flies included in the color plates in this edition are from the Capstick Collection. Originally owned by the author, they are included in this volume in memory and in tribute to Tom Capstick, a consummate collector and a consummate friend.

Following is the eulogy written by Tom's friend and fellow member of the Angler's Club of New York, Calvin Koch: "As we go through life and life swirls around us, from time to time we meet someone who, for many reasons, is a special person. Thomas Capstick, Jr., was one of these special people. He was a warm, generous man with a twinkle in his eye and a zest for life which he transmitted without effort to everyone near him wherever he went. When he entered a room, that room became brighter because he was there. Whenever he met a friend, no matter how many other people were there, he had the happy faculty of making that friend feel that he or she was the one person he wanted to see more than anyone else. Although Tom will not walk with us or talk with us again, his blithe spirit will always be with us. Tom Capstick was a kindly man, a devoted friend, companion, son, brother, husband, and father, an outdoorsman, a sportsman, and above all, a thorough gentleman."

Milton C. Weiler
1910–1974

Inspired by the world he loved, Milton C. Weiler is regarded as one of the finest painters of sporting art of his generation. Equally dedicated to gunning and angling, Weiler instilled in his paintings and carvings a rare authenticity and sensitivity.

Whether the subject is a chilly dawn or a surging salmon, the art of Milton Weiler reflects the artist's compelling sense of nature. He had a lifelong interest in conservation and the preservation of wildlife and was one of the founders of The American Museum of Fly Fishing. In addition to teaching fine arts, topography, and graphics, Weiler was also an illustrator whose sketches and watercolors graced many publications, including those of Derrydale Press, Winchester Press, Scribners, and Coward-McCann. His paintings, limited editions, and portfolios are cherished by collectors, as are his exquisite and lifelike carvings of waterfowl and shorebirds.

The drawings that appear in this edition of STREAMER FLY TYING AND FISHING have been generously provided by the Weiler family—as tribute to a man who created beauty in form, in color, and especially friendship.

Foreword

Of all the different types of fishing flies, none are more beautiful or more effective than minnow flies—streamers and bucktails tied to imitate small baitfish. Although information concerning the origin of these flies is somewhat hazy, it is clear that their popularity was nurtured and developed in the rivers and lakes of the state of Maine during the early part of this century. But unless anglers fished in Maine or had friends who did, it was unlikely that they would would be exposed to more than a dozen of the most popular patterns. All that changed in 1950 when Colonel Joseph D. Bates, Jr., wrote the first of his three books on streamer flies.

Joe Bates was fascinated with the long flies and often put them to use when he fished the wilderness areas of Maine. Joe got to know the fly dressers and guides of the region, people like Carrie Stevens, who developed many exotic streamer patterns, including the world-famous *Gray Ghost;* Gardner Percy and Bert Quimby, two well-known professional tiers; and top woodsman and Joe's favorite Maine guide, Ross McKenney. The more Joe associated with the people who tied and fished with streamers, the more he realized that important streamer and bucktail patterns and the history surrounding them should be preserved and passed on to all anglers. His enormous success in fulfilling that goal through his books is unquestioned.

A thorough and tireless researcher, Colonel Bates authored his first book, SPINNING FOR AMERICAN GAME FISH, in 1947. Until the time of his death in 1988 at the age of eighty-five, he produced sixteen books on various aspects of sport fishing but was always best known and respected for his work on streamers and Atlantic salmon flies. His 1947 book introduced spin fishing to Americans, a method that was not well known in this country at that time. The author and book quickly became the absolute authority on the subject, and the last chapter gave a hint of what was to come. In that chapter, entitled "Fly Fishing with Spinning Tackle," were dressing instructions for ten of the most popular streamer flies of the period. Joe had chosen the flies based on his correspondence with the leading streamer fly fishermen across the country. Pattern details came from flies tied by the originators in the author's growing collection that was established long before collecting became popular.

Joe Bates published his first streamer book, STREAMER FLY FISHING IN FRESH AND SALT WATER, in 1950. In his clear and easily understood style, Joe gave detailed information on tactics and tackle and the history and dressing instructions for over two hundred patterns. For the first time "the big fish flies," as Joe liked to call them, were treated in depth and a ready source of pattern recipes was available. Professional tiers and amateurs alike referred to this book as the authority for correct patterns.

At the time I was dressing streamer flies for a fly shop in New York City and remember frequently using Joe's book as a reference. The book eventually went out of print, but because the sport of fly fishing was growing the book was still in demand and prices for used copies, which were almost impossible to get, escalated. In 1966 Joe's second streamer book, STREAMER FLY TYING AND FISHING, was released. This book followed the same format as its predecessor but was updated and expanded to include a fly-dressing section listing over three hundred patterns, with details on their origination and use. This was Joe's most important work on the subject. A specially bound limited edition of six hundred copies was also published; these books have become very valuable collector's items.

It was in the early summer of 1965, while he was gathering material for STREAMER FLY TYING AND FISHING, that I first met Joe. As an advertising executive, he was doing some work for the Nestles company of White Plains, New York, just a few miles from my home. A

Foreword

mutual friend who knew of my efforts in designing the Thunder Creek Series of Baitfish Imitations, a group of flies tied to represent particular species of forage fish, arranged for us to meet to discuss the patterns. We had a good session and found we had many mutual friends in the fly fishing community. We met a number of times after that, corresponded regularly, and became good friends.

As time went on, the 1966 edition also became scarce and available only in the out-of-print market at high prices. It was time once more for a new edition. STREAMERS AND BUCKTAILS: THE BIG FISH FLIES, Joe's third streamer book, was published in 1979. Although this book contains important material from the two earlier books and an expanded pattern section, the emphasis is on how to choose and use streamers and bucktails under varying conditions to attract those larger game fish that we all enjoy catching. This book now too is rather scarce.

With the sport of fly fishing still expanding, especially with the explosive growth of saltwater fly fishing, it seems timely that new editions of Colonel Bates's classic works on both streamer and salmon flies be reissued. Although Joe is not here to do that, we are fortunate that his daughter, Pamela Bates Richards, follows in her father's interests. It's through Pam's efforts that this current edition is published. Pam has made it possible for anglers who read these pages to fish shoulder to shoulder with her father, Colonel Joseph D. Bates, Jr., the most knowledgeable angler and accomplished writer of his time on the versatile streamer fly.

KEITH FULSHER

Eastchester, New York

Preface

At a military service in the fall of 1988, taps sounded the end of the life of my father, Joe Bates. Along with the sixteen books he wrote, the meticulously inventoried and annotated collections of flies, tackle, books, art, decoys, and guns that he left were eloquent evidence of a life that had been devoted to the out-of-doors and dedicated to the world of angling. He left, too, an accumulation of correspondence spanning both the world and the decades, letters that reflected his determined effort to gather and to record as much information as possible relating to the mystique of the flies.

Typically, Joe's quest was for information regarding patterns and their histories, and the letters, together with the responses to them, became the foundations for the books that were to follow. The correspondence, collectively, is a chronicle of personalities and of friendships. These letters were written when North American streamer flies had little documented history. This point is clarified by the simple fact that, unlike later Bates books, STREAMER FLY TYING AND FISHING has no bibliography. In addition to establishing a base for the history of North American streamer flies, published quotations from the correspondence added a dimension to the flies that might have been otherwise ignored. I can't help wondering if the excitement of catching a fish on a *Gray Ghost* streamer would be quite the same without an awareness of the lore surrounding its origin, the story of Carrie Stevens and of Upper Dam. Those who care are captivated by the now legendary tale of the milliner from Maine who abandoned her tasks in camp to design a fly and proceeded to land a six-pound, thirteen-ounce trout with it—only after she "had hastily changed into a more suitable dress."

In going through my father's papers to do research for this book, I found tucked away in manila envelopes, tied with string and dusty with decades, letters from numerous and notable individuals of the era. Dad's absence was softened by his handwritten memos within his self-edited filing system. Cryptic notations such as "Destroy upon my death" left little question, but these were balanced by lighter messages such as "Good stuff in here" or "Pay close attention to this." Succinct reminders of responsibility continue to pop up in both likely and unlikely places, making it clear that the Colonel is still in charge. The process of discovery rivaled the magic moments of childhood. A large rabbit had definitely left something in my basket! Without permission given or needed, I had the opportunity to peek into the past.

Invaluable resources surfaced from the desk Joe had used for over half a century. For the early books, my father had been his own photographer. Using a camera that looked like an accordion, he captured the woods as they were. In the depths of a long-used drawer, I found negatives of photographs from the 1930s to the 1980s. They shared space with tiny pieces of art by Weiler, DeFeo, Burke, and Hogan as well as other memorabilia that included fly envelopes with notes from Stevens, Grant, Glasso, and Boyd, fishing diaries, three-cent stamps, and a lifetime supply of rubber bands. There seemed to be no end to the trove—and there still isn't. I have yet to look through a collection—feathered, written, or photographed—without unearthing something new or previously unrealized or unappreciated. Initially the care I gave to organizing the treasures of a life past was as positive as it was cathartic. Now, in the bittersweet manner of change, the challenge has developed into a fascination that my family is welcome to call obsessive.

Shortly after my father's death, I met Peter Castagnetti and Bob Warren through our mutual association with The American Museum of Fly Fishing. From caring for the collections my father left to inspiring the publishing of his work, Peter and Bob have been an integral part of compounding projects. Ultimately they succeeded in thoroughly complicating my life by introducing me to salmon fishing. In his gentle way, Peter tempers my growing fixation with keeping my waders wet

Preface

with his shared appreciation of lichen and lupine, and his innate sense of propriety keeps us on the less-traveled road. With the alacrity of an osprey, Bob Warren tackles every task with a sense of precision and a goal of perfection. On the river, in the woods, or at his tying vise, his success is obvious. I know that Dad would have had nothing but respect for the attention to detail that Bob has given the project. Had these two men met, they would have found a common bond in their dedication to the finer elements of flies and fishing.

Whether we are endeavoring to conquer the challenges of the collections or of the rivers, a good and rare partnership has developed. When the idea of publishing this book advanced into a contract with Stackpole Books, we began to realize a new level of commitment. The trio of Castagnetti, Warren, and Richards became a team with the welcome additions of Mark Waslick, armed with his own impressive talents at the fly-tying bench and angling bookcase, and Michael Radencich, with his extraordinary talents and fresh approach to fly photography. Spurred on by liberal raillery, we get together as often as possible to sift and sort both ideas and flies—and occasionally to apply feathers to hooks.

In the early stages of planning this edition of STREAMER FLY TYING AND FISHING, we decided to leave the text as its author had written it twenty-eight years before. Nick Lyons, who had generously offered to be a friend to the project, suggested that we augment the text with new color plates, combining Michael Radencich's expertise behind the camera with the treasures that continued to emerge from my father's files. Linking the past to the present and the tiers to the flies, we wanted to parallel visually what my father had accomplished in the text.

Once the decision to add new color plates was made, the never-ending treasure hunt through memorabilia took on new purpose. Slipped into the author's copy of STREAMER FLY TYING AND FISHING was a small sepia photograph of Carrie Stevens taken in the 1920s. It became the background for Plate 3. In that book I also found the pattern page that Edgar Burke had submitted to Herter's Catalogue, accompanied by a beautifully detailed painting of one of Doctor Burke's original flies. Together they became a part of Plate 11. The files of correspondence provided unlimited material, such as letters from Chief Needahbeh simply signed "the chief." Others dated themselves with three-digit telephone numbers, and a very special letter from Carrie Stevens told her own story of the origin of the *Gray Ghost* streamer fly. The mounted trout that appears in a photograph with Herbie Welch's flies in Plate 5 had presided over my father's study for many years. Dad said it was one of Herbie's last.

When I found an article my father had written during the forties about Shang Wheeler and White-nosed (or Pin Cushion) Pete, the elusive and legendary trout of Upper Dam Pool, I felt driven to locate Shang's painting. Don Palmer at The Rangeley Lakes Region Historical Society suggested that it might be in Connecticut in Dixon Merkt's fine collection of Shang Wheeler's work. It was, and Dixon kindly allowed White-nosed Pete to join the flies named for Shang in Plate 4. During one of my many pleasurable conversations with Ted Niemeyer, he revealed that a *Bumblepuppy* dressed by Theodore Gordon was part of his impressive collection. That fly was soon on its way across the country.

Borrowing time from writing her own books, Linda Warren painstakingly developed from the author's negatives many of the black-and-white photographs that appear in this edition. When artist and friend John Swan heard of the project, he offered a fly wallet that had belonged to Bill Edson, a friend of John's grandfather. In this wallet were several Edson patterns that are being published here for the first time.

With the assistance of these individuals as well as many others, the project had indeed become a collaborative effort. The union of the memorabilia with the histories of the flies that Joe had written almost thirty years before brought a new reality to the past. Instead of merely enhancing the text with the new color plates, the availability of such remarkable material made it possible photographically to bring the past into the present.

We encountered, however, one distinct and possibly insurmountable problem. The extensive collection of streamer flies that my father had acquired for the production of his three books on the subject had been traded years before to accommodate his transition to collecting salmon flies. To maintain the integrity of the text, I felt it was essential to find original flies of the era. Although I am not necessarily a believer in providence, divine or otherwise, there have been occasions

Preface

as I have worked on the book when the project has seemed ordained. Resolving the dilemma of the flies is one such example.

For too short a time my father enjoyed the friendship of Tom Capstick before he died of a heart attack at the early age of forty-nine. Tom was as avid a collector as Joe was, and each aspired to acquire the best of its kind for their respective collections of trout and streamer flies and salmon flies. A great deal of horse trading went on between them, each periodically claiming to have made the "best swap" as the shopping bags shuttled between New York and Longmeadow. Tom will forever hold a very special place in my heart, as I know he did in my father's. It was through his friendship and that of his wife, Carolyn, that I learned that those immersed in the world of what Dad referred to as "piscatorial pleasures" were not necessarily from a different planet. Tom kindled my first independent interest in flies and fishing, and he also suggested to me that meeting Dad on his own turf might prove interesting. As a result of Tom's advice, I made an effort to speak Dad's language, and, ultimately, we shared many happy hours either tying or talking about flies. Carolyn and I recognized in one another a kindred spirit that we continue to share. Her friendship is one of life's gifts, and her generosity has made this book complete.

When Carolyn handed me the ponderous binder that had been my father's and contained the patterns and notes established during his streamer years, it was too much to hope that the accompanying flies would also be available. But indeed they were, just as both Joe and Tom had left them more than a dozen years before. Selected flies from the collection that both men treasured are now a part of the new color plates presented in this book.

Finding the Capstick-Bates collection was the first of the true triumphs in the production of this edition. The reunion of the Bates and Weiler families was the next. My father was not alone in regarding Milt Weiler as one of the finest sporting artists of our time. As fellow Army officers, Dad and Milt met at West Point, where Milt was teaching topography, but angling soon became their common bond. Always Dad's illustrator of choice, Milt prepared the art for many of the Bates books, and they were friends, personally and professionally, for a lifetime.

In comparing the 1966 edition of STREAMER FLY TYING AND FISHING to the 1970 edition of ATLANTIC SALMON FLIES AND FISHING, there is a distinct lack of interpretive art in the streamer book. Discovering that Milt's sons were both as interested as I in preserving the work of our fathers was yet another gift to the production of this edition. The Weiler family has graciously made it possible to unite Weiler and Bates once again for the enjoyment of the next generation of angling enthusiasts.

As fortuitous events continued, another in the succession was contacting Keith Fulsher. As both resource and friend, Keith has given generously to the project. Having known some of the individuals now appointed to legendary status, Keith is always fascinating to talk with. As entertaining as he is encyclopedic, his stories of time spent with my father, Herb Howard, and Charlie DeFeo give an insight that is invaluable both personally and practically. As a contributor to the 1966 edition of this book, Keith had provided firsthand information regarding flies, patterns, tiers, and methods. His library of lore seems without limit, and he has given to this edition a depth and a credibility for which I am grateful.

Just as it was never possible to separate Dad from his work, I now find it impossible to separate the pleasure from the purpose in completing this edition and that of its companion, ATLANTIC SALMON FLIES AND FISHING. It has for me been the greatest of privileges and honors to be associated not only with my father's books but especially with a volume that is dedicated with these words: "For my wife, Helen Ellis Bates—with devotion." I can only underscore and amend the author's words: For my mother—no measure of devotion could be comparable to that which she has given. As consort, diplomat, hostess, wife, and mother, she has nurtured each of the Bates books, and she continues to do so now. Graciously and generously inspiring confidence, she is lovely in every way and is, indeed, the very heart of the matter.

PAMELA BATES RICHARDS

Newburyport, Massachusetts

Contents

PART ONE   The Tactics and Tackle for
Fishing with Streamers

I. Why Fish Take Streamers   3

   Basic Reasons Why Fish Take Streamers — Importance of Exact
   Imitations — Reasons for Unusual Designs — A Method for Teas-
   ing Fish to Strike — Importance of Streamers in Early Spring
   Fishing — Visibility of Flies in Flood Water — Exact Imitations
   vs. Attractor Patterns — Locator Flies — Value of Form, Flash,
   and Action — Importance of Shape — Significance of Colors —
   Requisites of Salt Water Patterns

II. Streamers, Simple and Otherwise   20

   Notes on Early American Fly Fishing — Theodore Gordon's
   Bumblepuppies — The *Fort Wayne Bucktail* — Other Early Streamers and Bucktails — The *Scripture* and the *Donaldson* Bucktails —
   The *Rooster's Regret* of Grand Lake Stream — Progressive Evolu-
   tion of the *Colonel White, Ordway, Bonbright, Dana*, and the *Ross
   McKenney* — Definition of a Bucktail; of a Streamer — Suggestions on Construction — Importance of Translucency and Sparseness — Comparison of Eastern and Western Patterns

III. How to Select Streamers   38

Value of Imitating Minnows — Varieties in Typical Baitfish — Imitating Baitfish with Flies — Development of Natural Imitation Patterns — When a Fly Is "Right" — Influence of Water and Atmospheric Conditions on Fly Selection — Determining Proper Sizes of Streamers — The "Injured Minnow" — Relationship Between Hook Size and Fly Length — Proper Hooks for Streamers — Eastern and Western Fly Types — Difference Between "Fast Water" and "Slow Water" Flies — Weighted Flies — How to Sink Flies Quickly — Notes on Visibility of Colors — Small Flies vs. Bigger Ones — Streamers and Bucktails for Trout — Fishing for Steelhead — Flies for Landlocked Salmon — Will Atlantic Salmon Take Streamers? — Flies for Bass — Pike and Pickerel Bucktails — Crappie and Panfish Flies — Shad Flies.

IV. How to Fish Streamers in Fast Water   69

Making the Upstream Cast — Casting to Bottom Feeding Fish — How to Fish Around Rocks — Making the Quarter Upstream Cast — Value of Drift Fishing — How to Mend the Line — Making the Cross-stream Cast — Use of the Floating Line — Making the Quarter Downstream Cast — The Downstream Cast — Notes on Riffle Fishing — Unusual Ways to Fish Streamers — Fishing in the Dense Undergrowth.

V. How to Fish Streamers in Slack Water   88

Tips for Early Spring Trolling — Trolling Lines and Trolling Speeds — When to Use Rod-holders — Why Lakes Turn Over — Effects of Water Temperatures on Fish — When to Fish the Surface, and When to Fish Deep — Value of a Thermometer — Selecting Trolling Flies — Keeping Weeds off Hooks — When Not to Roll-cast — The Fan-casting Method — Trout and Salmon Fishing — How to Fish the Shore-line — Big Fish in Spring Holes — Warm Water Pond Fishing — Catching Landlocked Salmon in a Blow — Where to Find Fish — How to Fish for Bass — Bucktails and Streamers for Bass — Night-time Fishing for Bass.

VI. Western Salt Water Streamer Fishing   106

Experiences in Trolling for Chinook and Silver Salmon — Habits of Silver Salmon — Trolling Tackle — Comparisons Between Eastern and Western Trolling — Western Salt Water Bucktail Patterns — Bucktail Color Combinations — Use of Spinner Blades in Trolling — Patterns in Trolling Flies — Fishing for Cutthroat Trout — Bucktails for Cutthroat Trout — Steelhead in the Estuaries — Flies for Steelhead — A Record Striped Bass on a Fly Rod — Flies for Pacific Shad and Other Salt Water Fish.

VII. Eastern Salt Water Streamer Fishing   122

Fly Rod Tackle for Striped Bass — When and Where to Find Stripers — How to Fish a Tidal Current — Flies for Striped Bass — Light Tackle for Mackerel — How to Find Fish When Boat-fishing — Boat-fishing for Striped Bass — More About Finding Fish — Habits of the Voracious Bluefish — Flies for Bluefish — The Rare Weakfish — Suggestions for Chumming for Weakfish — A Mixed Bag at Barnegat — Pollock on a Fly Rod — Flies for Pollock — Notes on Tackle — The Catherwood Natural Imitation Patterns.

VIII. Southern Salt Water Streamer Fishing   139

Stalking Bonefish by Boat and Afoot — Favorite Bonefish Flies — Tackle for Bonefish — Experiences with Tarpon in the Mangroves — Tackle for Tarpon — Flies for Tarpon — Fishing for Barracuda and Channel Bass — Night Fishing for Ladyfish — Experiences with Snook — Flies for Snook — Tackle and Tactics for Dolphin, Jack Crevalle and Pompano — Tiny Tackle for Snapper and Mullet.

IX. Notes on Types and Dressings   165

Names of Parts of Bucktails and Streamers — Books on Fly Dressing — Hooks Recommended for Dressing Bucktails and Streamers — Choice of Hackles for Wings — How to Apply Wings — Mrs. Stevens' Secret Fly Dressing Methods — Names of Carrie Stevens' Patterns — The "Reverse-tied" Bucktail — Fulsher's "Thunder Creek" Series — How to Dress the "Thunder Creek" Patterns — List of Lew Oatman's Patterns — Lew Oatman's Comments on Flies and Fishing — Sam Slaymaker's Trout Patterns — The "Trout Fin" — Austin Hogan's Color Blending Tips — Chief Needahbeh's "Biplane" Streamer — Value of Splayed-Wing Types — "Life Action" Bucktails — Matuku Streamers — How to Dress the *Silver Garland Marabou* — How to Dress the Schwab Weighted Body Bucktails — Applying Metal Bodies and Bead Heads — Jim Pray's "Optic Bucktails" — Propellor Heads and Wiggling Discs — Weedless Bucktails and Streamers — Dressing Mylar Cheeks and Bodies — How to Make Tandem Mylar Bodied Flies — How to Apply the Wire Linkage to Tandem Flies — Splayed-Wing Flies — The "*Engells Splay-Wing Coachman*" — The "Brooks Blondes."

PART TWO
The History and Dressing of Famous Patterns
Containing Detailed and Authentic Instructions for Dressing Famous Patterns of Bucktails and Streamers — Descriptions of Important Variations — Historical Notes and Originators' Comments on Each Streamer Fly and Bucktail.   211

Appendix   361

Index   385

Color Plates

PLATE	I	Flies Designed Primarily as Baitfish Imitations
PLATE	II	Flies Designed Primarily as Attractor Patterns
PLATE	III	Prominent Eastern Fresh Water Patterns
PLATE	IV	Original Patterns by Mrs. Carrie G. Stevens
PLATE	V	Well Known Salt Water Patterns
PLATE	VI	Imitator Patterns Designed by Lew Oatman
PLATE	VII	Historic Northeastern Streamers and Bucktails
PLATE	VIII	Prominent Western Fresh Water Patterns

PLATE	1	The Bumblepuppy
PLATE	2	Flies That Have Endured
PLATE	3	Original Patterns Dressed by Carrie Gertrude Stevens
PLATE	4	Shang's White-nosed Pete and Streamers for Upper Dam
PLATE	5	Streamer Flies Originated and Dressed by Herbert Welch
PLATE	6	Original Patterns Dressed by Bill Edson, with His Fly Wallet
PLATE	7	The Chief

PLATE	8	Streamer Flies Originated and Dressed by Bert Quimby
PLATE	9	Cains River Streamers Dressed by C. Jim Pray
PLATE	10	Streamers and Bucktails Originated and Dressed by Ray Bergman
PLATE	11	Streamer Flies Originated and Dressed by Edgar Burke, M.D.
PLATE	12	Streamer Flies Originated and Dressed by Preston Jennings
PLATE	13	Streamer Flies Originated and Dressed by Austin Hogan
PLATE	14	Salt Water Patterns
PLATE	15	The Thunder Creek Series Originated and Dressed by Keith Fulsher

Introduction

Since streamer flies and bucktails imitate the baitfish on which big game fish feed, a knowledge of how to choose them and how to use them is most necessary for successful fly fishing both in fresh water and in salt. The dry fly, the wet fly, and the nymph all enjoy cherished places in an angler's bag of tricks; but all except the most opinionated will agree that streamer flies and bucktails, when properly selected and employed, hook more and bigger fish more often and in more places than any other type of fly rod lure.

My interest in them began shortly after the First World War, when they were just beginning to become popular. Since then I have been privileged to know and to fish with many of the great names in American angling—men who developed original patterns of streamer flies and bucktails that later became standard, and who also developed the techniques and tackle for using them successfully.

Fortunately (since many of the originators of these famous patterns have gone where good anglers eventually have to go), I have for many years collected flies dressed by the originators or dressed exactly to their specifications. These, with authentic facts about them, now comprise a library of many hundreds of patterns—a library unduplicatable today.

The interest of other fishermen in how to catch bigger fish more often with streamers and bucktails moved me to write STREAMER FLY FISHING—IN FRESH AND IN SALT WATER in 1950. In the ten or so years that the book has been out of print it has become a cherished collectors' item valued at many times its original price. The demand for it became so incessant that it finally seemed imperative to publish this new book, containing the better parts of the older one and much new material besides.

In retrospect, I see so much to be improved in the former book that I wonder why people like it so much. Anglers read parts of it for pleasure and parts for information. Fly dressers still refer to it as the "Hoyle" on the subject and use it to settle opinions on the components of authentic bucktail and streamer patterns—patterns dressed exactly as the originators wanted them to be. In this, I tried to provide detailed and precise information. Evidently this effort was successful, because one gentleman dressed all the two or three hundred patterns in the former book from the instructions given in it without ever having seen the patterns themselves. He showed them to me one evening, and we compared them with my originals. The duplication was so exact that I am now sure anyone can dress any pattern correctly from the information provided in the book without having to have a sample of the fly to copy.

While angling methods and styles in flies have changed during the past fifteen years, much of the information and many of the patterns remain as standard today as they were then. But new ways of fly fishing, better ways of dressing flies, and improved fly patterns have also been developed. What has become outmoded in the older book has been eliminated here. Everything new and useful that I have been able to find has been added—many new fishing methods, new fly dressing techniques, and over fifty new fly patterns which should stand the test of time.

Thus, I hope and think, modern anglers and fly dressers will find in this new book a great deal of valuable information that they can't find anywhere else. I hope they will enjoy the eight full-page color plates, which show in accurate color over one hundred of the most famous streamer and bucktail patterns either dressed personally by their originators or dressed exactly to their specifications. For their inclusion I am indebted to the Stackpole Books, and also to my friend and neighbor Walter W. Whittum, president of Walter Whittum, Inc., who is a genius in color photography, color plate making, and color printing.

Introduction   xxxi

   This book has been a labor of love which has kept me at my desk for many months when I would rather have been out fishing. If other anglers and fly dressers find it of value, I shall consider the time to have been well spent, and I shall be very grateful.

J. D. B., Jr.

Longmeadow, Massachusetts

EMERALD MINNOW   SPOT-TAILED MINNOW   SILVER MINNOW
Originated and dressed by Mr. Keith C. Fulsher

LITTLE BROOK TROUT   LITTLE BROWN TROUT   LITTLE RAINBOW TROUT
Originated by Mr. Samuel R. Slaymaker, II
Dressed by the Weber Tackle Company

JESSE WOOD
Originated by Mr. Jesse Wood. Dressed by Mr. Ray Bergman

BLACK NOSED DACE
Originated and dressed by Mr. Arthur B. Flick

MARABOU PERCH
Originated and dressed by Mr. Arthur W. Fusco

GRIZZLY PRINCE
Originated and dressed by Mr. Austin S. Hogan

MUDDLER MINNOW
Originated and dressed by Mr. Don Gapen

HORNBERG
Originated by Mr. Frank Hornberg. Dressed by the Weber Tackle Co.

POLAR CHUB
Originated and dressed by Mr. E. H. Rosborough

LEECH
Originated and dressed by Mr. Frier Gulline

SILVER MINNOW
Originated by Mr. Al Giradot. Dressed by Mr. Maury Delman

MIRACLE MARABOU BLUEBACK SHINER   MIRACLE MARABOU LONGNOSE DACE
Originated by Mr. Robert Zwirz and Mr. Kani Evans
Dressed by Mrs. Zwirz

PLATE I
Flies designed primarily as Baitfish Imitations

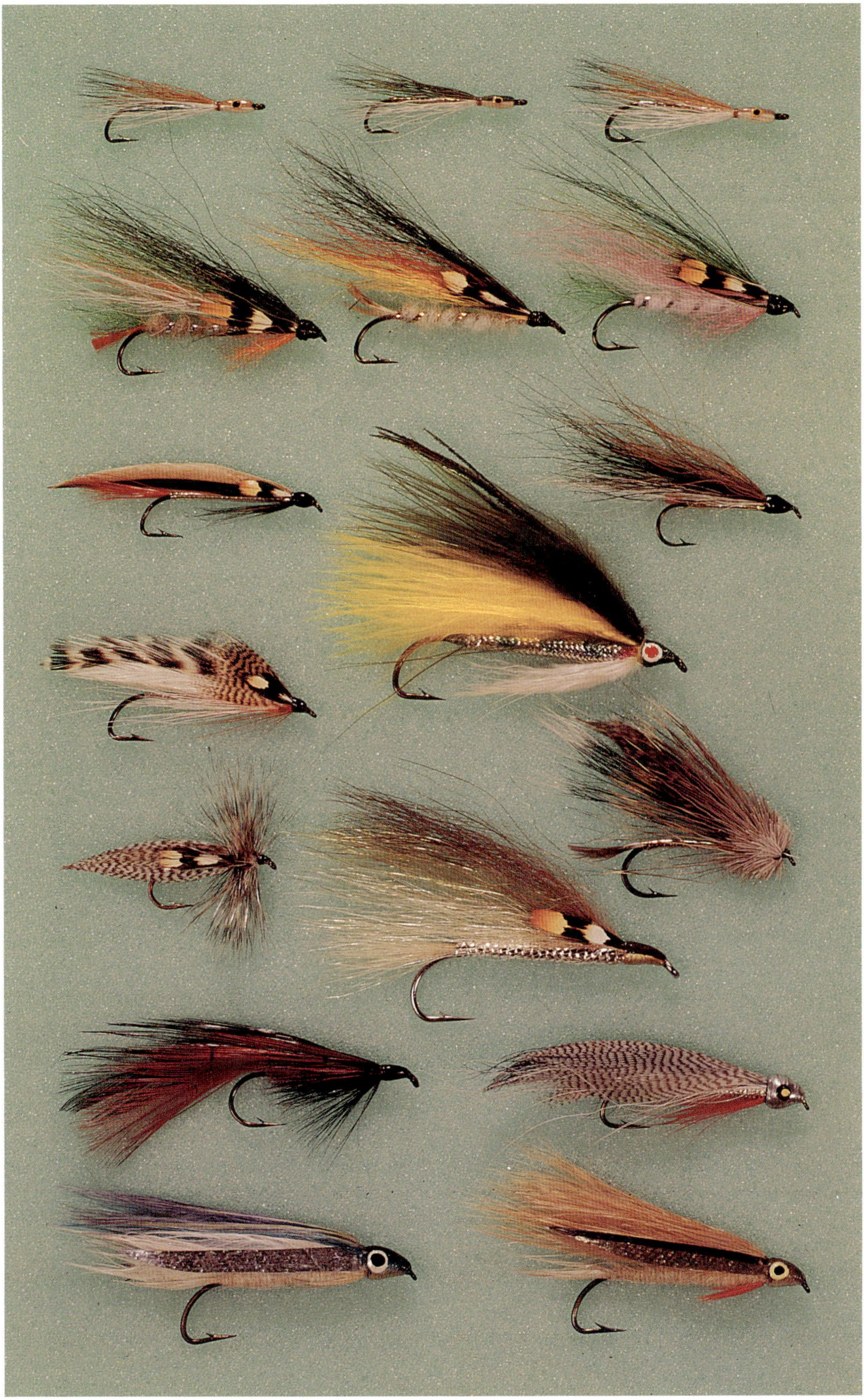

ALEXANDRA
Of English origin
Dressed by Mr.
Frier Gulline

PARMACHEENE BEAU
Originated by Mr.
Henry P. Wells. Dressed
by Fin, Fur & Feather, Ltd.

BLACK & WHITE
Originated and
dressed by Mr.
Austin S. Hogan

ROGAN ROYAL
GRAY GHOST
Originated and dressed
by Mr. Alex Rogan

BINNS
Originated and
dressed by Mr.
Frier Gulline

DR. BURKE
Originated and
dressed by Dr.
Edgar Burke

GRAY PRINCE
Originated and
dressed by Mr.
B. A. Gulline

CAMPEONA
Of South American
origin. Dressed by
Mrs. Elizabeth Greig

CAIN'S RIVER MIRAMICHI
Originated by Mr. Fred
N. Peet. Dressed by Mr.
C. Jim Pray

HARLEQUIN
Originated and dressed
by Mr. B. A. Gulline

SANBORN
Originated by Mr. Fred
Sanborn. Dressed by Mr.
Gardner Percy

ROYAL COACHMAN
Of English origin
Dressed by Fin, Fur &
Feather, Ltd.

GOLDEN ROGAN
Originated and
dressed by Mr.
Alex Rogan

BARTLETT'S SPECIAL
Originated by Mr. Arthur
Bartlett. Dressed by the
Weber Tackle Company

CHIEF NEEDAHBEH
Originated and dressed
by Chief Needahbeh

PLATE II
Flies designed primarily as Attractor Patterns

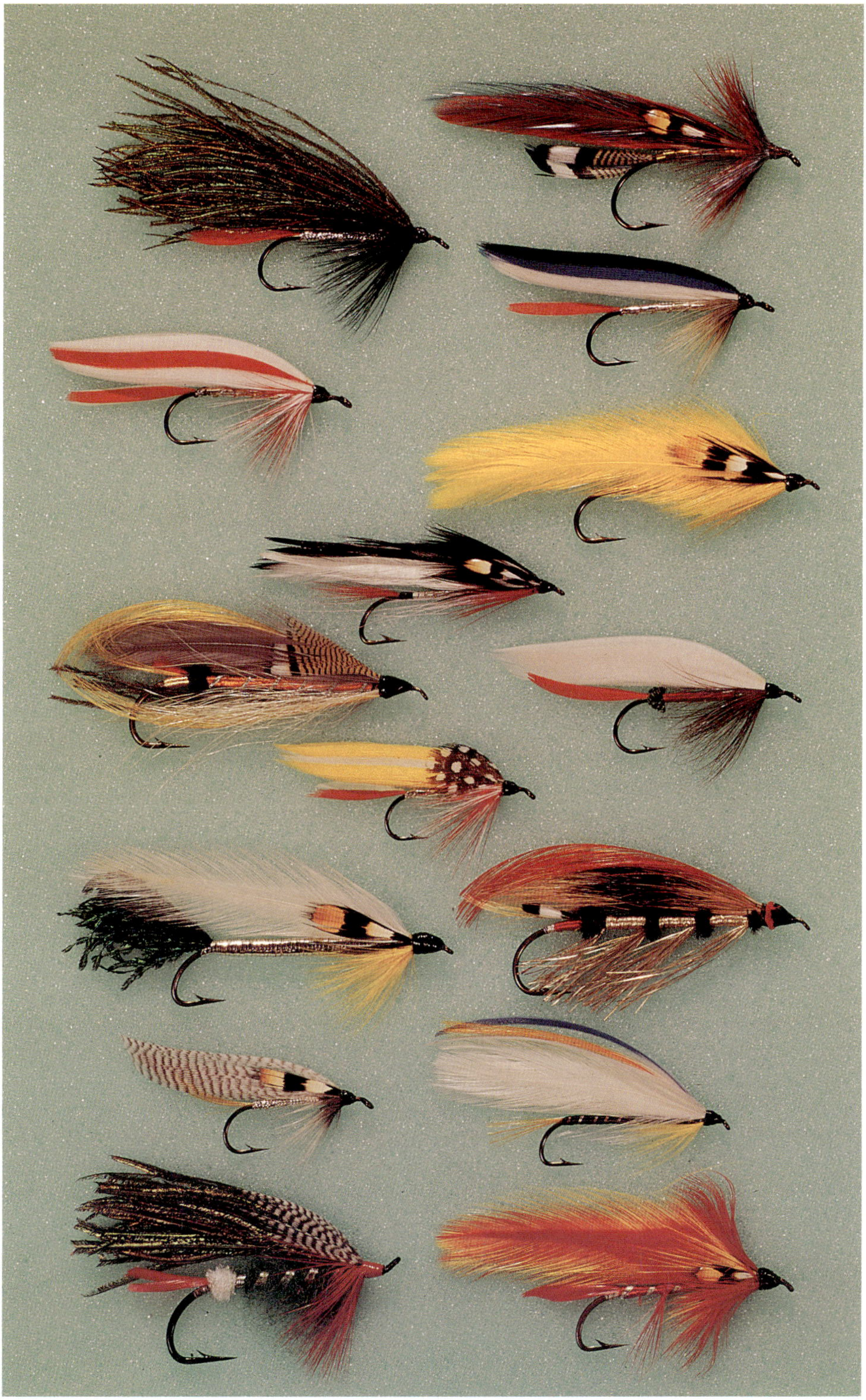

NINE-THREE
Originated by Dr. J. H.
Sanborn. Dressed by Mr.
Austin S. Hogan

GRAND LAKER
A development of the
"Rooster's Regret" type,
dressed by Mr. Benn
Treadwell

TROUT FIN
Originated by Mr. B. A.
Gulline. Dressed by Fin,
Fur & Feather, Ltd.

STEWART'S HAWK
Originated and
dressed by Mr.
Austin S. Hogan

SATIN FIN
Originated and
dressed by Mr.
Keith C. Fulsher

SILVER TIP
Originated and
dressed by Mr.
Keith C. Fulsher

MILLER'S RIVER SPECIAL
Originated by Mr. Paul
Kukonen and Mr. Henry
Scarborough. Dressed
by Mr. Kukonen

MASCOMA
Origin unknown. Adapted
and dressed by Mr. Paul
Kukonen

BLUE MARABOU
Originated and dressed
by Mr. Paul Kukonen

REDHEAD
Originated and dressed
by Mr. A. I. Alexander, III

COCK ROBIN
Originated and
dressed by Mr.
Joseph Kvitsky

GOVERNOR AIKEN
Named for Senator George
Aiken. Dressed by the
author

THE THIEF
Originated and dressed
by Mr. Dan Gapen

COSSEBOOM SPECIAL
Originated by Mr. John C.
Cosseboom. Dressed by
Mr. H. L. Howard

COWEE SPECIAL
Originated and dressed
by Mr. Stanley Cowee

LADY GHOST
Originated and dressed
by Mr. Bert Quimby

SPENCER BAY SPECIAL
Originated and dressed
by Mr. Horace P. Bond

PLATE III
Prominent Eastern Fresh Water Patterns

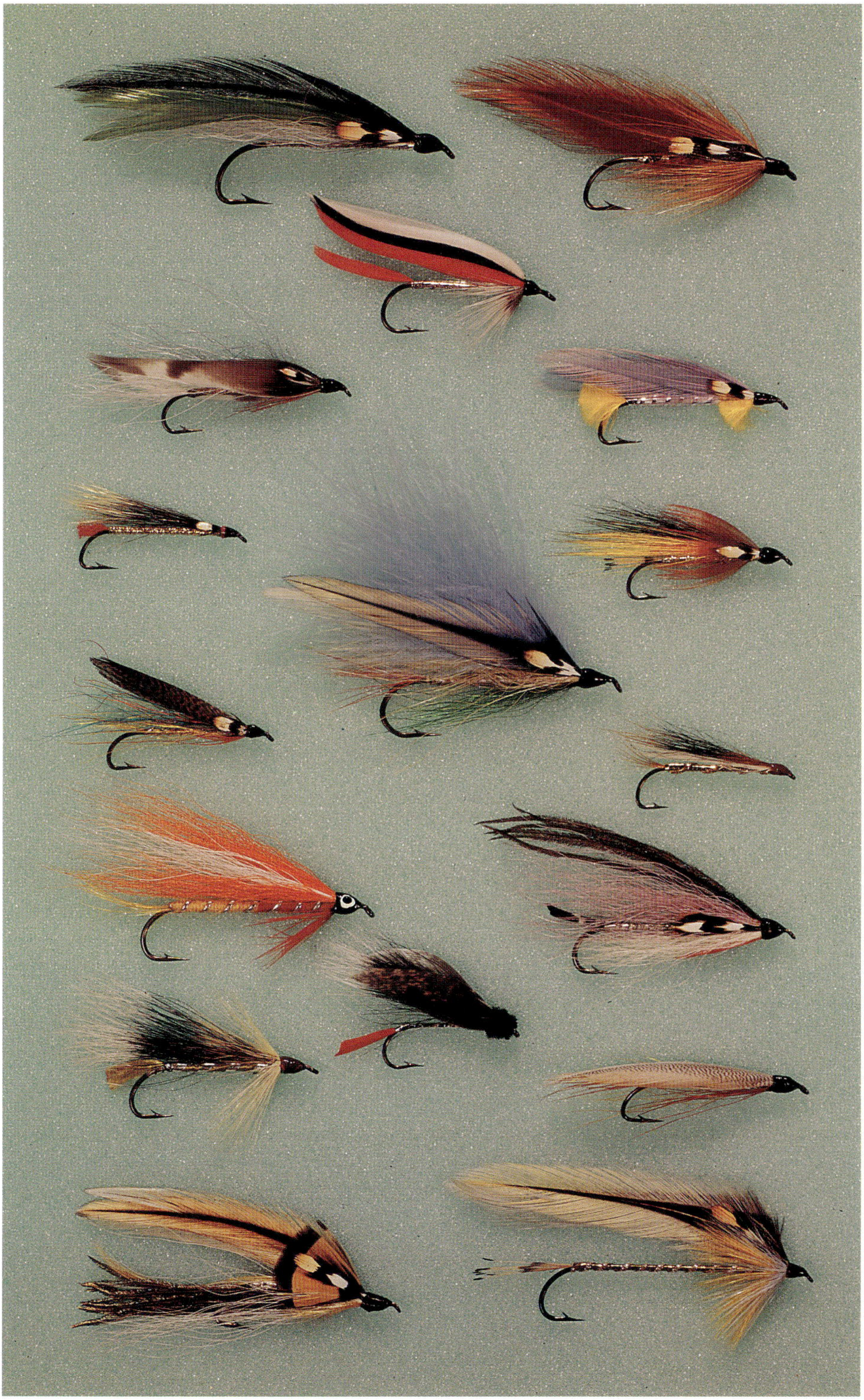

WIZARD	GOLDEN WITCH
BLUE DEVIL	DON'S DELIGHT
SHANG'S FAVORITE	COLONEL BATES
GRAY GHOST	
GENERAL MacARTHUR	GREEN BEAUTY
MORNING GLORY	ALLIE'S FAVORITE
SHANG'S SPECIAL	GREYHOUND

The Patterns on this Plate were Originated and Dressed by Mrs. Carrie G. Stevens

Plate IV
Original Patterns by Mrs. Carrie G. Stevens

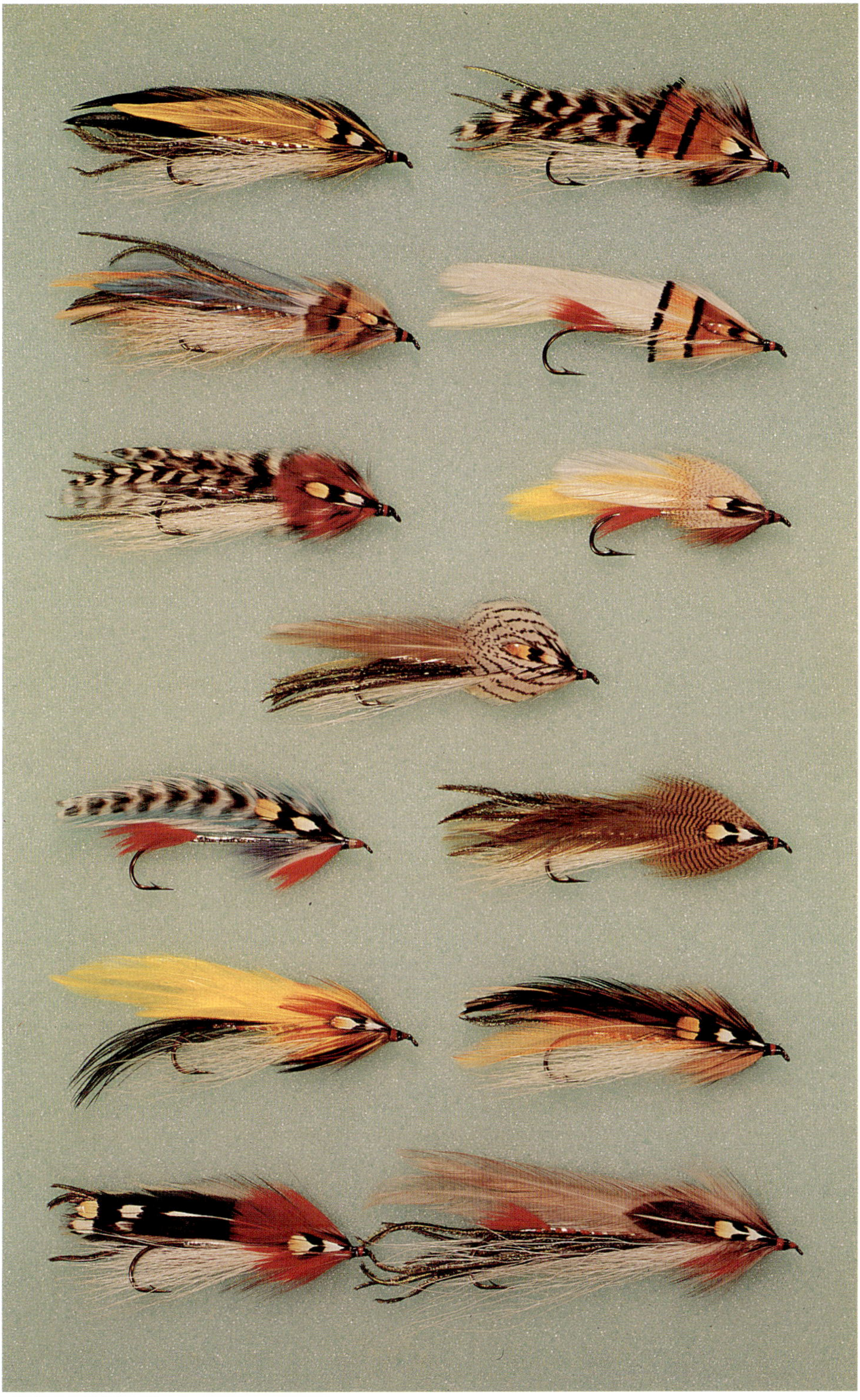

CHESAPEAKE BAY SHAD FLY
Originated by Mr. Burt Dillon.
Dressed by Mr. William Upperman

BROOKS' BLONDE
Originated by Mr. Homer
Rhode and Mr. Joe Brooks.
Dressed by Mr. Austin Hogan

SILVER MINNOW
Originated in British Columbia.
Dressed by Mr. Don C. Harger

MYLAR BODIED BUCKTAIL
This example of the type
was dressed by Mr. Arthur W. Fusco

BONBRIGHT
Dressed by Mr. Steward Slosson
(*of Abercrombie & Fitch Company*)
for Mr. G. D. B. Bonbright

CORONATION
Originated in the Puget
Sound Area. Dressed by
by Mr. Roy A. Patrick

GIBBS STRIPER
Originated and dressed
by Mr. Harold N. Gibbs

HAGEN SANDS BONEFISH FLY
Originated and dressed by
Mr. Hagen R. Sands

SILVER GARLAND MARABOU
Originated and dressed by
Mr. E. H. Rosborough

HERRING
Originated in the Puget
Sound area. Dressed by
Mr. Roy A. Patrick

CANDLEFISH
Originated in the Puget
Sound area. Dressed by
Mr. Roy A. Patrick

PLATE V
Well-known Salt Water Patterns

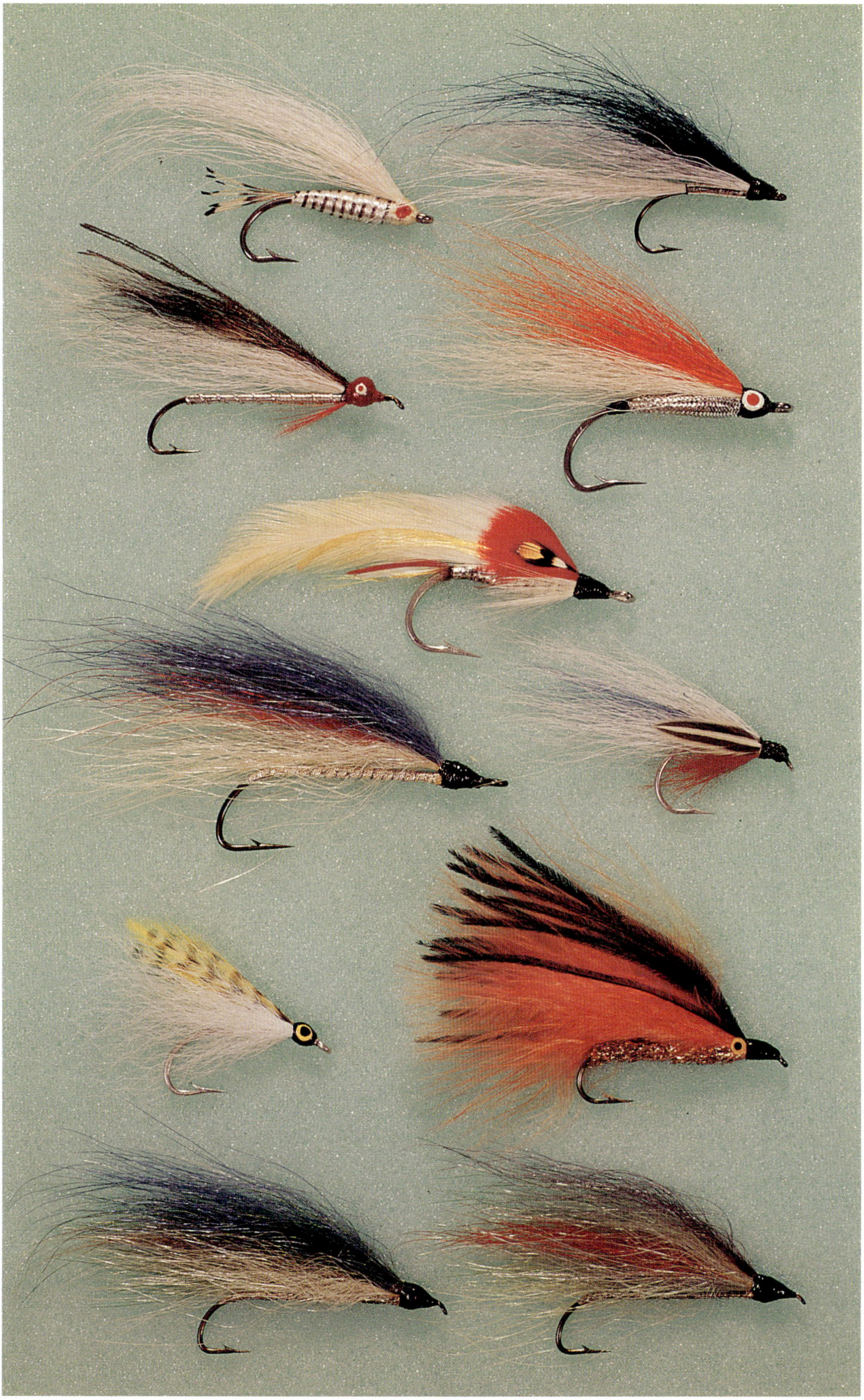

GOLDEN SHINER

DOCTOR OATMAN

RED FIN SILVER DARTER

BATTENKILL SHINER

BROOK TROUT

CUT LIPS

RED HORSE

GRAY SMELT

GOLDEN SMELT

TROUT PERCH

YELLOW PERCH

MALE DACE

GOLDEN DARTER

MAD TOM

SHUSHAN POSTMASTER GHOST SHINER

The "Silver Darter" and the three flies below it are originals dressed by Lew Oatman. The surrounding patterns are exact copies of originals, dressed by Keith C. Fulsher from information provided to him and to the author by Mr. Oatman.

PLATE VI
Imitator Patterns by Lew Oatman

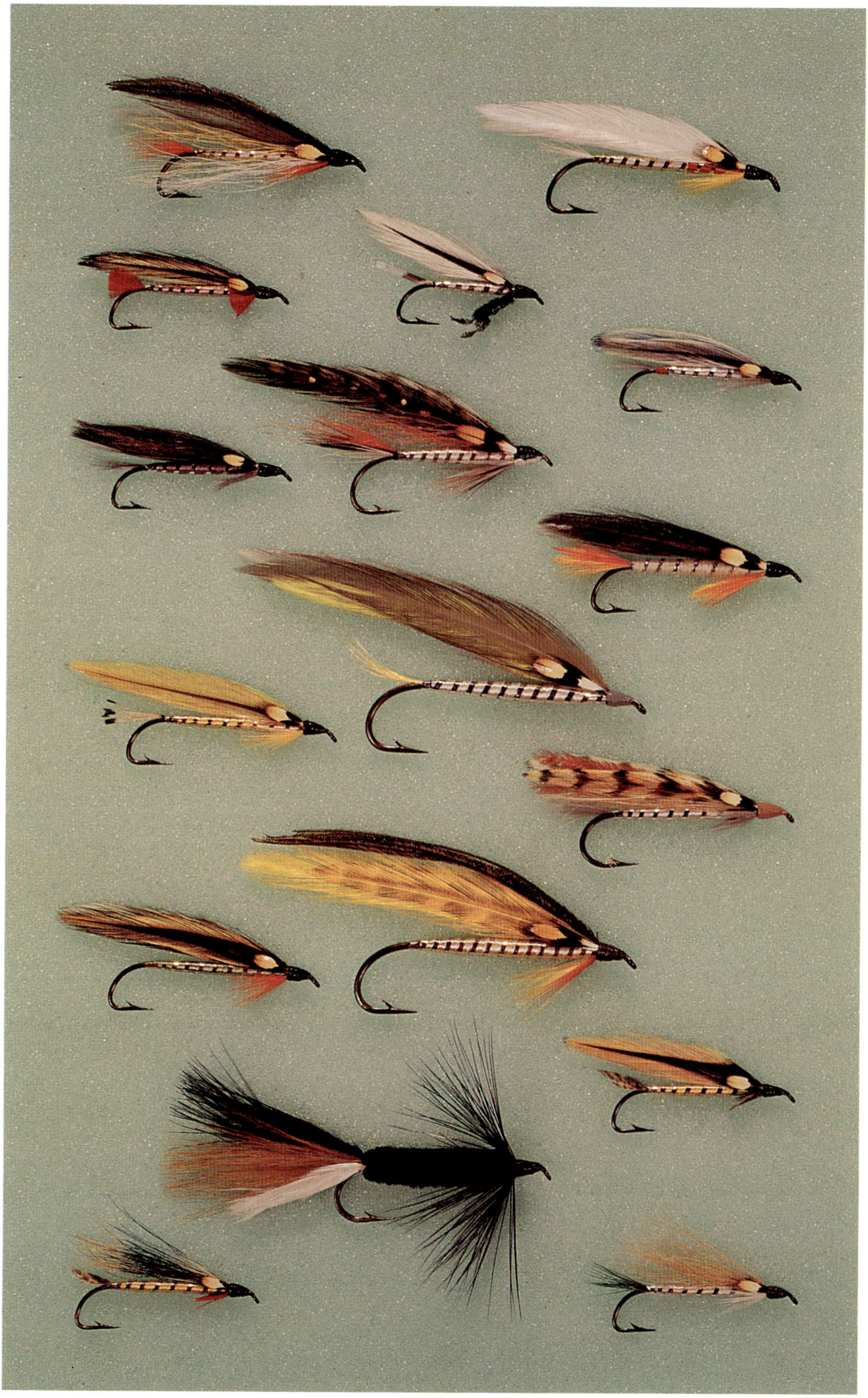

WARDEN'S WORRY
Originated by Mr. Joseph
S. Stickney and dressed for
him by Mr. Gardner Percy

WELCH RAREBIT
Originated and dressed
by Mr. Herbert L. Welch

BUMBLEPUPPY
Originated by Mr. Theodore
Gordon. Dressed by Mr. Herman
Christian, one of Mr. Gordon's
angling companions

PARMACHEENE BELLE
Originated by Mr. Henry
P. Wells. Dressed by
Fin, Fur & Feather, Ltd.

LORD IRIS
Originated by Dr. Preston
Jennings. Dressed by Fin,
Fur & Feather, Ltd.

BALLOU SPECIAL
Originated and dressed
by Mr. A. W. Ballou

MICKEY FINN (Streamer)
Originated by Mr. John
Alden Knight. Dressed by
Fin, Fur & Feather, Ltd.

LADY DOCTOR
Originated by Mr. Joseph
S. Stickney and dressed for
him by Mr. Gardner Percy

EDSON DARK TIGER
Originated and dressed by
Mr. William R. Edson

JANE CRAIG
Originated and dressed
by Mr. Herbert L. Welch

EDSON LIGHT TIGER
Originated and dressed by
Mr. William R. Edson

SUPERVISOR
Originated by Mr. Joseph
S. Stickney. Dressed by
the author

BLACK GHOST
Originated and dressed
by Mr. Herbert L. Welch

PLATE VII
Historic Northeastern Streamers and Bucktails

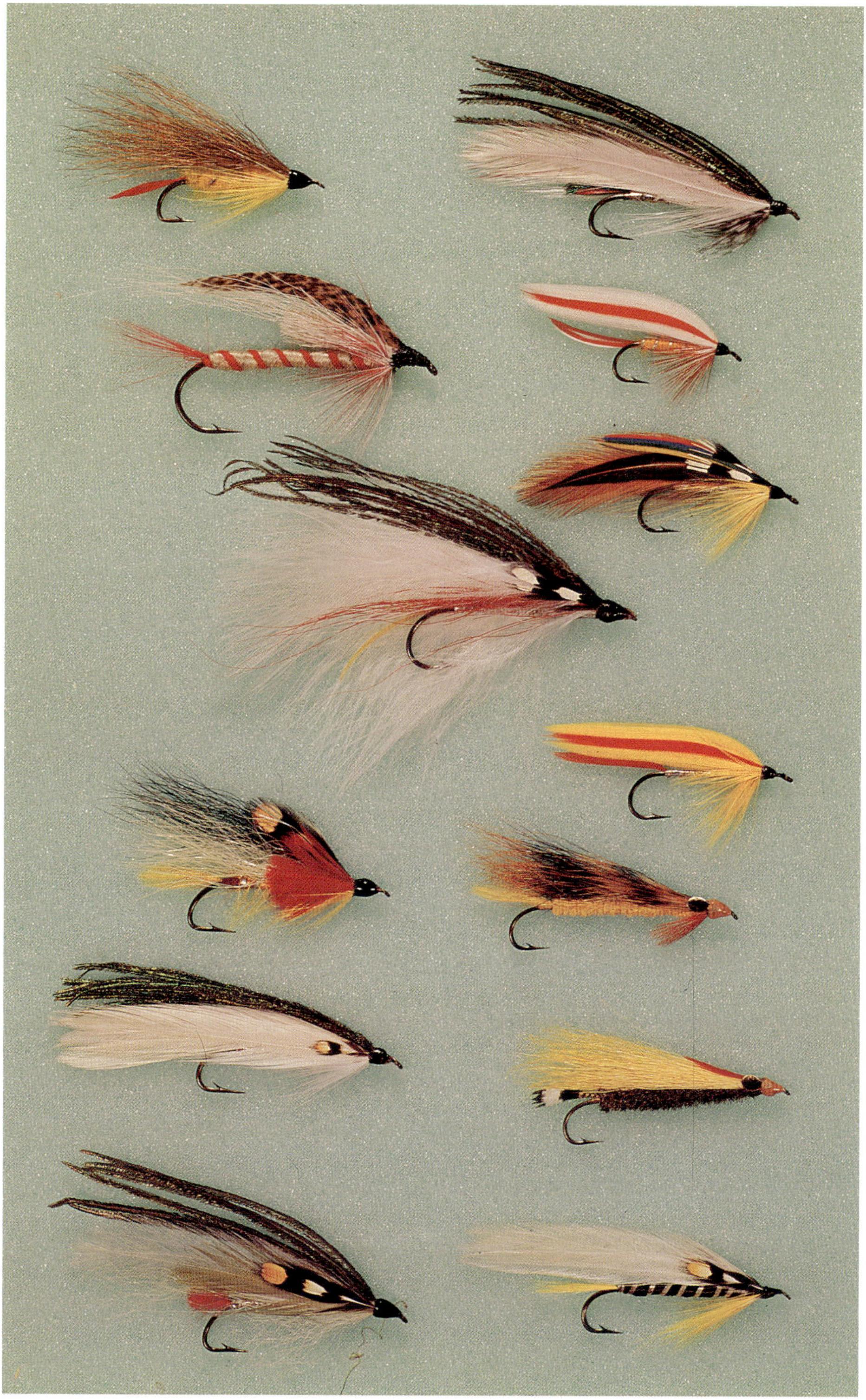

ALASKA MARY ANN
Originated and dressed
by Mr. Frank Dufresne

ASHDOWN GREEN
Originated by Mr.
Ashdown H. Green.
Dressed by Fin, Fur
& Feather, Ltd.

THOR
Originated and
dressed by Mr.
C. Jim Pray

BELLAMY
Originated by Mr. George
B. Bellamy. Dressed by
Mr. Peter J. Schwab

ROYAL COACHMAN
An English pattern,
dressed by the author

BLACK DEMON
Originated and
dressed by Mr.
C. Jim Pray

CHAPPIE
Originated and dressed
by Mr. C. L. Franklin

CARTER'S DIXIE
Originated and dressed
by Mr. C. Jim Pray

UMPQUA SPECIAL
A northwestern pattern
dressed by Mr. Don C. Harger

OWL EYED OPTIC
One of a series, dressed
by Mr. C. Jim Pray and
originated by him

IMPROVED
GOVERNOR
Of English origin, dressed
by Mr. C. Jim Pray

RAILBIRD
Originated by Mr. John
S. Benn. Dressed by
Mr. C. Jim Pray

SPRUCE
Of unknown origin, dressed
by Mr. Dan Bailey

ORANGE STEELHEADER
Originated and dressed by
Mr. Fred A. Reed

ATOM BOMB
Originated by George and
Helen Voss. Dressed by
Mr. E. H. Rosborough

RED PHANTOM
Originated and dressed by
Mr. E. H. Rosborough

PLATE VIII
Prominent Western Fresh Water Patterns

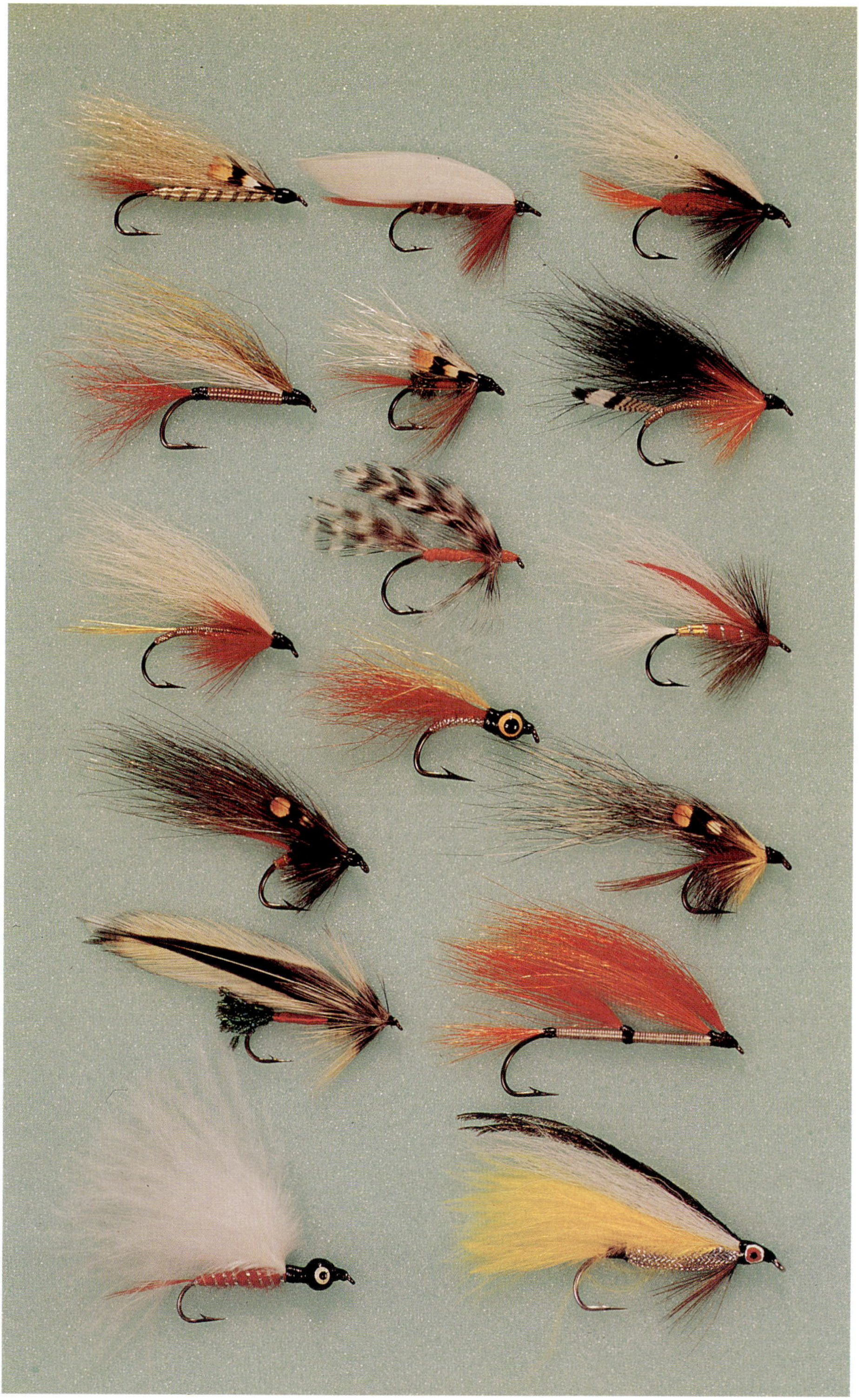

PART ONE
Tackle and Tactics

I

Why Fish Take Streamers

The sun had set in a profusion of red and golden glory that reminded the young angler of the colors of a male brook trout at spawning time. Lazily drifting mists were making up below the spruce and balsam slopes of Maine. They crept softly over the placid water of the lake while growing twilight obscured the reflections of the hills.

One by one, canoes eased into the landing, the "V" of their wakes disappearing beyond into the darkness. The drone and whine of outboard motors stopped abruptly as fishermen reached their temporary homes for the night. Lights appeared in the log cabins tucked amid the evergreens. The fragrant smoke of hardwood fires curled from the fieldstone chimneys, combining its perfume with that of the balsams into an essence which the young angler inhaled with thankfulness and satisfaction. The warm day of early June had been good. Maine's big trout and leaping landlocked salmon had struck savagely at the *Gray Ghosts* and the *Edson Tigers* the young angler had cast for them.

Chuckling laughter and the clink of glasses came from the porches of the other cabins. With chores and dinner finished, the old angler appeared on the porch. He tamped down the tobacco in his pipe. As he carefully lighted it, he looked with pride and pleasure at the young angler standing by the cedar porch rail. The two men gazed quietly down the big lake at the afterglow, dimming beyond the distant mountains. When darkness had settled, the old angler plumped down into an ancient bentwood rocker, put his moccasined feet securely on the cedar rail, and blew a wreath of pipesmoke toward the porch roof. The young angler took a chair beside him. They sat for a time without talking.

"Too bad you lost that big squaretail at the inlet this afternoon," the old angler finally remarked. "If that dead tree hadn't been in the water, you might have got him. Your leader tippets are a bit too fine for this kind of fishing. Around the dry-ki* I don't usually go finer than 2X. Long and strong! When you use dry fly leaders to fish for big trout and salmon with streamers, you're sending a boy on a man's errand!"

"I'd have lost him anyway," the young angler replied. "He had the leader snubbed tight around the branch, and he had broken away before I pulled loose. I'll tie some stronger leaders tonight."

They sat again in silence, thinking of the big trout which had bored to safety amid the branches of the dead tree.

"Here's a thing I can't figure out," the young angler said. "Take this matter of streamers and bucktails. There's every possible size, shape, and color combination. How can you tell which one to use? You say, 'Try a *Black Ghost*,' or 'Try a *Gray Ghost*,' or 'Try an *Edson Tiger*,' or you tell me to try something else. You tell me to fish 'em one way one time and another way another. The thing makes no sense to me. Do you really know what fly to use and how to fish it? If you know, how do you know? You usually catch more fish than anybody else. You always know exactly how to go about it. It can't all be 'by guess and by God!' What's back of all this streamer and bucktail business, anyway?"

The old angler thought for a minute, and chuckled softly.

"Son," he said, "you have bitten off for yourself a discussion of the first magnitude. Streamer flies and bucktails became popular in Maine about the year 1920. Since that time I have used them constantly, fishing these waters nearly every day of the season. I usually prefer them to dry flies or the shorter wet flies because they imitate the small food fish on which the big game fish feed. These big old busters care little for dainty, tiny flies. They want something with meat on it. They want smelt, minnows, or some other baitfish. They think a streamer or bucktail is a baitfish, so they usually prefer

---

* This is an Eastern term for weatherbeaten timber drifting on a lake or piled up by wind action on its shoreline.

Why Fish Take Streamers

it to anything else. Remember the big salmon we killed for dinner? When I tapped his head on the gun'l, what popped out of his gullet? A brook trout about nine inches long, scarcely dead! I opened up the trout and what was in his stomach? Three tiny shiners! Maybe it's not the case in all waters. I've heard here and there that it isn't. But in Maine and in most other places, give a big fish something that looks like a minnow, and is fished like one, and he'll strike at it most every time. That's only part of the story. There's lots more to it than that."

The old gentleman relighted his pipe and shifted his tall lean bulk for greater comfort. In the light of the match, lines caused by the laughter and the suns of seventy years fanned out in deeply engraved "crow's feet" in the well-tanned skin around his steel-blue eyes. The young angler lighted his own pipe and pulled his chair closer in respectful attention. Down the lake a harmonica searched out the tune of the United States Marines' Hymn, and contented voices joined in the chorus. The cooling night was agleam with stars, filled with the fragrance of the woods.

"I've said this many times before," the old angler continued, "and it is a fact well known to many; but I shall repeat it because of its importance. I shall repeat it because it is the starting point to what I have learned. I am convinced, and science says it is so, that fish will strike at an artificial lure for four reasons. First, they will strike because they think it is something to eat and because they are hungry. If they don't happen to be hungry, they may strike at it from curiosity, or from anger, or in a spirit of play.

"This we know, and because we know it we can divide all streamer flies and bucktails into two very different classes. There are those designed exactly to imitate a baitfish; and the nearer they imitate it in size, shape, and color, the more successful the fly will be. The closer we come to choosing a fly which imitates the type of baitfish in the waters where we are fishing, the more likely we are to get our share of strikes. In these waters we usually try to imitate the Smelt, because the Smelt is the most important baitfish for our trout and salmon. In other waters we may try to imitate the Northern Muddler minnow, the Barred Killifish, the Black-nosed Shiner or "pin-minnow," the Bridled-minnow, the Stickleback, or any of the many other kinds of forage fishes. In salt water we may imitate the Western coast Candlefish, the Herring, or some other type of baitfish which is prevalent where the game fish which we seek are feeding. Each of these has pronounced characteristics of color, size, and shape. If we work under the supposition that our game fish are hungry, the closer we can imitate their favorite baitfish, the better off we will be. That calls for a bit of knowledge and observation, but knowledge and observation are two of the factors which help to make fishing the most interesting and popular of sports.

"Now," the old angler continued, "let us assume that we have tried the exact imitation method on the supposition that the fish are hungry. The fish aren't hungry and the idea doesn't work. What do we do then? We cancel off the word 'hunger' from the reasons why fish in this case should strike a fly, and we have the other three reasons remaining. For the sake of simplicity we can fortunately group these three reasons into a separate classification. When fish will take a fly from anger, curiosity, or in the spirit of play, we can use a fly entirely different from anything which imitates a baitfish; the more different, the better. If whatever we use makes the fish angry enough, playful enough, or curious enough, he will strike. He will strike the same fly regardless of which of these three reasons he strikes it for!"

"That explains why the smallmouths hit that crazy fly they told me to use on Lake Maranacook," the young angler reflected. "The fly had a bunch of long, thin saddle hackles of red, green, white, and blue. It had a heavy hackle collar of the same colors, mixed. When it hit the water, the feathers splayed out like the arms of an octopus. I never thought anything would strike at it, but I cast it to the shoreline, under the bushes. I let it lie on the water for a few seconds and then twitched it under. A big bass would smash at it almost every time!"

"The queer shape and color and the unusual action probably made him angry," the old angler replied. "If he hit it hard, it probably was from anger, and it was your cue that day to fish that kind of a fly in the most unorthodox manner possible. Bass often act like that, particularly when they are near their spawning beds. If he really hit the fly hard, it evidently was not from curiosity or playfulness. Anyway, it doesn't matter."

"Can you use the same fly for all four reasons?" the young angler asked.

Why Fish Take Streamers

"Sure, you can," the old man said; "but for that, some flies are better than others. Let's take a marabou streamer, for example; either the *Ballou Special* which is so popular in Maine or one of Polly Rosborough's *Silver Garland* marabous which are very famous out West. This type of fly can be fished to imitate a minnow exactly. The *Ballou Special*, for instance, has a silver tinsel body to represent the silvery underbelly of a Smelt. When it is wet, the white marabou wing provides lifelike action to the fly, at the same time giving it the substance and color of a Smelt's body. The peacock topping imitates the Smelt's dark, greenish back; the jungle cock cheeks look like head and gills, and the bit of red bucktail and golden pheasant crest seem to add to the illusion. All the fisherman needs to do it to make it *act* like a Smelt. If it darts away like a terrified baitfish when a big game fish is nearby, the hungry game fish will have it in no time. It must be fished so fast that all the game fish sees is a flash of color, shape, and action.

"Now take this same fly when the fish are not hungry," the older man went on. "To be specific, let's take an actual instance of brown trout fishing in a New York state stream. The anglers I was with knew that a big brown trout lay near some cover by the bank. They had tried naturals of all sorts, but the trout didn't react to a thing. I thought I'd see if I could make him angry enough to strike, so I went in about sixty feet above him and cast the marabou streamer across stream with sixty feet of line. A small rainbow took it on the swing and I had to cast again. I guided the fly to a few feet above where I thought the big trout lay and left it there. Then I lighted a cigarette. The fly worked in the current near the bank, but the trout wouldn't take it. I kept slowly raising and lowering my rod tip and could imagine the fly's marabou wing fluffing and closing in the water. I'd let it drift down a few feet and then bring it up again, keeping the rod tip and the fly busy. Just before I finished the cigarette the big brownie struck. He weighed five pounds and two ounces. Now, surely that trout wasn't hungry and the fluffy marabou streamer was not being fished to imitate a baitfish. The trout stood the thing jerking near his nose as long as he could. Then he got mad and struck at it. It took five minutes, nearly. With brown trout it often takes that long, but by the time five minutes has gone by he will either strike or go away. Usually you can make a rainbow trout angry much quicker.

It just goes to illustrate that there are two types of reasons why fish will take a streamer, and there are two basic ways to fish them, plus a lot of variations. Unless we have evidence to the contrary, it seems preferable to start with reason number one: the hunger motive, matched by exact imitation of local baitfish in the fly selected and in its action. If that fails, try reason number two: the combination of anger, curiosity, or the spirit of play. Then, almost any fly will do; but some are better than others. It's the way you fish 'em that counts."

The night grew colder, and the two anglers went indoors. While the old angler lighted lamps, the young angler threw some logs on the fire and assembled several coils of monofilament on the table for tying leaders. The old man pulled up a chair, put a soft cushion into it, and sat down to watch the work.

"I think your comments about the four reasons why fish take streamers and bucktails explain more than you have said," the young angler remarked as he tightened a Perfection Loop in a heavy strand of the leader material. "If we are using small wet or dry flies or nymphs, or even live bait, it strikes me that we can appeal only to a fish's sense of hunger. How can he get angry or curious about any of these things? How could he get playful?"

The old angler chuckled softly. "That's another reason why I like streamers," he said. "It's pretty hard to appeal to a fish with a dry fly or wet fly or nymph if he isn't hungry. It's pretty hard to make him angry or curious or playful with a worm or a grasshopper or a half-dead shiner. But slap a streamer fly or bucktail in his territory and make it dart around like a strange little fish on the prowl, and the old tackle buster is likely to tear over and chew it to pieces! He will not want to eat it, but he will strike at it and then spit it out.

"I've seen the same thing happen to fish instead of flies," he went on. "I watched a wounded little trout in a pool, swimming around near the surface. Up came a four pound squaretail and hit it, but he didn't swallow it. He just took a good, solid slap at it and then went back under his favorite rock. The little trout drifted downstream and when he gave another wiggle or two, another big fish came up and did the same thing! I flipped a *Black Ghost* in there and took both fish. Before that little trout had drifted down, I had spent an hour or so fishing that pool with everything in the book except streamers and bucktails. I'm

Why Fish Take Streamers

darned if I know whether those two fish were curious or angry or whether they took the little trout because they were just being playful. It doesn't matter. They surely weren't hungry because they hit the streamer when they would touch nothing else.

"Curiosity is just as natural to a fish as it is to a woman," the old angler continued. "Is a big fish curious about a worm or a little fly or any other lure of that sort? Usually not. But work a streamer fly in front of him and fish it with a darting motion, and he wonders what strange new kind of minnow is in his domain. He strikes at it to satisfy his curiosity. His curiosity lands him in the pan!

"Big fish are playful too. They will play with a smaller fish like a cat plays with a mouse. Not hungry, not angry, and probably not curious. Just playful! Do they want to play with a worm or a tiny fly? No. They want to play with a smaller fish, and that's where streamers and bucktails come in again. Just fish 'em with a 'now you chase me' motion and that big old buster is a cinch for the creel!"

"All this explains a trick used in salmon fishing," the young angler remarked as he pulled a Barrel Knot tight on a leader. "It happens many times under conditions of low, clear water that Atlantic salmon will not take ordinary salmon flies at all. But use a big bucktail or streamer, even 4/0 or 5/0, about four inches long or more, and slap it down on the water and the salmon often will rise and take it. Probably makes them so angry they can't stand it!"

"That reminds me of the episode of the cigarette when I was at Ted Crosby's camp on the Miramichi," the older man reminisced. "I'd been casting over some big salmon all day. They were lying in a pool where I could see them, but I couldn't get a rise. Finally I broke off the fly and started to wade ashore, throwing away a cigarette butt as I did so. What happened? You guessed it. One of those salmon which had been eyeing my flies all day rose up and took the cigarette! Of course, I did the obvious thing. I put on a low water fly, hooked half a cigarette to it, and let it float down to the lie of the salmon. He swirled up and took the cigarette, and I waded ashore and took the salmon. Sometimes curiosity works both ways! It hasn't a thing to do with streamer fishing, but maybe it shows that most anything will work at one time or another."

The old angler threw a log on the fire, turned over his cushion, and picked up one of the leaders the young angler had made. He inspected the strength and length of the sections and the manner in which the knots were tied. He carefully coiled the leader, secured the end, and placed the finished product under the lamp with the others.

"Down home," the young angler remarked, "most fishermen are sure that streamers and bucktails are the best artificial lures for early season fishing, when there is a minimum of insect life on the streams. The water is cold and the trout are lazy. They don't seem to want to be bothered with ordinary flies, but they will take streamers—small ones usually—which imitate the minnows in the stream. Maybe it's the flash and action of the streamer, or perhaps it represents the most natural and most substantial food prevalent at the time. Probably the trout are tired of the bottom food they have been taking when they feed in the winter.* When spring comes and the water begins to warm up, they have a desire for a square meal, so they pass by the smaller stuff and take streamers and bucktails if they come near enough. You have to get the fly to the trout though. He won't go far out of his way to take it until the water warms up.

"It's a rather peculiar thing," the young angler added, "but some of my friends in the West tell me that in certain sections there seems to be no minnow life in the streams and therefore streamers and bucktails are ineffective. They say they have opened scores of trout and have never found a minnow in their stomachs."

The old angler puffed at his pipe for a moment. "It may be that what they say is so," he conceded, "but I have never seen it and I have fished a great many western streams. Fished 'em with bucktails. Usually I've taken more than my share of fish too. There are several bucktails in my fly book with the barbs pinched off the hooks. Each of them has taken many a trout in many a western river.

"Maybe there were minnows there and maybe there weren't," he pondered. "The fact that no baitfish were in evidence does not prove that the game fish would not take bucktails or streamers. Oftentimes trout live in streams where there are minnows close by for the taking,

---

* To illustrate that trout do not feed regularly in the winter, Mr. Eugene Connett says, "I saw a steam shovel working in the Willowemoc dig up brown trout that had been buried a foot deep in the pebbles and stones of the bottom."

Why Fish Take Streamers

but evidently they are never touched, as far as observation and the study of fish stomachs can prove. I have fished such streams and caught trout in them, with bucktails. Try it yourself sometime. Use minnows for bait, or use bucktails or streamers preferably. Regardless of their ordinary habits, when the trout see something that looks like an injured minnow in the stream, they will slash at it. That's why I have pinched some of the barbs off those flies. You can take it as a fact that big fish have no mercy on a minnow in distress—or a bucktail or streamer that acts like one. Try it for yourself and don't believe all you hear.

"It could be," he added, "that the western trout your friends mention feed on baitfish more than they think they do. It may be that your western friends could add to their knowledge of streamers and bucktails and how to fish them. This type of fly is relatively untried in many places in the West. Many anglers who have fished bucktails have done so as they would fish an ordinary wet fly. You and I know that there's a bit of science in the method. Just as there is science in fishing the dry fly, and a separate science in fishing the nymph, so there is an individual method in fishing streamers and bucktails. There are tricks of the trade. We like streamers and bucktails because we are successful with them. We are successful because we have studied the method and know how to apply it under various conditions. We live and learn!"

"I presume it is true in the West, just as it is true in the East," the young angler said, "that when streams are in flood or when they are discolored, fish take streamers more often than they will take the smaller flies or nymphs."

"Fish take streamers under those conditions," the old man answered, "because they can see them better; also usually because they represent their favorite food, as we have said. The situation is true virtually anywhere. When streams are high, the greater amount of water makes a larger fly necessary. Maybe the fish would take a smaller fly or nymph just as readily, but they surely can't take it if they can't see it. Streamer flies and bucktails are larger and usually have added glitter. They show up better in flood water, and therefore they catch more fish. They show up better in discolored water too. Under those conditions, in any part of the country, I'll take streamers or bucktails every time!

If the fish won't take 'em, we might as well give up fly fishing entirely and use spinning tackle or some other method of casting spoons and spinners.

"And here's something else," the old man continued. "We learn as we go. When I was younger, we fished the brightly colored flies almost exclusively—streamers and bucktails adapted from old wet flies like the *Parmacheene Belle*, the *Coachman*, and many others. Today we would call these bright flies 'attractor' patterns. Their advantage is that fish can see them from longer distances. They may swirl at them but not take them. Thus they often are used as 'locator' flies. If a fish swirls at an 'attractor' pattern, your cue is to switch to an exact imitation of the size and type of prevalent baitfish in the water, and to cast to him again.

"We've designed some pretty smart exact imitation patterns recently," the old man went on. "Lew Oatman's *Brook Trout*, *Gray Smelt*, and *Yellow Perch* were some of the earlier ones. More lately, Keith Fulsher's *Thunder Creek Series* of bucktails are as true to life as artificials can be. Sam Slaymaker's *Brook Trout*, *Rainbow Trout*, and *Brown Trout* also are tops. In fact, my young friend, the little things are deadly!"

"You seem to divide streamers and bucktails into two classes: the 'exact imitations' and the 'attractors,'" the young man remarked. Are all either one thing or the other?"

"Some quite obviously are either one or the other," the old angler said, "but some have characteristics of both types. The ones we just mentioned very definitely are exact imitations. The well-known *Mickey Finn* is a good example of an attractor, although many fishermen say that fish think it looks like a little sunfish. The *Lady Doctor* and the *Colonel Bates* are good attractors too. There are many. Those which have characteristics of both types have a semblance of baitfish imitation, but the colors and design are not exactly so. I'd put the *Ballou Special*, the *Black Ghost*, and the *Edson Tigers* in that category."

"Do you fish the 'attractors' only as 'locator' flies?" the young man asked.

"Not at all. Some of these so-called 'locators' were pretty hot patterns in the old days when fish were less sophisticated. In the Canadian backwoods and under many conditions down here they still

Why Fish Take Streamers

are. They often do well when waters are high and discolored, because fish can see them easier. Try them in very fast streams, because they are highly visible and fish must strike quickly without taking time to look them over."

The young angler put away his newly made leaders in his canvas kit-bag and took from it a large aluminium fly box. He opened it and handed it to the old angler. It was fully packed with about two hundred beautiful streamers and bucktails of every size, type, and color.

The old man fingered them carefully, poking one and then another. Occasionally he took one out and held it up to the light, then replaced it carefully in the box.

"Streamers are made to catch fishermen as well as fish," he observed.

"Some I tied years ago," the young man said. "Some I bought and some were given to me. What do you think of them?"

"You can throw away half of them," the old man said. "You can select about twenty of the others, and with them you can catch any fish that swims in fresh water that can be taken with a fly. Trouble with you is the same that's with most fishermen. You've got collectoritis. Fun, though, isn't it!"

The young man contemplated the treasured collection. He knew there were too many, but he loved them and they took up negligible room and weight. "Better too many than too few," he thought; and then aloud he said to the older man: "You say twenty streamers or bucktails will be as good as two hundred, for any fly-taking fish in fresh water anywhere. What are the twenty?"

The old man smiled broadly. "Twenty is a rather arbitrary number," he said. "Maybe ten would do. Maybe thirty would be better. It's a matter of opinion, and my opinion is no better than that of others."

"Your opinion," the young angler reminded him; "is the result of more than thirty years of experience in fishing streamers and bucktails more intensively than anyone else I know. Your opinion is good enough for me. I'll put a log on the fire and mix us a nightcap while you give out with the facts."

The old angler rose from his chair and went to his fishing vest, hanging on a hook on the wall near a leather rod case containing several superb fly rods. He extracted a small and battered fly box. Opening it, he laid it on the table. The young man was on the porch of the cabin. Gazing briefly at the crisp black and silver beauty of the night, he pulled a rusted ice pick from the log near the icebox and filled the glasses. As the door closed behind him, a loon far up the lake laughed harshly and there was an answer from much farther away. When the glasses were filled, he sat down again and picked up the older man's fly box. It contained not over thirty streamer flies and bucktails, many of them obviously old and battered from the teeth of countless fish.

"We'll decide on the most suitable streamers and bucktails before we have finished," the old man said; "but let's not put the cart in front of the horse! A list of names of flies will help little unless we first know how to tell a good streamer from a bad one. You and I can dress our own flies, but many anglers cannot, or they lack the time to bother with it. They must buy 'em. Unless they know the good from the bad, they are in trouble before they put their money on the counter. What are the indications which distinguish a good fly from one of lesser value?"

"Shape," the young man ventured, "and color combination—and size and quality."

"To an extent correct, but not entirely," said the old angler. "Quality is important and we shall define it as we go along." He selected a battered streamer from his fly box and tossed it on the table. "That streamer has quality," he said. "I saw the man who tied it catch and release fifty-nine large landlocked salmon with it before he gave it to me. I've taken enough big fish with it to make more than an even hundred, and the fly still is good. It has quality of construction, which makes it stand up under unusual abuse. But it also has other qualifications which help it to catch fish when another fly of the same pattern will not interest so many. You mentioned size as being important. Size is a matter of opinion and we shall come to that later also. There are 'yardsticks' by which we can determine the proper size to use on any water; but let's confine ourselves tonight to the essentials. The essentials, I am very sure, are form, or shape, as you say, and flash and action. Those are the essentials, and let us remember them. Form, flash, and action.

Why Fish Take Streamers

"You didn't mention color," the young man reminded him. "Isn't color important?"

"Color is important," the old angler replied; "but form is more important than color. Flash is more important than color, and action is more important than them all!

"Fish take streamers and bucktails," the older angler continued, "partly because they represent a baitfish. Yet many streamers which anglers make or buy lack the form of any known fish. We find them dressed with stiff neck hackles which, even when wet, make the fly too deep at the head. An excess of hackle throat or collar, or an excess of underbody, often contributes to this. Most flies are badly overdressed anyway. They lack the trim, streamlined appearance of the forage fish they are made to imitate. As a result, they catch fewer fish than streamers which are slimmer, more like the shape of a minnow. Fly tyers put on a bucktail wing of a big bunch of squirrel tail or deer tail or something else. The ends do not taper; the forepart is too heavy; and the whole thing looks and acts more like some sort of a brush than a lifelike fly. Form is a matter of proportion, and proportion is dictated by the fish we desire to imitate and the water we desire to fish."

"Form seems also to be dictated by custom," the young angler observed. "Take Pete Schwab's steelhead bucktails which are so popular in the West and Bill Edson's two *Tiger* flies which are killers in the East. Pete's have a high wing riding at an angle of about 40 degrees. Bill's have a low wing, very close to the body."

"Custom may have a bit to do with it," the old angler agreed; "but the form of both types of flies is ideal for the waters where they are fished. Western bucktails are dressed more heavily and with a higher wing than are eastern bucktails. They are dressed that way for a reason. I think the reason is that western bucktails usually are fished in fast, turbulent rivers which require a fly to be dressed more heavily in order to be seen more clearly. The swift current pulls down the high wing of a Schwab pattern and forces the fly to take the streamlined appearance of a minnow. That's why it is made that way—and also so that the wing will not mask the flash of the body. It 'works' in the fast water and provides action there which an *Edson Tiger* could not possibly give. One might be called a fast water fly and the other a slow water fly. Both have 'form' for the type of water for which they are made.

"As a matter of fact," the older man went on, "we think of the Schwab patterns as 'western' flies, for steelhead mostly. Those flies were originated by a world-famous angler who spent about forty years evolving the qualities which would give them form, flash, and action. The color schemes are basic. We use them in many eastern patterns. Red and white, yellow and white, brown and yellow, red and yellow, and so on. The form, flash, and action which are built into those flies are what make them famous patterns. They are as good in the East as they are in the West. They are good in either fresh water or salt—if the water is fast enough to bring out their action."

"That brings up a point," the young angler observed. "I was fishing an *Edson Light Tiger* in a backwater near a brookmouth on a lake in Canada. I cast the fly to a piece of dry-ki near the brook—fooling, more than fishing. The little fly lay in the quiet water just like a minnow resting. I twitched it a bit to watch its action. It was lifelike, all right. When I twitched it again there was an awful commotion. A big three and a half pound brook trout I had not seen waddled over shallow water scarcely deep enough to float him and snatched the fly like a shipwrecked sailor grabs a glass of water! That fly had the proper form for slow water. In that back eddy I don't think a Schwab pattern would have looked so lifelike."

"No," the old angler said, "and your *Edson Tiger* probably wouldn't have proved a thing on the Deschutes or the Klamath! Yet there is a Schwab pattern with the same color combination as the *Edson Tiger*. Form is more important than color, and form is influenced by the type of waters where we fish and the baitfish we want to represent.

"Now, let's take the matter of flash," said the old angler. "Flash also is dictated by water conditions and the conditions of light and weather. Watch the minnows in a quiet pool. Usually you can't see them until they turn to pick up a speck of food. Then you see a flash from their silvery bodies. The flash makes you notice them. It makes the game fish notice them too. Flash is what attracts a game fish to a baitfish, and to a streamer fly, but you then need form and action to make him take the fly. Flash is a relative matter. You need lots of it when the stream is high or discolored. Otherwise few fish will notice

Why Fish Take Streamers 17

the fly at all. That is why many streamers and bucktails are dressed with oval silver ribbing over the flat silver tinsel: to give added flash. You need less flash under clear water conditions or in small streams or on bright days. It is very possible to select a fly which has too much flash under such conditions. Then too much flash may scare a fish rather than attract him.

"What we have said," the old angler added, "pretty nearly covers the element of action. The fly must have action suitable to the water where it is being fished. In fast water the current may provide much of the action. In slack water, action is provided by the fly and by the angler who fishes it. If it is a bucktail, the hair wing must act 'alive' rather than cling to the body in a sodden mass. It must 'breathe' as the angler works it in the water. The quality and quantity of hair and the way it is applied to the fly helps, or detracts from, the lifelike action which the angler can give it. If it is a streamer, the feather wing must accomplish the same purpose. That is why most fly dressers prefer saddle hackles for wings rather than neck hackles. Saddle hackles are more streamlined and flexible. They react in a more lifelike manner to the action of the water and the angler. They are more translucent. Some slack water streamers are dressed with a splayed wing, for example, so that the 'V' thus formed in the wing will open and close as the fly is fished, giving added action. The fine strands of a marabou feather do the same thing. The hackle throat or the underbody may add even more. All of these things influence the choice of the fly we select for the type of water we intend to fish. Form, flash, and action are all-important. Color selection and color combination are important too, but they are least important of all!"

"Lots of us know these things," the young angler observed, "but few of us realize how important they are or how to apply them. Take the famous *Gray Ghost* streamer as an example. The average angler goes to a tackle shop and asks for a *Gray Ghost*. Rarely does he get one that is tied true to pattern, like Mrs. Stevens, its originator, ties it. Usually it is a pretty feeble imitation, improperly dressed and lacking in your three cardinal principles of form, flash, and action. Yet the fisherman buys it—any *Gray Ghost*, without regard for how it is made—and then wonders why he has such poor 'luck' with it!"

"I often think that a beautiful, well-made fly is a lot like a pretty girl in the results it gets," remarked the old angler. "I'm not so old but what I notice those women who have the same qualities as those needed in a streamer fly or bucktail. Form, flash, and action! When a girl has those things, the men all come a'running. When a fly has 'em, the fish do too." He yawned. "It's nearly twelve o'clock. Let's go to bed."

"How about salt water flies?" the young angler asked as they put their gear away.

"Salt water streamers and bucktails need the same qualities as fresh water ones do," the old angler replied. "Maybe they are a little bigger and dressed on larger non-corrosive hooks, because the baitfish usually are larger and oftentimes so are the gamefish. Salt water flies can be dressed very simply, frequently in the same patterns as fresh water flies. The all-important food for salt water game fish consists of various baitfish, so streamers and bucktails are almost the only types of flies with which the fly fisher can take salt water fish on the fly rod.

"You know," he added, "streamers and bucktails don't need to be elaborate to catch fish in either fresh water or salt. Simply dressed flies will do the job just as well, provided that they are selected for the qualities we have discussed. Let me repeat that fish take streamers because these fundamentals in their dressing excite their hunger by making them think the fly is a baitfish. Or they take them because the form, flash, and action of the fly excite their curiosity, anger them, or tempt them to use it as a plaything. Fish don't take streamers because they are dressed with the feathers from many varieties of rare birds and the hair from unusual animals. Fishermen buy 'em for that reason, however. Fishermen usually want 'em pretty, so fly dressers make 'em pretty. But that's all part of the fun of fishing, I suppose."

The young angler and the old angler walked out on the porch for a breath of air before turning in for the night. They stood quietly by the cedar railing and watched the clouds scud before the moon, casting deep shadows from the hills over the mist-enshrouded lake. Lights had gone out in the cabins along the water's edge, and even the loons were quiet.

"We bit off a big discussion tonight," the old angler said. "We chewed it only part way through. We'll keep on with it. You know things. I know things. Other people know things. Nobody knows everything. Fishermen have a way of swapping dope on what they know

Why Fish Take Streamers

about fishing. They learn from others who have been at it longer, and it is their choice to use what they learn or to leave it alone. Usually I like to try it anyway. I've noticed that some fishermen who don't look overly bright are a lot smarter than you think!"

The young angler laughed in agreement. "People look at all those flies in my fly box," he said. "They say, 'How in the world do you know how to pick out the right one to fish with?' Talks like this seem to make the problem jell. Maybe it's not quite as hard as it looks!"

They went into the cabin again and put the screen before the dying fire. "Call me if you wake up first," the old angler said as he turned down the wick and blew out the light. "That big squaretail you lost may be in a co-operative mood tomorrow. Anyway, there are others!"

Some who read this book surely will ask who the young angler and the old angler are. To satisfy their curiosity it should be stated that the young angler could have been myself, because I have enjoyed many a discussion such as this in a place such as is described. If he were meant to be myself, the word "young" would have an element of wishful thinking in it unless the conversation took place many years ago, as a part of it most certainly did. It could be that the "young angler" is he who reads this page. Youth is a relative state anyway, and the Red Gods give an ample share of it to those who enjoy fishing.

The old angler is the important one, and he is a composite of many famous fishermen I have been privileged to know. The remarks he has made in this chapter are true remarks, uttered by one and endorsed by others. What they have agreed upon would be true even if I had not enjoyed enough years with the streamer fly and the fly rod to prove these things to my own satisfaction. Although I am not old enough to have the wisdom of the "old angler," I am old enough to enjoy a bit of reminiscence. It is pleasant to ponder upon the fireside talks I have had with a few of the truly great in American angling—the names of Herbie Welch, Pete Schwab, Bill Edson, and Joe Stickney are only a few. It is because I know that these, and others less well known, have endorsed the old angler's remarks, that I feel it of value to write them. The opinion of one man is only as good as his experience, but the opinions of many can become so stabilized as to be contributions of considerable value to angling knowledge.

II
Streamers, Simple and Otherwise

The old angler and the young angler have observed that flies which imitate baitfish often catch game fish when no other types of artificials are successful. Before learning how to enjoy better fishing with them, we should learn about the various kinds of flies themselves. The choice of the right fly, in size and type more than in color and pattern, can result in a profitable day, while the wrong variety will usually impose the retribution of fruitless fishing. When fish are hungry and unsophisticated, almost any fly of any kind—regardless of how it is employed or dressed—may bring results. When fish are few or hard to catch, the situation is quite different. It is then that the angler is appreciative of his skill and thankful that he has inherited a share of the knowledge of those who have gone before him.

Insofar as catching fish is concerned, the history of streamers and bucktails obviously is of minor importance. It does, however, illustrate the point that properly dressed flies of these types have evolved through many years of trial and error, culminating in numerous basic and successful patterns which the fly dressers of today may adapt to their own purposes as they desire.

Contrary to the claims of many eminent fishermen, the origin of both the streamer fly and the bucktail is lost in the dim history of the past. It is probable that crude "long flies" were used by the ancient Macedonians. It is certain that the American Indians used similar flies in the first half of the nineteenth century. Explorers report having seen

Streamers, Simple and Otherwise

bone and hair lures, somewhat similar to the modern bucktail, in use among the Alaskan Eskimos (see *Alaska Mary Ann* bucktail), but how old they are is both unknown and unimportant.

Sport fishing in America is a development of the nineteenth century. Prior to then fish were caught only for food, and refinements in tackle almost were unknown. In 1833 Dr. Jerome V. C. Smith, in the second part of THE FISHES OF MASSACHUSETTS, describes standard patterns of flies (chiefly English) and advises the angler to learn to tie his own. Apparently the sport of fly fishing was well established in parts of the United States by that time. In 1849 Frank Forester described taking shad in fresh water on "a gaudy fly." Although these are but two of many instances of early fly fishing, the sport did not become more than regionally popular until after 1850, and the development of the streamer fly, and the bucktail followed that of other types of flies. So we must skip to the latter part of the nineteenth century to learn anything valuable about streamers and bucktails from an angling point of view.

Those conversant with the history of flies will not be surprised to learn that the great Theodore Gordon, father of the American dry fly, was one of the first to dress and to experiment with the bucktail and streamer fly as we know it today. For this valuable bit of research we are indebted to John McDonald, who edited the papers of Theodore Gordon and published them in THE COMPLETE FLY FISHERMAN (Charles Scribner's Sons, New York, 1947), a book of the greatest interest and value to every serious fly fisherman. Mr. McDonald has allowed me to quote these pertinent lines from Mr. Gordon's letters:

January 24, 1903, "... Some years ago we tried [for pike] some flies on an entirely different principle, our notion being to turn out something that would have great life and movement and resemble a small bright fish in colouring. If you could see one of these large flies played, salmon-fly fashion, by a series of short jerks of the rod top, and notice how the long fibres expand and contract, how the jungle fowl feathers [in a line with the hook] open and shut, you would see at once that it must be very attractive to any large game fish. White and silver predominate, but are toned down by long badger hackles and jungle fowl feathers.... We have taken, with a companion, sixty pike in an afternoon with these flies. Usually the big fish prefer the fly well sunk, but it is more sport when the fish can be seen when they rise. . . . They will kill all kinds of game fish, salmon included."

The fly Mr. Gordon mentioned in 1903 as having been evolved and tried "some years ago" was one of his various versions of the *Bumblepuppy* which is discussed in detail in Part II of this book. There it will be noted that Mr. Roy Steenrod, a lifelong friend and fishing companion of Mr. Gordon, wrote to the author, "I know that Gordon was tying these flies *as early as 1880.*"

In a letter written by Mr. Gordon on April 25th, 1903 (as quoted from Mr. McDonald's book), he said, "The *Bumblepuppy* is great medicine—there is no doubt of that, after years of trial. Attach a well-made specimen to the end of your cast and play it in clear water. You will see at once that it is very much alive and shows up wonderfully. If jungle fowl feathers are put on, they should open and shut with each movement of the fly. Years ago I sent samples of this fly, dressed salmon fly fashion, to the Editor [of the *Fishing Gazette*], but it is difficult to induce anglers to try new patterns if they are peculiar or display combinations not usually approved of."

This letter (or letters) to the Editor of the *Fishing Gazette* may have borne fruit, or it may be that the next allusion to streamer flies and bucktails was developed independently. In either case, six years or so after the emergence of the *Bumblepuppy*, Mr. John P. Hance, of Fort Wayne, Indiana, brought forth a long hair-wing fly for bass called the *Fort Wayne Bucktail*. I am indebted to Mr. Harold H. Smedley, author of FLY PATTERNS AND THEIR ORIGINS (Westshore Publications, Muskegon, Michigan) for research on the subject. In a perusal of old bound copies of *Forest and Stream* magazine, he found a letter written by Mr. Hance to its Editor describing the *Fort Wayne Bucktail*. Stating to the author, "The pattern, as I have given it, is just the way he wrote it," Mr. Smedley comments in his book as follows: "The orange body was bound with gold. The tail was red, yellow, and a strip of Wood duck feather. A large lock of deer hair extended as a wing beyond the end of the tail and was the most prominent part of the fly. This hair was not put on like a hackle but like a wing. It is dated 1886."

Those of us who love to fish for striped bass with the fly rod and salt water streamer flies may be interested to know that Mr. Gordon seems to be one of the first to try this also, because on July 19, 1915 he

Streamers, Simple and Otherwise

wrote to a friend: "The striped bass of the American coast is one of the finest game and food fishes in the world. On the same tackle he makes longer runs and fights as well as the Atlantic salmon. Large striped bass were at one time fished for at the Falls of the Potomac with large flies. I have killed them with *Bumblepuppy* flies. I sent you patterns years ago."

Also in 1913, in a letter to Mr. Roy Steenrod, Mr. Gordon says, "I have taken bass, bream, rock fish, perch, sun fish, pickerel, etc, on *Bumblepuppies*, not to mention big trout in the Esopus. Good when they are feeding on minnows."

In these early days, despite the work of pioneers such as Mr. Gordon and Mr. Hance, it appears that this new type of fly was so little known that others considered they had originated it independently. For example, Mr. William B. Sturgis, in his book FLY TYING (Charles Scribner's Sons, New York, 1940), quoted a memorandum commenting on the fact that a bucktail was tied in 1901 from the hair of a red spaniel and some worsted taken from a rug. This was done by a gentleman named Mr. A. S. Trude, a rancher of Idaho, who mentions the fact that this fly filled his creel to overflowing with cutthroat trout.

In 1902, during a week or two of guiding an English angler who was fishing for trout and landlocked salmon on Maine's famed Kennebago Stream, Herbert L. Welch, nationally known as a guide, artist, taxidermist, and fly caster, tied several flies to imitate Smelt. He showed me one in his studio on Mooselookmeguntic Lake. Herbie related that there were no long-shanked hooks in those days and, rather than make the flies with ordinary short hooks, he cut down and reforged bluefish hooks for the job. This was inspired by the fact that the Englishman had brought along several very lovely *Silver Doctor* salmon flies which were size 6/0, much too large for Kennebago fishing. They were useless as they were and seemed much too beautiful to discard. With the reforged bluefish hooks (originally made four or five inches long, so that the sharp teeth of the bluefish could not cut the leader) and the long multicolored feathers of the abnormally large salmon flies, Herbie made several streamers which took big fish. There is no doubt that he arrived at the idea independently, and there is no question that these flies were the most elaborate and beautiful streamers produced up to that time.

Other records show that Mr. William E. Scripture, Jr., a lawyer of Rome, New York, dressed bucktails in 1907. Soon after this the killing power of the new long flies began to become regionally known as anglers travelled from place to place leaving samples for other fly dressers to copy and adapt to their own requirements.

One of the grand old gentlemen of American angling is Harvey A. Donaldson, the famed firearms expert from Fultonville, New York. In letters written to the author in 1958 he enclosed three ancient bucktails, with the following comments:

"Strange as it may seem, my first fly fishing was done with a brown and white bucktail fly, so I was using bucktails before 1900. Our Mohawk River [in the Mohawk valley of New York State] was famous for smallmouth bass and we caught plenty with bucktails. One of the flies I am sending you* I believe was tied around 1875, maybe earlier. Note the fat body and the hook. These were Pennell hooks from England. At that time, no long-shanked hooks were available. Around 1905 I used bucktails on the Mohawk River above Rome, New York, for *big* brown trout. It was at this time that I met and fished with Bill Scripture. I knew his brother but never met his father, who was a judge and an old-time bird hunter.

"The only reason we used feathers instead of bucktail was for fishing in fast water. We found that long white feathers tied back to back and thus curved outward (as in the 'Ordway' pattern) gave a lot more action, and the big brook trout really went for them. This started about 1898 when my fishing companion, a lawyer from Fultonville, New York, named Leonard F. Fish, decided we needed something with more action than the bucktails in the swift water below Wakeley Flow Dam on the Cedar River. The cook had been cleaning some

---

* The bucktail which Mr. Donaldson states is dated 1875 has a short red wool tail with a fat buglike body wound (evidently) with silver wire. The wing is a bunch of natural dark-brown bucktail about twice as long as the hook.

The two bucktails of 1893 vintage are dressed as follows: No. 1 has a short red wool tail with a body of black thread windings over and almost concealing the wool, ribbed with silver wire or narrow silver tinsel. The wing is natural brown bucktail over white bucktail, about twice as long as the hook. No. 2 has a tail of olive-green wool with a body of the same wound with white thread as a ribbing. The wing is natural brown bucktail over white bucktail about twice as long as the hook. Both flies are crudely dressed. Mr. Donaldson relates that he often tied flies while standing in a stream. Comparison of the Donaldson bucktails with the Scripture bucktails indicates that they are quite similar.

FIG. II–1

THE SCRIPTURE BUCKTAILS are single-color flies of the simplest sort, yet their success with big Brown trout in the Mohawk River area of New York State is a matter of history. The Scripture bucktail No. 1 has a silver body with a short red wool tail and a white bucktail wing. The Scripture bucktail No. 2 has a gold body with a short red wool tail and a natural dark-brown bucktail wing.

chickens, so we tried tying some feathers on top of the bucktails. This didn't work, so I eventually tied four feathers (two on each side, back to back) on a bare hook. That really worked! We used these flies *only* in fast water.

"The reason the old flies I'm sending you have lasted so long is that I was taught to use fine tobacco dust sprinkled over the flies to preserve them from moths. This does not evaporate like moth balls, and it keeps flies for years. The other two bucktails enclosed were tied before 1893."

There are many who have had the impression that the streamer fly and bucktail originated in the state of Maine. While this does not seem to be so, it is certain that the fly tiers, anglers, and guides of Maine did much to promote the great popularity which these flies enjoy today. Their start in Maine seems to have taken place on Grand Lake Stream prior to 1910, because in the April, 1910, issue of *National Sportsman* magazine an army officer by the name of Brigadier Philip Reade writes: ". . . There was a time when the chanticleers of Grand Lake Stream used to rule the yards with uplifted white tails; but their pride was crushed when a guide named Alonzo Stickney Bacon demonstrated that hen's long feathers made attractive lures for ouananiche (land-locked salmon). This is how it came about.

"Alonzo was in his canoe, fishing with artificial flies. He could not get a rise. He was seated on a cushion filled with hen's feathers. There was a hole in the cushion and a long white feather protruded. Alonzo plucked the feather from the cushion; tied it to a hook, and used it as a lure. The ouananiche took it with avidity. Other fishermen copied the lure. Soon in all the barnyards of the plantations all of the hens were rifled of their caudal appendages, and the stream was flecked with anglers using a long straggly fly, misnamed by Boston flymakers the *Morning Glory*. All things great are wound up with some things little, but I am convinced that this recital is true. The fly makers of the great cities adorn the hook with white bristles in addition to the white hen feathers. The Grand Lake Stream people cut off these whiskers when sports let them. The lure is supposed, when jiggled in rapid water, to look to fish like a Smelt."

It may be true that Alonzo Bacon tied the first streamer used in Maine, although I dare say that there are those who will dispute it. Whether this was his original idea or a suggestion from a sportsman who learned of the new "long flies" somewhere else probably will never be known. In any event, the genesis of the streamer fly, insofar as Maine is concerned, seems to be at Grand Lake Stream—now, as then, a favorite angling water for big trout and landlocked salmon, the famous *Salmo salar sebago* of Maine.

Just as Theodore Gordon's *Bumblepuppy* was tied in many patterns, so were the original streamer flies of Grand Lake Stream. They usually were identified by the rather apt name of *Rooster's Regret*, which meant almost any fly which was tied from the long feathers picked up around the henhouses of the farms along the stream. Mr. A. W. Ballou, originator of the *Ballou Special* (the Maine version of the marabou streamer), sent me a rather ancient fly which he said was the first streamer he ever saw and ever used; it was tied by an Indian guide on Grand Lake Stream. It is made from two or three curved mallard body feathers crudely laced to a hook with string. I do not doubt that it caught fish, but I must say that it appears that the trout and salmon of those days were a lot less sophisticated than they are now!

Evidently the colors of these early streamers mattered very little, although white seemed to predominate. The colors were the simple barnyard colors, and the shape and action of the fly were what interested the fish. In those days simplicity seemed to serve the purpose, and in many instances this still is true today. There are guides on the Miramichi who insist that the best salmon fly is made by tying black bear hair

Streamers, Simple and Otherwise

to a bare hook. The guides say that they catch more fish on these simple flies than they do on the fancy patterns which the sports give to them. The basic requirement in their minds is having long hackles or hair to give form and action. They do admit, however, that when few fish are in the river, a bit of added flash from tinsel or silk seems to enhance the result.

From here on, the family trees of streamers and bucktails become rather complicated. In the cases of those flies which are of special interest I have added to the detailed specifications for their dressings whatever historical notes seem to be of value. The fly dressers of Maine were quick to exploit the new flies; and the fly dressers of other states, either independently or in imitation, followed suit. In the years that have gone by, the prolific result has brought the joy of acquisition to countless fishermen, at the same time confounding their minds and depleting their pocketbooks. How much these many patterns have aided their fishing is a question rather hard to decide. Without doubt there are far too many. Some are extremely valuable, designed with science and knowledge. Others are mere brainstorms of pretty colors, conceived by fishermen or fly dressers who wish to become fathers of what they hope may some day become famous patterns. This book gives authentic and detailed dressing for considerably more than two hundred streamers and bucktails which are of sufficient value or of enough national or regional prominence to make their inclusion seem advisable. In selecting this rather large number, a multiplicity of others of seemingly lesser importance were left out. Even so, from this more than two hundred carefully chosen patterns about two or three dozen could be selected which would provide good fishing to any angler, for any species of fish, anywhere in the United States.

As an example of this, let us start with the lowly *Rooster's Regret*, when one of its versions was so crudely fashioned by a guide on Grand Lake Stream from several white hackles stolen from a Leghorn and a bare hook with a bit of thread. This fly was made beautiful and legitimate by a Maine angler who added silver tinsel to the hook and embellished the wing with red shoulders. The fly, still called the *Rooster's Regret*, took more fish than its cruder forebear because the tinsel and the more carefully selected feathers enhanced its form, flash and action.

Professional fly dressers always are on the lookout for worthwhile patterns. This one was made even more salable by Gardner Percy who, until his death in 1949, was the proprietor of the Percy Tackle Company of Portland, Maine, and the most prolific of that state's fly tiers. Mr. Percy added a white throat and silver ribbing, calling the now fully developed creation by the name of the *Colonel White*. This was because the fly reminded him of the famous *Colonel Fuller*, except that it had a white wing instead of a yellow one.

Shortly after this accomplishment a gentleman from New Hampshire came to the Percy Tackle Company and said that he wanted some *Colonel White* streamers, but he wanted them dressed with splayed wings in order to give the fly greater action in slow water. Mr. Percy did as requested and, liking the adaptation, put it in his list of patterns. He called it the *Ordway* in honor of the gentleman from New Hampshire.

Following this occurrence, Mr. G. D. B. Bonbright, President of the Seaboard Airline Railway, was going tarpon fishing in Florida. As a pioneer in fly fishing for tarpon, Mr. Bonbright recognized the value of the color combination for this type of fishing. He commissioned Mr. Steward Slosson, then a famous fly dresser for Abercrombie and Fitch Company in New York, to dress the fly on tarpon hooks. It is probable that during the conference a few added refinements were decided upon because the fly emerged beautiful to behold! A tail was added of red and white duck wing sections and a short golden pheasant crest feather was included for good measure. Above the wing appeared a topping of a long golden pheasant crest feather. Horns of blue macaw tail fibers and cheeks of jungle cock completed its embellishment.

The fancy fly became known as the *Bonbright*. It caught many tarpon, was included in the Abercrombie and Fitch catalogs, and was copied for the use of all who desired to fish with such a combination of brilliant and rare plumage. That it caught more tarpon than the *Colonel White* or the *Ordway* would have is very much open to doubt. That it pleased a wealthy gentleman more is a foregone conclusion.

Eventually the fame of the *Bonbright* reached Boston, by way of Florida and New York. In Boston a tackle dealer by the name of Mr. L. Dana Chapman thought it very pretty, as in truth it was. Perhaps not knowing its name he sent an order to Mr. Percy to make up

Streamers, Simple and Otherwise 29

a few dozen, tied on fresh water hooks for the trout and salmon of Maine. I am sure that Mr. Percy must have recognized his former baby, even in its new silks and satins, but in any event he named it the *Dana* and it is famous by that name in Maine today.

The sequel to the story is short and I trust that there will be no occasion to add to it in later years. I purchased a *Dana* from Mr. Percy and dressed a few duplicates. One spring in the 1930's I went into the Allagash country of Maine to fish for trout. My guide was Ross McKenney, so famed as a woodsman that he taught the subject at Darmouth College later on. I gave Ross a sample of my home-tied *Dana* and he gave it to Bert Quimby, who at that time was second only to Gardner Percy in Maine's professional production of streamer flies. Next year the identical fly emerged in Mr. Quimby's catalog, but now it was called the *Ross McKenney*. The *Bonbright*, *Dana*, and *Ross McKenney* are identical in dressing. All have stemmed from the *Colonel White* and the *Ordway*, whose common parent was the *Rooster's Regret*, conceived on Grand Lake Stream!

Thus new flies are born, some to reach lasting fame and others to be deservedly ignored. Perhaps the vast numbers of good, bad, and indifferent patterns is a reason why no one before now has attempted to evaluate and classify them in a book such as this!

In understanding the dressings and uses of streamer flies and bucktails, just as in learning a language or a business, it is most convenient to start with elementals. With an understanding of these, it is simpler to understand which variations in dressings are necessary and helpful and which are not. Even the simplest dressings vary in their suitability for taking certain species of fish under certain definite weather, water, and seasonal conditions. That is a subject in itself, and it will be dealt with in the following chapter. It seems logical to understand the dressings first and then to learn how to use them most profitably.

The pedigree of the *Bonbright* and its less glamorous relations was given largely to indicate these two points: that patterns in streamers and bucktails have become unnecessarily voluminous and complicated, and that it is not necessary to use complicated patterns in order to catch fish. Many elaborate patterns are very successful; perhaps even more so than simpler ones. Anglers enjoy their beauty, and they have confidence in them. Enjoyment and confidence are primary factors, making expensive and detailed patterns worth their higher price, regardless of whether or not something simpler could do as well.

When a game fish sees a flash of silver and a touch of color dart by him in a swift stream, or even in a placid lake, he lacks the opportunity to inspect it carefully. If the general effect impels him to strike at it, it makes no difference whether it is composed of a multiplicity of rare feathers or something less complicated and expensive. If it has form, flash, and action, and if it is fished properly, in the right place at the right time, it will do its work well, be it elaborate or simple.

The point where a hair fly becomes a bucktail and a feather winged fly becomes a streamer is an arbitrary one. Peter J. Schwab, the famous angler and writer, defines it this way: "A hair fly becomes a bucktail when the wings are roughly twice the length of a *standard* length hook and thus give pronounced swimming action to the lure." This is generally true, and his definition applies to feather winged streamers as well as to hair winged bucktails.

A hair wing fly may be termed a bucktail, even though the wing is scarcely longer than the hook, providing that the hook is sufficiently long so that the fly, in action in the water, gives the effect of a swimming baitfish rather than of an insect or something else. This is true of feather winged streamers as well. As an example we may take the two *Edson Tigers*, which are acknowledged by everyone to be bucktails and to imitate a baitfish. When these are correctly dressed, the hook is abnormally long, such as 4X or 5X. The hair wing is scarcely longer than the hook. This is to prevent the hair from being able to catch under the bend of the hook while the fly is being fished.

It would seem more logical to consider as bucktails any hair fly, regardless of size, which is of a shape that gives it the appearance of a baitfish in the water. Streamers should enjoy a similar definition except that their "wings" are predominantly composed of feathers.

Of course there are both hair winged flies and feather winged flies which are so shaped that they can be fished by one method to imitate a baitfish and by another to imitate an insect. There is no doubt that the familiarly termed "wet flies" of many types are taken by fish to be tiny baitfish when the water current or the angler employs them so as to appear so. Such cases may be decided by determining what they are

Streamers, Simple and Otherwise

made to represent. There are few which can escape falling into one classification or the other.

The words "streamer flies" and "bucktails" are loosely used by many fly dressers and writers. It seems suitable to define the streamer fly as "A fly possessing a predominantly *feathered* wing and having shape and action which are intended to represent a baitfish." As such, a streamer may have a bit of hair of any length dressed over or under the hook. If the feathered part of the wing predominates, it should be termed a streamer. By the same token, a bucktail would be "A fly possessing a predominantly *haired* wing, whose shape and intended action are to represent a baitfish." It may have a feathered topping or shoulders (and frequently does), at the same time remaining a bucktail. A hair wing fly of this type is called a bucktail regardless of the kind of hair used. Both streamer flies and bucktails are known as "flies" even though the term may not be strictly correct. The words have become common in usage and are convenient. Since the necessary repitition of the words "streamers" and "bucktails" may become tiresome in this book I occasionally have grouped both types under the name of "streamers" for the sake of simplicity, and I do not mean to destroy their individuality by so doing.

The simplest of all such flies is the single color bucktail. Normally it is dressed on a hook 2X, 3X, or 4X long, but it can be dressed on a short hook if the wing is made long enough to provide minnow-like action. Usually the body of the hook is concealed by silver tinsel because the majority of baitfish have a silver underbody. It may, however, be dressed with tinsel of another color, silk, chenille, wool or other materials. The wing is a small bunch of hair of any sort or color provided that it gives suitable appearance and action. If the hooks used are 2X or 3X long, the wing should be about one and a half times as long as the hook. Shorter or longer hooks will require that the wing be longer or perhaps shorter than this.

The single color bucktail need have no tail, throat, shoulder, topping or other embellishment. If it is correctly dressed with a suitable color of hair, it will catch fish—a surprising number of them. The colors to be chosen, and the reasons for selecting them will be discussed in Chapter III.

Although such a bucktail surely will catch fish, I am convinced that the addition of a few more refinements will make it more successful, because these refinements aid in giving it the appearance of a minnow. However, I would prefer a simple fly such as this, if it is suitably dressed, to a more elaborate one which is so badly tied that it is relatively lacking in the inherent form, flash, and action which are so necessary to tempt strikes.

In passing on to more complex or elaborate bucktails, the fly dresser can go in either of two directions, or in both of them at the same time. He can build up the wing in two, three, or more colors, or he can embellish the fly with tail, throat, shoulders, and other decorations. My preference in the matter is merely individual judgment, but it has been sufficiently successful so that I shall discuss the steps in the order of their importance to me, leaving it to others to change them if they wish.

Fish in relatively unfrequented waters, certain pond fish, and many salt water fish usually will strike the simplest bucktail or streamer just as readily as one which is more ornate. When fish learn to be suspicious of anglers and their flies, greater attention must be given to the dressing and selection of the flies and the ways in which they are used. Whether or not the single color bucktail will obtain results, it always has seemed to me that the double color bucktail is better because it more nearly gives the impression of the dark back, light midsection and glistening underbody common to most baitfish. The double color bucktail is made by applying the same total amount of hair as in the single color fly, but the hair is composed of two distinct colors, one added on top of the other. Normally the darker color is on top. Thus, while the single color bucktail may be dressed with white or brown or yellow or some other resultful color, on a silver tinseled hook, for example, the double color bucktail may have brown over white, black over white, yellow over white, red over white, red over yellow, black over brown, or many other similar combinations. The single color often is good. The double color usually is better.

The next step is to add shoulders or cheeks or both. (The names of the parts of a fly are included with a drawing, Figure IX-1.) The shoulders imitate the head and gills of the baitfish, and the cheeks represent the eyes. Cheeks normally are the tips of feathers from a jungle cock neck, since these best seem to convey the illusion. Jungle

Three-color bucktail

Two-color bucktail with peacock herl as top color

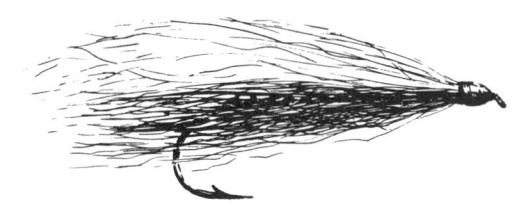

Two-color bucktail

FIG. II-2

SIMPLE BUCKTAILS

cock is expensive and sometimes difficult to obtain, so many fly tiers leave it off or substitute some other bit of feather for it. Shoulders normally are the tips of body feathers, dyed or natural, from ducks or other birds. They should conceal the fore part of the wing to between a quarter and a third of its length. Either shoulders or cheeks add greatly to the appearance and effectiveness of the fly, but the inclusion of them both is more of a luxury than a necessity.

Of following importance is the throat and/or the tail. The throat, with or without the shoulders, adds to the appearance of the fly and

33

enhances the illusion of gills. It normally is rather short, not heavily dressed, and its stiff fibers are made to splay out so that they will "work" in the water, providing added action to the fly. Technically, all material which is tied in at the head and applied under the hook is known as the "throat." Actually, the long hair or feathers of the throat represent the underbody of the baitfish, while the short hair or feathers imitate the underpart of the gills. In addition to this, the throat gives a more finished appearance to the fly. The tail may be of very short hair, but usually it is a small bunch of hackle fibers or a section (or combination of sections) of a feather. It adds color and attractiveness, and some anglers feel that it seems to provide the illusion of the tail of the fish. This last part of the statement, if taken from the fish's point of view, always has appeared to me to be doubtful. I am sure that it adds color and attractiveness, but otherwise its inclusion seems to me to be superfluous.

A topping adds to the appearance and resultfulness of many streamer flies and bucktails. Frequently it is a few strands of peacock herl, as long as the wing, but it may be of other materials. I doubt that many of these "other materials" do very much to assist the fly to catch fish.

It usually is important to add tinsel ribbing when the body of the fly is made from chenille, silk, or similar substances, because the tinsel provides the flash which makes the fly noticeable to the fish. If the body is of tinsel, the added ribbing enhances the flash by providing additional reflecting surfaces. This usually is an advantage, but on bright days in clear water it may not be so. If the dressing of the fly includes no tinsel in body or ribbing, a bit may be added as a tag.

The patterns of many elaborate streamers and bucktails call for butts, horns and the feathers of rare birds for toppings and for other embellishments. To my mind, these are decorations only. They make the flies beautiful and thus please the fishermen, but I am sure they make no difference whatsoever to the fish. Butts are supposed to represent the egg sacs of flies which imitate insects. Horns correspond to their "feelers," if they have any. Quite obviously these have no place in flies made to represent baitfish, but they occasionally are added for decoration.

A third color, or even a fourth, may be added to the bucktail wing

Streamers, Simple and Otherwise

at any stage of the game. This has resulted in such simple and extremely effective flies as the *Mickey Finn* and the *Black Nosed Dace*. An additional color often assists in the imitation of certain minnows, particularly those having a dark lateral line or stripe. On some flies the inclusion of (usually peacock herl) topping takes the place of another color of hair in the wing.

The steps in embellishing the streamer fly are almost identical with those of the bucktail. It frequently is customary to add a very small bunch of bucktail, or other hair, to the hook before tying in the feathers of the wing. Streamer wings usually are dressed with four saddle hackles of identical size, although the outer two may be a trifle shorter than the two in the middle, or of a different color. Matching sections of two identically opposite swan or goose wing feathers may be tied together into a streamer wing in a similar manner to that by which the wings of the smaller wet flies are dressed. This method is relatively rare in the United States, but rather common in Canada. The *Harlequin* and *Trout Fin* are examples.

Since baitfish are translucent, it is important to add as much translucency as possible to streamers and bucktails. In bodies, this is best obtained by using spun fur (one color or mixed) which can be picked out to break up the usually opaque body lines and allow light to shine through. Fly dressers should not avoid fur bodies under the impression that they are difficult. A minute or so does the job. Merely arrange the cut fur or dubbing on a flat surface in a long triangle, so that when the material is picked up by the thread it will be tapered slightly. Waxing thread is more or less obsolete. Many fly dressers use a preparation called "Fur Grip," which is a lacquer-like liquid applied to the thread with a toothpick or something similar. Merely roll the dampened thread over the cut fur, and the fur will adhere firmly to the thread, ready to be wound on the body. ("Fur Grip" is obtainable where fly dressing materials are sold; for example, from Paul's Fishing Tackle, 110 Green Street, Worcester, 8, Massachusetts.)

Polar bear hair also adds to translucency. It has a good taper and adds life to any fly. Use hair that, when cut close to the hide, is of the right length. Use as much of the underfur as possible to get bulk at the shoulder, tapering towards the tips. When using hackles, select those with little or no web (so newsprint can be read through them). Other materials which add translucency include marabou, mallard, teal, and peacock herl.

In dressing flies, the beginner invariably uses too much material, especially for the wing. Sparsely tied flies usually are much more productive because they provide a more streamlined appearance. When streamers and bucktails become wet, they increase in bulk; so flies which seem too sparsely dressed when dry may be just right when wet.

The streamers and bucktails so far mentioned have been of the eastern type, very long and with wings dressed fairly close to the hook. While these are used also in the West, the turbulent rivers of the western coast have caused a rather different type of bucktail to be more popular. Flies of the streamer type are rarely used in western rivers for steelhead and salmon, because it has been found that the bucktail variety is more serviceable on the fast rivers. This is partly due to the savage strikes of the big steelhead and salmon. Their teeth tear the feathers and give the streamer a relatively short life. It is also due to the fact that the stiffer wings of bucktails can be dressed at an angle of about 35 to 40 degrees from the head of the fly. This angle of dressing makes it possible for the wings to open and shut in the swift current, giving greater action to the fly in that type of water. These western coastal patterns would be as lacking in action on quiet eastern streams as the eastern type of bucktail would be in the torrential rivers of the coasts of California, Oregon, and Washington. There are a few rather turbulent stretches on many eastern rivers also. While this type of water in the East usually does not harbor many brook trout and brown trout except in the occasional "pockets," there are numerous fast water stretches in which rainbows are to be found. The western bucktail is very effective in such places, but few eastern anglers at present are acquainted with it. There is no reason why western flies, such as the Schwab patterns, should not be extremely valuable in swift eastern waters, particularly for rainbow trout and landlocked salmon. I should like to recommend them for the purpose.

Following the dedication of this book appear the names of many illustrious anglers and fly dressers who have contributed authentic dressings and/or methods to its pages. The majority of the flies herein listed are patterns which aggregate many years of study and streamside experience. If I may make two suggestions to younger anglers who

Streamers, Simple and Otherwise

are interested in dressing their own flies, I would say that it is most important to dress each fly faithfully to pattern and with the greatest of care. As an amateur fly dresser myself, I have made the error of trying to "invent" new patterns. Before I learned the wisdom of accepting the experience of others I had made dozens of pretty but illegitimate flies, most of which I have never used. On the stream side my desire for the best opportunity of catching fish led me to the wiser course of using established patterns, with the result that the earlier "inventions" remained untried. It is fun to improvise if we desire to do so; but it seems more advantageous to dress authentic flies which others have proved will catch fish.

This book is in part an attempt to remedy a situation touched upon in the introduction. One of my difficulties in dressing authentic patterns was that I rarely knew what was authentic and what was not. The books containing dressing formulas were either too lacking in detailed instructions to make it possible to tie a pattern accurately from them, or they were so much in error in these instructions that the result, even if faithfully followed, was a far cry from what the true dressing was meant to be. I hope that this book will be a contribution toward eliminating that difficulty for others.

Lacking proper information, in self-defense I began a collection of flies tied by the originators of the patterns. These, now numbering hundreds, have been the greatest aid in tying my own flies properly. Even if this book accomplishes what I have hoped that it will do, my second suggestion is that anglers and fly dressers obtain, as occasion permits, authentic dressings from the finest fly tiers, keeping this collection properly labeled and intact for future reference. If the fly dressers and their patterns are well known, as many of them surely will be, the collection will become more valuable with age, affording inestimable assistance and pleasure to its possessor.

III
How to Select Streamers

Many years ago I came upon an old gentleman who was sitting on the little wooden dock where I had left my canoe. He was gazing downward so intently that I also stopped to watch, fully expecting to see a giant bass cruising among the grasses which grew deeply into the water around the little lake. When he looked up and noticed the fly rod in my hand he smiled in greeting.

"I've been watching the minnows," he explained. "I'm trying to decide what kind of a streamer fly I shall use for these bass."

That was the day when I stopped selecting streamers and bucktails by sheer guesswork and began to use a little common sense in picking the right one for the fishing I was about to do. The old gentleman took stock of my ignorance and pointed to the minnows hovering nearly motionless near the sanctuary of the grasses. As they lay in little schools, fins erratically quivering, one and then another would flash the silver of his underbelly as he dipped to the bottom to pick up a morsel of food. A small pickerel cruised out from the grasses and the schools scattered, darting to safety.

"A fisherman could sit here watching minnows," the old gentleman said significantly, "and learn a lot about what fly to choose and how to fish it. All you have to do is to imitate the minnows."

We watched for awhile and then we went fishing together. The old man used a home-tied bucktail with coloring which imitated the baitfish in the lake. He fished it in a very minnow-like manner, and he came

How to Select Streamers

in with as nice a string of smallmouths as I have seen in many a day. I have been learning how to select and use streamer flies by noticing minnows ever since.

In common parlance, all small fish may be called "minnows," regardless of kind. Actually, of course, minnows are but a single family (*Cyprinidae*). While this is probably the largest of the many recognized fish families, there are many other baitfish which are not "minnows," as the scientists use the term. To avoid being technical we shall use the words "minnows" and "baitfish" interchangeably to include all small fish which game fish use as food.

From an angling standpoint, there is no need to become familiar with their names and habits. The only interest the streamer fly fisherman need have in minnows is to imitate them in size, shape, colors, and action. Flies can be matched to them merely by observing the type of baitfish in the waters where the fishing is to be done. All that is important is to realize that there is great variation between them in appearance, and that the fly which looks most like the minnows currently available is ordinarily the fly which is most apt to catch fish.

In common with many of the larger fishes, minnows become more brilliant in coloration when they are ready to spawn. Since this usually is in the spring, their spring colors are so pronounced that one hardly would recognize them as being the same kind of fish later on. Many brightly colored streamer flies or bucktails are spoken of as being "good early in the season." Duller flies are mentioned as being ideal in the summer and fall. In some cases the radical change between bright spawning colors and dull normal colors may influence this selection.

To understand how baitfish vary in color, it may be of value to mention a few which are fairly common. They are described in their bright spawning colors, so it must be realized that this coloration is much duller and less pronounced during the remainder of the year.

The Golden Shiner is common to most lakes and ponds throughout the United States. Although it is not a stream fish, it often is found in big rivers. The middle half of its body is golden yellow, with a very small expanse of silver underbelly and a similarly small area of blue-gray back. A bucktail with a silver body, yellow hair wing, and a topping of blue-gray hair or even of peacock herl should imitate it fairly well. The Golden Shiner is a fairly deep fish, which infers that a rather heavily dressed fly might be preferable to one with a sparse wing.

The Red Bellied Dace is one of the most colorful of minnows in streams throughout the Midwest. Over its yellow underbelly is a broad band of red. It has a wide, black medial line with pale-green shading to brown above. A corresponding fly might require a gold tinsel body, a wing of two red hackles with a golden badger hackle on each side, a topping of peacock herl, and a bit of added red in throat and tail.

The Spot-Tailed Minnow is a river and lake baitfish having a rather pronounced black spot on its tail. Its underbody is pinkish silver, above which is a lateral line of olive green surmounted by a bluish-purple back. This minnow is much used by bait fishermen in the East, who refer to it as "River Bait."

The Horned Dace and the Fallfish are two distinct species often grouped together under the common name of "chub." The Horned Dace has a pink underbelly, above which is a yellow medial line and a back of blue green shading to olive brown. After its spawning season, the Horned Dace is primarily slate-colored and could be imitated fairly accurately by the *Gray Ghost* streamer. The popularity of the *Gray Ghost* in certain waters may be attributed to this.

In general, minnows can be divided by type into three groups. The largest group has no pronounced medial line, but has a dark back shaded to a lighter color below. These would be imitated by streamers having a single color feathered wing and a topping, or by bucktails having a light-colored wing and an upper wing of a darker color. There are many suitable color variations in such flies, of which the often used *Brown and White* bucktail is an example.

The second group comprises the minnows having a distinctly banded lateral line, such as the Black Nosed Dace. Mr. Arthur B. Flick, author of STREAMSIDE GUIDE TO NATURALS AND THEIR IMITATIONS (New York: C. P. Putnam's Sons, 1947), is the originator of a bucktail called the *Black Nosed Dace* which is an excellent imitation of that baitfish. The fly is unusually successful on streams where it exists.

These laterally banded minnows, as in the case of the *Black Nosed Dace* bucktail, are imitated by flies (as shown in Figure III-1) having a pronounced lateral band obtained by the application of three layers of hair of separated colors. The popular and productive *Mickey Finn*

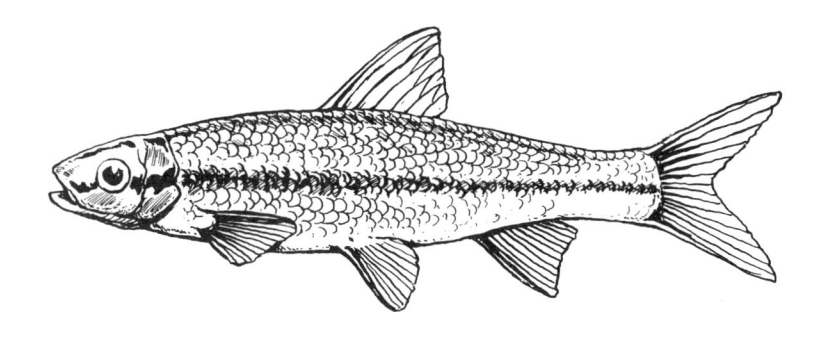

Blackstripe Minnow

Bucktail when dry

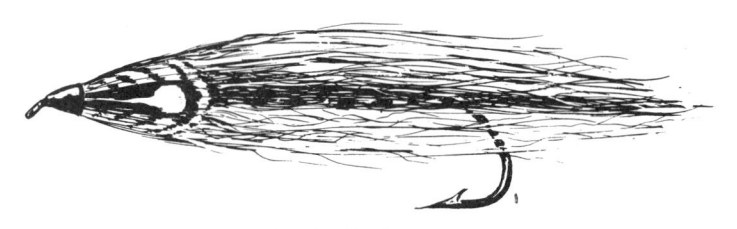

Bucktail when wet

Fig. III-1

SKETCH OF COMPARISON OF ACTUAL MINNOW WITH
BUCKTAIL WHEN DRY AND WHEN WET

is another example. In streamers this type of minnow is usually imitated by heavily banded feathers, of which badger hackles are the most common.

41

The third group of baitfish is less prevalent and is identified by vertical bars such as may be noticed in the Barred Killifish. In a bucktail these vertical bars are difficult to duplicate. It may be done rather poorly by using squirrel tail hair, which has a dark bar and a light tip. A better method is to imitate the bars with feathers, either dyed or natural, of Plymouth Rock or something similar.

In the 1950's and 1960's, several experienced anglers studied the principle of exact imitation and developed flies which have been referred to elsewhere in this book as "deadly." Keith Fulsher's "Thunder Creek Series" provides excellent imitations of some of the baitfish just mentioned. These include the *Silver Shiner*, *Red Fin Shiner*, *Golden Shiner*, *Emerald Minnow*, *Spot-tailed Minnow*, and *Black Nosed Dace*. Sam Slaymaker II, realizing that trout have no compunction about dining on their own fry wherever they exist, developed after considerable research a series called *Little Brown Trout*, *Little Rainbow Trout*, and *Little Brook Trout*. These can be obtained in both regular and small "streamerette" sizes from the Weber Tackle Company, of Stevens Point, Wisconsin. This rather pronounced trend toward exact imitation was influenced by the work of pioneers such as Art Flick, with his *Black Nosed Dace*, and the late Lew Oatman, who developed about seventeen exact imitation patterns discussed in Chapter IX. It has, however, been progressing ever since the first streamers and bucktails were crudely dressed on hand-forged hooks well over a hundred years ago.

Scuba diving has been helpful in providing a fish-eye view of streamers and bucktails—which often look very different when seen from under water in various conditions of atmospheric brightness, water turbidity, and current action. All this should be considered when one is selecting a fly. For example, famed author and angler Roderick Haig-Brown has spent countless hours under water in his favorite Campbell River in British Columbia to observe the migrations of salmon and the effect various colors, sizes, and shapes of flies have on them under varied conditions. Others have done similarly elsewhere, and they agree fairly well on several conclusions.

The expert fly dresser or angler instinctively knows when a fly is "right," but even he will often thoroughly soak it to see how it looks when wet. He will cast it close by to observe how it swims, and will fish

How to Select Streamers

it to see how it looks in action. This provides valuable information, particularly in the cases of commercially dressed flies, which may be improperly constructed in one respect or another.

The construction of a fly greatly determines its ability to catch fish. If one does not dress his own flies, he should look with suspicion upon those he buys, particularly if they seem to be "bargains." Commercially tied flies run all the way from being absolutely worthless to being so superbly dressed that it seems a shame even to get them wet, let alone allow fish to chew them up!

We have learned that if we wish to use imitator patterns, we should imitate the prevalent baitfish in size, shape, and color combination. Now we should consider effects of atmosphere and water conditions. If the day is bright and sunny, and if the water is clear, a duller fly may be called for; one with a minimum of tinsel or bright colors. If the day is dull, but water clear, one a little brighter or with a small amount of flash should be appropriate. If waters are badly discolored, a much brighter fly should be the thing, perhaps even one of the attractor patterns.

In matching the size of the fly to the size of the baitfish, a little variation usually is sensible. When waters are low and clear, try a somewhat smaller fly. When they are high, put on a somewhat larger one. If in doubt between two sizes, the smaller one is usually preferable.

These comments on sizes bring to mind an experience of my friend Paul Kukonen. He was trolling flies in the early spring on a squaretail (brook) trout and landlocked salmon lake in Maine. The fish were following schools of smelt along the shoreline. Since smelt in this region usually do not exceed four inches in length and often are much smaller, Paul put on a small tandem-hooked *Pink Ghost* streamer (which is the famous *Gray Ghost*, except that the wing is a faded gray pink instead of gray). This fly is usually an ideal choice under such conditions, and an occasional fish swirled to it, but none was hooked. The mystery was solved when a dead smelt was noticed floating on the lake. It was over six-inches long.

Paul, who goes on such trips fully equipped for almost anything, had his fly tying kit with him. That night he tied a few trolling streamers of the same pattern, all fully six inches long and with wings on both hooks to provide the length. The next morning he put on the smaller fly to see if the trout and salmon would take it. They wouldn't. Then he put on the long fly, and hooked several large fish. To be sure this was not coincidence, he alternated the small and large fly hourly during the remainder of the trip. He reported taking only one small salmon on the small fly and said he lost count of those taken on the larger one. On another trip to the same region the large trolling fly hooked nothing because the smelt at that time were less than two inches long. Small flies did the trick. Yes, size often does make a difference!

Ingenuity sometimes pays dividends when everything else fails—which brings up the story of the *Injured Minnow*, a streamer fly about as "far out" in design as one can get. Paul and a friend were trolling streamers on Maine's Moosehead Lake one morning during a flat calm when it was impossible to raise a fish. However, every few minutes the arching back of a large trout or salmon would break the surface a hundred yards or more from the boat. In searching for evidence of what the fish were feeding on, Paul noticed a three inch long smelt floating almost dead on the surface and just feebly moving. The conclusion was that the fish were attacking schools of smelt under water and that an injured one occasionally escaped and floated, later to be picked up by one of the larger fish.

Back at camp that evening Paul opened his fly tying kit and tied a clipped deer hair body on a No. 2, 8X long hook in the general shape of a smelt. He says it took about twenty bunches of deer hair to do the job. The "fly" was also dressed with a half-inch tail of brown impalla (calf), a throat of yellow hackle wound on as a collar, with a little unclipped deer hair around it, and a wing of four medium blue saddle hackles extending to the end of the tail, as the sketch shows. Finally, he soaked the *Injured Minnow* in dry fly oil and dried it.

Later in the week he encountered the same conditions of feeding fish rising to injured smelt on the calm surface. Using a ninety-foot floating fly line and a 100-foot-long six-pound test monofilament leader, he placed the *Injured Minnow* on the water and slowly paddled the canoe until line and leader were extended. When the ripples quieted he moved the canoe just enough to keep the line straight and to give very slight action to the fly. On about the tenth twitch of the fly a five-pound salmon arched up and took it solidly, putting on a spectacular jumping exhibition. Paul reports that he hooked and landed

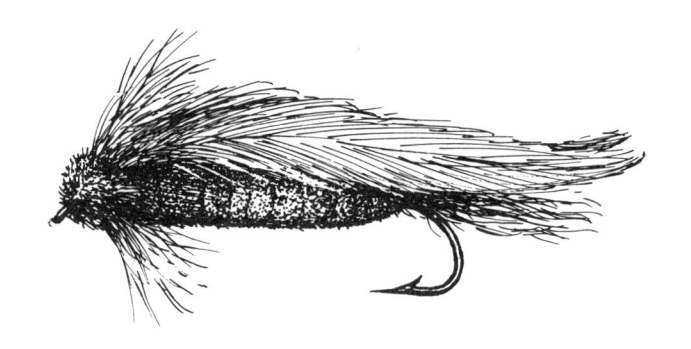

FIG. III-2

THE "INJURED MINNOW"

two more large fish before the wind came up, and that he has used the same fly (tied in various sizes and color combinations for lakes, ponds and streams) very successfully on other occasions.

In dressing streamers or bucktails, there is a rough relationship between the size of the hook and the length of the fly. This, with certain exceptions, is decided by the gap (distance from shank to barb) of the hook, rather than by the length of the shank. In standard flies, where the wing is half again as long as the standard 2X long hook generally used for streamers and bucktails designed for casting, the fly usually is six times as long as the gap of its hook. Thus, for example, the wing of a standard fly dressed on a No. 4 hook would be about two-and-a-quarter inches long regardless of whether the hook is of regular length or much longer.

Hooks for streamers and bucktails usually are Limerick, Sproat or Model Perfect forged patterns with turned-down eyes. Turned down *looped* eye hooks are preferable when available, because it is easier to dress flies on them and because they are less inclined to chaff the leader when being used for large fish. Oval wire salmon hooks, due to their greater strength, are ideal for large fish. Hooks for trolling flies usually are 6X long. The trailer hook on tandem-hooked trolling flies should be two sizes smaller than the leading hook, with dressing covering both.

46   Tackle and Tactics

It may be well to stress a point made previously, that streamers and bucktails should also be chosen for the type of water in which they are to be fished (Figures III–3 and III–4). I have never heard of them being referred to as "fast water flies" or "slow water flies," but it might be appropriate if these terms were used to identify them. A fly whose wing is fairly stiff and dressed close to the hook (such as our previous example of the *Edson Tiger*) is primarily a slow water fly. Its manner of dressing gives it action and life in slow water, but the action and life are usually destroyed on fast streams. Fast streams call for bucktails having wings dressed high on the hook (such as steelhead flies) or

FIG. III–3

EASTERN AND WESTERN TYPE BUCKTAILS. The Pi-Way Squirrel (left) is an example of a properly dressed low wing bucktail as used principally in the East. The Atomic (right) is correctly tied with a high wing for the fast water of western coastal rivers

FIG. III–4

EASTERN AND WESTERN TYPE STREAMERS. The Grand Laker (left) illustrates the predominantly eastern type of long winged streamer, dressed low on a long hook. The Chappie (right) is typical of successful western type fast water streamers, dressed on a regular hook with a highly set wing

How to Select Streamers

streamer flies with long, stiff hackles, enabling the fast water to enhance their action by "working" the fly. Certain flies are designed with splayed wings (such as the *Ordway* and the *Spruce*) so that the "V" of the wings can be used by the angler to give an opening and shutting motion as the fly is fished in slow water, thereby increasing its action. The splayed wing method of fly dressing can be adapted to both streamers and bucktails. Many salt water patterns are tied in this manner, and I am surprised that there are so few well-known fresh water flies made with splayed wings.

High, swift water conditions frequently demand flies which will sink readily, because under such conditions big game fish are usually near the bottom, resting in the protection of large boulders or similar obstructions. The fly must sink well down into the water or the fish will not see it. This is particularly true on western steelhead rivers in the winter season, but it is also true on many eastern rivers, especially in the spring. I doubt that the amount of dressing does a great deal of good to remedy this condition. Even if an excess of dressing does not hurt the appearance and action of the fly, the dressing may add to its bouyancy rather than doing the opposite.

The heaviest part of an ordinary fly is its hook. To make the fly sink, a very heavy iron should be used. When it is allowed by the rules of the river (and it is not allowed on many eastern salmon rivers and trout streams) the hook may be weighted. This may be done by winding it with strip lead or metal wire as explained in Chapter IX. The body dressing is applied over the lead and may be dressed over the wire, but the latter is not always necessary. The majority of Peter J. Schwab's celebrated steelhead patterns (such as the *Queen Bess* and the *Princess*) are dressed with heavy wire body uncovered. If it is desirable to add weight of this sort to flies, it is important that no more weight be added than is necessary to get the fly properly down into the water. An excess of weight is very bothersome in casting and usually impairs the action of the fly by making it logy. When spinning with the fixed-spool spinning reel first became popular in this country, many very heavily weighted streamers and bucktails were offered for use with this type of tackle. My observation has been that their weight detracted so much from their action that they took very few fish, and I know of no accomplished spinning anglers who favor their use today. It is prefer-

The old days.

How to Select Streamers

able to add a bit of lead to the leader a foot or two ahead of the fly. A split shot or two is equally useful in fly fishing if weight is permitted.

Another way to sink a streamer or bucktail quickly is to use a fast-sinking line. All of the major line manufacturers offer these in a large selection of sizes, weights, materials, and tapers. Whether it is the fly that is made to sink quickly or the line, or both, depends greatly on the speed of sinking desired, the depth to be fished, and to a large degree on the opinion of the angler. Whenever possible, my own preference is for a non-weighted fly used with a fast-sinking line such as will be described. This reduces the number of flies to be carried and seems to make them cast farther, easier, and more accurately.

Flies predominantly black in color, such as the *Blackbird*, the *Thief*, and the *Black Marabou*, are extremely popular under conditions of high or cloudy water, especially for bass. Bass take these flies under clear water conditions also, perhaps because they associate them with the color and shape of the several species of pondfish which are predominantly black.

One might wonder why a black fly would have good visibility in high or cloudy water. The reason may be due to its great intensity of color (if we may call black a color), giving the fly a pronounced silhouette which, under certain conditions such as in milky streams, may provide greater visibility than even yellow or white.

One of the staunchest advocates of black flies is Robert McCafferty, of Hershey, Pennsylvania, who illustrates his propensity for them—and particularly for the *Black Marabou*—with this observation: "The value of the *Black Marabou* is in its visibility in dark or dirty water. We used to hunt with an all-white English setter and a predominantly black Gordon setter and noticed how well we could follow the dark dog late into the evening after the sun had gone down; in fact we could watch the Gordon when we couldn't see the English setter at all. This caused us to experiment with black flies for dark or dirty water. We found that the *Black Marabou* is more visible than lighter colors under these conditions. Angling results proved that the trout seemed to see black flies better also. In this section we have limestone streams which are always murky. They have a milky color, and black flies almost always are productive."

In summary of these notes, my years of angling have brought me to the following conclusions, borne out by the great majority of fly fishermen with whom I have discussed the matter. When waters are clear and not in flood, flies in exact imitations of baitfish in size, shape, and color may be assumed to be most productive. While we should use a size of fly similar to that of the predominant baitfish, we also may draw the conclusion that small streamers and bucktails are usually better than larger ones for low water and for small streams or in ponds and lakes where the game fish are not large. In the early spring, and particularly when waters are high or discolored, larger flies are more productive, especially in the extremely visible color combinations of white, yellow, or red. When streams are milky a fly in a white or yellow combination may not be as visible as one of dark brown or black.

With these many facts in mind, it seems relatively easy to inspect a fly box containing almost any number of patterns and to decide upon a very few selections which should do the work of the moment. Fortunately for the pleasure of angling, I doubt that the rules ever will be laid down which are of such a definite nature as to preclude a reasonable amount of judgment, intuition, and guesswork in the choice of flies. To narrow the question down a bit further, however, the following notes may be of value in arriving at the basic colors and color combinations preferred by each species of fish. With these notes are certain other observations which may be helpful in deciding how effective streamers and bucktails are for these fish normally caught in fresh water.

BROOK TROUT

Under normal conditions in well-filled streams, brook trout seem to prefer natural imitations to the exclusion of brighter colors. When these less pronounced blending hues fail, combinations of red and white, red and yellow, yellow and white, brown and white, or brown and yellow normally accomplish good results; the brighter of these colors usually increase in relative merit as waters become high or discolored. My fly book always contains a liberal range of these combinations in the simple bucktails, particularly in the smaller sizes and often with a bronze peacock herl topping. Since most of us fish in well-fished streams, where smaller trout predominate, small flies tied on

How to Select Streamers

10 or No. 12, 2X long hooks generally prove most successful. Keith Fulsher's "Thunder Creek Series" and Sam Slaymaker's trout-imitating "streamerettes" should be in everybody's book, as well as the remarkable *Muddler Minnow* in its smaller sizes. We usually save the larger flies for lake and big stream fishing, although even here the smaller ones are often more productive. Unless necessary because of high water or turbid conditions, we reserve the brightly colored flies for backwoods fishing, where the less sophisticated trout often prefer them. But—as this is written in the mid-1960's—I must admit that one must go pretty far into backwoods waters to find trout that are not highly selective.

BROWN TROUT

All the previous combinations are taken by brown trout from time to time, but the most attractive colors to them seem to be combinations of yellows and browns or browns and whites, occasionally with a little black added as a topping. The brown trout has a greater preference for the sombre colors of baitfish than for the bright colors which the brook trout frequently enjoy. Since brown trout tend to be more cannibalistic than either brooks or rainbows, exact imitations of their own species (such as Slaymaker's *Little Brown Trout*) or exact minnow imitations of other species should be effective. Brown feathered streamers with gold bodies are popular for brown trout, with or without the addition of a bit of brown, yellow, or white bucktail or a bronze peacock herl topping. Because of the frequently larger size of brown trout and the larger baitfish commonly found in their waters, these flies are often tied relatively large, on No. 4, 6, or 8 hooks.

When trout are fished in big waters such as lakes and rivers, the matter of visibility should be considered in the choice of flies. When flies are viewed from under the water, the relative loss of light tones all colors down drastically, especially when flies are fished deep or in discolored water. Brilliance, or high visibility, is the result of contrast. For example, a black streamer or bucktail, when viewed from under water in the evening dusk, has more visibility than one of lighter prismatic tones. Very dark flies thus are popular for evening fishing. The same comment applies to white in many instances (which is one of the reasons for the effectivness of the famous *Black Ghost*). When a fly is highly visible under water, it is so essentially because of the background from which it is viewed. Bright colors fished near the surface, especially in sunlight, lose very little of their color. But in many instances, and especially in lake trolling when fish are deep, pronounced colors such as black and white are much more visible than prismatic colors because of their contrast. The *Nine-Three* is another example of a fly often used in such instances.

RAINBOW TROUT

All the flies recommended for brook trout will do nicely for rainbows, which have the same liking for bright colors that the brook trout does. For all these fish the merits of the marabou streamer should not be ignored. On western streams the predominantly white marabou is extremely popular. It is an acknowledged producer in the East also where a close competitor is the plain marabou with a silver body. The development of the marabou streamer in the West has been championed by Mr. E. H. Rosborough of Chiloquin, Oregon, who is an expert commercial fly dresser of the highest quality. His *Silver Garland Marabous* are made in several color combinations, and are distinguished by an unusual body made of heavily lacquered Christmas tinsel, thickly dressed and fuzzy, with hundreds of light-reflecting facets. (Note the comment in Part II in connection with Rosborough's *Polar Chub*.)

Mr. Ted Trueblood, a nationally known angler and author, prefers the white marabou for Idaho rainbows. His dressing of it is simplicity itself: merely a few wisps of white marabou feather as an underbody and a few tips of peacock herl as a wing, either with a silver body or dressed on a plain hook, to which a few turns of gray hackle tied on as a collar is added. He comments on this as follows:

I put the marabou, which represents the minnow's white belly, below the hook. I use gray hackle to give the fly a little body toward the front in the spot where the minnow is the thickest—at his head. I don't use eyes, because I am convinced they make no difference as far as catching fish is concerned. The fly is fully as good without any body at all as it is with a silver body. It looks a little more complete with a body, but it doesn't contribute to its fish-catching qualities one iota. I tie it without a body for my own use but usually include it on the flies I give away. This fly is a top-

How to Select Streamers

notch fish catcher all over the country. It catches trout in streams when they are feeding on minnows and it catches them in high mountain lakes where there are none. I tie it in all sizes from No. 12 to No. 4 but use the small sizes more. It should be tied quite sparse. I usually fish it like any other streamer or bucktail, but I have caught plenty of trout on it when it was drifting freely or being worked very slowly in a stream, and when it was sinking in a lake. It takes all kinds of trout from the littlest to the biggest. It is only fair for bass.

LAKE TROUT (MACKINAW)

This fish can be taken on an unweighted fly directly after ice leaves the lakes in the spring and usually again when the water becomes cold in the fall. When surface waters are warm, he sinks to lower, colder levels and is then caught only by deep trolling. In many of our cold northern lakes, the smaller sizes of lake trout (usually up to four or five pounds) frequently can be caught near the mouths of brooks all year through. Lake trout depend primarily upon smaller fish for food and thus take streamers and bucktails avidly. They are not particularly selective in their choices of colors in flies and will take any of the patterns recommended for landlocked salmon.

CUTTHROAT TROUT

Sea-run cutthroat have a decided preference for flies with a lot of white and a little red, to which a touch of yellow often is added. This combination normally will prove successful, but may be varied by using orange instead of yellow, or brown instead of red. Gray, particularly as it comes from natural Plymouth Rock feathers, is an occasional wise substitute for the white.

Flies for both sea-run cutthroat and non-migratory cutthroat are of two rather distinct types: the high-winged, relatively short steelhead variety and the low-winged, longer flies which are more common in the East. The former usually excels in fast water, while the latter may be preferred for the slow water stretches. The color combinations given above are primarily for what I have termed the fast water, or steelhead type, flies. Oftentimes they are dressed with bodies of chenille, usually ribbed with silver tinsel, and they occasionally are palmered with a hackle of one of the colors mentioned. The dressings of many of them which may not properly be termed as streamers or bucktails are given in William B. Sturgis' book FLY TYING (New York: Charles Scribner's Sons, 1940).

The wide variety of minnows common to eastern and mid-western streams and lakes is not always found in the West. Usually the baitfish in western waters are confined to relatively few varieties, and in some streams even these are rare. Regardless of this, anglers who fish streamers and bucktails properly find that they take more than the average number of fish with them, and frequently much bigger fish. A wide variety of long flies is not needed, as evinced by the following quotation from a letter to the author written by Mr. E. H. Rosborough, of Chiloquin, Oregon:

"Streamers! Boy, do I love 'em! But a lot of eastern favorites are a total loss on most western streams for trout and salmon. Most any combination will do the trick on bass. But when you are after the *Salmo* family, it will as a rule be in streams or lakes where the minnow life is restricted to two or sometimes three species: chubs, suckers, and the little Stonecat or Madtom.* So there is need for only two wing combinations: black and white, to imitate the sucker or Stonecat; and various olive greens and white for the chubs—all with a silver body.

We have no minnow life in our better trout rivers that corresponds to the dace or many other forage fishes common to the East. Thus the aforementioned colors are all that it takes to tempt a hungry fish. Most of ours usually are hungry for something that imitates as closely as possible a minnow native to their streams."

Regardless of this, the experiences of many western anglers indicate that a variety of eastern patterns are highly acceptable to both sea-run and non-migratory cutthroat trout.

DOLLY VARDEN TROUT

I shall dispose of this fish as quickly as possible with the remark that fishermen who are interested in catching him are advised to use spinners or bait. He is generally considered to be a notorious scavenger whose destructivness surpasses his value. He may be taken with streamers or bucktails near the mouths of streams, or in the streams themselves, particularly during the spawning seasons of other fishes,

* These are members of the catfish family.

How to Select Streamers

which he habitually follows into the rivers in order to pick up their ejected roe. The Dolly Varden normally is found near the bottoms of streams, and it is necessary to fish flies (or other lures) as deep as possible. Nearly any streamer or bucktail recommended for steelhead or cutthroat trout will interest him, but preferably it should be one which closely resembles one of the smaller fishes most prevalent in the stream at the time.

STEELHEAD TROUT

The steelhead is a rainbow trout which has spent a period of his life in the sea. He returns to western coastal rivers in the fall or winter to spawn. At that time he has a dark back with bright silvery sides, closely resembling a salmon; but as he remains in the river, he gradually reverts to his rainbow coloration. I have described his habits and the methods of catching him at considerable length in my book TROUT WATERS AND HOW TO FISH THEM (Boston: Little, Brown and Co., 1949).

While the eastern streamers and bucktails are used for steelhead, particularly in down stream reaches of rivers where waters are wider and less turbulent, most anglers prefer the high winged bucktail, due to its better action in fast water and because it has less air resistance, allowing it to be cast more easily to the great distances which often are necessary. Bucktails are used almost exclusively (to the exclusion of streamers), because hair has been proved to be more durable than feathers in contact with the mouth of this superb game fish.

The steelhead shares with the cutthroat trout a decided preference in the colors of the flies he will take most actively. Red and white is the favorite combination, closely followed by yellow and white, orange and yellow, or red and yellow. Perhaps the most popular of all is the *Royal Coachman* bucktail, with its white wing and predominantly red body. This combination is carried out in one way or another in many other steelhead flies—such as the *Thor* and the distant cousin of the *Royal Coachman*, the *Van Luven*. Many anglers prefer black wings or bodies, usually combined with a good deal of red. Others use a bit of the California gray squirrel hair in the wing, and many evince a decided preference for "a little brown in the fly," usually applied as a topping. Fishermen who are addicted to a certain river have decided preferences in the flies they use on that river and what is a favorite in one place may be frowned upon somewhere else.

Steelhead "holding water" is near the clean river bottom of the main current where there are rocks, sand bars, and similar spots, either out in the stream or in the protection of the banks, where the fish may rest without having to combat the main force of the flow. During a steelhead run, when a fish is taken from one of these holding positions there is always another to take his place in the favorable spot. Anglers know these positions by experience and instinct. In well-fished rivers, such as the Klamath of California, it is customary for fishermen to enter riffles at the head and to keep in motion to the tail of the riffle, so that other anglers following them may have an equal chance at the favorable spots. I have fished riffles on the Klamath when each one held a constant procession of anglers, waist deep in the middle of the stream, rhythmically casting to holding water behind rocks and along the bank. In most such places a long, powerful rod is needed to reach the good spots, even when a Power Cast is used.

In fishing such rivers, it soon becomes apparent that the time to expect a strike is when the fly cast cross stream has drifted quartering down current. If the strike does not take place there, it often happens just as the fly completes its swing and changes motion to waver erratically directly downstream. On fast rivers the current gives sufficient action to work the fly properly. When the swing is completed, it is advisable to work the fly a bit before retrieving it for a new cast, because there may be an undecided steelhead who has followed it from his holding position and who can be made to strike if the fly is given a radical change in action. Such strikes at the completion of fishing the cast are rarely strong. The fish are inclined to nip the tail of the fly and frequently are not as securely hooked as in the savage strike made while the fly is completing its swing. In either case, the long runs and the spectacular jumps of this most noble of the several species of trout have earned them a reputation unsurpassed even by the revered Atlantic salmon, who can offer superiority only in size. Many men maintain that the steelhead is the king of fly rod game fish. Others choose to give these laurels to the Atlantic salmon, and still others vote for the striped bass. I do not wish to take sides in such a discussion except to say, after having battled all of them, that no one should be-

How to Select Streamers

come dogmatic on the subject, at least until he has taken a sizeable bonefish with a fly rod and a streamer fly.

Steelhead rarely will take a fly on the surface, and then only under exceptional conditions of relatively low and warm water. Usually the streams are deep and fast. The fly must be cast quartering upstream, with plenty of slack to allow it to sink and drift near the bottom. On a trip to the lower reaches of Oregon's famous Deschutes River, I accompanied an accomplished angler who fished all day for an entire week without getting a strike, because his fly did not sink down to the level of the fish. Other anglers using sinking lures caught steelhead every day. For this reason many steelhead flies are weighted as described in Chapter IX. Most famous of these is the series developed by the master angler, Peter J. Schwab, who has been kind enough to assist me with some of the material for this book and to furnish me with several authentic patterns, including the *Bobby Dunn, Bellamy, Princess, Queen Bess, Brass Hat,* and *Paintbrush,* all originations of his, which he usually dresses with bodies weighted with wire.

LANDLOCKED SALMON

Like the steelhead, the landlocked salmon (the *Salmo salar sebago* of Maine or his close cousin, the Canadian ouananiche) has rather pronounced favorites in the colors of his flies. When he is hungry, any fly with a yellow wing and a silver body will produce a strike. Yellow is his color, particularly for dark days or discolored water. The yellow often is combined with a little white or red; these three combinations being perhaps the most generally acceptable. This preference has given prominence to such well known streamers and bucktails for landlocked salmon fishing as the *Colonel Fuller, Colonel Bates, Edson Tiger, Sanborn, Lady Doctor, Mickey Finn,* and a host of others.

When yellow fails, as it sometimes does, the landlocked salmon fisherman will turn to one of the many flies designed to imitate the smelt, a baitfish common to most landlocked salmon lakes and most necessary to the growth and well-being of the salmon. These natural imitations vary considerably in colors, but the great majority of them have a peacock herl topping to represent the dark-green back of the smelt. Among the most popular are the *Ballou Special* (the original eastern marabou streamer), *Supervisor, Jane Craig, Welch Rarebit,* and many others, with bodies predominantly white or green. A brown fly, such as the *Grand Laker* or the *Brown Ghost*, often is successful, particularly on a bright day. So are the famous *Gray Ghost* and *Nine-three*, the latter imitating the smelt by its black over green feathers and its silver tinsel body, above which is a bit of long white deer hair.

It seems obvious that some of the bright yellow flies, notably the *Colonel Fuller* and the *Sanborn*, are taken by salmon less because of hunger than because of their other instincts of anger, curiosity, or playfulness. It may also be that at certain times they are abnormally easy to please, because on one occasion I took a five pounder with a "fly" made by tying cellophane from a cigarette package on a bare hook. More usually, however, the most exact smelt imitations are the most successful.

Because the smelt is long and slim, landlocked salmon flies should be longer than normal and very sparsely dressed. I have seen occasions when a heavily dressed fly would not take fish, while the use of a larger, sparser fly would result in many strikes. Ultralong flies are difficult to cast easily, so they are usually used in trolling, as discussed in Chapter V. Such flies often are dressed with tandem hooks. Upon becoming familiar with the cohoe type of fly, so popular for cohoe (or silver) salmon in the Northwest, it has seemed to me that these flies could be used very profitably for landlocked salmon, and I have used them most successfully for the purpose.

All of these flies have been designed with the paramount qualities of form, flash, and action in mind. With these qualities, regardless of whether they are dressed as exact imitations or otherwise, at one time or another they will take fish.

ATLANTIC SALMON*

When anglers speak of Atlantic salmon the old discussion is usually renewed as to whether these fish will ever take streamers or

---

* Silver (cohoe) salmon and chinook (king) salmon flies are discussed under "Western Salt Water Streamer Fishing" in Chapter VI, since these species are most frequently taken in salt water or tidewater. The fishes discussed under Chapter III are fresh water fish or sea-run species most commonly taken in fresh water.

How to Select Streamers

bucktails in preference to the shorter flies. The argument has a habit of reverting to the question of whether salmon take any sort of fly as food or whether their occasional rises are prompted by one of the other basic instincts. In an attempt to resolve these two points, I must depend upon anglers who have had far more experience with Atlantic salmon than I, because my limited fishing for them would make it extremely presumptive for me to venture any opinions which I may have.

Anglers who have fished many of the famous salmon rivers in the northern provinces say that Atlantic salmon will take streamers and bucktails very satisfactorily in some rivers while in others they will not. Mr. Lee Wulff, an acknowledged authority on salmon fishing, wrote me as follows:

Streamers are poor flies for Atlantic salmon, falling behind usual wet and dry fly patterns except for black salmon, which is a highly publicized but small and inferior section of the sport. Streamer flies are most effective in high water. They are the preferred fly for spent fish (slinks or black salmon) in the early season and will work well on bright fish when the rivers are in flood and there's so much debris coming down the stream that a big fly is essential to draw the salmon's attention. All colors seem to work to some degree. Red is not a favored color, but yellow is generally good, and white, gray, brown, black, and mottled (barred rock) streamers seem most attractive. Yellow and black make one of the most effective color combinations for Atlantic salmon. Streamers for them should be dressed fairly sparse.

The comments of Mr. Wulff agree with those made by others, that fresh-run Atlantic salmon *will* take streamer flies, particularly in certain rivers and under certain conditions. Under ordinary circumstances the use of some other type of fly may be preferable, but even so the qualities of the streamer for these fish should be considered. Mr. Herbert L. Howard, an eminent fly dresser and salmon angler of New Rochelle, New York, is one of several who have mentioned the advantage of using a streamer for bright salmon when they will not rise to ordinary flies under conditions of low and clear water. In fishing this "augmented fly," anglers have obtained rises by slapping it on the water and manipulating it in an extremely unorthodox manner, as one occasionally does when fishing for bass. Evidently the salmon's reaction is from anger or curiosity, and the color of fly used seems to be of minor importance.

This subject of using streamers and bucktails for Atlantic salmon merits a bit of development, because flies are perhaps too often recommended for them from habit. In the early days of Atlantic salmon fishing, fancy and expensive English patterns were used almost exclusively; Americans and Canadians had not experimented enough to develop patterns of their own. Then the guides, who could neither afford them nor dress them, found they could dispense with such fripperies in favor of patterns much simpler.

A guide (I think it was at Jack Russell's old camp on the Miramichi about in the 1930's) tied a fly on a salmon hook with a black yarn body and red wool tail (pulled from old sweaters) and with a black bear hair wing (clipped from a rug by the fireplace), and he used this crude and simple creation with amazing success.

In 1963 I fished from Ted Crosby's camp at Blissfield, New Brunswick, in his famous Wasson Bar Pool on the Miramichi and found the popular flies there were very simple. My friend Paul Kukonen, who thinks this is the best pool on the river, gave me two samples which I shall describe as examples. He calls them the *Green Assed Bastard* and the *Red Assed Bastard* (if you'll pardon the expression).

The *G.A.B.* has a tail of a few black hackle fibers; a butt of fluorescent green yarn; a body of black spun fur, picked out and ribbed with narrow oval silver tinsel; a throat of black hackle; and a black squirrel wing. The *R.A.B.* has a tail of a few brown hackle fibers; a butt of fluorescent red yarn; a body of brown spun fur, picked out and ribbed with narrow oval silver tinsel; a throat of brown hackle; and a red squirrel or fox squirrel wing. Similar patterns are tied with orange spun fur bodies and gray squirrel wings. The flies are dressed in several sizes, usually on 4X long hooks.

In discussing these flies, Paul writes (in 1965): "These two flies are the guides' favorites and the ones most used on the Miramichi and Cains rivers. There, they have taken thousands of salmon from July through the middle of October. My personal success led me to try them tied bucktail pattern for trout, and they produced equally well. I believe that Ted Crosby (owner of Wasson Bar Camps) orig-

How to Select Streamers

inated the fluorescent butts, and the famous angler and fly dresser Harry Smith, of Chesterfield, Maine, certainly had much to do with the popularity of hair wing salmon flies."

The author's own experiences on the Miramichi indicate that fluorescent butts bring many more strikes than do flies dressed without them. Perhaps fly dressers and anglers should increase their experimentation with them for other species of fish.

Anglers who fish salmon rivers are usually there for so short a time that they use locally popular flies rather than chancing fewer strikes by doing much experimenting of their own. Paul Kukonen is an experimenter, and the trend from fancy English patterns to the modern simpler ones can perhaps be carried a step farther to the more prevalent use of streamers and bucktails, as these instances related by Paul will illustrate:

"Although, currently, 95 per cent of bright salmon are taken on wet flies, with a few on drys, there is much experimenting to be done. Five of us were fishing a long pool on the Cains River in October, with no results. At the tail of the pool an angler hooked three fish in rapid succession. He was using a *Gray Ghost* streamer a good two inches long, tied on a No. 4 hook.

"On another occasion, all of us spent three days making occasional casts to a rising salmon who never left his lie. After over a thousand had been made to him, a new man arrived in camp and, on seeing the bulge, took him on the first cast with a large white bucktail. Evidently no one had told either the angler or the salmon that salmon never take streamers or bucktails!

"These are two of many instances to which I do not need to add several of my own to prove that Atlantic salmon *will* take streamers and bucktails more frequently than some of us might think."

So if, as some say, Atlantic salmon do not feed after entering the rivers, why do they take the type of flies which imitate minnows?

It is acknowledged that salmon feed very little in fresh water but the fact that they *do* feed occasionally has become well established. For example, Mr. John E. Hutton in his book TROUT AND SALMON FISHING (Little, Brown and Co., Boston, 1949) gives repeated instances of noticing the feeding of bright salmon on plankton, flies, worms and *minnows*. He advances proof that salmon disgorge their stomach contents upon being hooked, and that their rapid rate of digestion would account additionally for food rarely being found in their stomachs. Thus it may be inferred that salmon will take streamer flies and bucktails from hunger as well as because of the other basic reasons.

Black salmon, the slinks, or "unclean fish" which formerly were bright salmon but which have spent a winter in the river, will take streamer flies or bucktails avidly. The color, size, or shape of the fly matters little or not at all. Their impelling desire is to satisfy their ravenous hunger after being imprisoned in the river during the winter months.

BASS

Flies for the popular smallmouth bass are many in shape and varied in color. In years gone by, extremely large patterns of the orthodox wet fly type were used almost exclusively with the fly rod. As the value of streamers and bucktails became generally known, their importance for bass fishing became so apparent that they have now virtually supplanted flies of the older designs. When surface waters are moderately cold and bass are feeding on the surface, many anglers prefer the added action of taking them on floating lures. This can be done with the streamer fly if bushy hair wing patterns or limp hackled streamers are selected. The fly is dropped on the water, with as much of a "plop" or "spat" as possible, near the supposed sanctuary of a big bass and is allowed to lie there for a moment. Undoubtedly he notices the fly and is waiting to see whether or not it is alive. A light twitch of the rod tip settles his indecision, and as the now active fly is pulled an inch or two below the surface, the angler may expect a smashing strike.

It is often the case that bass do not take floating lures but will take a moving fly fished a foot or two under the surface. The similarity of the streamer fly or bucktail to a baitfish puts it in a class by itself in affording action at such times. The bass will strike from anger as well as from hunger, especially during his spawning season in the late spring. Thus, exact imitations in streamer flies rarely are necessary. Extremely colorful patterns are usually more effective. Yellow is my favorite, but many anglers prefer black and white, red and white, yellow and red, or flies with mixed hackles of green and blue combined with any of the above colors.

The productive colors in bass streamers and bucktails often vary markedly from one section to another. In streams where crawfish are prevalent red or orange winged flies usually are especially successful because of the red-orange color of the crawfish.* In other streams, such as the Shenandoah River, black flies are used extensively, because the bass feed on the black Madtom or Stonecat. For the same reason, black is a preferred color on many rivers in the Ozark region.

Bass flies do not need to be unorthodox, but they are often made so. They may be dressed in virtually any color combination. Hackles may be so long and limber that they would be frowned upon in flies for other fish. An abundance of palmered shoulder hackle is a common method of dressing, and splayed wing types are favorites from coast to coast. Fancy, expensive feathers and hair are decidedly unnecessary.

All this may seem to recommend certain color combinations and then leave the field wide open! My preference is for simple, standard streamers in the colors first mentioned, with yellow leading because of its unusual visibility. Either bass have a decided liking for yellow or it is so visible in the water that they will travel farther to strike a fly with which it is dressed.

It seems that the choice of fly is decidedly less important than the manner in which it is fished. If we know that bass are feeding near the surface and we still are not enjoying strikes, it is better to change the manner of fishing the fly than to change the fly itself. During warm surface water conditions bass may be feeding deep down during the heat of the day; but unless the water is too warm, they will move into the shallows in the evening for food. Regardless of the time of day, when they are near the surface they will take the properly fished

---

* A bright orange (or "hot" orange) fly also is very popular on many western steelhead rivers because of the large numbers of red-orange crawfish in these waters. These often become dislodged from their hiding places in the stony river bottom and are washed downstream, being visible in the water only as a red-orange blur about the size of the ordinary streamer fly, which for this reason often is mistakenly taken by fish if it is red orange in color. The crawfish's erratic manner of swimming is not unlike that of a minnow. A splayed wing bucktail in "hot" orange with a gold body should be an excellent imitation of the crawfish, but I have never seen a fly so tied.

FIG. III-5

TYPICAL LONG-WING BASS STREAMER

streamer or bucktail at least as readily as they will any other type of lure.

Many anglers prefer bass flies tied on ringed hooks (hooks with a straight eye, not turned up or down), because they sometimes find it advisable to cast or troll them attached to a spinner. While it may be helpful to have a few such flies, it is normally well to keep them to a minimum, because they are less useful for regular fly fishing. A wide variety is not necessary. When they are needed, the bass seem to be more interested in the spinner than they are in the fly. Along with these I like to have a few weedless streamers (see Figure IX-12), because it is extremely annoying to have an ordinary streamer constantly becoming caught on grass when one is fishing in weeds.

What has been said of the smallmouth bass applies, insofar as streamers and bucktails are concerned, to the largemouth. Being on the average a somewhat larger fish, capable of devouring big frogs, birds, mice, and other types of food in a mouthful, not excluding other fish nearly as large as he is, the largemouth needs flies which are likewise big and tied to large-sized hooks.

PICKEREL AND PIKE

Simply dressed streamers and bucktails are as useful for pickerel and pike as they are for bass, since these types of fish exist under similar conditions and seek the same kinds of food. My preference in pike and pickerel flies is for heavily dressed bodies of wool or chenille, with simple one color or two color hair or feathered wings. White is one of their favorite colors, particularly when a small bit of red is added. Yellow, or red and yellow, will usually be equally pro-

Fig. III-6

TYPICAL PIKE AND PICKEREL BUCKTAILS

ductive, but black and white or gray may be found to be effective, especially on brighter days. If these combinations fail, the addition of a spinner in front of the fly may add to its attractiveness to the fish (Figure III-7). Since walleyed pike are frequently to be found near

Fig. III-7

"LITTLE WONDER SPINNER" FOR WALLEYED PIKE. This model, which originated in the Lake Erie area, is used for casting. For trolling, a similar rig is popular except that the lead is placed on the leader two or three feet ahead of the fly

the bottom of the shallow parts of lakes, it is advisable to fish the fly for them as near to the bottom as is possible.

Mr. Lacey E. Gee, of Independence, Iowa, sent me three pike and pickerel flies that have proven themselves extremely successful. One is dressed with a thick white wool body with a red tail, a short red throat, and a fairly long wing of white bucktail. Another has a thick red wool body, with a yellow hackle tail and throat and a wing of red bucktail, with an equal amount of white below the red. The third has a body of white chenille with a white tail, red throat, and a wing of black over green bucktail. These flies were developed

FIG. III-8

TYPICAL CRAPPIE AND PANFISH STREAMER

by Mr. Lawrence Johnson for walleyed pike fishing in the Niagara River. Mr. Johnson states that he has caught a pike of twenty pounds with one of the flies and that they are equally successful for bass and crappies. Pike streamers should be an inch or two longer than pickerel streamers and should be tied to a 5X long hook at least No. 2 in size.

PANFISH

Virtually any small streamer or bucktail will take crappies, bluegills, bream, perch, and other panfish, particularly if it is in their favorite pure or combined colors of black, white and yellow, or in red and white, brown, or gray. The use of a spinner adds greatly to the attractiveness of the fly for perch and occasionally adds effectiveness for other panfish. At one time or another even the most inexperienced angler can catch panfish with the fly as easily as he can with bait. From this it must not be assumed that panfish, particularly the larger and more experienced ones, can be taken consistently with lack of skill and knowledge. To me, panfish are vastly underrated by most fishermen. It takes science to locate the big ones, and it requires skill with the fly and rod to bring home a noteworthy string. Here again, the manner of fishing the fly is more important than its choice. My favorite panfish for streamer or bucktail fishing are the perch and crappie, since they feed on minnows to a greater proportionate extent than do bluegills and certain other small pondfish which prefer bottom food or insects. Flies for bluegills should be tied on size 12 or 14 hooks, but the hooks for other pondfish, most of which have large mouths, can be two or three sizes larger.

Connecticut River Shad Flies are used both with and without tails. These are shown with glass beads attached to the leader. This type frequently is called the *Silver Yank Shad Fly*

McCredie Special Shad Bucktail is popular in Northwestern coastal waters.

FIG. III-9

SHAD STREAMERS AND BUCKTAILS

SHAD

Shad has been termed "the poor man's salmon." This rather belittling appellation seems unfair to him, because he is a fighter and leaper well worthy of his place among the game fish. The shad enters coastal rivers of both oceans in the spring, following them as far as dams and pollution permit, for the purpose of spawning. His entry into southern rivers is early in March and in the northern streams as late as May or June. Fly fishing for him has become extremely popular in recent years. Although favorite flies vary widely in color and appearance in the rivers where they are fished, these three may serve as typical examples.

The *Chesepeake Bay Shad Fly* was originated by Burt Dillon of Baltimore, Maryland, in 1942. It has a thick body of white yarn ribbed with silver tinsel and a long wing of white deer hair. Its dressing is completed by a tail of a few fibers of a golden pheasant tippet and a red painted eye, as illustrated in Color Plate V.

The *Connecticut River Shad Fly* is dressed with silver tinsel extending partway around the bend of the hook. A wing of a section of a red duck flight feather is tied full, but extremely short, occupying about half the length of the hook. A quarter-inch red glass bead is always strung on the leader ahead of the fly. Orange or yellow wings and beads are alternate and less used combinations but they are occasionally effective. They may be dressed on a hook wound with gold tinsel.

A shad fly popular on the West Coast, particularly around the Coos Bay area of Oregon, is called the *McCredie Special*. It is dressed on a short-shanked hook wound fairly thickly with red silk and ribbed with silver tinsel. It has a long throat of white polar bear hair and a high wing of equal length sparsely dressed with black bear hair, both extending well beyond the end of the hook. A black head with white painted eye and black pupil completes it. Heavy hooks in size 2 or 4 are preferred for all three patterns, the first two calling for hooks 2X or 3X long and the third for a regular length hook.

Shad normally rest in the protection of rocks in the current. The fly is cast cross stream and allowed to swing. The fish usually take it as the swing is completed, just before the fly is retrieved. When shad are near the bottom in fast water, as they often are, it may be necessary to add a bit of lead on the leader ahead of the fly in order to make it sink, or to use weighted patterns. The mouths of these fish are very tender, making it advisable to handle the fish lightly so that the hook will not pull out.

IV

How to Fish Streamers in Fast Water

Once in a while I go fishing with an angler whose name is well known to many and whose passion for using the streamer fly or bucktail is almost an obsession. He has fished a fly for more years than I have lived. He fishes with constant patience, following the season to find the most productive of north-eastern waters in spring, summer, and fall. When his native streams are no longer open, he is a familiar figure on the historic salmon and steelhead waters of the Northwest—forsaking them only to enjoy a month or two with the bonefish, snook, and tarpon of the Florida Keys before returning to Maine for big landlocked salmon and trout as soon as the ice leaves the lakes in the spring.

"Do you ever use anything but streamers and bucktails?" I once asked him.

"Only when big fish won't eat little fish," he answered. "Never knew 'em not to. I started with wet flies and I fished dry flies when they first became popular on the Beaverkill. Then I learned about streamers. Haven't used anything else since. Never felt that I needed to."

"Why?" I inquired.

"Because wet flies, dry flies, and nymphs are productive only occasionally," he said; "but streamers and bucktails will take fish all year through. I've learned how to fish 'em and I've learned that they invariably help me to catch bigger fish. I like to catch big fish, and big fish will strike at streamers more often than they will at smaller flies."

The many years of experience of this angler entitle his remarks to be taken with respect, but I shall go along with him only a part of the way. When trout are rising to a dry fly, I can think of no form of fishing which is more enjoyable than to try to catch them with tiny floating bits of fuzz and feathers. I have tried to like all forms of fishing and have tried to avoid being a purist in any of them. Bias is a handicap in a sport which offers so many means for its enjoyment. Variety in fish, in fishing locations, and in methods is a key to maximum pleasure with the rod and reel.

There are anglers who have the opinion that streamer flies and bucktails are useful only under conditions of high or cloudy water, or when fish can find little or no drifting food early in the spring. Those who have fished fairly consistently with streamers will agree that they are the best of artificial flies for these situations. They also will agree that these flies are good under low and clear water conditions, and that they will invariably take big fish almost any time and anywhere. I have found situations when I could not get strikes with streamers, but in these instances it is rarely the case that the fish could have been taken with anything else. I do not think it an overstatement to say that streamers and bucktails are the most consistently productive of artificial flies. Certainly, if I were confined to only one type at all times and in all places, they would be what I would select.

It has been noted that this type of fly is easiest to use in fast water, because the current aids the angler in fishing the fly. How it should be fished is to a large extent a matter of opinion. There are many methods, some of which should be used in certain circumstances and for certain kinds of fish, while other techniques are superior in other cases. Some of them can be pinned down and some cannot. I have read several books wherein angling authors become rather dogmatic in advising a single technique for a defined type of water. I have found that in most cases several techniques will work; usually one better than the others, but it is rare that one can forecast the proper method in advance. I shall try to describe all the methods and to recommend certain ones in certain cases, but it must be left to the

Fig. IV-1

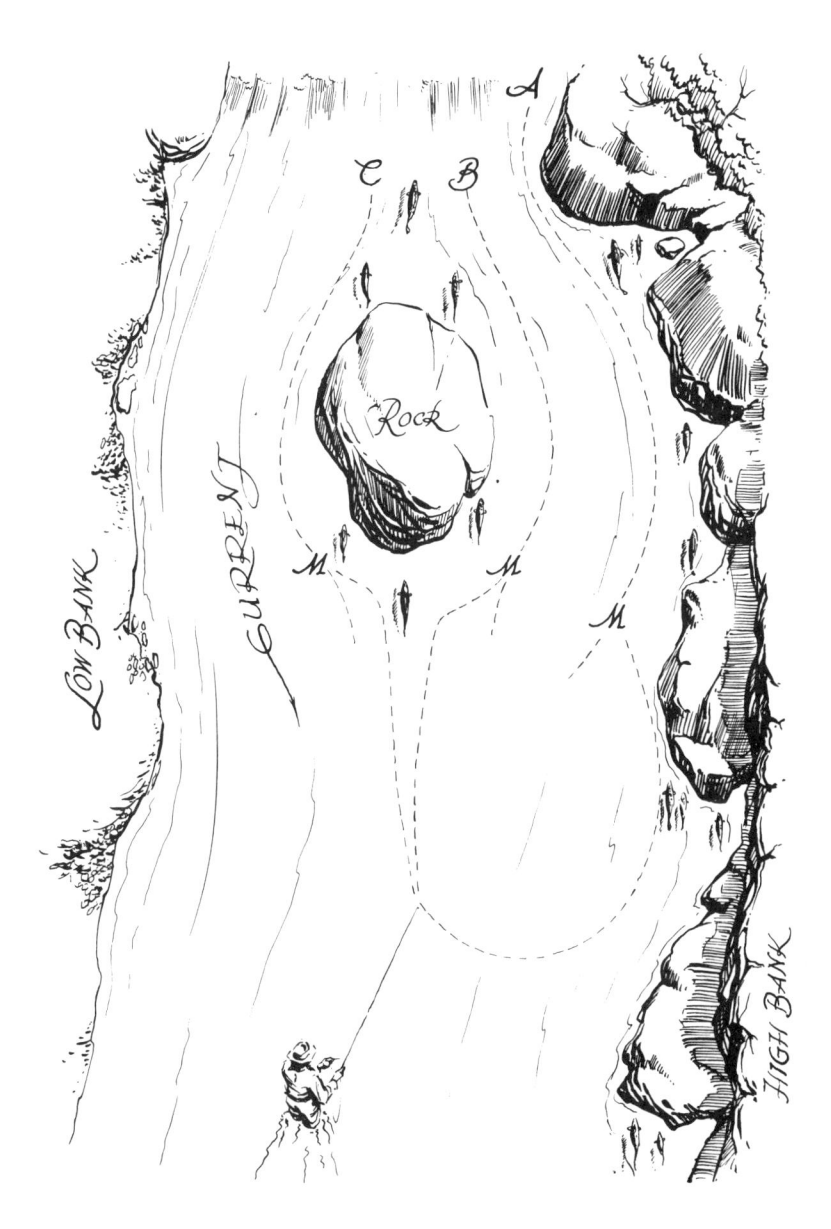

THE UPSTREAM CAST is used to deeply sink the fly

71

experimentation and intuition of the angler to decide what is best in the situation he faces.

When fish are not feeding on or near the surface, as usually is the case in the early spring, and when the current of the stream is slow enough to make it feasible, the upstream cast is worth trying. It has the advantage of allowing the fly to sink deep in the current, and it thus helps the angler to direct his fly near where the fish may be lying in the protection of rocks and other obstructions. It has the disadvantage of forcing the fisherman to constantly recover line in order to keep the fly moving slightly faster than the current, so that it will appear natural and so that he can feel a strike when it occurs. It is necessary to work the fly with a lifelike motion, because it will not drift in simulation of a minnow when it is being washed downstream head first. In a fast-moving stream this combination is so difficult to accomplish satisfactorily that I usually give it up, unless deeply sinking the fly to bottom feeding fish is the prime objective. In a slow-moving stream the operation is much easier and more likely to be successful.

To fish the streamer fly upstream, the fisherman must be in the stream, unless it is very narrow or unless it has enough curves and promontories so that he can cast from the bank. If we take Figure IV-1 as a typical case, he may notice on his right some large rocks and a deep run near them where some of the stream current is directed to the right bank. He may correctly assume that fish are lying in the protection of the rocks near the fast water of the current. He therefore makes a reasonably long cast to a point such as "A," where the current moves into a deep run near the bank, and he allows the fly to be borne into the run toward the bank by the current. As the fly drifts downstream, he simulates the action of a minnow by raising and lowering his rod tip to give the fly a series of short and erratic jerks. Each time he lowers his rod tip, he recovers sufficient line to keep himself in control of the fly. The raising of the rod tip is done by a series of sharp and short twitches rather than by a sweeping motion.

In fishing across a current to slower water beyond, as in the cast to the far right to position "M," the faster current will put a downstream bow in the line which will pull the fly downstream much faster than it should be fished. Unless this is corrected, the excess speed of

Fig. IV-2

MENDING THE CAST

the fly usually repels fish rather than attracting them. To correct this, the angler "mends" his line. That is, he keeps the line on or very near the surface and, by a flip of the rod tip in the opposite direction to that which the bowed line is taking, he reverses, or partially reverses, the bow in the line, thus regaining control of the line from the current and allowing the fly to be fished in a normal manner. Mending the line under such circumstances is of extreme importance.

Abnormally large rocks in a stream are favorite sanctuaries for fish. They lie in the protection of the slack current around the rock, usually just above the rock or on its downstream side in the position shown on the sketch in Figure IV-1. Thus, a cast to a position above the rock to point "B" will direct the fly deep into the water near where the fish are presumed to be. As the fly begins to pass by the rock, it may be possible, if a sufficient length of the line is on top of the water, to mend the line to the left to keep the fly as near to the downstream side of the rock as is possible. This should throw that part of the floating line which is nearest the rod into the current to the left

73

of the rock. This current should pull the line to the left and direct the fly through the quiet fish-holding area on the downstream side of the rock.

When one side of the rock has been covered, the other side should be fished in a similar manner, as is indicated by the cast to position "C." Mending the line is an alternative to making a new cast. Sometimes this is advisable in cases where low overhanging branches make it impossible to place the fly near the bank by ordinary means. Many very large fish are found in the protection of rocks near shore, so these places should not be ignored in favor of mid-stream locations.

It often happens that a fish will follow a lure and not take it unless the method of fishing the lure is varied. Therefore, just before the cast is completed, anglers often find it of value to change the action of the fly by giving it a series of longer and slower, or of shorter and sharper, motions before it gets near enough to be picked up from the water. I have seen many cases where this change of action brought a quick strike from a good fish, his indecision probably being settled by a feeling that his prey was about to escape.

In all degrees of current swiftness, and particularly under very fast water conditions, the quarter upstream cast has several advantages. It usually makes it possible to fish from the bank in places where it is not desirable to wade. It allows the fly to sink deep in the water. It gives the angler better control of his line and his fly. Being fished more nearly broadside to the current, the fly drifts in a more natural manner, tempting more strikes with a minimum of manipulation of the fly. Its main purpose is to allow the fly to sink. Therefore, on completion of the cast the fly should usually not be fished immediately but should be allowed to drift and sink on a fairly slack line until just before it reaches a place where a fish may be expected.

There is a spot on Vermont's White River where a big brown trout habitually lives below the large rock shown in Figure IV-3. Other smaller trout usually rest in the protection of the fallen tree slightly downstream. An angler with whom I was fishing noticed the big trout one evening but could not catch him, so the next morning it fell to my lot to try him with a bucktail. After casting for him from downstream I walked up to position "A" and made a quarter upstream cast to point "C," allowing the fly to drift deep and

Fig. IV-3

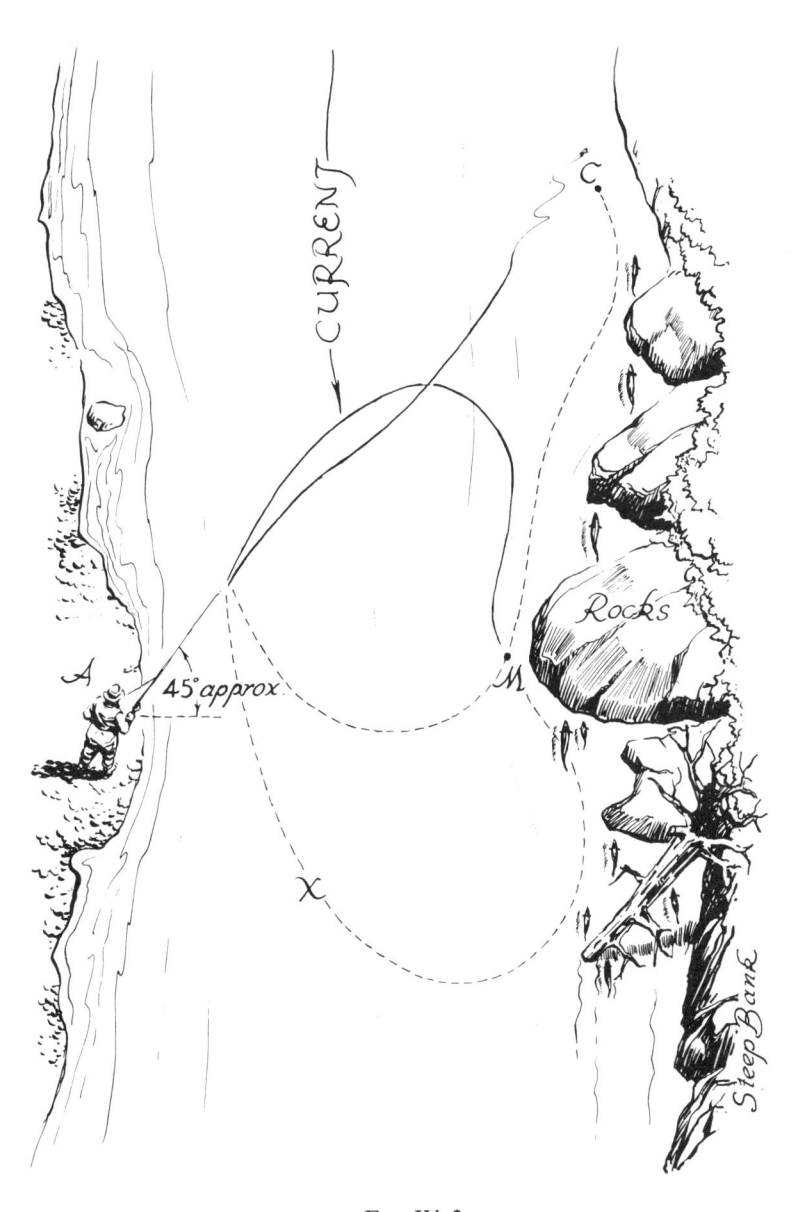

THE QUARTER UPSTREAM CAST both sinks and swings the fly

pass by the big rock. The water was cold and slightly muddy from spring rains. The fly took the path of the upper broken line in the sketch, but the current took it away before it could pass near enough to the downstream face of the rock. Since I had cast directly into the position previously, I assumed that I had put the fish down; so I went farther upstream and returned an hour later to try for him again.

On the next cast I mended the line at point "M" so that the fly was carried nearer to the pocket than in the previous cast. The fly passed out of the pocket and drifted by the fallen tree in the curve shown by the lower dotted line. When the fly had reached point "X" I noticed that a big trout was following it. He came along directly behind the fly, seemingly interested, but rather obviously suspicious. When I saw him in pursuit of the little brown and white bucktail I gave it a series of short, quick jerks rather than using the slower method I had adopted previously. The trout immediately became more interested, increasing his motion to stay directly behind the fly. At this point I had about given up the idea that he would take it, since he was now so close that my presence must have been noticed. Just before I had to take the fly from the water I gave it several even shorter and sharper twitches and the trout took it less than fifteen feet from the rod tip. He weighed nearly four pounds but did not put up a fight of any consequence. Evidently the water was so cold that he was extremely logy and disinclined to feed. It was only the extreme variation in fishing the fly which seemed to make him take it, and my opinion was that he was not as smart as most big brown trout are supposed to be.

Undoubtedly he was the big trout I had been fishing for, in spite of the fact that another angler took another fish from the same position next morning, in addition to several smaller brook trout from around the fallen tree. Usually it is the case that a good holding position is inhabited by a fairly large fish. When one is taken from it another ultimately moves up to take his place. The fallen tree always is an excellent spot for smaller fish, but the fly must be worked within a few inches of the log to make them take it.

When a streamer fly or bucktail swings in the current on a tight line, it drifts broadside or quartering to the current, which will keep it in motion with little or no help from the angler. We can note a

How to Fish Streamers in Fast Water

similarity between this maneuver and the frequent habit which minnows have of drifting downstream for a short distance quartering against the current. In the case of a streamer fly or bucktail drifting in this manner, the fish may not strike the fly even though he may be observing it, but it is probable that he will strike when additional action is imparted.

When a fly is drifting in the proper current, a large amount of action given to it by the angler may drag it from the current into a less favorable location. In such a situation it usually seems wise to try a complete drift, without giving the fly added motion. In this case its nearness to suitable rocks or the river bank may be more desirable than increased action in a less desirable path. I believe in fishing out the cast first and allowing the fly to complete its swing and hover for a minute or so in the current downstream. At this place it pays to work the fly rather energetically. It frequently happens that a fish will follow the fly on the swing, and will take it only when the swing has been completed and there is a change in the fly's motion as the line trails downstream. If there is no strike at this point, it is well to vary the action of the fly as much as is possible while retrieving the line. The indecision of many fish can be counteracted in this manner, as was that of the brown trout mentioned above.

The upstream cast and the quarter upstream cast have so many means of employment that no book ever could list all the typical situations which arise from time to time. So I shall confine myself to relating a single example. There have been repeated instances of its happening. Usually it recommends the use of the dry fly, but this book is about streamers and bucktails and they will serve just as well.

In stream fishing the angler may come upon a situation where trout are feeding in the tail of a pool. They may be picking up nymphs or hatching flies, and it is possible that they will be feeding rather selectively. A small bucktail or streamer often works well, even in a case such as this. It happened, for example, one year when I was fishing a small wilderness stream in Maine. The deep upper part of the pool provided little action, but there seemed to be activity in the shallow water where the tail of the pool fanned out. I walked through the brush and waded into the riffles below, so as not to disturb the water. From this position several minutes' inspection showed four or five large trout feeding on the bottom, their tails and dorsal fins occasionally showing. After locating the fish, I made a quarter upstream cast to a spot just above the nearest one. The fly worked in front of him without his seeing the leader, and he took it instantly. I coaxed him over the lip of the pool and netted him there so as not to disturb the others. Then I cast for the next nearest fish and ultimately took three before those remaining had moved away.

In this case an upstream cast was of no advantage, because the fly would not have worked as well in the fast, steady current, and particularly because the line and leader would have been seen by the fish before the fly arrived where he could take it. The quarter upstream cast was the only one which could be used from that position and allow a proper presentation of the fly.

I enjoy most of all the cross stream cast, as shown in Figure IV-4, because it is adaptable to shallow water or to deep water when fish are feeding near the surface. With this cast I like to use a floating line so that I can mend it at will. One can see the fly and watch the strike of the fish, all of which adds greatly to the fun of angling.

The cross stream cast may be used from the side of a deep pool, as is indicated in the sketch. It may be used across a stream or river just as well. In this case, and ordinarily, the angler will elect to fish the nearby water first, casting to points "B," "C," "D" and "E" before he makes a final cast to point "F." He may try a few casts with a slack line and allow the fly to explore the depths of the pool. He also may allow the fly to swing on a tight line until all of the fishable water is covered, or until the fly has been borne downstream to point "H," where it should be worked for a few moments before being retrieved. In doing this he will find it advantageous to so handle his line that the fly will work close to the rock at position "G" because a rock such as this is an excellent place to find large trout.

I think the floating line should be used in surface fishing with streamers more commonly than it is. With it one can pick up the fly almost at will, if occasion demands it, without disturbing the water. If the leading portion of the line sinks, this is of minor consequence. When one can watch the line on the water, the position of the fly is clearly indicated. In a slack line cast, the motion of the line often will indicate a strike before it is felt by the angler. The floating line allows

FIG. IV-4

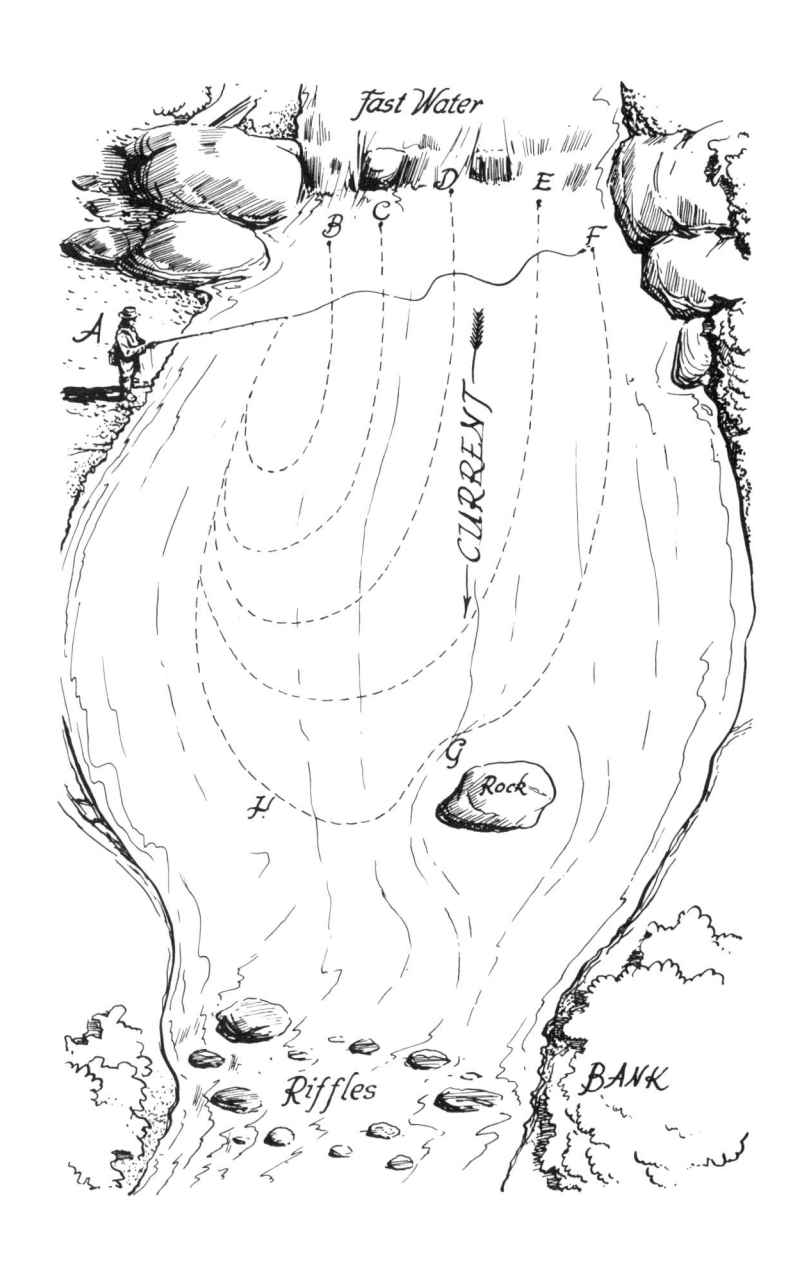

THE CROSS STREAM CAST is excellent when fish are surface feeding

Fishing when the author "roamed the Maine woods when it really was the Maine woods."

How to Fish Streamers in Fast Water

the shallow spots to be fished without the line becoming caught up on the obstructions which may be a few inches under water in the stream. This allows us to fish over shallow rocks where it would not be possible otherwise.

With the floating line I like to use a leader about nine feet in length. A short leader restricts operations and frequently discourages a fish which might strike. A longer leader is often inconvenient and usually unnecessary. The nine-foot leader allows a streamer or bucktail to be fished to a depth of a foot or so, which is usually sufficient when fish are feeding on or near the surface. At this depth the floating line will not hamper the action of the sunken fly, particularly since a few feet of the leading portion of the line will most likely be under water.

The quarter downstream cast is useful when it is desirable to cover a definite position downstream or to cover places in a restricted area. If one wishes to fish a rock or run, for example, it may not be necessary to cover other parts of the water with the cast. It may also be unwise to cast directly to the spot to be fished, for fear of the disturbance which might be caused by the fly and leader landing on the water. Thus the quarter downstream cast is made to land the fly in a current which will swing it into the spot to be fished. In such a place the fly is handled as it would be in a cast directly downstream. This cast is valuable in covering riffles, a pool, or any other restricted area from upstream. Examples of it are illustrated in the casts to positions "B" and "D" in the sketch in Figure IV-5.

The remaining of these five casts is the downstream cast, which also has rather distinct advantages. It, as well as that discussed above, may be used with a floating or a sunken line, depending on the depth and turbulence of the water to be fished. As shown in Figure IV-5, one of its uses is to cast between obstructions (in this case, rocks) and fish positions which could not be reached as well with casts made across stream. Quite obviously the downstream cast is the opposite of the upstream cast and may be used in covering similar positions. The difference is that the upstream cast tends to sink the fly much deeper than the downstream cast does.

In Figure IV-5 the angler is on a jutting ledge, attempting to cover the holding positions in the sketch. He makes a cast as near the left bank as possible and allows the fly to swing and to work the water at point "B." He may let out line and try to reach the fish on the downstream side of the rock, and undoubtedly he has first covered the position on the upstream side. When this is done to his satisfaction, he will cast to point "C" and allow the current to fish the fly between the two rocks, extending and shortening his cast or the length of his line to explore the upstream area first and then work the lower positions. When he casts to point "D," the current will immediately move his fly to the right of the middle rock, and by letting out a bit of line he can reach the fish on the right of its lower side. After this, he should lay a cast to spot "E" and allow the current to swing the fly to the left to fish the nearby rock on that side.

In a previous discussion of the marabou streamer, we mentioned the fact that a fish may rise to a streamer and be seen to be interested in it even though he will not take it. This is an ideal spot for such a thing to happen when fish are not hungry, or if the appearance of the lure does not appeal to them. I should like to make the point again that when an extra good feeding position is noticed, it should not be fished superficially and too quickly passed by. If there is a good reason to think that a worthwhile fish is there, he may be induced to strike if you repeatedly work the streamer in front of him. When I find such a place I usually make it a point to light my pipe and not to stop fishing the place until the pipe goes out. When we think of the time taken to explore a stream, five minutes does not seem too long to invest in fishing a good feeding position. In any event, the practice has paid dividends in big fish that other anglers did not catch because they preferred to hurry to newer places around the bend.

Downstream fishing offers more latitude in working the lure than with any other type of cast. On some days, and for certain kinds of fish, this method will do so well that further experimentation is useless. Frequently it is only necessary to place the lure in the right position. The current will fish it in a lifelike manner, especially if the current is fairly swift. The rod may be twitched occasionally and moved from side to side in order to cover more water.

If this does not work, it is well to drop the lure back a few feet and then make it undulate forward by an upward sweep of the rod tip. This causes the fly to sink down into the current and then to

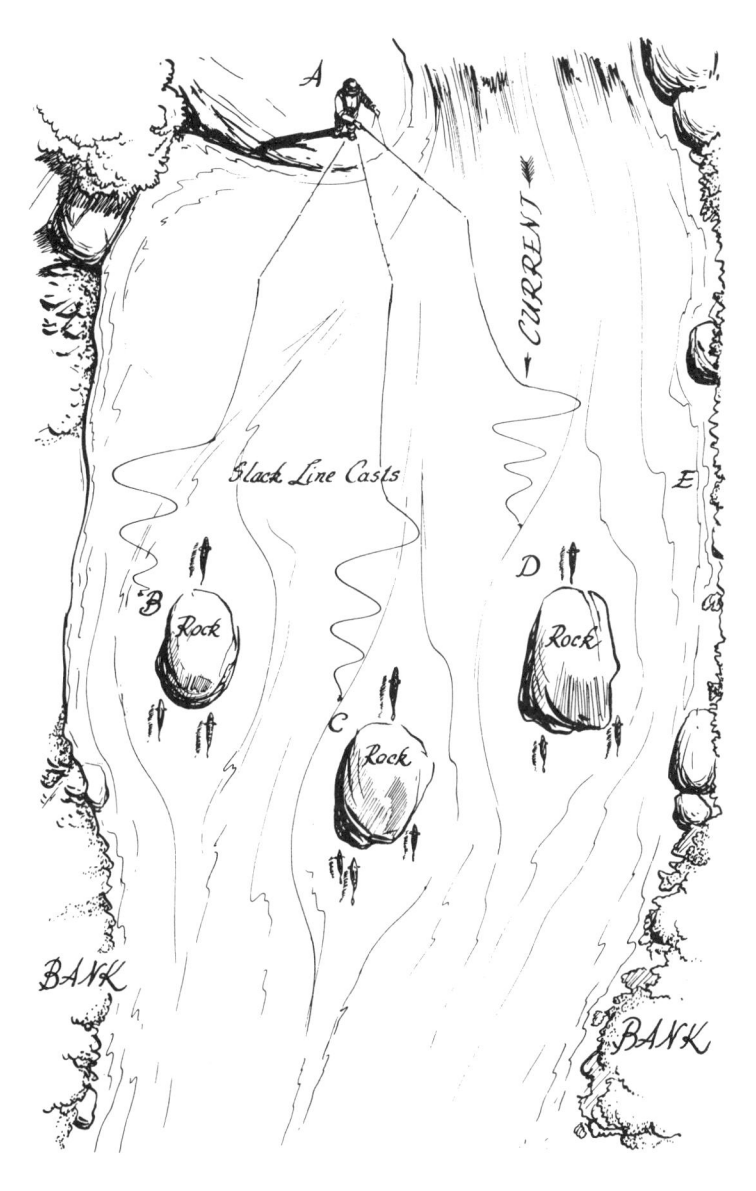

FIG. IV-5

THE DOWNSTREAM AND QUARTER DOWNSTREAM CASTS
are useful in restricted places

83

work upward like a minnow trying to reach the surface in a current that is too swift for it. To cover the water thoroughly, this may be done in alternation with moving the rod from side to side while the angler is gradually recovering line by the hand twist method preparatory to regaining it for a new cast.

When one can fish a split riffle, there is a great deal of advantage in wading the riffle and casting to the bank rather than attempting to fish from the bank. In riffle fishing the large game fish normally are near the midstream rocks or along the deep runs and protected positions of the shore. In fishing from the bank the angler often is at a distinct disadvantage, because he is on top of the good spots before he sees them; the situation is just the opposite when he is able to wade the riffles.

The motion of a sick or injured minnow can easily be duplicated with the streamer fly. When an actual one is observed, he will be seen to drift and waver, occasionally to summon his strength and try to dart for cover, only to loose his balance and repeat the procedure. The point cannot be stressed too strongly that the easiest way to learn the various methods of making a streamer or bucktail act like a live or injured baitfish is to devote a considerable amount of time, perhaps in the often unproductive noonday period, to watching the methods of swimming which the various baitfish employ, and then to fish a bucktail nearby until it is observed that the action the angler imparts to it is a reasonably accurate simulation of the minnows' varying action in the water.

It may also be well to repeat here the point that, once a suitable fly has been decided upon, it is more advantageous to change the method of fishing it than to change the fly itself too often. I have fished with anglers who use a fly for a few minutes and then impatiently break it off and try a new one. The result is that they spend too much time fussing with their tackle and too little time working their fly in the water.

I have noticed, as others have, that big trout (and other fish, too) have a habit of traveling in pairs all year through. When an abnormally big fish is taken, it is well to keep on covering the same water. Very frequently another can be caught. In watching the actions of a hooked fish, I have often seen the rather frantic behavior of another

How to Fish Streamers in Fast Water

which followed the hooked fish in. Perhaps he is too disturbed to be caught, but very often he is there.

When an angler is fishing the ordinary wet fly or the dry fly and another chooses to use streamers or bucktails, it is better for the former to fish ahead, followed by the latter. A streamer fisherman frequently can spoil the water for a wet fly or dry fly man, but the opposite rarely is the case. Many of us have followed anglers using small flies and have taken large fish right behind them. A trout often will strike at a small fly only once, but he may come for a streamer again and again. Perhaps this is due to his feeling that he has lost it the first time and when it comes into his field of vision again he assumes that it is injured and makes a renewed attempt to take it.

When one fishes a streamer or bucktail without success, it is more important to change the size of the fly than it is to change the pattern. Many cases have been noticed when fish (and trout particularly) will take a small streamer and will refuse a larger one of the same pattern. It is also true that fish will refuse a bucktail but will take a streamer of identical size and color. This often is due to the bucktail being overdressed, or appearing too bushy in the water, while the hackles of the streamer may give a more streamlined appearance and greater variety of action.

As we have noticed in the cases of bass and Atlantic salmon, it is possible to get results by fishing in an unorthodox manner when ordinary methods fail. If it is impossible to take a fish by the procedures which have been described, we might as well attempt the unorthodox practice of slapping an ill-shaped fly onto the water and fishing it with complete disregard for common sense. It is true that this should be a last resort, but it often has taken fish which can be made to strike from anger, curiosity, or playfulness rather than from hunger. If the current is swift, or if there is a lot of surface wave action, strikes sometimes can be obtained by adopting a very fast retrieve and skittering the fly on the surface so that it will jump from wavelet to wavelet like a minnow which has been driven to the surface and is trying to escape a large game fish underneath.

Small streams usually call for the use of small streamers and bucktails, and this type of fly often produces extremely large fish which no one would suppose could be living there. I like to fish small streams if there is a prospect of taking a big trout by doing so. I am inclined, however, to pass up spots overgrown with bushes where one has to crawl and creep laboriously for fifteen minutes or so in order to reach a place from which a decent cast can be made only with the greatest difficulty.

One of the best and most consistently resultful anglers I know adopts an entirely opposite view. When he asks me to go fishing with him he is sure to ferret out the most inaccessible place imaginable. After crawling and scratching our way the last few hundred feet he signals for silence and stalks to the stream with a degree of care which would seem absurd if one did not know his methods.

When we have arrived finally at the scene of operations he usually whispers, "Look at this wonderful water. No one has been in here for years!"

The first time I went with him I replied rather dryly that I didn't wonder, and I resisted the temptation to add that I was sorry we had been the first in so long a time. I sat on the muddy bank with my feet in the water and my head in the bushes and suggested that he show me how he could possibly cast in such a dense tangle of undergrowth.

He took out his jackknife and cut a branch of lead pencil size and about one-third as long. The branch had a single leaf on it. He hooked the barb of the fly through the edge of the leaf and let out line while he carefully guided the floating branch and fly to a dark pool near an undercut bank.

When the fly had arrived at the proper point he delicately twitched it from the leaf and carefully worked it through the holding water. There was an immediate swirl and he was fast to a large brown trout which for some reason or other he succeeded in working around the maze of roots and branches to a spot where he could raise his rod tip high enough to take him from the water. This accomplished, we slowly worked our way downstream to another spot where he suggested that I try a similar procedure. He knew there was a fish in the location he pointed out, and after three attempts to float the fly down to him I succeeded in hooking him. He broke me off around a stump and we gave up the spot to labor our way farther downstream. When darkness stopped operations he had three large brown trout and I had one. On comparing notes in the beer parlor of a nearby general

How to Fish Streamers in Fast Water

store it appeared that we had done better than had any of the local anglers that day.

One of the commonest mistakes made by inexperienced anglers is to note a rising fish or a good holding position and to cast directly to that spot. A minnow does not come to a fish that way: that is, it does not drop on his head. A better procedure is to utilize the currents of the stream to guide the fly from the right or left to the place the angler wishes to fish. By manipulating the rod tip, if necessary, the fly is presented in a natural manner, and it is normally able to accomplish the desired result.

I shall conclude this chapter with two general rules which may serve as the essence of streamer and bucktail fishing in fast water. First, fish the fly slowly when water is cold and the fish are inactive. Fish it more actively when the water is warmer and when fish are more disposed to travel faster for the fly. Second, study the minnows and imitate them in form, flash, and particularly in their action. If a bucktail or streamer is handled to copy the erratic motions of a startled minnow, and if it is fished in the right places at the right times, it is almost certain to produce far more than its share of results.

V

How to Fish Streamers in Slack Water

Several of the secrets of success in trolling streamers were impressed upon me many years ago when I was one of three anglers who visited a lake in Maine for the early spring trout and landlocked salmon fishing. One of the group was an elderly columnist who sometimes goes under the pen name of "The Old Fisherman," so that is what he will be called here. It was the Old Fisherman who gave us some of our first lessons in how to catch fish while trolling a streamer fly or bucktail.

The first day on the lake was annoyingly cold with a brisk breeze which made the water choppy and discouraged casting. After the wind had caught a few lines on the backcast and brought the flies dangerously near the occupants of the boat, we gave up the project in favor of trolling with three rods. I was given middle position to fish directly off the stern.

"Don't let out much line," the Old Fisherman advised. "Put out just enough to keep your fly in the end of the wake of the boat."

That kept the fly in plain sight, only twenty or twenty-five feet astern. "Doesn't seem far enough," I remarked dubiously.

The Old Fisherman took a pull at his pipe and directed the boat along the shoreline. "It's all right as it is," he replied. "Let's try it that way for a while."

The other two lines were let out sixty or seventy feet with the rods nearly at right angles to the boat so as to keep the flies and lines

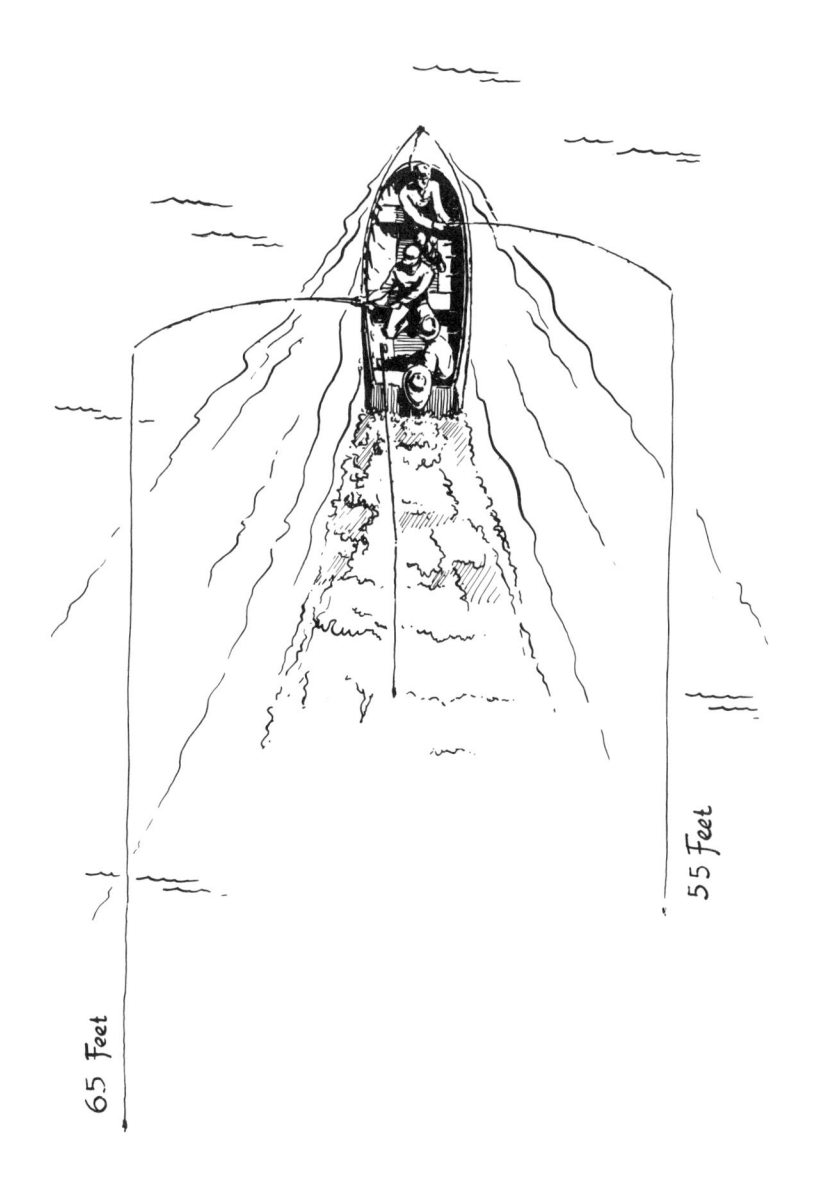

Fig. V-1

WHEN TROLLING TWO OR THREE LINES the middle fly should be in the wash of the boat, with the outboard lines much longer.

separated and to cover as much water as possible. A few split shot were added to the leader of one of the lines to make the fly ride a bit deeper than the others.

The Old Fisherman speeded up the Johnson 5.5 motor, sending the little Rangeley boat along the shoreline at a clip of four or five miles an hour. While he puffed on his pipe, he discussed the strategy of trolling.

"Fish are often attracted by the wake of a boat," he said. "They may come up to the middle fly as it rides in the wake. If they don't like the looks of it, one of the two outboard flies may appeal to them when they follow along. When fish are taking on the surface there's no need to put lead on the leaders, but adding it to one of them is a good experiment. After we hook a few fish we'll know what works best."

There was a solid strike at the *Edson Dark Tiger* fly on the left rod, and a salmon immediately leaped into the air. We reeled in the other two lines and watched the angler play his fish. The salmon jumped three times and came to boat. When he saw the angler, he tore away again and took to the air twice in rapid succession. The jumps of a landlocked salmon are every bit as spectacular as those of his anadromous cousin, the Atlantic salmon. What he may lack in size he compensates for in energy, boring up three or four feet into the air with rapid gyrations of his wide tail and powerful silver body. When he has reached the height he falls off and dives straight into the water, perhaps immediately to jump again. Once I counted seventeen leaps from a little *Salmo salar sebago*, but four or five are more common. To me, he is a better jumper than the steelhead and every bit as energetic as the tarpon, whose great size is the only reason why his aerial antics are more awe inspiring.

The salmon swirled near the boat. The Old Fisherman, his net wet and ready, waited until the angler signaled to take him aboard. At the sight of the net the fish bore down so deeply and quickly that the rod was pulled to its ferrule into the water. Before the angler could raise it, the fish had traveled under the boat, demonstrating the valor of his fighting heart by another jump in that direction.

The Old Fisherman quickly turned the boat to free the line and bring the salmon astern. Now exhausted, he was led in and lifted

How to Fish Streamers in Slack Water

from the water in the net. He weighed nearly five pounds, which is better than average for his species.

No sooner had we put the lines out and resumed speed again than a second salmon fell to the same rod.

"Take the lead off the other line," the Old Fisherman advised. "We don't need it, particularly so near shore."

I decided to try the lucky pattern and tied an *Edson Tiger* to my leader. The other angler removed his lead and did the same. The *Edson Tiger*, in both its variations, always has been a favorite of mine. It is as good for trout and bass as it is for salmon. When the day is bright I like the Dark *Tiger* better than the Light one. The name "Dark" or "Light" refers to the wing rather than to the body, and of the two the yellow wing of the Light *Tiger* makes it the brighter fly.

We soon learned that the salmon were not following the schools of smelt, as is their spring custom. They were feeding along the gravel of the shoreline, in water so shallow that one had to use care in handling the boat. This change in their habits may have been due to the fact that the smelt had not started their usual spring spawning run. Undoubtedly it was influenced by the relative warmth of the shallow water along the shoreline and the fact that food was to be found there.

That night we came in with eight salmon, after having returned many more to the water. Since this was far better than the luck of the other boats, everyone at the camp insisted on knowing what fly we used. A local fly dresser had set up temporary quarters at the camp and was kept busy all night tying *Edson Tiger* bucktails for all and sundry.

The next day was like the first, except that the first fish fell to a *Ballou Special*; so we all used that fly and reported its success at dinner that night. *Edson Tigers* promptly were forgotten, and the fly dresser burned the midnight oil to turn out dozens of orders for the new white marabou pattern. On the third day we switched to the famous *Gray Ghost* with equal success, to the consternation of the other fishermen and the profit of the fly dresser. Someone rumored that there was a conspiracy afoot between the fly dresser and ourselves, so around the fire that night the Old Fisherman undertook to explain matters.

"Probably any of those flies would have taken an equal number of fish," he said to those in the circle of chairs around him. "They all are good flies for these waters. I switched patterns several times today and took salmon on all of them. The fly is of less importance than where you fish it and how you fish it. First you must find the salmon. Then you must know how to fish the fly!

"Most people troll flies altogether too slowly," he said. "In the early spring, when the water is cold, relatively slow trolling is all right but, as the water warms up, faster trolling is necessary. When the wind makes the water choppy—a 'salmon ripple,' we call it—slower trolling is good, but even in that case speed up the boat occasionally and slow it down occasionally. A fish may be following the fly and not taking it because it may be going too slowly or too steadily. Speeding up the boat often makes him change his mind.

"From five to seven miles an hour, or a bit faster than a man can walk, is a good average trolling speed," the Old Fisherman continued. "You run the motor a bit slower when going with the wind, and a bit faster when running against it."

"What about holding the rod in a rod-holder, as compared to hand-holding it?" someone asked.

"When the water is choppy, a rod-holder usually is all right," the Old Fisherman replied, "but it probably won't give the fly enough action in calm water, particularly when travelling at a steady motor speed rather than the more erratic speed caused by rowing or paddling. I like to fish from a canoe whenever possible on this unpredictable lake. The erratic action of paddling works the fly. Paddle on a serpentine course to cover as much water as possible. But when the water is flat, the fishing usually is poor near the surface. If you fish the surface, use a long line and a hand-held rod. Fish the fly very actively, and travel at a faster clip. Some folks prefer to fish right on top. That may be all right on a ripply surface, but usually three or four feet down is better. Use a sinking line, or at least a forward section that will sink and work the fly deep enough. Whenever in doubt, give more action to the fly. If the waves and the boat don't do it, you have to do it. Generally a rod held in the hand and actively manipulated will bring twice as many strikes as you would get by merely dragging the fly."

How to Fish Streamers in Slack Water

"We found our fish in the shallows," someone said. "I thought they were supposed to be following the smelt."

"The smelt runs haven't started yet, evidently," the Old Fisherman observed. "The water is cold, so the salmon feed on something else in the shallows where it is warmer. The wind was blowing against the shoreline we were fishing. That brought food to the fish. It rippled the surface too, and that helped the fishing. We haven't had enough wind to turn the lake over, so surface water is very cold. When she turns over she'll warm up a bit, and we'll have better fishing."

"When she turns over?" a young man exclaimed. "What do you mean by 'when she turns over'?"

"You are here at just the right time to find out," the Old Fisherman said. "Didn't you ever hear of the good fishing on our northern lakes a week or so after the ice goes out? Don't you know the reason? Well, the reason is this, and it has to do with water temperatures, because trout and salmon feed more actively in temperatures of from 50 to 70 degrees than they do when the water is near freezing as it is now.

"Water reaches its maximum density at 39·2 degrees Fahrenheit," the Old Fisherman continued. "That's the temperature right now, down deep; and it has been so all winter, because water at freezing temperature is lighter and thus stays on top. So most of the fish are deep, and the hungry ones which have come up are feeding in the warmer water along the shoreline.

"Then what happens? The ice gets mushy from spring suns. Suddenly a little surface action breaks it up, and it dissolves. But the surface water still is near freezing, and the water down below still is at 39·2 degrees, and the fish mostly are deep. Then a good wind comes up. It churns the water enough for the warmer, deeper water to mix with the colder surface water, and all the water mixes until it's all at about 39·2 degrees. Limnologists say the lake 'turns over,' and I guess that's just about what it does.

"So then, with the water all at about the same temperature, the fish come to the surface, where there is more food. After being down deep for the winter, they are hungry and feed actively for a time. This continues, off and on, until the surface water gets too warm for them. Remember that water colder or warmer than 39·2 degrees is lighter, and stays on top. So eventually, as summer comes on, we get a layer of warm water that becomes too warm, and the trout and salmon don't like it. While some stay in the cooler water around stream mouths for a while, most of them go deeper, to an intermediate layer, where temperatures are more to their liking and where enough sun reaches down to make the plants and algae grow which baitfish feed upon. So then we either troll deep or fish the spring holes and stream mouths where the water is colder. The same thing, in reverse, happens in the fall when cool temperatures bring the surface water down to 39·2 degrees again. We're here at the right time," the Old Fisherman said happily. "We should get a blow tonight that may stir things up a bit. If so, the fish will be boiling tomorrow!"

"In that case, we don't fish the shallows any more?" the young man inquired.

"We fish all over the place," the Old Fisherman said. "But mainly we fish where the food is—along the shoreline the wind is blowing against; around islands and reefs; in the coves; and out in the lake near stream mouths.

"One more thing, while we're on the subject," the Old Fisherman continued. "Later on in the year, when the water has reached 70 degrees or more, we know that many of the big fish are down deeper where it is cooler. The warm top layer may extend down from ten to twenty feet deep or more, depending on how big the lake is and other factors. Just under this warm layer there is a shallow middle layer of rapid temperature change where temperatures suit game fish—in between the surface, where it is too warm, and the very deep water, where it is too cold. If we're smart, we'll find out the depth of this layer of rapid temperature change with a thermometer. The depth will stay about the same all summer. We'll troll at about that depth along the shoreline and around islands. Many use bait for the purpose, but a good-sized tandem streamer fly or a tandem bucktail trolled on a very long leader at the end of a wire line is deadly; that is, if you like that kind of fishing."

A gentleman from New York who had been listening to the conversation brought over his streamer fly box and opened it before the old Fisherman. "Would you tell me," he asked, "why I'm not getting many strikes on these tandem flies? I bought them from one of the best dealers I know of."

How to Fish Streamers in Slack Water

"Well, let's assume the trouble is with the flies, rather than with the way you fish them," the Old Fisherman said. "Now take this one, for instance. It's tied to gut or monofilament which has become so warped that the two hooks are not in line. A trolling fly with a bent linkage is almost impossible to straighten. It won't act right in the water unless the two hooks and the linkage are straight and in the same plane. Lots of fishermen nowadays dress tandem flies with Sevenstrand stainless steel wire because it won't kink or warp as nylon or gut or other monofilaments will.* You'd better not use it any more.

"Here's one that is too heavily dressed," the Old Fisherman remarked as he selected another. "It won't troll with the slim appearance of a baitfish. Maybe we can trim some of the dressing off and make it work better. And this one: the dressing is too long. It should just cover the rear hook, and it's over an inch longer than that. Fish will hit it, but you'll probably get short strikes and not hook the fish, because many of them will nip the tail." He pawed through the collection and selected several properly dressed tandem flies. "Use these tomorrow," he advised, "and you should do a lot better."

"I was trolling for trout in Allsop's Pond," the New Yorker said after thanking the old man. "I got some trout, but picked up too many weeds on the hooks."

"If you're going back there," the Old Fisherman said, "I've got some weedless flies, and I'll give you a few at breakfast. But here's a little trick that will help when you don't have any. Tie a small treble hook on your leader about six feet above the fly. It will keep most of the grass off the fly when the grass travels down the line. The treble hook won't keep it all off, but it will help a lot."

That night the wind blew hard, just as the Old Fisherman had said it would. In the morning the lake was heavily white-capped, with waves breaking into froth along the shore.

"Take your waders," the Old Fisherman said over coffee the next morning, "and let's take the trail to the cove. It will be calmer there, and easier than trying to manage a boat."

In the sheltered cove a small rocky point of land jutted out where casting could be done without interference from the dense tangle of

* See page 203 for dressing tandem flies.

spruce which came down to the water's edge. The old man studied the rippling cove carefully.

"One place is as good as another," he said to the younger man. Go out on the point and fan-cast the whole area as far as you can. I'll fish farther down, if I can wade out far enough to keep my back-cast from the trees."

"You can roll-cast from shore," the young man suggested.

"Too calm in here," the Old Fisherman said. "Unless it's windy and the water is choppy, roll-casting disturbs the surface too much and puts the fish down. I roll-cast only when the surface is disturbed anyway; never when it is as calm as this, unless I have to. That's why I said we should bring waders."

The young man walked out on to the point and looked at the water. The day was bright, and small minnows with dark medial lines and lighter backs darted about in the shallows. He selected a small *Black Nosed Dace* and tied it with a Turle Knot to a nine-foot finely tapered leader. The old man had taught him how to fan-cast, and he did it methodically. As sketch V–2 shows, he didn't disturb the water farther out until he had covered the area nearby. Starting at his left, he made a series of short casts to his right until all the area about twenty feet from his rod tip had been covered. He fished one cast near the surface, retrieving rapidly with short jerks of the rod tip, and was pleased to see the little fly dart inward as the little baitfish had done. His next cast was allowed to sink deeper, and he fished it in more slowly. The third cast was deeper still and fished very slowly. The fourth cast was deep and was fished faster. As he activated the deeply sunken fly with a twitch of the rod there was a silvery flash where the fly had been, and he was fast to a trout. The trout bore down deeply, first one way and then another, taking a little line from the reel. He rose to the top and swirled. After a few minutes of scrappy resistance he was led to water near the rock, on his side and feebly shaking his head against the fly and leader. The young man admired his bright colors, watching him for a moment or two. Then he kneeled down and drew the trout to him. His fingers slid down the leader until they held the fly, impaled in the trout's upper jaw. He grasped the fly as far back on its shank as possible and turned it over as he lifted the trout from the water.

Fig. V–2

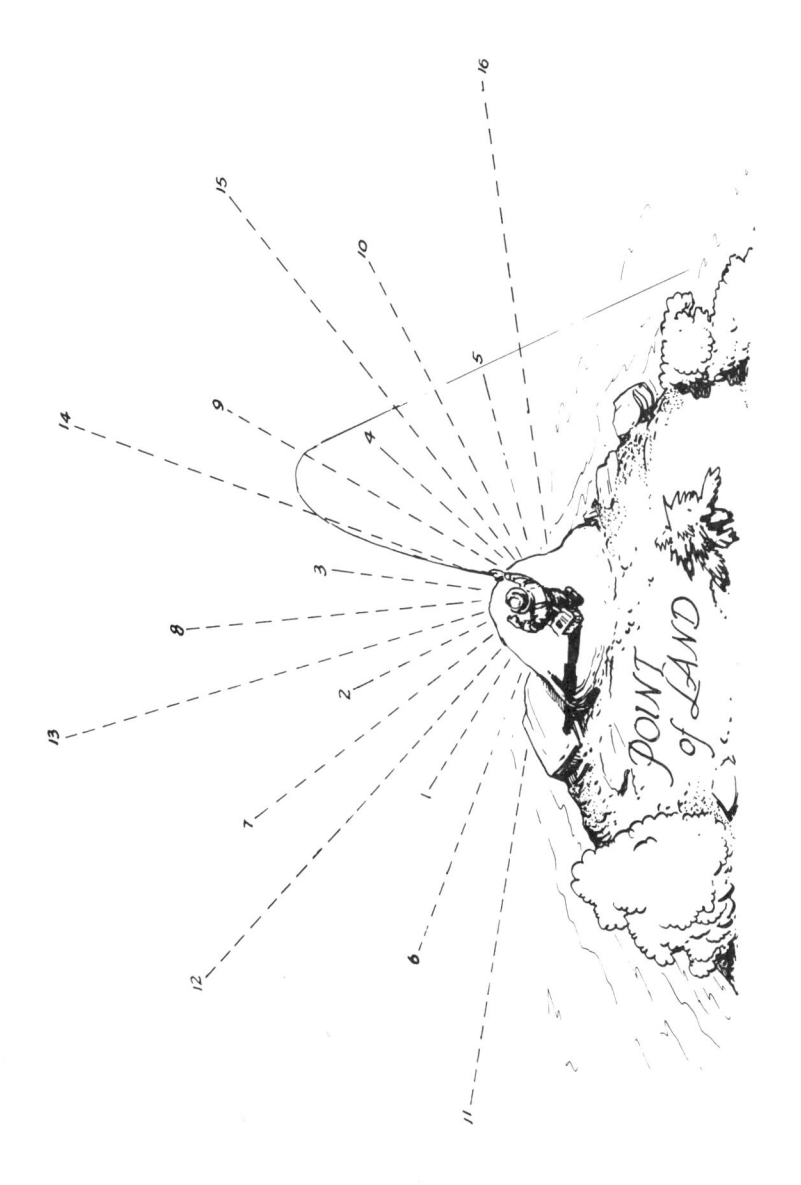

THE FAN-CASTING METHOD of covering a large area

"Now shake loose," he said softly. The trout, twisting against the firmly held fly, dropped off and flashed away.

The young man stood up and, smoothing the fly, looked at the Old Fisherman. The Old Fisherman was waist-deep in the water, sending long Power Casts toward a mass of floating logs farther down the shore. As the young man watched, the old man dropped his fly within inches of one of the logs. The water boiled and the strike resounded like the slap of a beaver's tail. The old man's reel whirred as the trout bore down under the logs. The taut line went limp and the bowed rod flicked straight as the fish snubbed the leader around an underwater branch and broke off. The old man snapped his fingers in a gesture of disgust and, turning, grinned at the younger man.

"Damn!" he called fervently, "That one was a real danged honest-to-God buster!"

The young man laughed and, with a few false casts to extend line, he increased his distance to forty feet. He covered the arc of the extended area precisely as he had done with the nearer one, alternating shallow retrieves with deeply sunken ones, and fast stripping of line with slow retrieves made by recovering a few inches at a time with his fingers.

He extended his casts to sixty feet and covered the more distant area as he had covered the nearer arcs. On his third long cast the fly was taken by a salmon which seemed to jump into the air to reach it as it landed. The young man's reel whined and his rod against the tight line jerked convulsively as the salmon made his run. Far out in the cove he swirled on the surface and somersaulted into the air, water flashing from his silvery sides. He jumped again and again, and as he leaped the angler dropped his rod tip slightly to decrease line tension for fear the jumping fish might break the leader with his body.

Raising the rod high, the young man regained line. The salmon jumped twice more and raced about, but he was tiring now. Soon he was nearby, lying feebly fanning his tail and fins on his side in the water. The young man, seeing that the fish appeared to be well hooked, led him to a sandy spot between two rocks and, walking backward with rod held high, he beached him on the gravel. He picked up the flapping fish by his gills, killed him, and held him up for the Old

How to Fish Streamers in Slack Water

Fisherman to admire. Then, reaching into his jacket, he produced a small pair of scales and weighed the fish.

"Five-and-a-quarter pounds!" he called to the old man proudly.

The old man had waded from the water. "That one sure is a keeper," he said admiringly. "You know, I was hoping we'd get a big salmon. I wish you'd see fit to have him filleted and broiled for lunch. Let's get back to camp. I'm getting hungry. The lake is calmer and will be just about right for fishing at sundown. The water seems warmer and I guess last night's blow destratified it. If so, we'll get some great fishing during the rest of the week."

That evening, as the purring motor steadily pushed the dark-green canoe across the spruce-bordered lake, the great copper-red globe of the sun, slowly-setting behind the dense forest marking the horizon, flecked western cumulous clouds in pastels of pink, purple, and gold. The Old Fisherman, seated in the stern with his hand on the tiller and with his pipe trailing wisps of fragrant smoke astern, noted it with satisfaction not only for its beauty but because it portended good weather. The young man, seated in the bow with fly rod ready between his knees, drowsily absorbed the monotonous slap slap slap of wavelets breaking under the bow as the canoe pressed forward. To his left a pair of loons were diving, and nearer off the port bow there suddenly appeared the swirl of a large feeding fish.

The young man quickly became alert, raising his fly rod into false casts as he extended line. The old man, stopping the motor to let the boat drift nearer to the spot, watched as the young man expertly dropped the little streamer in the center of the widening ring made by the fish.

"Right on target," the young man exclaimed, as he fished in his cast.

"Too damn near right on target," the Old Fisherman objected. "You know you never should cast directly to the rise. Haven't I always told you to cast beyond it and a bit to one side or to the other? Now you've gone and put that fish down, and you didn't even have a chance to fish the fly past him correctly. They don't like those things dropping right on their noses!"

The canoe reached the opposite shore, and they very slowly cruised along it within casting distance of the rocks, logs, and holes which should be sanctuaries for feeding trout at that time of year. As shown in Fig. V–3 (which shows a rowboat because it is roomier, more stable, and easier to handle for this type of fishing), the angler in the stern has cast to a fallen tree, which should be a good lie for a fish. As he fishes his cast in to point "X," the angler in the bow casts to point "A" between two large rocks. As he completes fishing his cast, the rearward angler may try the same place—because a difference in the fly or in its manner of presentation could tempt a strike where the first angler had failed.

When the rearward angler has completed his cast to point "A," the boat's progress will permit the forward angler to cast to point "B." By thus alternating casts, only one line is in the air at a time to prevent possible tangles. Also, all the good spots can be easily and alternatively covered. In case of a strike, the boat would be allowed to drift while all nearby positions would be fished more thoroughly.

"It doesn't apply to this time of year," the Old Fisherman said, "but I'll never forget a day in late June when Ross McKenney and I were fishing Snake Pond many years ago. We cruised the shoreline several times, and on each trip Ross would hook and land a big brook trout of about four pounds. At the time, I'd never caught one that big, and I was getting pretty exasperated because all I could hook were small ones. Well, on the next trip along the shoreline Ross bet me a dollar he could hook another four pounder on his next cast. Naturally I took him up on it. I lost the dollar.

"Then Ross let me in on the secret. 'See that bunch of very green foliage in the pocket where I hooked the fish?' he said. 'See that trickle of cold water running down from the bank? Well, that's a spring hole, and there are several big trout in it. Maybe you didn't observe that I hooked each of the big fish in exactly the same place, one on each trip by. Now, I'll bet you a dollar you can do the same thing on the next trip.'

"On the next trip I cast to the spring hole, and I caught a four pounder. So when surface waters are warm, I always look for spring holes. Ross taught me a lesson I'll never forget."

"Did you keep all those four pounders?" the young man asked.

Fig. V-3

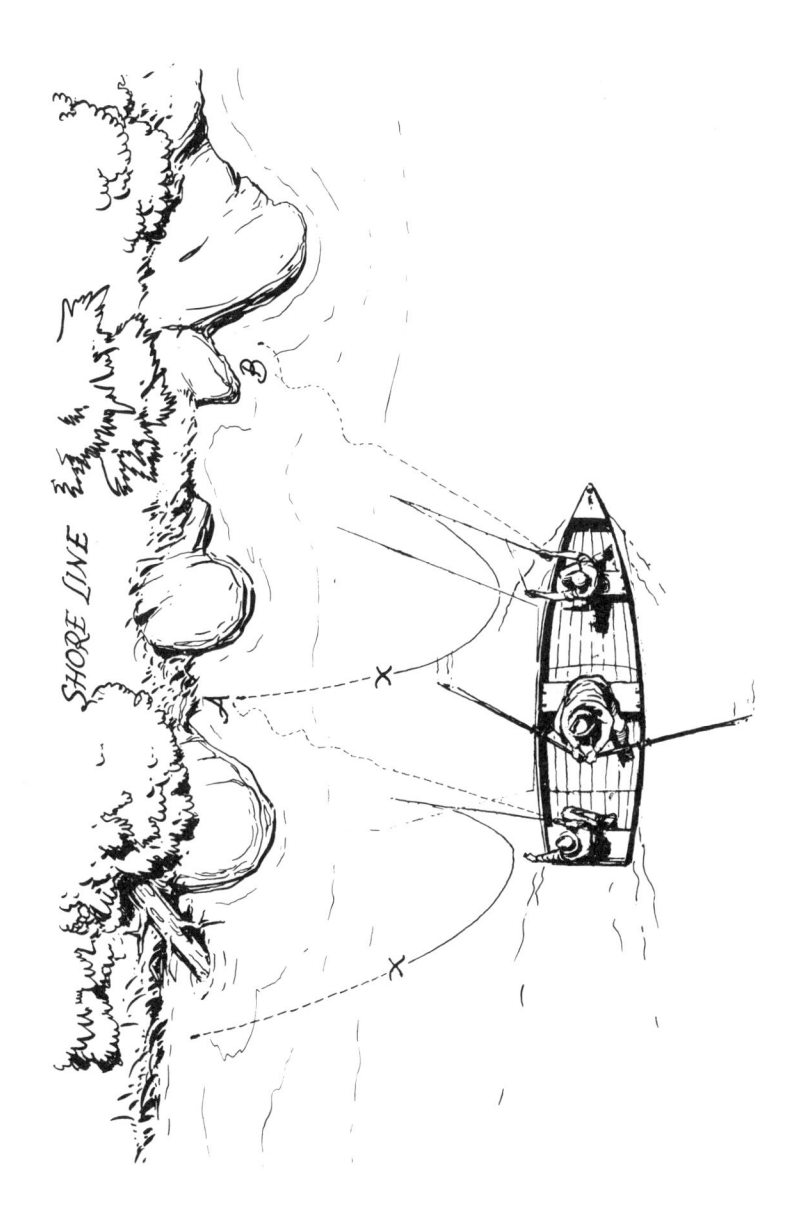

METHOD OF COVERING SHORELINE from slowly moving boat

"I kept mine because I wanted to have it mounted, but Ross released all of his. If people had fished Snake Pond since then more for fun than for meat, the fishing would be about as good today. It isn't. Aircraft and game hogs have ruined it."

"Speaking of warm water fishing, I remember a lesson an old-timer taught me one late spring day on Pierce's Pond, here in Maine," the young man said as they slowly fished the shoreline. "Trout weren't taking on top, and I hadn't hooked a thing, so I was letting the canoe drift and just fooling around. This old-timer came out and anchored his canoe. When she was steady with the breeze he made a long cast, put down the rod, and lighted a cigarette. When he had smoked the cigarette he took up the rod and stripped in with fast jerks. He caught several nice trout that way."

"Nowadays he wouldn't need to take so long to let his cast sink," the Old Fisherman observed. "He would be using a fast-sinking dacron line and could do it in less than half the time. Probably the pond was stratified and the fish were staying in the cooler water down about ten feet deep or so. Maybe they would have fed on top in the evening. Sometimes a very small streamer or bucktail, fished very slowly but in the same manner, will do well too."

"We're fishing the shoreline," the young man noted, "and this is a week or so after the ice has left the lake. The ice has gone, and the blow we had has destratified the lake, so why not fish out in the lake itself?"

"The top water is warming a bit," the Old Fisherman said. "That boil you cast to on the way over means that fish are starting to cruise around. The shoreline and the coves and islands have been the best so far, but the deep water should produce for the next week or so. I was dragging a thermometer on the way over. The top water is about 50 degrees. It's starting to be the way the fish like it.

"I remember a day about this time of year, maybe a week or so later," the Old Fisherman continued. "It was many years ago, when fishing for squaretail trout and landlocked salmon was really good on Mooselookmeguntic Lake. We were at the head of the lake in a small boat. A blow came up, and even the larger boats started in. So we decided to go in too, but we couldn't start the motor. While Bud was working on it, I began to cast a *Ballou Special* white marabou streamer, because that's one of my favorite smelt imitations for salmon. I was taking a fish on almost every cast. They were jumping and tearing under the boat and pulling the rod tip under sometimes, and the boat was pitching about in the white caps. Really exciting!

"Bud decided the boat could weather the blow, and he couldn't fix the engine anyway, under the circumstances, so we both fished while the wind blew us from one end of the lake to the other. Usually we both had salmon on at the same time. Must have been drifting with a school of them. We caught salmon all the way down the lake, releasing all but three or four. Finally the wind blew us near a cove, and we put out the oars and got into it. We made a little fire and broiled a salmon. Then we fixed the motor. The lake became less rough about sundown, and we got back all right. Quite an afternoon! It reminded me of old Chief Needahbeh and how much he liked rough water for salmon fishing when he bounced his peculiar *Biplane Streamer* from white cap to white cap. The fish often get ravenous when it gets rough."

The sun long ago had disappeared, and the afterglow had faded into darkening purple shadows deepening over the lake. A light flickered in the cabin on the opposite shore. The old man and the young man had caught several trout and salmon, but they had killed only two. The old man put them in a plastic bag under the stern seat of the canoe, turned the motor handle to full throttle, and swiftly headed for home against the cool night breeze.

The Old Fisherman would readily admit that conditions occasionally exist which, for unknown reasons, make fishing very poor or non-existent regardless of the knowledge an angler may possess. But the experiences related in this chapter indicate that knowledge of the habits of fish is as important as knowing how to select a fly, how to cast it, and how to fish it in. Fish are like people in that they collect where they find suitable temperatures, adequate protection, sufficient oxygen, and access to a food supply. Protection may be a rock, an undercut bank, a fallen tree, or a mass of underwater plants. The food supply may be provided by an incoming stream, a gravely bottom, or the baitfish which seek protection in aquatic growths. Fish will not stay in water that is too warm or too cold if they can find temperatures more to their liking. We have noted that trout and salmon usually prefer water temperatures from 50 to 70 degrees. If surface waters are warmer, they will go deep to cooler places—except perhaps in the coolness of the early morning or late evening, when they may come to the surface to feed. If surface waters are colder, they probably will be deep down and more or less dormant. Consideration of these factors, with the use of a thermometer, helps greatly in deciding when, where, and how to fish.

What has been said about landlocked salmon and trout applies in general to bass and other pond and lake game fish. The largemouth bass thrives in reservoirs, farm ponds, lakes, slow rivers, swamps, sloughs, and bayous all over the United States. He wants the protection of logs, stumps, rocks, reefs, or rocky lake edges with deep dropoffs. He usually prefers water temperatures of between 70 and 75 degrees, but often tolerates 80 degrees or slightly above. He eats almost anything, including small snakes, frogs, small birds, little animals, crawfish, and almost any other fish he can devour, including his own relations and offspring.

Smallmouth bass are found east of the Mississippi except in some of the southernmost states, where in many areas the Kentucky (or Spotted) bass takes his place. He likes somewhat cooler water than does the largemouth, and he prefers cool streams or lakes with plenty of rocks and high oxygen content.

Bass spend most of their time, especially in midsummer, in deep water, coming to the surface to feed in the early morning, late evening, or during the night. Predominantly they are minnow eaters, so exact imitations in streamers and bucktails (often in fairly large sizes) are usually productive. Frequently the reverse is true. One of my favorite bass streamers is a floppy, long-winged monstrosity of red, blue, and yellow hackles that no self-respecting trout would look at. The fly can be slapped down near lily pads or weed beds and allowed to lie on the surface until the ripples have subsided. Then, when it is twitched into action, a strike from a hungry, curious, or angry bass often results.

In bass fishing, quietness and slowness are vital. The bang of a tackle box or oars or feet in a boat, and even knocking out pipe ashes on the side of a boat, can discourage nearby fish from striking for half an hour or more. When one learns the characteristics of bass, one learns to go where the fish are supposed to be: in places such as above and in surface waters at the edges of weed beds, along weedy or rocky shorelines, and over reefs. The best time usually is an hour or so before

How to Fish Streamers in Slack Water

and after dawn and from an hour before dusk until well into the night. During the day one usually has to fish deep, so flies may be less effective than metal lures or deep-running plugs.

At late dusk or during the night, flies of non-pastel colors seem to work best, because their contrasts against the dim light are more pronounced—flies such as those which are all black or all white, or combinations of black and white like the *Black Ghost*. At other times we have noted that exact imitations (including the *Muddler Minnow*) and garish attractor patterns, such as orange marabou, may be equally effective. Bass fishing is leisurely fishing; it is quiet fishing; and it is contemplative fishing. When the big ones are feeding, they often do so noisily, swirling and slopping in search of their prey. Thus an observant, quiet angler can often hear and see where the bass are and cast to individual fish. When the bucktail or streamer quietly lands, rests for a moment, and then is pulled under and set into motion, the result often is a resounding strike and a sturdy battle—which will prove that bass, of all species, are high on the list of the best game fish of them all.

Established as a sporting camp in 1904, Cobb's Pierce Pond Camp in North New Portland, Maine, is one of the state's few remaining traditional fishing camps. The Maine Watershed Trust is working to protect the Pierce Pond watershed and enable future generations to enjoy Maine's rich angling heritage. *(Photograph by Dorothy Douglass)*

VI

Western Salt Water Streamer Fishing

In the breaking dawn of a cold September day a lone angler stowed his fishing gear aboard a sixteen foot outboard boat, adjusted his motor, and gave the starter cord a lusty pull, startling a few gulls and sea pigeons which had been peacefully perching on the mossy barnacled piling of Seattle's docks. As he eased his boat through the fogbound, oily slick of the protected waters of Puget Sound, he contemplated his ill fortune in having to return two hours later to start his daily labors. He munched a pre-breakfast chocolate bar and then lighted his pipe, at the same time gazing intently through the rising mists with the hope of noting the raucous activity of sea birds as they wheeled and dived in a constant circle to indicate a school of Herring or Candlefish driven to the surface by the feeding silver salmon below.

In the boat was rigged a six-ounce fly rod with a reel which held about 300 yards of eight pound test monofilament line, to the end of which was attached a small swivel and five or six feet of nylon monofilament testing six pounds. On the end of this was a long silver-bodied bucktail in the colors of blue, pink, and white which was attached to the nylon leader by a small weighted spinner.

"A fifteen-pound silver," the angler thought to himself, "will be all we'll need for dinner. When I catch him I'll hurry home for breakfast so I won't be late for work."

The sea birds suddenly began their frenzied crying and darting as they wheeled in a compact flock far out over the rippling waters of the sound. The fisherman dropped his fly into the water and allowed nearly 100 feet of line to run from the reel. He cut his motor to half speed as he neared the excited birds and began to troll his fly in a wide circle around the scene of activity. Small bait fish flurried to the surface here and there, rippling the slow swell of the sea and scattering thousands of droplets with the effect of rain.

The fisherman tested the drag of his reel and watched the slight quivering curve of his rod, resting in a rod holder and pointing nearly at right angles to the axis of the boat. Scarcely had he made a half-circle when his rod tip shot backward and the reel began a slow whine which increased in pitch as the hooked fish gathered speed in the start of his run. Instantly the angler shut off his motor and picked the rod from its holder. He struck as hard as he dared and held back on the rod in an attempt to turn the fish. Two hundred yards of line whirred off his spool before the initial rush could be stopped. This fish seemed much too heavy to be a silver salmon. He bored deeply down into the sea, holding his position so doggedly that the angler was forced to slap the rod butt and to strum the line in an effort to goad him into motion. Finally, up to the surface he came and leaped into the air.

The angler's jaw dropped in amazement to see, not the expected silver salmon, but a giant chinook, king of all the salmons, and this one a veritable behemoth of his kind!

The sun rose in the sky. Breakfast and work were forgotten. Boats had seen the jumps of the giant fish and returned to spread the news of the battle. Soon a crescent of them had collected to watch the lone angler as he stood and valiantly tried to check the inexorable rushes of the great fish. He gave the salmon all the tension of line which the tackle would stand. His arms ached from constantly arching the rod. Needles of hot pain stabbed the muscles of his wrists but still he held on. When the salmon gave a derisive jump near the boat the angler noted the flash of two spinner blades in his jaw in addition to his own. The sun reached its zenith as the boats of the spectators came and went. The fisherman licked his parched lips and blinked his eyes to blot out the glare of its reflection on the water. Eight hours had gone by, yet the fish showed no signs of tiring. He was one of those giants of his kind which had survived far beyond his normal span to reach monstrous proportions from added years of gorging upon the hosts of baitfish in the sea. He was a record fish, and boating him would win rich prizes and national renown.

Hour after hour still went by. The fish took line from the reel and grudgingly gave it back. As the sun set in the West, he electrified the gallery of spectators by making his fourteenth jump. The exhaustion of the angler became beyond comprehension, but still he held on. He held the great fish until darkness fell and lights appeared in the distant city. He held on until all but two of the boats had left; until his aching arms and wrists could stand no more. Then he pointed the rod at the fish and locked the reel. When the fish stretched the nylon to its limit, there was a rubbery snap and all was over. The fisherman flopped down on the seat of the boat and sadly licked his parched lips as he reeled in his line. The last remaining boat drew alongside. A reporter handed the fisherman a Thermos from which he took a grateful draft.

"Fourteen hours and sixteen jumps! What a story!" the reporter said admiringly.

"Guess I never could have landed him with a fly rod," answered the fisherman dejectedly as he started his motor. "But what a fish!"

True stories of great Pacific salmon illustrate that there are bigger ones in the coastal waters of the Northwest than ever have been caught on a fly. Men who fish with the fly rod and the fly for silver salmon occasionally catch chinooks (also called "king" or "spring" salmon, or "tyee" salmon when they reach a weight of thirty pounds or more) and one or two other species, but the favorite fly rod fish of all is the silver salmon, called the coho (or cohoe) in Canadian waters. Silver salmon have been caught with the fly rod and the fly since the turn of the present century, especially in the Vancouver Island area of British Columbia. In the early days of silver salmon fly fishing this was a sport confined to the adventurous and experimental few, but since the Second World War it has become popularized as one of the most spectacular forms of fishing possible with the fly rod and the fly.

Silver salmon are distributed extensively up and down the northern Pacific coast. The majority of them make very limited migrations into the sea and often grow to full maturity within a relatively small area. They migrate to salt water as yearlings. At this time they frequently are caught and referred to as "sea-trout." Upon reaching adulthood in their third year, they return to the rivers to spawn, usually doing this

Tandem Trolling Bucktails

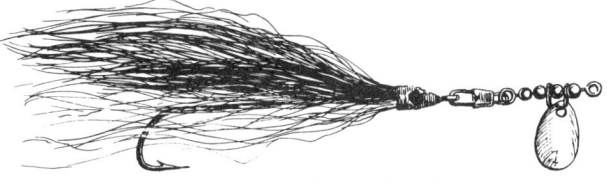

Single Hook Trolling Bucktail and Spinner

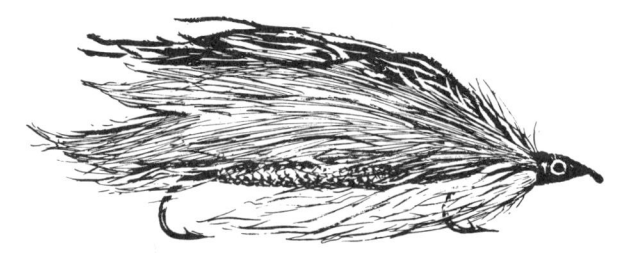

Tandem Streamer with body of Mylar Tubular Cord

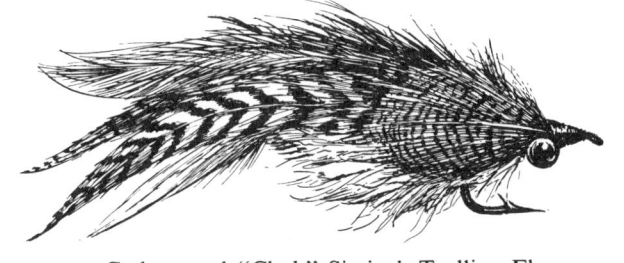

Catherwood "Chub" Six-inch Trolling Fly

FIG. VI-1

BUCKTAILS AND STREAMERS
ESPECIALLY DESIGNED FOR TROLLING

on the gravel bottoms of very small creeks far up in the source waters of the rivers. In the Puget Sound area, fishing starts about the middle of June, with catches averaging between three and five pounds. Their growth continues at such an amazing rate that by the middle of September they reach a weight of ten or twelve pounds, with many much heavier. In this area September is the peak fishing month, because the salmon will usually have traveled up the streams to consumate their spawning activities by October and November.

Although the silver salmon will take a cast fly when conditions are suitable, they take a trolled fly very much better. A streamer or steelhead rod about nine feet long and approximately six ounces in weight, with a torpedo tapered line to match, is the favorite tackle for fly casting. Casts are often made to rising fish, much the same as in angling for trout. Bucktail flies with wings between three and four inches long dressed on 3X long hooks in sizes between 1 and 3/0 are most popular for fly casting.

Although trolling equipment varies rather widely, the tackle described earlier in this chapter is popular with a great many fishermen. An eight foot two-piece steelhead rod, with double cork grips and a screw locking reel seat, also merits considerable favor. Those who prefer this equipment feel that the usual fly reel takes up line too slowly when a fish is coming towards the angler. They prefer a reel larger than the conventional fresh water plug casting reel but of the same multiplying type, accommodating about 300 yards of nylon monofilament line testing in the vicinity of eight pounds.

One of those who have done the most to promote silver salmon fishing in the Puget Sound area is William Lohrer, owner of Bill Lohrer's Sport Shop in the University district of Seattle. He is one of the many anglers who use spinning rods with the fixed spool spinning reel both for casting and for trolling. He prefers a glass rod because of its lightness and because it is more durable for salt water fishing. He says: "We run the nylon right to the spinner and let the spinner and fly troll right in the propeller wash about twenty-five feet behind the boat. We go so fast that the lure almost skips out of the water, making fast, sharp, frequent turns with the boat and working the rod tip with jerks at intervals. Often one can see the salmon following, upon which

Western Salt Water Streamer Fishing

we let out a few feet of line quickly or sweep the rod back to induce him to take the lure. Generally no lead is needed although sometimes an ounce or less is helpful. We keep changing flies until we find the color and style which the fish seems to want under the conditions which exist. Occasionally, chinook or humpback salmon will take a lure trolled in this manner."

It is interesting to observe the comparison between the most accepted methods of trolling for chinook and silver salmon on western coastal waters and trolling for land-locked salmon and big brook trout on the inland waters of Maine. In both cases many experienced fishermen agree that for best results the boat must be run at the relatively high speed of about five miles an hour, and that the fly should be trolled on a relatively short line in or directly behind the propeller wash of the boat. If more than one rod is used, the flies on the additional one or two rods may be trolled at a somewhat greater distance, so that a fish which misses the first fly may strike at the other trailing behind.

In the early days of silver salmon fishing the flies for the sport were more varied in color than those currently popular. The use of bucktail for wings gradually gave way to polar bear hair, because it was found to be less brittle, more brilliant, more attractive, and much more prone to take dyes in a satisfactory manner. As this book is written polar bear hair is considered far superior to other types of hair and to feathers, although these also are used to a minor degree.

The great increase in fly fishing for salmon has served to standardize patterns of flies to a considerable extent. A group of anglers including William Lohrer, George McLeod, Letcher Lambuth, Zell Parkhurst, and Roy Patrick, determined that the most successful salmon flies were those of the bucktail type which represented in color and shape the two principal bait fishes of the area: the candlefish and the herring.

The candlefish, sometimes known as the needlefish or sandlaunce and more correctly named the eulachon, ranges from northern California to northwestern Alaska. It enters the rivers in spring to spawn and apparently dies after spawning. It furnishes food both for salmon and for the fur seal. The candlefish is used extensively for food and for making cooking oil by the Indians. The term candlefish comes from the fact that the Indians dried the fish and fitted them with wicks to

Joe Stickney (center) with Ross McKinney and friend. *(Photograph by the author)*

Western Salt Water Streamer Fishing

serve as candles because of the large amount of oil which they contain. The herring is so commonly known that it seems to need no introduction.

Bucktails in imitation of the candlefish and the herring have become standard patterns, with silver bodies and white polar bear hair wings shading to greens, blues, and other colors above. The two favorite flies are named the *Candlefish* and the *Herring* and are included in the descriptions of fly patterns in Part II of this book. A third standard pattern is the somewhat simpler *Coronation* bucktail, which seems to appeal to salmon as representing a baitfish and which also is described in Part II.

Mr. Roy A. Patrick, a member of the group mentioned above and a well-known Seattle fly dresser, has described to me the general color schemes and sizes of Pacific salmon flies in a letter from which the following quotation is taken:

"In my mind the person who has done the most toward the original standardization of both the *Candlefish* and the *Herring* bucktails is Mr. Letcher Lambuth, although it has been my pleasure to keep a finger on all the alterations and group of patterns which have been fishably effective since these two flies were originated. Changes made by fishermen, simplifications in dressing, and experiences in fishing have resulted in a flood of color combinations, some of which have been found to be very good while others have been discarded. The preferred combinations are as follows (dressed on silver tinsel bodies with polar bear hair unless especially noted):

Green over white
Blue over white
Orange over white
Brown (bucktail) over white
Green over yellow over white
Blue over green over white
Blue over red over white (*Coronation* pattern)
Green over red over white
Gunmetal gray over medium green over fuchsia over white
Blue over green over yellow over white
Grey over green over peach over white

"You will note that embossed tinsel has been used on some of these flies. My inclination is to the pastel shades rather than the bright ones. We prefer long-shanked hooks in sizes 2/0 and 3/0. Sometimes a tandem or trailer hook is snelled to a lead hook of a larger size by a very short piece of fifteen or eighteen pound nylon monofilament. In recent years the trend has been to more or less do away with tandem hooks in favor of a single hook with an over-all length of approximately two-and-a-half inches, ranging in size from 3/0 to 5/0. This hook has a looped or ringed eye so that a spinner may be attached. A great deal of success has been obtained with the fly and spinner tactics."

Some silver salmon anglers maintain that when a spinning blade is not attached to the fly, the productivity of the lure is decreased to about 10 per cent of the effectiveness it would have with the spinner. When a spinner is used, the fly must be dressed on a hook having a ringed eye; that is, an eye that is neither turned up nor down. Some of these tandem trolling flies are as long as six inches, with the trailer hook concealed in the hair about an inch from the end of the wing. Many of them are wrapped with silver colored foil, folded to make a ribbon about three-eighths inch wide. The nylon snell and the body of the lead hook usually are built up slightly, and the foil is wound from the base of the snell to the head of the fly to give the effect of the body of a baitfish. In a fly called the *Kandlefish Kate*, the wing is tied down to the body of the trailer hook about an inch from the end of the wing. Ordinarily I doubt that this would enhance the action or appearance of the fly, but in the case of the *Kandlefish Kate* the white polar bear hair wing has a topping of peacock herl, and tying down the wing over the built-up silver body results in a fly with a very close resemblance to the colors and shape of a baitfish.

The nylon monofilament linkage between many of these tandem flies is so short that patterns not over four inches in length can be tied on tandem hooks and used in fly casting without a spinner. Hooks for flies used in fly casting should have a turned down eye. Experiments with the *Candlefish* and *Herring* flies have indicated that these patterns are very effective even without a spinner. Wesley Drain, a prominent angler of Seattle, Washington, says of them: "I cast to my fish the same as you would cover a rise in a lake or pool, and have never felt the need or urge to attach a spinner to these patterns."

In dressing bucktails for silver salmon the hair wing is of moderate fullness, extending an inch or so beyond the bend of the hook. The head is usually decorated with a painted eye. Silver tinsel bodies are most common. The tinsel occasionally is eliminated from flies dressed on nickeled or chrome-plated hooks, and on some patterns chenille is substituted for it.

The fact should be stressed that these comments about flies and angling methods apply nearly as well to the king (or chinook) salmon and to humpback (or pink) salmon as they do to the silver (or coho) salmon. Since the silver salmon does not reach a size normally considered excessive for the fly rod, and because he is gifted with renowned fighting ability and a pronounced propensity to take the fly, he is considered by most anglers to be the favorite of all the Pacific salmons for fly fishing. When one fishes for the silver salmon, he also may take one of the other species, so it has seemed expedient to discuss them together.

The migratory cutthroat trout commutes so frequently between salt water and fresh water that, like the anadromous rainbow called the steelhead, he only partially belongs in a chapter on salt water fishing. Like his landlocked counterpart, he is marked by a V-shaped red line between jaw and gills, this marking often being concealed unless the gills are spread. Unlike his fresh water brother, he is silvery of side and dark of back, very similar in appearance to the salmons and the steelhead. In Oregon he is called the "blueback" and in other places is known as the "harvest trout," "Rocky Mountain spotted trout," or by several other names. He rarely grows to a great size and is most often caught weighing in the vicinity of two pounds.

The sea-run cutthroat differs from the steelhead and the salmons in that, rather than traveling into fresh water only for the purpose of spawning, he travels often between salt water and fresh in search of food. Usually he spends his first two years of growth in the river and then travels to the sea for another two years, during which he lives in the estuary of his river and makes frequent trips into the fresh water for a change in diet. When he is three or four years old, he is an adult fish. At this stage of his life he usually will go into his river in the early fall and travel to the source waters to spawn in the late winter or early spring, after which he returns to the estuary again. During this annual migratory season many young cutthroats and some adult fish will remain in tidewater.

The travels of the cutthroat are of interest to the fly fisherman be-because they indicate when and where fly fishing will be best. Fly fishing in the rivers is best in the fall and early winter, when the greatest number of cutthroats are in the streams. Fly fishing in bays and estuaries is best in the late spring and through the summer until the fall migration begins.

The travels of the cutthroat into the rivers are not entirely influenced by the urge to spawn, as is the case with the steelhead. They come into the rivers to follow the migrations of the several species of salmons and to feed on salmon fry when they are making their trip to the sea. Thus there are several minor migrations of cutthroat trout; but these vary so widely because of conditions of temperature, food, and the river itself that it would be dangerous and misleading to attempt to draw specific general conclusions.

Salt water fishing for cutthroats in the late spring and summer is dictated largely by the actions of the tides. The fish travel into the estuary on the outgoing tide and return up the mouth of the river during the flood. It is easiest for the fly fisherman to locate them during the last of the ebb and the beginning of the flood tide, when many fish should be concentrated in the pools of the channel. In some places wading is possible, but in others a boat must be used if one is not to get caught far out on the flats and risk a ducking.

Flies quite obviously must be fished deep in such places. Baitfish form a large part of the cutthroat's diet, particularly in salt water, so streamer flies and bucktails are popular for this type of fly fishing, just as they are for all other salt water species that can be taken with the fly rod. Non-corrosive hooks in sizes 2, 4, and 6 are ideal. Small sizes of any streamer or bucktail with coloration resembling a prevalent baitfish will take cutthroat trout in salt water. Flies of the *Candlefish*, *Herring*, and *Smelt* types are good examples. Here, as in many other forms of fishing, the fly is of less importance than where and how the angler fishes it. Usually there is a pronounced current in the pools and eddys of river channels at the end of the ebb tide and at the beginning of the flood. If the fly is cast up-current and across on a slack line, it will sink and swing with the flow of the water, just as it

Western Salt Water Streamer Fishing

will when one is fishing the currents of inland rivers. In doing this it is rarely necessary to give much action to the fly, since the flow of the tide usually provides all the motion which is needed.

What has been said of the cutthroat trout applies to a large degree to the steelhead as he exists in the estuaries and tidewater areas of northwestern rivers. Unlike the cutthroat, he makes a single annual upriver run, usually coming into tidewater from the sea in the late summer, fall, or early winter. Like the salmons, he waits in the estuary until rains swell the river and make it safe and easy for him to travel upstream. In his journey, and during his resting periods in eddys and pools, he keeps to the well-scoured main channel and shuns the silt laden, weedy places. His usual holding position is in the protection of rocks or below sand bars near the bottom of the channel, so the fly must be fished deep to enable him to see and take it. In such places one can fish for the steelhead either from a boat or by wading, as conditions allow. Boat fishing is more popular in most locations because few estuary and tidewater areas offer the opportunity for wading that would make it possible for the caster to reach the fish, even during the most favorable time of the tide.

When the fish are in the estuaries, many steelhead are caught while trolling or casting for cutthroat trout or for silver salmon. For trolling, the same tackle as described for silver salmon is ideal. For fly casting, a rod nine or nine-and-a-half feet long, with fairly stiff action, is necessary to make the long casts needed in tidewater fishing or in upriver fishing from riffles to the banks of wide rivers.

Most angling and fisheries authorities maintain that steelhead do not feed after leaving salt water, probably being too preoccupied with their primary instinct of procreation. They have said that Atlantic salmon do not feed in the rivers either, although competent anglers have proved that they do feed to a very limited extent. Whether steelhead feed or not, it is certain that they take food so seldom after leaving the estuaries for their destination up river that the angler may assume that they take the fly because they are made angry by its presence and perhaps by its color and movement. In any event, if steelhead do not take the more common northwestern salt water bucktails, such as the *Candlefish*, the *Herring*, and the *Smelt*, it may be safely assumed that they are not feeding and that they can be made to take a fly only through the instinct of anger. When this is the case, bright flies should be used—chiefly in the colors of red, white, and yellow, since these seem to influence the anger instinct more than any other colors. These are the flies commonly used for steelhead in fresh water, as described on pages 55 to 59.

In estuary fishing the bead-head bucktail is often used. Its western champion was Mr. C. Jim Pray, of Eureka, California, considered by many to be the finest commercial dresser of steelhead flies who ever lived. He called it the *Owl Eyed Optic* and dressed it with a plain body of oval silver tinsel and a wing of red, red and yellow, red and white, or with the hair of squirrel, badger, or something similar. The one-quarter-inch brass bead which is clamped to the head is painted black, with a yellow painted eye having a large black center. Hooks usually are extra heavy and extra strong because the savage strikes of the steelhead may straighten or break anything less sturdy.

Since I shall treat the striped bass in the next chapter, I will not dwell upon it here, except to describe the capture of what may be a world's record fish and to call attention to the growing importance of striped bass fishing with the fly rod in western coastal waters.

I believe the fly rod was very little used for stripers on the West Coast until Mr. Joe Brooks, Jr., popularized the method on a trip there with me in the fall of 1948. Coos Bay in southwestern Oregon, had been recommended to us as one of the finest of striped bass locations. When we reached it on an afternoon late in September, a cold drizzling rain and banks of fog enshrouded the picturesque little city, making the prospects of catching a bass that afternoon appear rather discouraging.

After we had traveled across the continent largely for this occasion, it would have taken more than bad weather to dim the ardor of Joe for his big bass. He had confided to me that he hoped to catch a record fish, so time was not to be wasted.

We hired a charter boat and went down the bay with our two angling companions, Mr. Don Harger and Mr. Chandler Brown, both of Salem, Oregon. The boat captain cast disdainful glances at Joe's six-and-a-half-ounce fly rod equipped with a large capacity Otto Zwarg fly reel and a GAF line spliced to 200 yards of backing. If one could read his thoughts, fly fishing in salt water for such big fish was

Western Salt Water Streamer Fishing

an inadequate method which only a rank novice would presume to try in preference to the usual practice of trolling bait with much heavier tackle.

As we passed under the highway bridge, the boat captain pointed to a series of narrow channels and announced that the incoming tide was right for us to locate large schools of bass traveling inshore to feed. Joe's practiced eye took in the part of the shoreline which could be seen through the mist.

"The school bass are too small," he said. "I'd like to try for a big one. Let's run the boat as slowly as possible, about ninety feet off the breakwater by the airport, so I can cast to the rocks."

"There are no bass there," declared the boat captain. "If you want to catch any, I'll take you to the right places."

We went to the breakwater. Joe, encased in oilskins, unlimbered his fly rod and sent neat casts directly to the rocks, allowing the white bucktail to rest on the water for a moment after each cast before pulling it under.

On the third or fourth cast the water beneath the fly erupted and a gigantic bass leaped into the air amid a splashing shower of spray. The white bucktail flew high in the air and fell back on the foamy ripples. Joe fished it slowly in an effort to duplicate the laboring action which a wounded baitfish might assume. Instantly there was a smashing strike, and he was fast to his bass.

The fish made a long and ponderous run to the middle of the channel, taking out all of the fly line and more than half of the backing. The boat backed slowly toward the fish so that the angler, facing his adversary, could regain part of his line.

After two or three such runs the bass changed his tactics and deeply sounded, hugging the bottom of the channel until it seemed that nothing the angler could do could raise him. Joe slapped the rod butt and strummed the tight line as the rod bent in what would have seemed a dangerous curve if the fisherman had not known the mettle of his bamboo. This goaded the big bass to action again. He broke water near the boat to show the intent anglers his great length, his ponderous girth, and the narrow black stripes which identify his species.

The bass by then was tired. He halfheartedly attempted to run and sound, but the strength to do so was no longer in him. Twenty-six minutes after he had been hooked he was netted and taken into the boat. He weighed twenty-nine pounds and six ounces, which I believe was a record for striped bass taken on a fly rod at that time.

The sun had set when the bass was boated, but Joe tried a few more casts along the breakwater before we returned. On the last of these there was a second nerve shattering strike, and Joe was fast to his second bass. The tactics of this one were very much like those of the first, except that just before he could be netted he succeeded in throwing the fly. He looked fully as large as the earlier one and may have been a bit bigger.

At the risk of an anticlimax I mention this aftermath to three hours of fishing at Coos Bay to indicate that taking the first bass was neither a rare nor an accidental occurrence. Anglers who know striped bass understand where they are likely to be found. They know that the biggest ones usually do not travel in schools but habitually lead a lone and roving existence, only a few of them being found together at most.

Catching this big striper on a fly rod was a nationally publicized event, which was a primary influence in inducing western salt water anglers to forsake their heavier gear and to adopt the fly rod and the streamer fly or bucktail for the greater sportsmanship and thrills which this combination offers to salt water angling.

Streamer flies for western striped bass fishing have not been standardized in the West as much as they have been in the East. I have not fished for western stripers to an extent that would indicate the right flies to use, but I know that it is a habit of bass to prefer the brighter colors of white and yellow, occasionally with a bit of red. Striped bass share with their fresh water cousins a desire for flies with a great deal of action, amply collared and fully dressed with flaring bucktail or with long saddle hackled streamers. When such a fly is properly fished before them, the anger of their smashing strike is a sight to behold!

The shad is a fly rod fish deserving a much better reputation than he possesses. In western harbors and tidewaters fishing for him is becoming increasingly popular. The technique is identical to the eastern methods described in Chapter VII, but the preferred flies are

Western Salt Water Streamer Fishing

quite different. One of the few western flies designed especially for shad is the *McCredie Special* bucktail illustrated on page 67.

There are few surface fighting tackle busters of any size which cannot be hooked with the fly rod and the fly. The variety of such fish is somewhat more limited on the West coast than it is on the East. In addition to those mentioned, the Pacific barracuda, yellowtail, ladyfish, snook, and white sea bass should be included among those which have been, or may be, taken with the streamer fly and the bucktail.

Many anglers who have tried this light tackle are now forsaking the heavier gear which they have preferred heretofore. The science of locating the fish, the skill of casting for him, the technique of handling him, and the thrill of giving him battle with a graceful wand, perhaps too fragile for the purpose, rather than a heavy pole and a line so strong that he scarcely has a chance for his freedom, comprise a sport considered by many to offer the greatest pleasures possible among the numerous methods of fishing.

VII

Eastern Salt Water Streamer Fishing

Fishing with the fly rod and the fly for striped bass and a few other species of salt water game fish is a sport which was popular with a few adventurous anglers even before the turn of the present century. In those days, heavy fish in stupendous numbers choked countless undammed and unpolluted rivers, making fresh water angling so productive that salt water sport fishing was all but ignored.

The increasing millions of fishermen, and the alarming decline in the productivity of fresh water angling, has influenced a constantly growing proportion of sportsmen to investigate the thrills which Father Neptune so lavishly provides. Those who seek them out intelligently rarely are disappointed. In coastal areas where inland fishing is poor, many virtually ignore the prospects of catching a few small trout or pondfish in favor of casting their flies for the savage striper, the leaping bluefish, the fast running weakfish or the playful mackerel. Heavy rods and lines, cumbersome plugs and the nuisance of bait are gradually being supplanted by gear much lighter, with equally rewarding streamers or bucktails as the favorite type of lure.

My own conversion to the use of the fly rod in salt water took place one October in the early 1930's on a trip to New England's Narragansett Bay.

"Bring along a fairly sturdy streamer rod," my host wrote; "and a line with about 200 yards of backing. Bring along a lighter trout rod too."

Fig. VII-1

FISHING A TIDAL CURRENT. Cast slightly up-current to "A" allowing fly to sink and swing. Fish the fly most intensively at "B", where the majority of strikes usually occur

As a safety precaution I packed a pair of the more usual heavy salt water rods and a tackle box filled with plugs, jigs and the voluminous array of other impedimenta customary to the conventional salt water fishermen. I found no need to use this equipment and it has been a much neglected element of my gear ever since.

The filmy disc of a full moon was rising as I reached my destination late in the day. My host pointed to it and then to the placid waters of the estuary.

"A full moon means high tides," he said. "High tides mean that fish will be feeding. The tide will be changing in exactly an hour. You'd better get into your fishing clothes right away. There's no time to lose."

As we walked down the beach to a point of land which marked the entrance of the river, he discussed the value of the tides in salt water angling.

"New fish work into feeding spots when there is a full moon and also when there is no moon," he said. "Fish feed most actively at these times, with increasingly diminishing activity as the moon continues to wane, so that the least advantageous times are when the moon is in the first or in the last quarter. The moon, of course, influences the tides. When the tides begin to turn, the fish begin to feed."

He waded into the water off the point of the inlet and kicked around in the sand. Two or three small crabs, dug out by his boot, scurried for safety.

"Shedders!" he said. "They shed on the full and on the dark of the moon, but mostly on the full. Crabs are an important reason why fish come into the shallows to feed. Fish seem able to scent crabs from a greater distance than any other kind of bait. They are as desirable a food for fish as ice cream is for children. After they drop their shells, they hide in the sand for a few days until the new shell hardens. Usually the shells of both sand crabs and rock crabs come off during the outgoing tide. The little crabs bury themselves in the sand or mud, with only their feelers and perhaps a bare outline of their bodies showing. This place is full of crabs. There are small baitfish in the eel grass too. If you want to find fish, all you need to do is to go where there is food for them, preferably at the right time of the moon and the tide."

He slanted his watch at the afterglow of the sun and then looked out upon the water of the bay.

Eastern Salt Water Streamer Fishing

"It's the right time," he announced; "and we are in a good place for a try at the stripers. The tide has changed, so they should be working in toward shore."

His fly rod was about eight feet in length, weighing approximately four-and-a-half ounces. He used a six-foot nylon leader tapered to eight pounds test to which he had fastened a *Gibbs Striper* bucktail, predominantly white with a medial line of blue, dressed on a size one salt water streamer hook. Deftly and without unnecessary motion he flicked the fly into action.

"A good current is beginning to run into the river," he said. "Cast up-current and let the fly sink and swing. You may get a strike at any time, but the chances are nine in ten that it will occur as the fly completes the swing. Fish it slowly and work it a bit before you start the retrieve."

I walked up-current beyond his casting distance and lighted my pipe, watching him while he fished. He held up his rod at a 45 degree angle to aid it in cushioning the strike when it came. As the fly swung with the current (Figure VII-1), he followed it with his rod tip, working it slightly before slowly beginning to recover his line.

Suddenly the rod tip shot down, and the loop of line disappeared from his fingers. His reel whirred in protest as the fish ripped line from the spool. Out in the bay the striper swirled, tugged, and sulked. The angler gave him all the pressure the tackle safely would stand. The fish was heavy and the current in his favor. Twenty-five minutes and several long runs later the bass was worked into shallow water, totally exhausted and lying on his side.

"I'll let this one go," my host said, as he removed the fly. "The one you're going to get will be enough to eat."

We fished until long after dark. My companion took four striped bass of between six and twelve pounds each, while I took two. Oftentimes they run smaller and occasionally much larger. Their fighting ability in every way is comparable to a trout of any species of equal size.

"Bass like to find spots where the current carries bait to them," my host said. "They feed in rocky pockets along the shore or in deep spots near the mouth of streams or backwaters. When the tide nears the flood stage, they work into the grasses along the shore, searching for any bits of food they may be able to find. When the tide is favorable, the best fishing hours are before sunrise and after sunset; but occasionally, and in some places, they can be taken at any time of the day. I have stood quietly waist deep near the shoreline and have had bass splash so near me that they covered me with water. Usually you can catch them, but occasionally they seem unwilling to take any bait or lure of any sort."

"What are the best flies?" I asked.

"In the Narragansett Bay area we have three favorites," he said. "The *Gibbs Striper*, the Brooks Blondes, and Mylar bodied bucktails. Usually, any predominantly white fly of the type dressed to imitate a baitfish, with dark back and white underside, will do. On dull days a yellow fly often is effective, especially when the water is discolored. On very bright days a fly with less pronounced colors, such as one that has some Plymouth Rock feathers in it, may give better results. Many fishermen use very simple flies, and some maintain that a red and white streamer or bucktail is as good as anything at any time in northern salt waters.

"Tomorrow we'll try fly fishing from a boat," he said. "We'll try the mackerel and we may run into a school of bass. Even in the middle of the day I have seen schools of as many as 2,000 bass surfacing and feeding. I have seen dozens of anglers fishing around a school, using all types of tackle and every kind of bait and artificial lures. In some instances they would take nothing but a streamer fly or a bucktail!"

The next morning's fishing began slowly, but our luck increased as the day wore on. Just before noon the sea birds collected as if by magic, wheeling in a compact flock and diving to the water to pick up the bait being driven to the surface by a school of game fish underneath.

"It may be stripers and it may be something else," my host commented; "but it certainly is worth investigating. You can always find schools of game fish if you watch the action of the birds."

We circled upwind of the commotion and stopped the motor, allowing the boat to drift to the place. It proved to be a large school of mackerel. Dozens at a time rushed to the surface, driving the disorganized bait before them; forcing the tiny fish to leap into the air, only to fall back into the jaws of the slashing mackerel below. The onslaught stunned or wounded many of the little fish, to the raucous joy of the hungry gulls and terns, which dived to pick each bit of bait from the surface as quickly as it showed itself.

We unlimbered our light rods and cast our flies into the scene of carnage. The fly used made little or no difference. As soon as it touched the water and was pulled under, a mackerel would have it. These were small fish, occasionally known as "tinkers." Greenish black of back and with bellies of shining silver, they are beautiful to behold as they rush up to take the fly and then as quickly attempt to reach the depths again. Few of them weigh over a pound each, but their fighting ability, in my estimation, exceeds that of trout or fresh water bass double their size. Fresh caught from the sea, they are a table delicacy difficult to surpass.

As the boat drifted down the harbor the school of mackerel remained around it. When the gulls and terns became satiated with their feast, they flew lazily to shore while others joined the flock to take their places. Each of us took between two and three dozen mackerel, rarely losing one and never bothering to change the fly.

As we returned home for a belated lunch I could not help making a mental comparison between the lavish abundance of these fighting game fish of the sea and the dwindling numbers of equally sporting, but usually smaller, fish which frequent northeastern inland waters. It seems logical to observe that if anglers living within easy access of salt water would pay greater attention to the many remunerations of that form of fishing, the future of inland angling would prosper in consequence.

A favorite companion on some of these salty excursions, when our respective duties permit us to combine forces, is Oliver H. P. Rodman, a specialist in salt water angling and one of the most versatile fishermen I have ever known. When "Ollie" Rodman speaks of angling, he speaks with the authority of many years of experience, as those who have read his books will testify. To avoid being accused of looking at the subject of salt water fly fishing through rose-colored glasses, I asked Ollie Rodman to record a few of his observations for this book. As usual, they are succulently to the point.

"Many game fish of New England's salt waters will take streamer flies or bucktails at one time or another: bluefish, snapper blues (the little six to twelve inch ones which come way back into the harbors and tidal ways), weakfish ('squeteague' to Rhode Islanders), mackerel, pollock, and striped bass. In fact, there are times when these fish will take flies in preference to other lures or when all other lures fail.

"Here is a case in point. We had been trolling eel skins, feather jigs, plugs, seaworms, and spinners for about four hours and had taken just one striper; this in spite of the fact that the bay was full of them. Other boats in the area were having the same experience. Bass were breaking everywhere but were not taking. My companion finally suggested that we run back to the car to get our fly rods. It seemed to be worth trying, so we gunned the motor and headed for shore. An hour later we were back in the 'hot spots' with our fly rods rigged, but there was no sign of any bass.

"We had seen this happen before when the tide was slack, as it was now. By and large, fly fishing for stripers is best on a running tide; one that has gained the momentum of two or three hours either on the ebb or flow. So we dropped anchor at one edge of the narrow channel where we could cover the distance from one bank to the other with a long cast and then we waited. It was low tide.

"Two hours later, looking down the bay, we saw a splash and then another. Soon afterward the whole bay seemed to be breaking wide open as the schools of bass started working back in with the tide and coming right towards us. My partner placed his fly over the first boil of a bass, barely ten yards away, and had just started to retrieve the fly when he hooked into a fish. On about the third cast after that I hooked one. By that time my companion was boating his. We had a full hour or so of fast and furious fishing. Even in the midst of the excitement, I noticed that, time and again, a bass would burst up through a school of hundreds of small bait to take our flies in preference to the natural bait. Maybe the fly looked easier to catch!

"It may be in order to point up the facts of this experience. First, it paid to take the time and trouble to go back and get our fly fishing tackle, which I now would carry along in the first place. Secondly, it paid to wait out the fish. Thirdly, you will notice that we anchored, with no motor running to scare the fish, and that our best luck was on the running tide.

"It was fortunate that all the bass working up into that section of the bay had to come through the main channel, so that we could wait for the fish to come to us. However, it you are fishing a bay or harbor where the fish may be breaking over a wider area, this is the best way to get them with fly fishing tackle (which does tie you down to a smaller area of fishing coverage because of the limited lengths of cast which even the best fly fisherman can make).

"There are many times when an approaching boat will put the bass down for a long time. Therefore, it is a good rule to work up on these fish slowly. Get uptide or upwind and cut your motor before you get into fly casting distance. Then drift into your fish. This requires a good deal of patience as it's a great temptation to rush into a place where you can cast immediately. Once in a while you'll get away with it, but the cautious approach pays off more often.

"Some of the best fly fishermen I know of confine their fishing for stripers to the following times and conditions: just before dark to after dark or before dawn to just after daylight, always on a running tide when fishing a tidal river. If the fish keep on biting after dark, you can take them all night if you have the physical stamina to stay with them. These are the cardinal rules, but often you can take them even around mid-day if you happen to catch them near the surface and adopt the cautious approach.

"One concluding bit of advice is that in fly fishing for any salt water species it is a mighty good idea to strike up an acquaintance with the local fishermen, since many salt water game fish, such as striped bass, strike best at different times or tides in different localities."

No salt water fish which can be taken with a fly is more unpredictable in his habits than is that wanderer of the seas, the voracious bluefish. One cannot travel to salt water and expect him to be on hand, but when the word is passed around among anglers that "the blues are in" it is a jaded fisherman indeed who will not attempt feverishly to arrange his affairs so that he can be at the fishing area with a minimum of delay.

The bluefish usually is true to his reputation of being "here today and gone tomorrow." One season will find him along northeastern shores in schools of untold thousands. Another will find him absent or with his species represented by an insignificant few. These rather undependable tendencies may be due to the temperature of the water, the degrees of abundance of the bluefish's favorite food, which is menhaden (often called "mossbunkers"), or to something else. Offshore he has been known to reach a weight of as much as twenty-five pounds, but in inshore waters it is rare to find one weighing over five. Even two or three pound bluefish, or the smaller "snapper blues" will give an account of themselves which would do credit to many game fish of at least twice their size.

When schools of bluefish are feeding offshore, or in the northeastern harbors and estuaries, they may be located by the action of the sea birds, as has been described. In the case of the bluefish, the excitement of the birds may be greater than usual, if that is possible, because bluefish are notorious killers; even a small school of them being able to slash a large school of baitfish to small bits, leaving the broken bodies of those they do not eat as food for the gulls and terns.

When the bluefish are in, small schools of them frequently are found in the shelter of estuaries and breakwaters, where they may pass for a time unnoticed by the birds. Regardless of where they are found, the tackle used for striped bass is fully adequate; and for small fish, including the "snapper blues," an average sized trout rod should give better sport than one of greater power.

The flies used for striped bass will do very well for bluefish. Harold Gibbs, former Commissioner of Fisheries for the State of Rhode Island and one of the most accomplished salt water fly rod men on the New England coast, is very partial to the *Bluefish* bucktail, which is ultra-long and light blue in color. Other anglers favor an all-white or a red and white fly. When a bluefish is hungry, which seems to be nearly all of the time, the color of fly seems to make very little difference. If it is given the action of a baitfish, he will take it with a shattering strike which will warm the heart of any angler.

The teeth of bluefish are so sharp and needle-like that they can sever monofilament or plastic leader material as easily as a human being can chew cooked spaghetti. These teeth, incidentally, are such formidable weapons that it is dangerous to put fingers near them while removing the fly. The solution to severed leaders is to use light stainless steel wire leader material (such as "Sevenstrand") which need test no more than eighteen pounds. From three to five inches is enough. The terminal end loop is usually equipped with a small snap, the other end loop with a small swivel, all of a black or dull color.

Of course the more unobtrusive this necessary linkage is, the better it is. Fishermen who fly fish for bluefish quite often, and who dress their own flies, sometimes lash the stainless steel wire to the hook shank when dressing special flies for bluefish, mackerel, and others having sharp teeth. The wire is bound to the hook with tying thread, leaving a final quarter-inch of wire near the bend of the hook. When the wire has been tied down to this point, this quarter-inch is bent forward, wound in, and lacquered. After the fly is dressed, a small loop is made in the forward end and a small swivel is inserted in it. One way of doing this (and one I like particularly) is to close the loop by using tiny metal sleeves available in tackle stores for the purpose. The sleeves are crimped tight with a Sevenstrand crimping tool or with "Sportmate" pliers. The loop should be tested to be sure it is secure.

In my younger days, sea trout (or weakfish) were a favorite oceanic fighter, quite equal to the bluefish in the battle they could offer. With sides like gleaming opal, they were beautiful to behold, and very delicious to eat. Then, for some evidently unknown reason, they disappeared to the extent that almost none have been caught in past years. As this is written (in 1965) there are signs of the weakfish coming back, so let's become acquainted with him briefly. I must confess to considerable favoritism for him, partly because he is an ideal adversary on a light fly rod and also because, since my fly rod went to sea, he seems in his appearance and manner of fighting to be the nearest thing to the eastern brook trout which I have found in salt water. His name is rather unfortunate because there is nothing "weak" about him unless it is his tender mouth, which calls for considerable delicacy in handling him and which therefore seems to add to his many sporting characteristics. I have never taken one weighing over four pounds, although weakfish frequently are caught which run much larger. Even a four pounder is, however, an excellent adversary on a medium strength fly rod.

The weakfish feeds on the surface as well as near the bottom. When they are known to be present in harbors and estuaries and are not surface feeding, they often may be induced to do so by the process of "chumming." This consists of anchoring a boat in the current of a suitable river mouth or channel and dropping overboard bits of bait. Shrimps are one of the favorites. Three or four quarts should be enough for a day's fishing for the occupants of a single boat. An accepted method of keeping shrimps alive is to mix them with about twice their volume of wood shavings, or sawdust, and place the mixture on a gunnysack over some ice in a covered box. The sawdust helps to keep the shrimp alive and serves to mark the direction of the chum line as well. A handful containing three or four shrimps dropped overboard every few minutes will suffice. It may take approximately half an hour for the fish to find the shrimp, but when they do so they will work up the chum line to within casting distance of the boat. A handful of shrimp and sawdust dropped over the side occasionally will serve to keep them there, allowing them to be taken near the surface with a fly. I have a preference for red and white streamers, or bucktails, for weakfish and I use them more or less consistently, even though I am sure that some of the other color combinations would do as well.

It is true that the fishing for these salt water game fish along the northeastern coast improves as the season advances. The fish seem to grow bigger, more numerous, and more inclined to take the fly in September and October than in the spring and summer.

It is sometimes possible to enjoy a mixed bag of striped bass, bluefish, and weakfish, even to the extent of catching one of each species on successive casts. This has happened to me only once, but there was so much excitement on that eventful day that it will remain indefinitely in my memory. It was late September on this occasion when I reached Atlantic City for a few days of fishing with Bill and Morrie Upperman, both accomplished anglers who need no introduction to fishermen in the Northeast.

We decided to try our luck at Barnegat Inlet, forty miles from Atlantic City and one of the most famous fishing locations along that part of the coast. The inlet, marked by Barnegat Light, is flanked by two stone jetties whose seaward ends converge to the open point of a triangle, providing a sheltered area for small boats entering the Inlet.

Eastern Salt Water Streamer Fishing

Along and between the jetties schools of striped bass, bluefish, weakfish, and other species collect, at some times so numerous that one "can walk from jetty to jetty on the fish," as the Chamber of Commerce rather optimistically likes to put it.

In the cold dawn giant waves were breaking over the jetties, the combination of wind and tide making a swirling cross-chop so intense that the smaller boats were not venturing out. I cast a dubious eye at the Maelstrom. We planned to fish between the jetties, but their presence did not seem to be accomplishing any useful purpose at the moment.

"Looks a bit rough for fly fishing," I commented as we pulled our tackle from the car.

Bill chuckled and winked at Morrie. "That's just a nice cross-chop to get the fly down to the fish," he announced. "Andy Bjornberg is a good skipper, and he has a staunch boat. He uses it for rescue work. There's no need to worry. We'll have good fishing and a lot of fun!"

Andy and his little motor launch both bred confidence. We came aboard, stowed our gear and backed out from the slip. Aft of the pilot house the boat was entirely open, without appointments of any kind and with a rail which was just short of being knee-high. The boat began to pitch as we left the protection of the Inlet and approached the breakwater.

"What do you hold onto when she pitches?" I asked.

"Nothing," was the encouraging answer. "You just dig your knees against the rail and lean with the motion of the boat. If you don't lean the right way, we'll try and fish you out!"

The skipper maneuvered the boat along the jetty so we could cast with the wind. Morrie's torpedo tapered line drove his fly out nicely, while I unlimbered my rod and attempted to follow his example. Bill preferred to try heavier salt water tackle.

The boat slowly made its way within casting distance along the breakwater. Occasional choppy waves crashing against the rocks sent deluges of salt spray cascading over all on board. Captain Andy, comfortably seated in the protection of his little pilot house, placidly smoked his pipe and expertly kept the rolling and pitching boat in position despite the turbulence of the sea. The combination of the erratic motion of the launch and the brisk wind made casting difficult. An error in equilibrium would have put a man overboard, a rather dismal prospect in such an angry sea.

At those moments which seemed expedient each of us attempted to cast. When the fly landed near the breakwater, it was immediately engulfed in foam; washed under by the churning waves and carried backward by the motion of the boat and the current of the incoming tide. Fishing the fly was neither necessary nor possible, but fortunately the elements did that for us.

Suddenly Morrie had a slashing strike. The fish bore deeply along the breakwater, easily taking all the power that the fragile rod could give. Twenty minutes later he was able to gaff it and haul it into the boat; a handsome striped bass of fourteen pounds. His handling of it was a rather noteworthy accomplishment in such a sea, with tackle so inadequate for the conditions which existed.

As the day wore on we seemed better able to stand firm with the motion of the boat, but on many occasions the line between being aboard and being overboard was drawn rather fine. Morrie took a second bass before either Bill or I had a strike. Then Bill hooked one on his heavier tackle. It seemed to be a big fish. The minutes passed while it took out line and then was brought back, sulking too far beneath the wildly heaving boat to be seen in the broken waves covered as they were with creaming foam.

I put down my rod and made my way to the pilot house to rest my aching knees and to get a bottle of soda pop from the pail which held them. There came a loud splash from behind, sounding as if a great fish had shaken himself on the surface. I turned to watch the battle again, and when I did so Bill and his rod were nowhere to be seen.

Morrie had dropped his fly rod on the deck and was ripping off jacket and rubber shoes while wildly scanning the violent water for a sign of his brother. I grabbed a coil of rope and hurried to join him. The captain reversed his engine and attempted to hold the boat in position.

In seconds that seemed like minutes, up from the sea slowly rose the tip of a fishing rod, not more than ten feet away. When it had reached its full height aloft. Bill's head and arm appeared at the other end. He looked around frantically, his back to the boat, before another sea engulfed him. Almost instantly he appeared again.

Eastern Salt Water Streamer Fishing

"Point the rod toward the boat, Bill," I called out. He turned and promptly did so. Morrie and I grabbed the rod tip and hauled him aboard. His rod lay on the deck unnoticed while he disgorged a quantity of sea water.

"Nice fish," he finally spluttered. "Sorry I lost him."

I glanced at his tackle. "Maybe you didn't. Your line is still in the water."

Bill jumped up and grabbed the rod, quickly reeling in the slack. The fish was on and he soon had it in the boat. It was one of the largest striped bass I had ever seen.

"Should go a bit over twenty-five pounds," said Bill with satisfaction. "I hope so, because the *Field and Stream* magazine qualification is twenty-five pounds and I want one of their silver award buttons."

On the heaving boat there was no way of weighing the fish accurrately. I suggested that we return to the dock, but Bill would not hear of it.

"We still have an hour to fish," he said. "Let's use every minute."

I flicked a red and white fly to the breakwater and watched the green seas carry it under. When my line straightened there was a heavy strike. Line ripped from the reel and a small fish jumped into the air.

"A blue!" cried Morrie excitedly. "The bluefish are in!"

It is well to keep a tight line on a bluefish. He is a spectacular jumper and frequently succeeds in throwing the hook. While handling him I marked where I caught him and made a mental note to try the spot again on our next trip along the jetty.

The leaps and runs of a bluefish remind me vividly of those of the renowned steelhead in western rivers. When they are taken with the same tackle, I cannot see that one is superior in fighting ability to the other. This one proved to be six-and-a-half pounds.

Another strike occurred on my next cast. The fish ran and swirled in the trough of a swell, but failed to jump. He was a lovely weakfish weighing slightly over four pounds.

The weakfish in northern waters is iridescent, with a body coloration between belly and back which I have described by likening it to an opal. In southern waters the weakfish are spotted and are commonly called "trout." These spotted weakfish are a different but very similar species. Both varieties are equally valiant at the end of a line.

It seemed that my luck had changed, and the next cast proved it to be true. My mixed bag was completed with a small striped bass weighing nine-and-a-half pounds. Before we returned to the Inlet, Bill and Morrie both took another bass while I boated a second bluefish and lost a third.

When the launch reached its slip Bill picked up his large striper and hurried to the scales. Each of us took turns at weighing it, but the fact remained that it was exactly twenty-four and three-quarters pounds.

"Undoubtedly the bass lost a quarter pound between its catching and its weighing." I said. "I should think you would be within your rights to call it twenty-five pounds. A difference of only one per cent in weight is neither here nor there, and you certainly deserve your silver button for handling him in that rough sea; not to mention the ducking you took in doing it!"

Bill smiled a bit ruefully. "The bass weighs twenty-four and three-quarters pounds," he said. "It does not weigh twenty-five. Seems as if every big bass I catch just falls short of the mark. One of these days I'll get a bigger one and have that button for my hat."

Morrie went to his car and reappeared with a flask. We drank to the early demise of Bill's prize-winning bass and called it a day.

The fishing at Barnegat Inlet frequently is better than I have described it, particularly late in the season. Rarely is it so rough that men are in danger of going overboard while handling a fish. I relate the story partly to indicate that salt water fly fishing can be carried on successfully, even under rather unusual difficulties. Partly, also, to pay a well-deserved tribute to the sportsmanship of Bill Upperman, who is the manufacturer of the *Upperman Bucktail*, the weighted-head jig for spinning, plug casting and surf fishing on which Bill's striper was caught.

One of our less appreciated fish is the pollock, which ranges offshore waters from Canada as far south as the Virginia capes. The pollock (frequently termed "Boston bluefish" on menus) is usually thought of as a commercial fish, and its value to sport is not yet generally realized. It reaches weights of twenty-five pounds or more, but five or ten pound examples are extremely common. Its long, fast runs compare very favorably with those of the striped bass.

Spring runs of pollock occur both in the spring and in the fall. The

Eastern Salt Water Streamer Fishing

fish school offshore but frequently swing into the deep water of harbors and estuaries, where they furnish fast sport for the fisherman with any type of tackle. The pollock will strike at bait or spinners, but those who have fished for him with the fly rod and the streamer fly or bucktail find that he will take these flies even better. The color of the fly is unimportant, since a pollock will strike at virtually anything, even including bits of cloth or tinfoil.

In concluding these notes on eastern salt water fly fishing it may be well to mention that if the fly rod is to be used consistently in salt water, it is advisable to have it equipped with non-corrosive guides such as those made from Monel metal. Nothing will ruin a fly line faster than rusted guides. Greasing corrosive guides before fishing, and a thorough cleaning afterwards, will help; but with a rod mounted with non-rusting guides this difficulty is eliminated entirely.

I have used my favorite Orvis split-bamboo eight-and-a-half and nine foot fly rods for salt water fishing, but no longer do so, because they are too expensive and too fine instruments for use when conditions suddenly can get rather rough. The less costly glass fiber rods are more sensible. Carrying long rod cases on trips by aircraft can be a nuisance. The Wright & McGill Company, Denver, Colorado, presented me with a four-section fiberglass fly rod which, in its aluminum tube, is only two feet long and thus can be packed with luggage. Despite its three ferrules, it has amazingly good action and is a most convenient expedient when carrying heavier tackle is unnecessary.

It is advisable to keep salt water streamers and bucktails separated from those used in fresh water, particularly if they are dressed on corrosive hooks. Unless carefully washed (and perhaps even then), they will rust and lose strength, meanwhile coloring hair and hackles a dirty, rusty brown. Considerable advancement is being made in non-corrosive hooks with stainless steel or high nickel content, notably in the United States by "Eagle Claw" (Wright & McGill Company), and by Allcocks, of England. Being of shiny, silver-like metal, the shanks do not need to be dressed. Most fly fishermen confine themselves to the sizes 3/0 and 1/0 and find they are satisfactory for the majority of salt water gamefish.

In the next chapter we will describe salt water patterns commonly used in Florida and other southern waters. Many of these are equally useful along northern coasts. We from the North have been very loyal

FIG. VII-2

CATHERWOOD'S *Needlefish*

to the simple bucktails which have been described, but perhaps we would do well to experiment more frequently with newer types, such as Joe Brooks' *Blondes* and some of the splayed-wing patterns.

Newer types occasionally are announced in sporting magazines and newspaper rod and gun columns, together with information on their success. An interesting innovation, for example, is the Catherwood series of exact baitfish imitations produced commercially by Bill Catherwood, of Tewksbury, Massachusetts. Usually dressed on special 2/0 short nickel hooks, these streamers are about six inches long; dressed unusually full forward, with several colors of marabou over which are six or more long varicolored hackles, all combining to provide the bulk, length, coloration, and action of various baitfish. These include balao, capelin, chub, herring, mullet, needlefish, sand eel, smelt, squid and tinker mackerel.

Bill Catherwood's patterns are amazingly lifelike when wet. They have successful records with big game fish along both coasts, northern pike inland, and with several South American species, including the tremendous rainbow trout in the Andean lakes. While necessarily large and somewhat bulky to provide properly sized baitfish imitations, they can be cast reasonably well with suitable tackle and are excellent for trolling or for fishing tidal currents. An example is shown here, and another in Figure VI-1.

VIII

Southern Salt Water Streamer Fishing

There are few places in the world, either on salt water or on fresh, which offer to the fly rod angler greater variety and abundance of fighting fish than do the colorful expanses of the Florida Keys. In these green and blue mangrove dotted shallows and in the deeper reaches around them cruise the bonefish, the tarpon and the snook; the channel bass, the weakfish, and the chiro. There also lurk the barracuda near schools of jacks, pompano, snappers, and mullet. Occasionally the angler may track down one of the finest game fish of them all, the deep and multicolored permit; or he may travel to the deep blue of the Gulf Stream and cast his fly into a school of graceful dolphin. One finds similarly fabulous fishing in many other parts of the Gulf of Mexico and along the southeastern coast, but to my mind nowhere is it as abundant as amid the myriad of tropical coral and mangrove islands of the Florida Keys. If a change from such an angling Utopia should ever be desired, the inland canals frequently teem with baby tarpon, snook, and gigantic largemouth bass.

Of this wealth of lordly game fish, the one which generally is conceded to excel them all in pound for pound endurance and in the express-train power of his long runs is that silvery ghost of tropic waters, the fabulous bonefish. When I sought him first in the spring of 1948, we were fortunate to have Captain Harry Snow, Sr., of Marathon, Florida, as a guide. Harry has the reputation of being able to spot a school of bonefish as far as the average man can see. He came to our cabin the evening we arrived to exchange a few pleasantries and to inspect our tackle in anticipation of the next day's fishing.

He looked with approval at my nine-and-a-half foot streamer rod and a somewhat lighter fly rod, together with the torpedo tapered lines to fit them, each wound on a sturdy reel large enough to hold the line and over 200 yards of backing. He took a rather dim view of the relatively light leaders I showed him, however.

"Ten or twelve feet is long enough," he said, "but you'd better taper them down to six pounds as a minimum, and eight or ten pounds would be safer. The fish may fray or break the monofilament against coral or mangrove roots, and you will need strength to hold them when they decide to run too far."

Early the next morning we put our gear aboard Harry's big boat and cruised down the channel along the mangrove islands with a skiff bobbing from a rope at the stern. The many islands make this part of the Keys usually as calm as a mill pond. From the deeper water toward the shores the flats stretch mile on mile. At low tide, many of these are out of water, and at half tide or full tide they ordinarily are not over a foot or two deep. The schools of bonefish work over them on the incoming tide, searching the ribbongrass and mud-covered bottom for crabs, shrimp, mollusks, baitfish, and other bits of food, which they crush between the bony plates of their mouths. Their dorsal fins and tails frequently appear above the surface as they grub along the shallow bottom. This habit of "tailing" makes them easy to locate, as do the patches of mud which they stir up as they slowly work their way in with the rising tide.

Suddenly, Harry pointed toward shore. "A school of about two dozen bonefish," he said excitedly; "and two of them are big ones!"

He anchored the launch while we put the necessary gear into the skiff. With powerful strokes of his long pole he pushed the smaller boat shoreward, carefully working far around the incoming school of bonefish until he had quietly maneuvered it between them and the shore. He signaled that I should stand up and be ready to cast. I shook out the necessary amount of line and with the slack coiled in my left hand, stood motionless, waiting.

The bonefish now could be seen clearly. Fifteen or twenty of them,

Southern Salt Water Streamer Fishing

seeming to average about eight pounds apiece, were slowly and casually making their way toward us in water not over a foot deep. Occasionally one would root on the bottom, his deeply forked tail and wide dorsal fin shimmering pale green and silver above the surface. Another would dart aside to pounce upon a delicacy, splashing quietly as he did so. The ranks of glistening tails waved aloft like ghostly banners, little disturbing the peaceful ripples of the green water.

One of the bonefish appeared larger than the rest. He seemed to be leading the school and I decided to cast for him. I glanced at Harry, who nodded imperceptibly. The big bonefish by now was not more than thirty feet away. I extended the line with a few false casts and attempted to drop the yellow, red and white streamer about three feet beyond and ahead of him.

Perhaps it was the pent-up excitement which got the better of me, although sometimes I ascribe it to an unfortunate gust of the breeze. In any event, the fly landed so accurately on the tip of the bonefish's nose that I could not have duplicated such improper perfection once in a dozen casts.

The water exploded. The big bonefish spun about as if he had been shot, his disarming lethargy instantly replaced by violent action. Flanked by his cohorts he streaked for deeper water. With a dozen lusty splashes, followed by as many torpedo-like wakes, every bonefish in sight had disappeared completely in a matter of seconds.

Harry chuckled softly as I reeled in my line and sat down.

"You can't hook one on every cast," he said, trying to appease my embarrassment and chagrin. "You'll have another chance in a minute or two. Look to your left!"

Bushes and individual sprigs of mangrove dotted the peaceful water. Their finger-like roots rising above the surface were heavily encrusted with barnacles. Among them, not more than 300 feet away, the tails of nearly 100 bonefish slowly waved in ghostly silence.

Harry pulled his pole from the mud and quietly worked the skiff within casting distance. I stood up and made ready again. The great school of fish were turning and working toward us. A small shark cruised about in the water to our right, and near him a ray two or three feet in diameter grubbed about, sending up clouds of mud. The sun beat down, hot and bright. Harry stopped the skiff in the path of the fish and we waited as the army of shimmering tails drew closer.

As the nearest of them came within casting distance I worked my line into the air again. The fly fluttered down ten feet ahead of a large bonefish and several feet beyond him. He was undisturbed. The streamer settled in the shallow water, a bit too far from the fish, so I worked it as slowly as possibly, still keeping it above the ribbon grass which would entangle it. The big bonefish was absorbed with something on the bottom. The red collar of the fly worked delicately, its white hackles opening and shutting with the slight motion of the rod. The oppressive silence was broken only by the quiet splashes of the silvery-green fish as they worked closer and closer.

My bonefish gave up his investigation of the bottom and cruised slowly forward. When he did so I worked the fly faster. The paths of fish and fly were converging. They were less than three feet apart.

Suddenly the big bonefish saw the fly. With a splash he turned and took it. His light touch tugged at the line and instantly I struck and had him.

When he felt the hook he turned and made for the sanctuary of deep water. As he did so, the vast school of fish turned as one, splashing and slithering away.

The line ran out from my hand and began to pay off from the reel as the bonefish increased his speed. I raised the rod-tip higher to cushion the run. Faster and faster went the fish. Now the tapered line was gone and the black backing was melting from the reel. Its whirring handle was an indistinguishable blur.

The bonefish traveled as straight and as fast as if he had been an express train on a track. Still the line ripped out. Half the backing had disappeared in a matter of seconds. I glanced anxiously at the reel. Only a little line was left. Then, as quickly as it had started, the run of the fish slowed and stopped. Far out on the glassy calm a fish swirled. It seemed too far away to be mine, but it was!

I held back on the fish and began to reel. Soon he was coming toward the boat at a steady pace. I looked at the reel and tried to estimate how much line he had taken. All together, it was very close to 175 yards. My backing returned to the reel and then a part of the

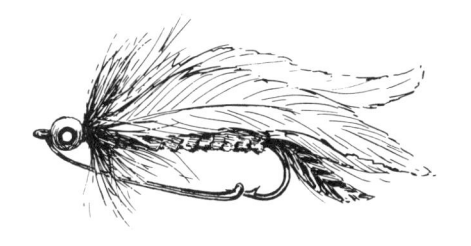

Gordon Dean Weedless Bead-Head Streamer

Homer Rhode, Jr. Splayed-Wing Bonefish Streamer

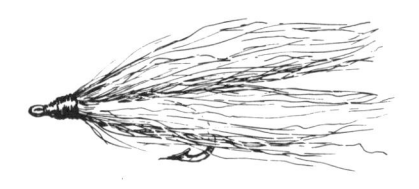

Joe Brooks, Jr. Splayed-Wing Bonefish Bucktail

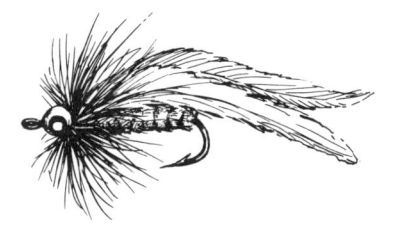

Gordon Dean Splayed-Wing Bead-Head Bonefish Streamer

FIG. VIII-1

STREAMERS AND BUCKTAILS
FOR FLORIDA SHALLOW WATER FISHING

The author discusses the evening's fly selection with "Uncle Will" McNally (center) and guide "Happy" Gardner (right) on the porch of Dana McNally's cabin, located where Chemquassabamticook Stream flows into Long Lake near the headwaters of the Allagash River in Maine.

144

Southern Salt Water Streamer Fishing

tapered line. Doggedly acceding to the pull, the bonefish wavered slowly toward me over the flats.

"Watch it now," said Harry softly.

As if that had been a signal, the bonefish suddenly saw the boat and turned quickly to run again. His second run was neither as long nor as fast as the first, but he made it between two mangroves whose barnacled numbers vie with the coral as hazards to the angler and his line.

When he stopped his run and swirled I drew him back the way he had come. He swam again between the mangroves which would have broken me and afforded him instant safety had he but circled them. He came to the boat, turned once more and ran anew, but his strength was unequal to his desire. Held by the line, he circled the boat again and again. The circles grew smaller and smaller.

Harry dipped the long handled net into the water. As I brought the exhausted fish nearer Harry slipped the net under him and lifted him out. He withdrew the fly, carefully keeping his fingers away from the crushers which could have mashed them to a pulp.

"About eight-and-a-half pounds," he said. "Not a bad fish. Took you twenty-one minutes. Do you want to keep him?"

"Let him go," I said.

Harry eased him into the water. He lay quietly among the ribbon grass for a minute and then slowly swam away.

"There are some more around the point," Harry announced. "You have about an hour and a half before the tide slacks off."

I decided to try for them by wading. The swifter luxury of fishing from a skiff is easier but, in the inner sanctum of the fly rod bonefishermen, taking a big bonefish is not considered to be of great importance unless the angler stalks him on foot and catches him with a fly.

Harry dropped me off near the point, pulled the boat to shore and settled back comfortably to watch. The water was nearly knee deep and comfortably warm. My rubber-shoed feet sunk into the muddy spots, crunched over the ribbon grass and picked their track around hummocks of brownish-grey coral. A few bonefish were making their way inshore. I slowly maneuvered to place myself in their path and then stood quietly, waiting. There was time to light a pipe and clean the specks of salt from the very necessary Polaroid sun glasses.

Three bonefish were steadily approaching. Record fish rarely are found in large schools, but the ones which travel alone, or in groups of a very few, often are satisfyingly big. Far down the shoreline a long-legged white bird which might have been an egret also stood silently. He was fishing in his way and I was in mine.

Finally the bonefish were near enough for a cast. I dropped the fly ahead of them and had fished it no more than a few feet when one of them swirled and took it. He began his customary reel scorching run and then deviated suddenly to turn around a small mangrove. Then he swerved again and tangled with another. The line was tight, but I could feel no sign of life at the end.

I followed the line, reeling it in and attempting to prevent it being chaffed more than necessary against the sharp barnacles of the mangroves and the coral. When the end was reached the leader was intact. The fish had broken off at the fly.

Farther down the shore I located several large fish and tried again. When they were within reach they ignored the first cast, but remained undisturbed for me to try another. A fish took it and made a long run to deep water. He kept me out of trouble and behaved very much as did the one I had taken from the boat. On his third and evidently what was to be his last run a small shark swept in to attack the tired and frantic fish. I snapped my rod tip back in an effort to break the leader to set him free, but it was too late. The fish was lost in a grey swirl of muddy water. Near the dark back of the shark the grey was tinged with crimson. The shark retreated with his meal, allowing me to draw in the dead weight of half a bonefish; his body cleanly severed near his dorsal fin.

On other days and in other places there may be fewer bonefish and fewer hazards to their catching. Many of the flats are a mile or two wide and several miles long, yet frequently on them there is not a bonefish to be seen. They go where food is most abundant, sometimes descending upon these places in vast schools of hundreds. I have taken half a dozen or more in fairly rapid succession, without losing one; but on other occasions something always seems to interfere with success. Other duties necessitate that my visits to the Florida bonefish flats be few and far between, but the element of chance and the incomparable excitement of battling these fabulous fighters will take me there again and again, as often as circumstances permit.

Fig. VIII–2

THE *Horror* AND *Frankee-Belle* BONEFISH FLIES

Anglers on the Keys and outlying islands are constantly developing new bonefish flies, so whatever is in style as this is written may be entirely out of fashion later. Al McClane currently swears by his *Golden Shrimp*, which he usually dresses on No. 4 or No. 6, 2X strong, 1X long Improved Sproat hooks. In an article in the September, 1965, issue of *Field and Stream*, he says: "It is tied with an antique gold mohair body palmered with grizzly hackle dyed the same shade, and has a V-shaped tail made from the dyed hackle. The marabou wing (about half again as long as the hook) is antique gold also." The palmered hackle is wound as a collar at the head to help hold up the marabou wing and to act as a throat extending to the barb of the hook.

Pete Perinchief, a highly experienced angler from Hamilton, Bermuda, evolved a very successful brown bucktail and yellow chenille fly called *The Horror*, which is dressed upside down to prevent it from picking up grass. As shown by the sketch, the body is very short, of double-wrapped yellow chenille about three-eighths inch long, wound near the eye. There is a one-eighth inch wrap of the chenille behind the bucktail wing, which causes the wing to cover the point of the hook. The wing, protruding from the rear of the chenille body, is about two inches long and is composed of a rather large bunch of brown bucktail extending about one inch beyond the bend of the hook. When cast and worked, the hook rides point up to prevent snagging on the bottom. Pete says, "The fly which is enclosed is my favorite but it can be varied by tying it with white or pink bucktail as well as blue and white, dark brown, yellow or even green. The chenille head also can be varied in color, but I am firmly convinced that the brown one is the best of the lot."

The *Muddler Minnow* also does well on bonefish; all these three being brownish flies because this is the general color of shrimp and other aquatic foods on the flats.

Standard bonefish flies are similar in shape, an excellent example being the *Frankee-Belle*, designed by the famous bonefish guide Captain Jimmie Albright and named for Frankee Albright and Belle Mathers. As in the sketch, this has a yellow chenille body and a one-and-a-half-inch long wing of two white hackles outside of which are two barred rock hackles. The throat is white bucktail extending half an inch beyond the bend of the hook. Hook sizes are from No. 6 to 3/0. Bonefish flies such as this usually are dressed in combinations of white, brown, black and gray, sometimes with green or green and yellow bodies and with yellow throats. A brighter pattern of red and orange sometimes does very well, especially in discolored water. They often are dressed with splayed wings to make them sink slower, thus being less inclined to pick up grass. Also, the pulsations of splayed wing streamers and bucktails provide more action. It is important that they be tied with wings short enough to prevent them from becoming caught under the hook. They should be fished in short, quick jerks to allow the wings to open and close with each strip-in while fishing the fly. If a fish doesn't take a fly fished in this manner, the fly should be worked faster. Patterns on small hooks are preferred for very shallow water, because they sink slower. The larger sizes are preferred when water is deeper. Flies should be selected not only for water depth but also for the species of fish, what they are feeding on, and how they feed.

Bonefish flies are tied both with feathered and with bucktail wings. Another top example of the feathered type is the *Hagen Sands* bonefish fly shown in the color plates. A popular bucktail type is Joe Brooks' series of "Blondes" (described in the next chapter). The high wing opens and shuts during the retrieve in a manner similar to that of flies of the splayed wing type.

Rods for bonefishing usually are nine-and-a-half feet long, with slow action; this length helps to keep the fly off the bottom and gives it good action. Such rods usually carry GAF lines in torpedo taper with from 250 to 300 yards of backing on reels with adjustable drag.

Southern Salt Water Streamer Fishing

Nylon squidding line of about eighteen pounds test is preferred for backing, due to its resiliency. Leaders are from twelve to fourteen feet long, tapered from thirty to about eight pounds in strength.

While we have discussed this tackle and these tactics for bonefish, it should be remembered that the same flies and tackle in general are equally suitable for all game fish which inhabit the flats, as well as for all but the very large fish elsewhere.

It was Harry Snow who also introduced me for the first time to the amazingly spectacular leaps of a tarpon with one of my flies in his mouth. If fighting a tarpon lacks the hair-raising excitement found in the extraordinary runs of the bonefish, ample compensation is provided by his amazingly beautiful and prodigious jumps. What a bonefish does to you in the water, the tarpon does to you in the air. The difference is in the element only. The electric thrills that tingle down the neck of the angler are the same.

Harry's big boat purred down the channel with the little skiff bobbing along behind as usual. We went down the coast and entered a small bay which gave the effect of a tropical lagoon. Here Harry anchored the launch, and we took to the skiff with a battered outboard motor to maneuver us in the deep water. Coconut palms rose above the mangroves of the shore. In the deep part of the bay the water had the hue of cobalt blue, shading to azure and a milky green at the shoreline.

"Usually there are a few tarpon in here," Harry said. "They are a good size for your fly rod; about twenty or thirty pounds. We'll see if we can find them."

He scanned the bay for minutes before finally pointing to a cove in the far end. "Bubbles!" he announced, "and I just saw a tarpon roll."

We slowed the motor as we reached the spot. Harry stopped it and we coasted in. I stood in the bow with my fly rod ready; a red and white streamer on the leader.

"Cast over the bubbles," Harry advised. "They are around here somewhere."

I sent the streamer as far as I could; let it sink a bit, and stripped it in slowly. There was a great swirl where it was. A blue-black shape flashed deep in the water. I struck but nothing was there.

"Too slow on the strike," Harry commented. "They'll take it and spit it out in an instant. They have bony mouths, too. Hit 'em as hard as you dare to, as soon as you see anything."

I began to cast the fly fanwise around the drifting boat. Deep in the water a dim black form cruised purposefully to the fly. When he reached it I fished it faster, felt him, struck, and had him.

Beside the boat an underwater explosion took place as the big fish crashed through the surface and snaked his gleaming, heavy body high into the air. With gills distended brightly red he leaped upward, shaking his head violently from side to side. Then he fell back into the blue water and was gone. The little red and white fly fluttered down after him, landing dejectedly among the foam and the ripples.

I said something softly as the shivers left my spine.

"I expect you must be praying, using those words!" Harry said, laughing. "If you can stay with a tarpon once in seven tries your average is better than most. We'll leave here for the moment and scout along the mangroves. Maybe we'll find some there."

He gunned the little boat to shallow water, stopped the motor, and picked up his pole. The mangrove border appeared from a distance to be dense underbrush. It was a network of tiny canals with quiet pools nestled in the dimness among them.

Suddenly Harry stopped the skiff. "Look in there!" he whispered hoarsely. Deep among the mangrove roots was a small pool and on it appeared a mass of bubbles. As I watched, the water swirled quietly.

"I'll move out a bit," he said. "You'll be needing room. Cast as close under the bushes as you can."

I sent the fly in there. It hit a branch and dropped to the water. As I pulled it under, a dark form shot out trailing a heavy wake. The tarpon took the fly and rushed toward the boat as I ripped in slack and struck and struck again. The point of the barb had been honed to needle sharpness, but it seemed logical to set the hook as deeply as possible.

Near the boat the tarpon jumped, covering us with salt spray. The hook held. He made a short run and jumped again. As I stood in the boat I seemed to be looking up at him, shaking his bulk of blue-black and shining silver in the air.

Again and again he jumped. As he left the water I gave him slack line, tightening it instantly when he returned. His runs were short

Southern Salt Water Streamer Fishing

because tarpon expend most of their energy in leaping. Their great size and burnished beauty, coupled with the spectacular height and the splashing power of their jumping, is an awe-inspiring sight peculiar to the tarpon alone. It is unduplicated by the bass, the steelhead, or the salmon, even though there is resemblance to a degree.

The tarpon cruised about slowly, bewildered and tired. By pulling up on the rod, I forced two more jumps from him. We brought him beside the boat, but the fly was so deeply embedded I could not get it loose, so I broke the leader at the eye of the hook and let him go. He swam dejectedly away to join his brothers under the mangroves. The last I saw of him was a flash of red and white from the fly as he took it under the leaves.

Next day I saw him again as we drifted beside the mangroves. I had hooked five tarpon and brought two to boat. Then nearly a dozen came in single file procession from their sanctuary to the deep water. One of them had a red and white fly tucked lugubriously under his nose. Of course I cast for him, but he was disinterested. He had one of my flies and, to judge by his expression, he seemed to think it was more than enough.

These tarpon of the mangroves may be termed medium sized fish. There are smaller ones in greater numbers in the numerous inland canals which open into salt water. There are vastly bigger ones in the winter and early spring in the channels between the mangrove-dotted islands of the Gulf, of the Florida mainland and its Keys. Several anglers have taken tarpon of over 100 pounds on streamer flies or bucktails. Joe Brooks took one weighing $148\frac{1}{2}$ pounds, which is or was a record. For this and for deep fighting fish which require "plenty of lifting, tugging, and hauling" he prefers a stiff action nine-foot split-bamboo rod weighing eight ounces or a nine-foot fiberglass rod weighing between six and six-and-a-half ounces. He also prefers thirty pound test dacron for backing because he wants rigidity rather than resiliency for this kind of angling.

Favorite flies for tarpon are bright ones. They seem to please the fish; and they help the angler, who must watch the fly and be ready to strike when the fish hits. As illustrated in Figure VIII-3, these may be either streamers or bucktails, with long hair or six or eight long feathers tied behind very fully dressed collars. Wing colors are white, yellow, red, brown, or grizzly, with collars of the same or of contrasting colors. For night fishing, an all-white fly is popular on bright nights, and a jet black one often is used when the sky is overcast, because these "colors" provide greater contrast against the dim light.

Hook sizes between 1/0 and 3/0 are adequately large for all but the biggest fish. Anglers who seek baby tarpon in the canals often use flies dressed on long shanked hooks as small as size 6, feeling that these miss fewer strikes than the larger sizes. Bucktails with bodies of braided mylar tubular cord, as described in the next chapter, provide a minnow-like flash and translucence which is very attractive to baby tarpon, as well as to snook and many other species. These are usually natural imitations, with a darker wing color over a lighter one. Joe Brooks' "Blondes" in suitable sizes are excellent flies for tarpon, as well as other game fish. The *Homer Rhode, Jr. Tarpon Bucktail* illustrated in Figure VIII-3 probably was the father of this type, because Homer gave me some of them prior to 1950, and they were illustrated in *Streamer Fly Fishing*, which was first published at that time.

Homer Rhode is an old angling companion and one of the earliest pioneers in salt water fly fishing. He wrote me comments in 1949 which are as good today as they were then:

"You will note that all of my neck hackle and saddle hackle flies are tied with very heavy collars. The divided (splayed) wing flies have the wings tied in as far back on the shank of the hook as possible, and the collar is started at that point. This helps to keep the wing from wrapping around the shank of the hook and thus keeps the fly from turning or spinning, at the same time assuring a natural action. In more than twenty years of experimenting with salt water flies, I have found that these features cause fewer refusals, less mouthing of the tail, and that I hook more and lose fewer fish. My flies are longer and larger than usual. The heavy collar is due to the fact that I fish very slowly, usually in very shallow water. The divided wing opens and closes like a pair of scissors, making the fly seem to breathe. The heavy collar vibrates when fished slowly, seeming to give the fly added life. Ordinary (unsplayed) flies will do this to an extent, but their principal action seems to be an undulating motion when the fly is worked correctly. When I dress flies on offset hooks I remove

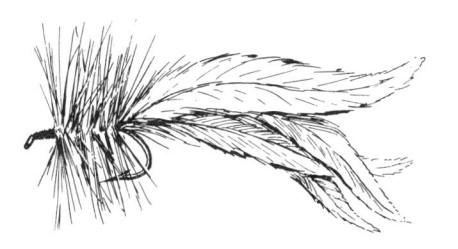

Homer Rhode, Jr. Tarpon Streamer

Gordon Dean Tarpon Streamer

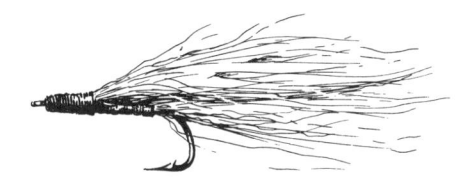

Homer Rhode, Jr. Tarpon Bucktail

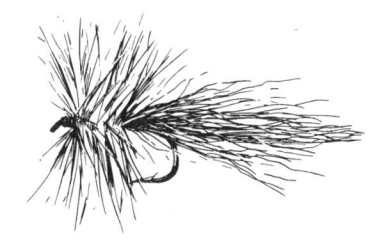

Homer Rhode, Jr. Tarpon Bucktail

Fig. VIII-3

STREAMERS AND BUCKTAILS FOR FLORIDA
DEEP WATER FISHING

about 90 per cent of the offset, which seems to give the best results in hooking and holding fish."

Tarpon often seem to like a fly fished one way on one day and another way on another. If they will not take what is offered it is usually preferable to change the method of fishing the fly rather than to change the fly itself. As a general rule, the "bonefish retrieve" seems to work best. This is a medium fast stripping in, ten or twelve inches at a time, alternating with short pauses to give the fly the darting motion of a minnow. With the smaller tarpon of the canals the retrieve may be made very slowly, particularly if the water is cloudy. This makes the fly flutter almost at a standstill, which often seems to interest them greatly.

Anglers seeking any species of fish in relatively shallow tropical waters occasionally feel a spine-jarring strike and retrieve their line only to find that the fly has been neatly bitten off. This may be accompanied by the momentary glimpse of a darting gray and silver shape which snakes out from the sanctuary of coral or mangroves to sever the fly and then as instantaneously returns to hiding. This is the barracuda, ace marauder of the deep; a powerful adversary which strikes like lightning, leaps like a salmon, and is very sporting on light tackle. This "Tiger of the Sea" is the pike of salt water; a sharp-toothed fish which averages in the neighborhood of five pounds but which frequently is much larger.

Small barracuda can be a decided nuisance to the fly fisherman, particularly if they are very prevalent when he is fishing for something else. As a rule, the barracuda is a slow-moving fish and often has to be teased into striking. At other times he is one of the fastest of all game fish, usually moving upon the lure from the side and hitting the head or the forward part of the fly. His runs are short, swift and violent but, like the pike and pickerel, usually not of long durations.

Barracuda strike at any fish which seems to be wounded or helpless, so the fly is worked slowly in imitation of an injured minnow. The relatively large ones used for tarpon are ideal, usually with wings of white or yellow with a collar of red.

In fishing for barracuda, a wire leader of six inches or more in length (preferably Sevenstrand stainless steel in a dark color) is all-important, because the fish can sever even very strong monofilament

Fig. VIII-4

MYLAR-WINGED BUCKTAIL

lines or leaders instantly. The barracuda seems partial to flies providing a great deal of flash, such as the *Mylar-winged Bucktail* illustrated here. This is essentially the simplest version of one of the "Blondes," with long silver mylar wings tied in at the head in the approximate shape indicated. Big barracuda of thirty pounds or so are found cruising bonefish flats and in many other places. But an almost sure location is around lighthouses built on metal stilts in the water, because they collect there to pick up whatever edibles are thrown overboard. Casts usually are made to individual fish. If one follows without striking, quicker action with the fly may induce him to do so. He probably will ruin the fly, so several should be on hand. One fish per fly may seem wasteful, but the flies are cheap and easy to tie—and a battle with a big barracuda is well worth the effort.

I have never tried the fly rod for large channel bass (redfish) in deep coastal waters, but in shallow water, on the "banks" or flats, the sport is very similar to bonefishing and is nearly as exciting. Perhaps it is done differently in some regions, but my experiences all have been in stalking them in places such as have been described as favorable to bonefish. Peculiarly enough, although the ribbon grass bottom of the shallow water is the same, I never have noticed bonefish when channel bass are in residence.

On a sunny day in the early spring we hitched an outboard motor to the skiff and purred through a maze of mangrove islands to the redfish flats. The flooding tide scarcely had covered the grass, but the area was laced with natural ditches or canals which allowed us to pole about and scout the region with little difficulty. Here and there a small splash, or the wavering of a bronze-red tail, indicated a redfish feeding. In such places they grub about very much as the bonefish do. Nearby a relatively large tail occasionally was showing, so we quietly moved up on the fish.

"You'll have to land the fly right on his nose," my companion advised. "The 'reds' have small eyes in proportion to their size and do not see too well. They are not as easily frightened as the bonefish."

The channel bass appeared to weigh about twelve pounds. We approached within twenty feet of him and watched as he attempted to worry something edible from the sand and grass. They are very much like a smallmouth bass in shape, although perhaps somewhat slimmer. In coloration they are very different, being of a coppery-pink or bronze-red, with the familiar identifying black dot at the base of the tail.

This one seemed to be totally oblivious of our presence. I let out sufficient line and kept the red and white streamer in the air. Finally the redfish concluded his investigation of the bottom and started to move off. I dropped the streamer in front of him and twitched it under. He took it with a splash and I set the hook as solidly as I dared.

The barb made the fish frantic. Over the grass he slithered, first one way and then another, erratically and aimlessly trying to run away from the bright feathers which held him so tightly. Failing this, he tailed repeatedly, trying to grub out the hook in the coral sand. It was necessary to keep him on an even keel to hold him, requiring all the pressure the six ounce rod could give.

Twenty minutes later he was beside the boat. We took him aboard for a bass dinner that night.

Farther on, another redfish was tailing. This one flushed when the fly landed too close. We found another and caught him. In some places it was difficult to work the fly without catching it in the ribbon grass bordering the shallow canals where the fish were feeding. I changed to a weedless fly (Figure VIII-2) and had no more difficulty, except that it was somewhat harder to set the hook.

I am told that channel bass give a much better account of them-

Southern Salt Water Streamer Fishing

selves in the surf than on the flats. The same flies work very well in all regions as far north as the Carolina coast, if the winds are favorable and the caster can reach the fish. Popular colors in streamers are pure white, white with a red collar, brown, grizzly and white, or yellow, which also may be mixed with grizzly. Hook sizes usually range between 1/0 and 3/0, the flies being tied rather full, with fairly long saddle hackle wings.

One need not go far afield for the spotted trout (or weakfish) or for the ladyfish (or chiro). Often they are caught fishing from the low bridges, from the causeways, or from boats within the limits of many Florida cities. The weakfish (or "trout" as he is familiarly called) differs from the northern weakfish in that he is spotted. He rarely weighs over three pounds, but is very trout-like in his appearance and manner of fighting. His mouth is rather soft, so the hook must be set very lightly. On many occasions the trout will not rise to surface lures. They must be fished deeply, usually necessitating the use of a weighted fly or of a split shot or two ahead of the fly on the leader.

One of the popular ways of fly fishing for trout is from a drifting boat. When a school of them is located, the spot is marked so that the boat may return to drift over them again and again. This usually is in relatively deep water, so the fly must be allowed to sink out of sight, after which a slow retrieve is started, with a distinct pause after each jerk, using the rod tip to work the fly. Any of the smaller flies in white, yellow or other generally preferred salt water combinations usually are satisfactory, preferably in sizes not exceeding 1/0.

Many fishermen confuse the ladyfish with the bonefish because the appearance of the two is somewhat similar and because, pound for pound, the two species generally are conceded to share the laurels as the greatest gamefish to be found in Florida waters. Ladyfish average less than three pounds. If they grew to the eight or nine pound weight of large bonefish, and retained their fighting ability in proportion, it is said that they would be practically unbeatable on light tackle. They jump, run, sound and bulldog a lure furiously, striking with great speed and ejecting the hook just as quickly.

Ladyfish are one of the few species which can be caught successfully with the fly rod at night. In some of the cities, such as Miami, they play and feed under the lighted bridges on the moving tide, affording unusual sport. Homer Rhode and several other Florida anglers have taken me fishing for them from the causeways, islands, piers and bridges within the city of Miami and in the vicinity of the Keys. Usually they are caught on a white fly in sizes 1 to 2/0, but they will take yellow almost equally well. The fly is fished slowly near the surface, with the usual darting minnow-like action, when the tide is moving strongly; otherwise fairly fast, with a strip retrieve.

It is a thrilling experience to accompany a few anglers to a lighted pier or bridge late at night to cast a fly for ladyfish. One can return late from a social evening and spend an hour or two of incomparable fly fishing, often within sight of home or hotel, without even bothering to put on fishing clothes. Frequently the angler must judge where his backcast is going and where his fly is landing, because often he cannot see it: but there is no doubt about the smashing strike of a ladyfish, or the frequency of the strikes when the time and the place is appropriate.

The ladyfish is very bony and is not considered a table delicacy so, like the tarpon and the bonefish, he is caught purely for sport and usually is returned to the water. This reminds me that perhaps I should have commented upon the edibility of bonefish, which have the reputation of being unfit to eat. I have eaten broiled bonefish and found them to be very good, although so far inferior in texture and flavor to many of the other species that I agree their value for the table should be ignored. They are very difficult to filet but, like the shad, when the bones are removed and when they are properly cooked, they definitely are in the edible class.

Northerners who go South for salt water fishing usually have their minds set on tackling bonefish and tarpon. We do not diminish the wisdom of these worthy objectives by saying that anglers miss a great deal if they don't devote part of the time concentrating on snook. The snook takes no prizes as a beauty and is down the list as a table delicacy; but if these are defects, he makes up for them on the end of a fly line.

The snook is a selective feeder, so selection of fly types and sizes is important and often calls for experimentation. He wants the fly sunk to his level, which is usually in fairly deep water. Because the snook is a fast-moving game fish, the fly must be sunk quickly and usually should be fished fast and with plenty of action.

Southern Salt Water Streamer Fishing

On a warm and sunny day in May we put tackle and lunch in the station wagon and headed for snook country. Although snook are found in pools in the mangroves, around docks in many areas, and in other places, the spot chosen for this foray was a deep ditch watered by the ocean-accessible canals near Florida's Tamiami Trail. The ditch seemed to lack flowage, and was so highly discolored that nothing under water was visible. Since a bright fly seemed logical, I put on a red and yellow splayed-wing pattern on an eight-pound test leader connected to a level floating line with a tapered fast-sinking forward section. The cast made the fly light on the water about forty feet across the ditch, where the sinking line quickly pulled it under. After letting it sink for half a minute, I pulled it into action by stripping in line a foot at a time, very fast and jerkily, with the rod always pointed above the fly. A snook hit the fly savagely on the second jerk, made a fast run, swirled a bit, and after a few minutes of very creditable activity was brought to the bank and released.

We took snook on nearly every cast. The ditch must have been loaded with them, because only those nearby could see the fly in the brownish water. All the fish were from five to eight pounds, and after we had caught and released a dozen or more, the abundance of fish became a bit boring.

"Well: five more casts," I thought, "and we'll go back to the car for a cold drink and some lunch."

On the second of the five something hit the fly with a jarring strike. The fish raced down the ditch so near the surface that his dorsal fin and part of his tail occasionally showed. The distance between them was impressive. He took out the line and some of the backing while I tried to pick my way along a bank studded with jack-palms to follow him; one eye on the fish and the other carefully watching for snakes.

The fish swirled far down the ditch, and then the power of the rod turned him and led him back. He swiftly passed by, going in the other direction and, when he was about 100 feet away, he swirled again. If he had been a smart snook, he could have broken the leader by snubbing it around a palm branch along the shore; but with occasional coaxing by my leaning back on the rod, he remained in the channel. Soon he was nearby, with the twelve-foot leader near the tip of the nine-and-a-half-foot glass rod. The other anglers had collected, and one of them brought him ashore. Pocket scales weighed him in at seventeen-and-three-quarter pounds. This is of course a big snook, especially when taken on a fly rod, but they come much bigger. He provided an exciting ending to a very active morning.

Other good flies for snook, especially in clear water, are the natural imitations dressed on bodies covered with braided mylar tubular cord, as mentioned previously in this chapter and as described in Chapter IX. "Blonde" patterns are occasionally effective. So are small tarpon streamers in bright colors, but these should be sparsely dressed to make them sink fast to the level where the snook are feeding.

While fast fly action is usually preferable, under some conditions it should be very slow. In the canals the fly may need to be cast under the overhang of mangrove bushes where snook like to lie, or close to the reeds which may line the shore. Big snook often want to inspect the fly carefully before taking it. They often may suck in the fly and remain still or may swim slowly toward the angler. So an angler sometimes needs to strike instinctively, because many strikes of the fish will be lost before they are felt. During the day, snook may lie on the very bottom of the canals. In order to get a strike, one must let the fly sink to the bottom and may need to retrieve it very slowly.

When conditions are suitable, snook fishing at night can be very exciting. Here again, jet black, black and white, or all-white flies usually are preferable because their more pronounced silhouettes are more visible in the dim light. Hook sizes usually vary between 1/0 and 3/0. The type of non-corrosive hook is a matter of opinion, but I am still partial to the popular O'Shaugnessy bend.

Many anglers who go trolling in the Gulf Stream for sailfish often take their fly rods along in the hope of catching a dolphin. Dolphin travel in schools, frequently remaining under the floating debris and sea weed which marks the landward edge of the Gulf Stream on relatively calm days. If a school is found and one of them can be caught, the usual practice is to tether him alive in the water, thus inducing the remainder of the school (who will not leave him) to remain nearby. The dolphin used for this decoying purpose either can be left on the hook or a light line can be made fast around his tail so that he can swim in the water off the stern of the boat.

Fly fishing for dolphin requires a sturdy rod because, while they

Southern Salt Water Streamer Fishing

average between about seven and twelve pounds, one occasionally catches them as large as thirty pounds or more. Long streamers in white, or yellow and white, tied on hooks from 2/0 to 4/0 are popular, fished with a slow strip retrieve. When a cast is made into a school the fly rarely moves more than five or ten feet before a dolphin has it. They are an exceptionally good fly rod fish, jumping profusely and making long runs. In addition to being one of the most beautiful of all salt water species they are delicious to eat. The vivid coloration of the dolphin changes rapidly to sombre tones upon being taken from the water.

The jack crevalle is a rugged fighter which, because of his bodily depth and strength, battles sideways to the angler, rather than head on. In addition to having to be "inched" up to the gaff or net, he is inclined to make sudden darts away from the angler; these darts often developing into long runs. When this situation is brought under control (or if it is!) the fish will begin to circle the boat in an ever decreasing spiral until he is brought in. Thus, a five pound jack crevalle provides considerable of a workout for the fly rod angler, while a twelve pounder would be in the record class. Jacks are inclined to "bulldog" on the end of a line and occasionally run fairly deep. Favorite flies for them are white streamers with red or red and white collars. Yellow and white streamers or bucktails also are good choices, especially in fast or rough water or at night. Grizzly and white streamers also are popular. These flies, in sizes 1/0 to 3/0, should be fished fast with distinct pauses, usually increasing the tempo as the cast becomes fished out. Fast fishing is especially important if the fish trail the fly but do not strike. When they decide to strike it is almost impossible to take the fly away from them.

The pompano is a winter-run fish in Florida, although a few will be found at most other times in sandy bottomed channels where tides move rapidly. I know of few anglers who have taken a pompano on a fly rod and a fly. The angler is Gordon Dean, who described it as follows:

"It is a bit difficult to fish for pompano with a fly rod because the lure has to be fished on the bottom and therefore must be rather heavy. Usually, the tide has a tendency to bring it to the surface, where it does no good. The usual procedure is to drift in a skiff and cast ahead of the boat. The retrieve is a series of short jerks, which make the weighted all-yellow fly skip along the bottom similarly to the familiar zig-zag retrieve sometimes used with weighted spinning lures by deep water bass fishermen.

"The pompano fights well but is tricky; somewhat reminiscent of a smallmouth bass in moving water. It is given to making sudden darts toward the bottom when close to the boat and, being of a deep-bodied, flattened shape like the jack, can be strong and rugged on a fly rod. Two pounders are average and three pounders are not uncommon.

"The cast should be made into the tide, which will help keep the lure on the bottom. When the lure appears near the surface it should be picked up and cast over again. Since the fish travel in schools and constantly move on the bottom, one must blind cast for them. It takes about three buckshot to keep an unweighted fly on the bottom when the tide is moving rapidly. Fishing for pompano is a lot of work, but it definitely is worth it. A yellow streamer tied on a 1 or 1/0 hook is about right."

I have not intended to describe these fishes in order of importance (or in any other order, for that matter), because what is of great interest to one angler may be a matter of no concern to another. There are many lesser fishes which can be taken in salt water with the streamer fly and the bucktail, and perhaps there are a few game fish valuable for the fly rod which have been ignored. Certain fishes are adaptable to this manner of angling, while others are less so, or are not adaptable at all. Fortunately, each type of light tackle fishing has its place and neither the fly rod, the spinning rod, the plug casting outfit or trolling gear is a cure-all for everything.

Homer Rhode, Jr. has sent me some comments on fly fishing for snapper and mullet which will draw me near to the close of this rather lengthy chapter. I shall never forget the day when Homer and I fished nearly the entire length of Long Key in an attempt to tie me into a big permit. This is a colorful giant of the pompano family which some time I hope very much to catch. We located four of them, but there was only one to which I could cast. When we saw him he was too close for a fair chance, but he had the upsetting affrontery to swim nearer and to bunt my lure before disdainfully swimming away! It is suspense-

Southern Salt Water Streamer Fishing

filled moments like that which add so much to the attraction of fishing. For me, its suspense and attraction vastly is increased by using a fly rod and a fly for these big fish. The fly rod adds thrills for the angler but it also gives the fish a sporting chance; much more so, certainly, than using tackle so heavy that he could not possibly get away.

Florida has many masters of the fly rod; many pioneers who love to try for new species and for bigger fish with this type of tackle. They enjoy the diverse bounties which southern angling has to offer, and they realize that while some of the larger species may be harder to land, some of the smaller ones may be harder to hook. The snapper and the mullet are in the latter category, as these comments of Homer Rhode may make clear:

"I often use a single or double spinner ahead of a fly for snapper, or occasionally a small split buckshot. I let the fly sink slowly next to mangrove roots or other cover, and start the fly slowly back at the instant the snapper start to boil around it. The timing must be perfect and it usually takes quiet a bit of practice, as they can be worse than tarpon about fooling you in taking a fly. The average man starts his fly far too fast. For this fishing I prefer a small fly, but larger ones in the same patterns can be used for the larger fish in the potholes on the flats. Here, the retrieve decidedly is faster because you must take him before he can think it over. He usually will strike violently if a good cast is made. A light wire leader is preferable for the larger of these sharp toothed fish. White polar bear hair bucktails with white hackle collars, the same in yellow with red and white collar, or a yellow, or yellow and white bucktail or streamer do well for snappers.

"The same style of fishing and of flies is appropriate around wrecks and shallow reefs. The snapper can become educated faster than most any fish I know of. I truly love to catch him and have had a hard time convincing other fly rod fishermen that he can be taken successfully and regularly under the right conditions.

"I have only seen or heard of two other fishermen who have taken mullet on light fly rods and artificial flies. The mullet in my estimation is a true *game fish*; a worthy opponent requiring considerable skill from those who fish for him. He will take tiny size 14 and 16 flies in white, light green, yellow or black. Leaders must be tapered to as fine as 2X or even 4X at times. I use the same methods that are used in northern fresh water trout fishing. The largest mullet I have taken weighed five-and-three-quarters pounds. He took out nearly 150 yards of line and jumped like a wild banshee. Sportsmen who ignore this fish really are missing something!"

I must apologize to anglers in the southern coastal states and in those bordering the Gulf for having had so much to say about Florida in this chapter. I realize that Florida does not have a monopoly on good fishing, but since it happens that nearly all of my angling in the southeastern quarter of the United States has taken place there I hope that I will be pardoned for attempting to discuss that with which I am acquainted, rather than that which I know little or nothing about. Although Florida is the location for the subject matter of this chapter, fishing elsewhere has taught that there are prefered lures and methods for each type of fish, no matter where it may be. I hope therefore that this material will be of as much value to anglers from Texas to the Carolinas as it will be to those in Florida or those who plan to go there.

Joe Brooks

IX
Notes on Types and Dressings

Since this book originally was written in 1950, several new methods of dressing streamers and bucktails have been devised which (in the opinion of many anglers) make these long flies more effective than ever. In reporting these variations, readers should be reminded that this book is not intended to be a manual on fly tying: a subject which has been treated competently by other authors, some of whom are listed in the references in the footnote below.*

In order properly to interpret dressing instructions such as are given in the second section of this book, it is necessary to understand the names of the various parts of a fly, as shown in Figure IX–1. In

---

* *Fly Dresser's Guide*, by John Veniard (London: A. & C. Black, Ltd.), $8.40.
Fly Tying, by William B. Sturgis (New York: Charles Scribner's Sons), $4.50.
Flies, by J. Edson Leonard (New York: A. S. Barnes & Co.), $5.95.
Fishing Flies and Fly Tying, by William F. Blades (Harrisburg, Penna: The Stackpole Co.), $8.50.
Fly Tying, by Helen Shaw (New York: Ronald Press Co.), $7.00.
Tie Your Own Flies, by Roy Patrick. Available from Patrick's Fly Shop, 2237 East Lake Avenue, Seattle, 2, Washington ($4.00).
Professional Fly Tying and Tackle Making, by George L. Herter (Herter's, Waseca, Minnesota), $1.50.
How to Tie Flies, by E. C. Gregg. (New York: The Ronald Press Co.), $1.95.
Trout Fishing and Trout Flies, by Jim Quick (The Countryman Press, Woodstock, Vermont), $5.00.
Pacific Northwest Fly Patterns, by Roy Patrick. Available from Patrick's Fly Shop, 2237 East Lake Avenue, Seattle, 2, Washington ($1.50).

these names there exists a partial lack of agreement which I hope will not be further confused by my own definitions, of which a few may need explanation.

The TAG usually is of metal tinsel, but may be of two or more parts, the lower of which usually is of metal and the upper normally one or more colors of silk (often called "silk floss"). In early patterns I used to think it very effective to dress the tinsel tag abnormally far down the bend of the hook. I have stopped doing this because the teeth of fish (even of trout) quickly tear it apart. The function of the tag is to add a bit of flash, but its use mainly is for decoration.

The TAIL normally curves upward, as an aid to the appearance of the fly. When a tail of a section of a wing feather is called for it should be cocked upward in the same manner as the wing of a wet fly is made to do. In streamer flies and bucktails, anything but a decorative purpose for the tail seems a little far fetched, although frequently it is used in a bright color as an attractor.

The BUTT of a streamer or bucktail also is added primarily for decoration. In flies made to imitate insects it represents the egg sac which, of course, has no anatomical place on a fly made to imitate a minnow. A very few streamers and bucktails have additional butts located forward of the tail section. Perhaps these properly should not be called butts, but they are applied in the same way, serve the same decorative purpose, and it seems confusing to refer to them by any other name.

The BODY and RIBBING seem to need no description other than the illustration in Figure IX–1 but a comment or two about them may be helpful. Bodies of peacock herl will be torn apart easily by fish unless, in dressing them, the herl is wound around the tying thread. The tips of the required number of herls of equal length are tied in and then twisted *with the thread* so that, when thread and herl are wound on, the thread binds each turn of herl and keeps it from unraveling in case one or more strands are broken in use. Bodies and ribbing add fullness and flash, simulating the belly of a baitfish.

Where a palmered hackle embellishment to the body is called for it is prepared in any one of the several ways described in fly tying manuals. If the materials permit it I like to lacquer the body thoroughly before tying in the end of the hackle and palmering (winding round

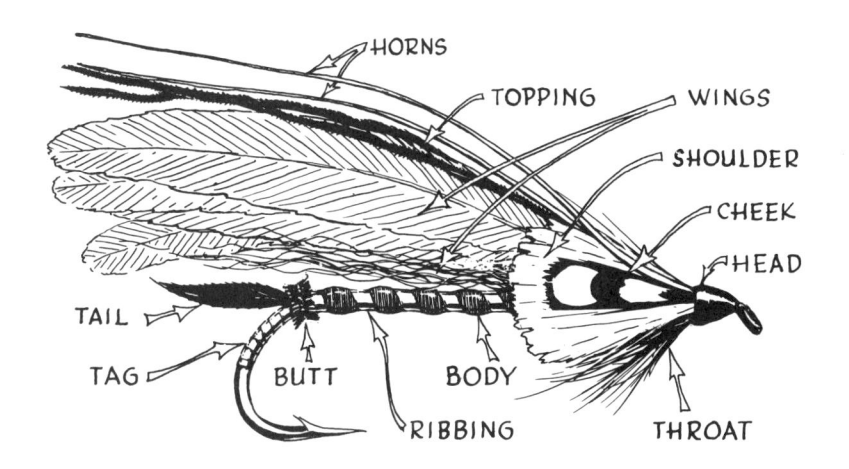

Fig. IX–1

ANATOMY OF A STREAMER FLY

and round) it toward the head. When the hackle is thus tied into wet lacquer, the rib of the hackle is cemented into the body and cannot be torn apart easily. Oval tinsel helps to protect the palmered hackle more than flat tinsel does. Usually the rib of the hackle is wound flush against the front or back side of the ribbing for added protection. I know of no case when it should be allowed to cross the ribbing. Bodies or ribbing of metal tinsel should be lacquered to build a secure fly and to prevent tarnishing. Properly lacquered tinsel will stay brilliant for years but unlacquered tinsel will corrode in a season. If the nature of the body is such that the tinsel cannot be lacquered, care should be taken to use non-corrosive tinsel.

The THROAT represents (to a greater or lesser degree) the underpart of the gills of the minnow. Where it is proper to do so I like to include a throat, whether it is called for or not, because it seems to give a more finished look to the fly, at the same time adding a fluttering action which probably is a further enticement to the fish. Throats are applied in several ways. Where a specific method of application is called for, it is included in the descriptions in Part II. Usually fairly stiff hackles or hackle fibers should be used, because they are more "alive" in action and less inclined to matt together in the water.

A throat sometimes is referred to as a SPIKE. There is a difference between the two in that the spike usually is dressed at a right angle to the hook by taking a few turns of thread under it to cock it down. Also, the spike normally is clipped off flat at the end and frequently is of hair instead of hackle. This method of dressing is used very seldom.

Although it has been said that a throat represents the underpart of the gills of a minnow, and therefore would be rather short, I have attempted to simplify dressing nomenclature by including another use for it. On many streamers and bucktails the throat (or a part of it) is of herl or hair, extending sometimes beyond the end of the hook. This, of course, is not a "throat" in its purer definition, being instead more like part of a wing tied under the hook shank rather than over it. However, the two are applied in the same place in the same way so I have taken the liberty of referring to them under a single name.

The WING, as has been said, may be of feathers, hair, or a combination of both. Where wings of a definite length are required in authentic patterns their specifications are included in the text. In this type of fly the word "wing" may be a misnomer, but it has come into common usage to indicate the part of a streamer or bucktail which represents the upper body of a baitfish, as well as (in the usual wet or dry flies) the representation of the actual wing, or wings, of an insect. The several types of wings, and how some of them are applied, will be discussed farther on in this chapter.

The SHOULDERS and the CHEEKS of a fly sometimes are defined differently in other books. In this one, the shoulders, each identical on both sides of the fly, are feathers (or occasionally other material) that cover a part or the whole of the forward section of the wing. They are normally less than half as long as the wing and frequently represent the head and gill covers of the minnow.

The CHEEKS are extremely short feathers (usually jungle cock) applied over the shoulders (if shoulders are called for) and of smaller size and length. They are applied partly for decoration and partly to imitate the eyes of the baitfish. Since jungle cock is expensive, there is a tendency to use too much of it, thereby making the cheeks so long that the feathers break off in use. In the discussion of Carrie Stevens' method of streamer construction farther on in this chapter, note that

Notes on Types and Dressings 169

she cements the jungle cock firmly to the shoulders, thereby usually preventing this difficulty.

TOPPING is anything (normally peacock herl or golden pheasant crest) applied over the top of the wing. Usually it is of the same length as the wing and sometimes (particularly in the case of peacock herl) is put on to represent the dark back of the minnow. Frequently it merely has the function of decoration. The words "topping" and "crest" often are used interchangeably. A "crest" ordinarily is of golden pheasant which, particularly in the case of Scotch and Irish salmon flies, has the functions of finishing the fly and of holding together the various elements of the wing, as made possible by the "V" shaped curve of the two edges of the feathers.

HORNS were inherited from salmon flies, where they were applied to imitate the "feelers" of insects. As such, they have no place on streamers or bucktails and are added to a very few purely for appearance. Usually they each consist of a single strand of a wide wing feather, such as macaw, curving upward, outward and backward.

The HEAD of the fly serves to bind all elements together and is made as small as secure construction permits.

Some of these definitions, I realize, are controversial. Where there hitherto has been no concrete accord it has seemed logical to definitely establish one meaning or another for clarity of description, insofar as this book is concerned.

A few words of comment may not be amiss on the hooks to be used in the dressings in Part II. I have avoided specifying types, lengths, sizes and strengths, because of their great variety and because it is rare that a certain kind should be used to the exclusion of all the others. There are a few patterns which would not be absolutely correct unless a certain hook was used. In these cases the hook has been specified. In other cases the matter has been left to the discretion of the fly dresser, who should use what seems most desirable or whatever is available.

Ordinarily, streamers and bucktails should be dressed on either Limerick or Sproat hooks with turned down eyes (preferably turned down *looped* eyes) in regular strength, 3X long. Ringed eyes (which turn neither up nor down) should be used only for flies which will be attached to snaps, rings or spinners.* In fresh water angling there is little choice between the Limerick and Sproat bends. The Sproat is bent into a rounder curve than the Limerick. My preference is for the Limerick, partly because the straight stem and the narrow bend prevent the hook from sawing about and pulling loose, but largely because it seems to be superior for penetration and strength.

Unless otherwise noted, it is recommended that all fresh water bucktails and streamers be dressed on 3X long hooks. In some cases, "extra long" hooks are specified. These should be 4X long or 5X long. Where more specific hook data is called for, the information has been included in the dressing instructions. Unless there are reasons to the contrary, I am opposed to abnormally long hooks because their extra length gives fish more leverage with which to work them loose.

As shown in Figure IX-2, the lengths of hooks are based on the "regular" or normal length, which is in proportion to the size of the hook. A hook "2X long," for example, is a hook which is as long as a regular hook two sizes larger. A hook "4X long" is as long as a regular hook four sizes larger. A hook "2X short" is as long as a regular hook two sizes smaller, and so forth.

A similar situation holds true for strengths. Each larger size of hook is made on a proportionately larger diameter of wire. A hook which is "2X strong" or "2X stout" is made on the strength of wire normally reserved for a hook two sizes larger. A hook "1X light" or "1X fine" is made on the strength of wire normal for a hook one size smaller.

Both Limerick and Sproat type hooks have straight bends; that is, they lie flat with the point bending neither to the right nor to the

* One of the exceptions is Keith Fulsher's series of "Thunder Creek" patterns discussed in this chapter.

Fig. IX-2 (*Facing page*)

CHART OF HOOK SIZES, LENGTHS AND STRENGTHS. The Mustad-Limerick hooks shown at top of page are in regular lengths. Differences in lengths of a size 6 Mustad-Viking hook appear in column at right. Lengths of other hooks are similar. Size 4 Limerick and Sproat hooks with regular and with extra long shanks are shown at left. The drawings are full size to serve as a guide for identifying actual hooks.

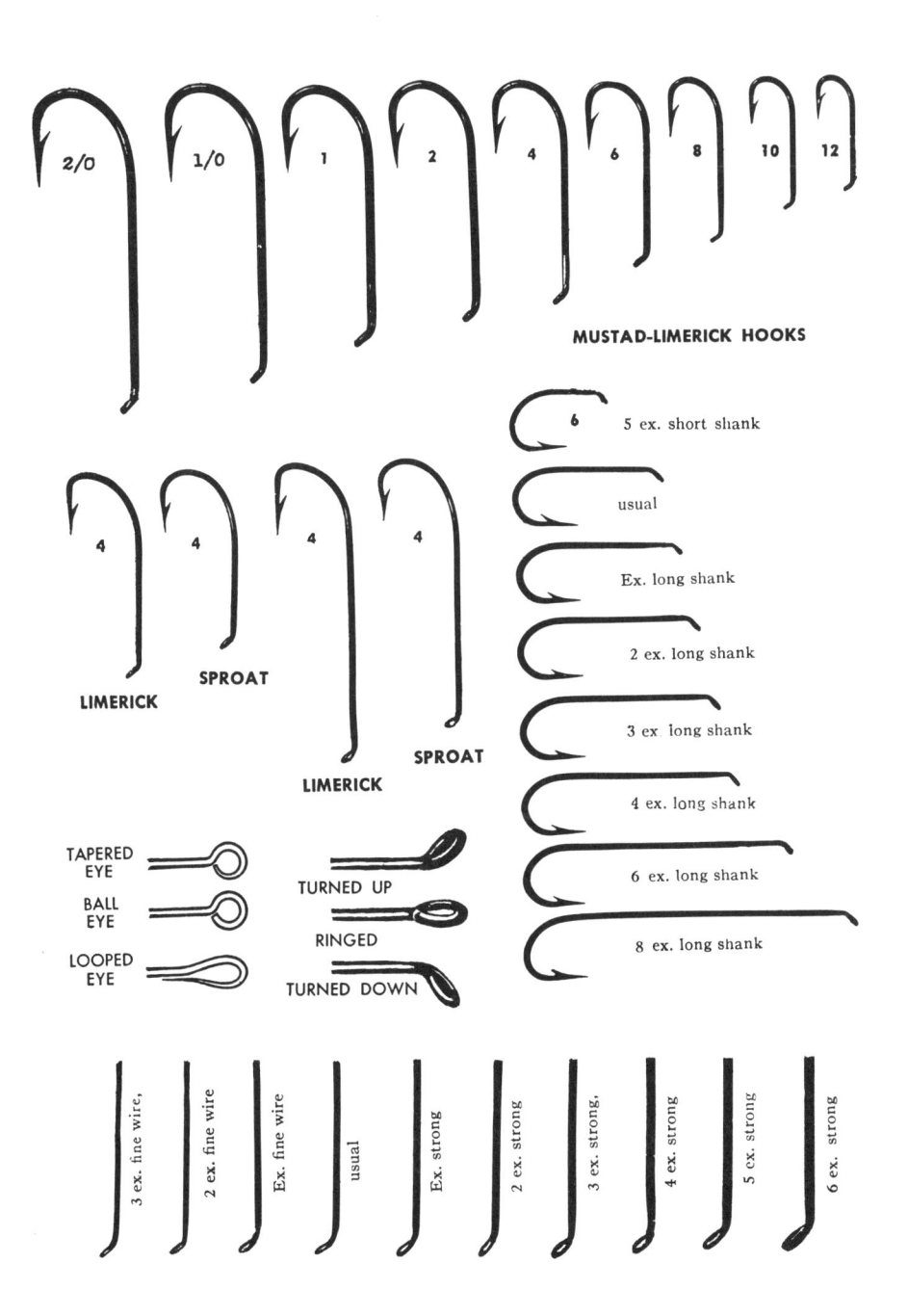

MUSTAD-LIMERICK HOOKS

2/0 1/0 1 2 4 6 8 10 12

LIMERICK SPROAT LIMERICK SPROAT

5 ex. short shank
usual
Ex. long shank
2 ex. long shank
3 ex. long shank
4 ex. long shank
6 ex. long shank
8 ex. long shank

TAPERED EYE
BALL EYE
LOOPED EYE

TURNED UP
RINGED
TURNED DOWN

3 ex. fine wire, 2 ex. fine wire, Ex. fine wire, usual, Ex. strong, 2 ex. strong, 3 ex. strong, 4 ex. strong, 5 ex. strong, 6 ex. strong

left. A straight bend hook is preferable for bucktails or streamers because it rides on a level keel in the water and has less tendency to twist or to spin than offset bend hooks do. Hooks lighter than regular are used on flies where buoyancy is desired without exceptional strength. Hooks stronger than regular are used for their qualities of quicker sinking, or where abnormally strong fish, such as steelhead, are encountered which might straighten a lighter weight hook, particularly in the fast water where they frequently are found.

The dresser of streamer flies and bucktails can adopt considerable latitude of choice in the methods of applying wings. Several eminent originators have distinctive methods which should be followed carefully if authenticity of workmanship is desired. In ordinary patterns, wings may be applied in many ways, each of which alters the appearance and changes the action of the fly.

The majority of the prominent professional dressers who specialize in streamer flies prefer to select wings from saddle hackles rather than from neck hackles, because saddle hackles are slimmer, more translucent, and more supple. These qualities give the fly a more streamlined, minnow-like appearance and a more pronounced fluttering or undulating action in the water.

Where economy is not the primary object it seems better to select hackles from a complete saddle (the tanned skin of the back of the bird with all feathers attached) than from loose feathers or strung bunches. It will be observed that the feathers on the two sides of the saddle curve slightly in opposite directions. When two feathers are selected from one side and two more from a similar position on the other, the two pairs can be joined with their backs facing outwardly so that they have a uniform and pleasing downward curve. Feathers thus chosen match each other in size, shape, texture and color pattern and thus result in an attractively designed fly. Feathers taken from plucked bunches are difficult to match in this way, and usually produce a fly with a wing improperly curved and bent, with the tips of the feathers presenting a random appearance rather than giving a more pleasing united effect. This is important in assembling a high quality streamer, but it should be of no concern in making some of the cruder bass and salt water patterns where a floppy, random wing is to be sought rather than to be avoided.

Notes on Types and Dressings

In applying feathers where a uniform, compact wing is desired an expert fly dresser showed me a trick which aids greatly in attaining this result, but which does not seem to be generally known. The feathers are matched together in the desired position and are cut to a uniform length, after which the ribs are stripped of herl to a distance of about a quarter of an inch from the ends. The matched feathers then are held tightly together near their butt ends by the thumb and forefinger of the left hand, so that the stripped ribs lie closely together, side by side, without overlapping. In this position they can be scored by pressing the thumb nail of the right hand against the tops of the ribs at the spot where the herl of the feathers begins. The pressure of the thumb nail against the forefinger will evenly score the bases of the ribs, bending them at a slight angle. Then, without disturbing the position of the feathers, they can be laid onto the hook and tied down with the bent portions of the ends acting as a base. The thread should not be tied over the apex of the angle thus made, but it should be tied closely to it, the ends having been cut off previously so that they are exactly of the right length for secure tying in.

This is easy and quick to accomplish. If done correctly the bases of the feathers will be tightly united without separation, and the wing will curve slightly upward at the desired angle. After three or four tight turns have been taken with the thread, the left hand can be removed to see that the feathers are applied correctly. If not, the job should be done over again. If the feathers lie correctly, it is well to add a drop of lacquer to the ends before additional winding, in order to cement them firmly in place. A very small amount of practice should accomplish the desired result speedily, without failures. This method is one I have used for many years. I have found it of great assistance in properly applying hackle wings.

In tying the *Gray Ghost*, the *Colonel Bates*, and other patterns originated by Mrs. Carrie G. Stevens, the above method of cocking and securing the wing should not be used. Her method (never publicly disclosed until now) is quite different. Carrie does not dress flies any more. In years gone by she sat by the hour at her table in her cabin at famed Upper Dam Pool (where Maine's Mooselookmeguntic Lake flows into Richardson Lake, and where these famous flies were originated) dressing her flies amid a clutter of hair and feathers on the floor while favored anglers sat nearby discussing fishing with her husband, Wallace (who was a popular guide there). But in all these sessions and despite surreptitious glances, we didn't learn her secrets until chance brought them to me much later. Carrie prided herself on being self-taught, which explains her unusual methods; methods so painstaking that only dedicated amateurs should bother with them. But dedicated amateurs will use them to dress very sturdy and surpassingly beautiful flies. They also will find that she had several little tricks which make considerable sense.

Since the flies used in the clockwise rotating current of Upper Dam Pool were fished more by the current than by the angler, and since others usually were dragged with fly rods behind boats in the Rangeley Lakes, Carrie specialized in trolling flies tied on long (5X and 6X) hooks as well as tandem hooked trolling streamers. Her streamers had little action, and thus had to be fished. Here are her secrets, using the *Gray Ghost* as an example:

She dressed each fly by combining three separately assembled sections, making up dozens of each section at one time. Both sides of the wing were made separately, as well as the bodies. To assemble either of the two sides of the wing, she would first prepare the shoulder of a Ripon's silver pheasant (narrow banded) body feather and would firmly cement it to the jungle cock cheek by coating the entire underside of the jungle cock with cement. Then she would prepare and lay on the two olive-gray saddle hackles, cementing all four together where they would be tied in. Many assembled and firmly cemented right and left sides would be made at one time by this means. Because of the cementing, the jungle cock rarely pulled out of place or became detached in use.

The dressing of the body was also unique. The tying thread was made tacky by wax, an extra piece of which was always stored in a convenient place where it would be kept warm by bodily contact. She wound the underbody on the hook with white thread, because other colors would affect the color of the silk overbody when wet. The overbody (of the *Gray Ghost*) was yellow orange silk, rather than red orange, and she stopped dressing the overbody four-fifths of the way to the head of the fly, leaving one-fifth dressed only by the white

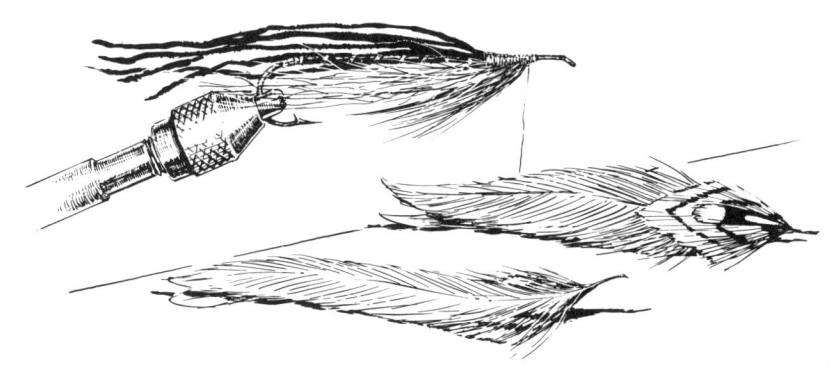

Fig. IX-3
STEVENS' METHOD

tying thread. She applied the narrow flat silver tinsel ribbing sparsely to allow three-fourths of the silk overbody to show.

Now the throat was tied in. A small bunch of white bucktail extending beyond the barb of the hook was tied in under the rearward part of the white underbody. This surrounded the white underbody and was applied here so it would point backward, rather than backward and downward. Immediately ahead of this a small bunch of white hackle (all of approximately the same length) was tied in, in the same manner, to hold the bucktail up and to extend the whiteness of the throat forward.

Next, from four to six strands of peacock herl as long as the wing were tied (usually) on top of the forward part of the white underbody to lie on straight and curve downward. These were cemented firmly in place where they were tied in. Then, over this, one heavy golden pheasant crest feather was tied in as a topping, so that it would be as long as the wing and would arch upward over the back of the body to meet the end of the wing. The white thread at this point was tied off and black thread was substituted for it. Using the black thread, a small golden pheasant crest feather was tied over the white hackle throat so that it extended backward half the length of the hook shank, curving upward. This completed the body.

Identical but opposite right and left wing assemblies once and a half as long as the hook were then selected from the two piles she already had made, and these two sides were laid on one at a time so

Carrie Stevens at her camp at Upper Dam, Maine, circa 1950. *(Photographs by the author)*

Notes on Types and Dressings

the shoulders covered the forward underbody windings and so that the upper sides met and combined at the top but allowed the throat to show. These assemblies were tied in usually more on the sides of the body than on top to achieve this effect. (The ribs of the feather assemblies were not scored, as mentioned for other flies in preceding notes.)

Carrie always dressed her flies with a two-color head, which she used as a trade-mark or signature. To do this, she covered all of the quill with black thread and, in winding backward, tied in a piece of orange thread. She finished the head with black thread, then whip-finishing three or four turns of the orange thread in the middle of the head to make a three-section head of black, orange, and black. A light coat of lacquer then was applied to the head, but not enough to conceal the orange collar. Finally, she adjusted the dressings as necessary, especially pulling up the golden pheasant topping just enough for it to show.

It seems proper to go into this detail to explain Carrie's method, because so many fly dressers and anglers have wondered about it. Her way took time, but it resulted in sturdy and beautiful flies for which she became nationally famous.

Carrie Stevens originated many streamers, including the *Allie's Favorite, Blue Devil, Colonel Bates, Don's Delight, General MacArthur, Golden Witch, Gray Ghost, Greyhound, Green Beauty, Morning Glory, Shang's Favorite, Shang's Special, White Devil, Wizard,* and *Yellow and Black,* plus several bucktail patterns. Of these, the *Gray Ghost* and the *Colonel Bates* have become especially prominent. I always considered the latter primarily as a courteous nod to me and rarely used it until this negative opinion frequently was disputed by anglers who found the fly unusually productive when a brightly colored pattern seemed appropriate. In recent years it has become a recognized favorite.

Mrs. Stevens occasionally dressed salt water flies by a novel method which seems to lack a name (as does the fly I shall describe), but which may be of interest to mention. We may as well call it a "Reverse-tied Bucktail," as shown in Figure IX–4. Beginning near the rear of the hook she wound the body evenly and compactly with red thread, which then was lacquered. At a point slightly behind where the wing

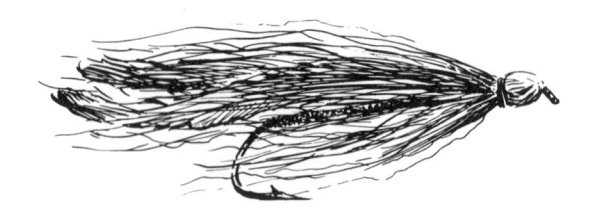

Fig. IX-4

MRS. CARRIE G. STEVENS' "REVERSE-TIED BUCKTAIL"

usually is tied in, she fastened two light blue saddle hackles. Just forward of this she tied in a bunch of white bucktail with the tips pointing *forward*. The bucktail was pulled uniformly around the hook and the ends were trimmed off as near as possible to where they were tied in. The winding was carried forward to just behind the eye and then was brought back at least three-sixteenths of an inch, where two half hitches were made.

The base then was lacquered. At this point the bucktail was gathered backward tightly and evenly, so that it concealed all of the winding done previously. The thread was brought through at a convenient place and the bucktail was lashed down by two of three turns of thread secured by a two or three turn whip finish. These turns of thread thus gave the effect of a band. The thread and the bucktail forward of it were saturated with varnish. The bucktail should be nearly as long as the feathers and should be thick enough to nearly conceal the shank of the hook, without overdressing the fly.

Mrs. Stevens believed that this *Reverse-tied Bucktail* made a stronger fly. She tied many of them in whatever colors seemed to suit her customers.

Early in the 1960's a banker from Eastchester, New York, named Keith C. Fulsher carried Carrie Stevens' idea to a most important conclusion by painstakingly developing and testing the "Thunder Creek Series" of exact baitfish imitations, some of which are shown on the color plate facing page 48. These indicate a continuing trend in streamer and bucktail design away from the earlier large, often overly dressed, gaudy flies toward smaller, more streamlined creations—a trend noticeable elsewhere in the development of the tiny

Notes on Types and Dressings

and sparsely dressed streamers and bucktails so successful in heavily fished waters where game fish are usually relatively small.

Keith's series of four primary patterns and three secondary patterns are so unusual and enjoy such an impressive record in taking game fish in so many regions that they deserve special attention as a notable contribution to American angling. The difference in them over the more conventional patterns is caused by the way the bucktail dressing is attached to the hook, which in turn leads to the shaping of the head and body. Color and proportion are important, providing a minnow imitation both rugged and lifelike, with a head in proper proportion to the body and with an eye placed in correct position on the head. The few turns of red thread at the neck provide the little flash of red so often seen in a live minnow as its gill covers open and close. Placing the bucktail completely around the hook adds an important third dimension, at the same time largely concealing the hook.

Tying the bucktails in the "Thunder Creek Series" is relatively simple. Since Keith's favorite is the *Silver Shiner*, let's use it as an example. Hook sizes Nos. 8 and 10, 6X long, are preferred, using ringed-eye hooks to act as an extension of the head. With red tying thread, dress the hook shank with flat silver tinsel. A small bunch of brown bucktail is tied to the top of the hook so that the tip ends extend *forward* of the hook eye. (In tying on the hair, slightly more room than normal is left for the head area; and the length of the hair should be such that when the tip ends are folded back toward the hook bend, they will extend slightly beyond the bend.) When applying the hair, allow it to rotate to cover the top 180 degrees of the hook shank, and trim the butt ends at the base of the head area. In binding the bucktail down, wrap the tying thread over the hair right up to the eye of the hook; then return the thread to the base of the head and cement the wrappings.

To dress the underside, turn the hook over in the vise and, using a small bunch of white bucktail, perform the same operation as with the brown hair, allowing the white to cover the bottom 180 degrees of the hook shank. Use bucktail sparingly because sparseness is most important.

The next step is to return the hook to its upright position and completely reverse all of the bucktail by folding it back tightly along the hook shank, so that in this reversed position it is firmly against the underwrappings of tying thread in the head area. In doing this, use care to keep the two colors of hair separate, and be sure that they completely surround the hook.

Now bring the tying thread through the hair at the base of the head and wind several turns, ending with a whip finish. This completes the fly except that several applications of clear lacquer should be applied to the head, followed by painting a yellow eye with black dot on each side of the center of the head.

When a lateral stripe is needed (as in the *Black Nosed Dace*), tie on a few black bucktail hairs conventionally on each side after the hook shank has been dressed. The *Black Nosed Dace* can be improved further by applying a narrow line of black lacquer along both sides of the head from the hook eye to the base of the head, following the dividing line of the brown and white hair. This is done prior to applying the eye, which is then centered on this line. (These black head markings blend in with the black hair previously put on and create an imitation with the exact markings found on the actual minnow.)

With the above method, one's imagination is the only limitation in developing new patterns. In fishing, the fly should be kept constantly in darting motion to provide minnow-like appearance and action in the water. The flies are most effective when thoroughly soaked, because the bucktail tends to streamline better and assume the minnow shape it is made to represent.

On page 181 are dressing instructions for Keith Fulsher's "Thunder Creek Series": (Three patterns are illustrated in Plate I.)

What the "Thunder Creek" patterns did to improve natural imitations in the bucktail is comparable to what Lew Oatman accomplished in improving natural imitations in streamer flies. Lew was not only a superb angler and professional fly dresser but also an early pioneer in developing feathered imitations of the forage fish common to the area where he lived (in Shushan, New York).

From his correspondence with Keith Fulsher and with the author, evidently he developed seventeen patterns which have become standard. Because of Lew's angling prominence, the beauty of his flies, and

PRIMARY PATTERNS

Name	Hook Shank Covering	Lateral Stripe	Back*	Stomach*	Eye
Black Nosed Dace	Silver Tinsel	Black Bucktail	Brown Bucktail	White Bucktail	Yellow Lacquer with Black Lacquer Pupil
Golden Shiner	Yellow Tinsel	Yellow Bucktail	Brown Bucktail	White Bucktail	Yellow Lacquer with Black Lacquer Pupil
**Red Fin Shiner	Deep Pink Flourescent Floss	None	Brown Bucktail	White Bucktail	Yellow Lacquer with Black Lacquer Pupil
**Silver Shiner	Silver Tinsel	None	Brown Bucktail	White Bucktail	Yellow Lacquer with Black Lacquer Pupil

SECONDARY PATTERNS

Name	Hook Shank Covering	Lateral Stripe	Back*	Stomach*	Eye
Emerald Minnow	Green Tinsel	None	Brown Bucktail	White Bucktail	Yellow Lacquer with Black Lacquer Pupil
Satin-Fin Minnow	Blue Flourescent Floss	None	Brown Part of Blue Bucktail	Pale Yellow Bucktail	Yellow Lacquer with Black Lacquer Pupil
Spot-Tailed Minnow	Gold Tinsel	None	Brown Part of Green Bucktail	White Bucktail	Yellow Lacquer with Black Lacquer Pupil

SENTIMENTAL PATTERN

Name	Hook Shank Covering	Lateral Stripe	Back*	Stomach*	Eye
Mickey Finn	Silver Tinsel	Red Bucktail	Yellow Bucktail	Yellow Bucktail	Yellow Lacquer with Black Lacquer Pupil

* This material also forms the head.

** The Silver Shiner imitation duplicates the female and immature fish of the silver or common shiner species, while the Red Fin Shiner imitation duplicates the mature male fish of the common shiner species.

THE "THUNDER CREEK" PATTERNS

the sound reasoning behind them, they are worthy of record, and are: *Battenkill Shiner, Brook Trout, Cut Lips, Doctor Oatman, Ghost Shiner, Golden Darter, Golden Shiner, Golden Smelt, Gray Smelt, Mad Tom, Male Dace, Red Fin, Red Horse, Shushan Postmaster, Silver Darter, Trout Perch,* and *Yellow Perch,* as described in Part II and as illustrated in Color Plate VI.

Both Lew Oatman's flies and his angling methods were based on his conception of sound reasoning. His skill and experience were such that a few of his notes in letters he wrote to the author (just before his death in 1958) should be of interest:

"The basic purpose of a bucktail or a streamer fly is to resemble a small forage fish. With plenty of opportunity to study the actual feeding habits of game fish, I concluded that this type of fly would be most effective, day in and day out, all season through, and under practically all conditions. Since I was familiar with the species of small fish the big ones seemed to like, and that were more or less common, I looked for patterns to imitate them. Aside from patterns designed in Maine to imitate the smelt, my search was unproductive.

"It is possible to design a fly of almost any combination of materials and colors that may take fish, but imaginative patterns lack the ingredient of sound reason. Mother Nature offers us patterns in the forage fish she created that are not only graceful and beautiful in color and design but are also easily recognized as real tasty bits by our game fish.

"Among the forage fish are found some species with the subdued coloring that is effective for wary trout in the clearest waters, and others that serve better as attractors when that type may be needed. So a fly tyer should be satisfied if he can imitate nature's patterns to a reasonable degree without attempting to surpass her creative ability.

"Working along this line, the resulting patterns have turned out to be very effective. Once the technique of handling this type of fly is learned, and confidence gained in its use, an angler can take his share of fish all season long with selections from this group. There are several species of forage fish more or less similar in coloring, including the long nosed dace, and some of the suckers, chubs, and shiners. These generally have light bellies and lower sides, with darker backs. They are imitated fairly well either by the *Ghost Shiner* pattern or the

Notes on Types and Dressings

old brown and white or black and white bucktail, depending on the shade of back wanted. Thus, there isn't much point in attempting to imitate each of these species individually. Being a practical fisherman, I have tried to boil down the number of patterns as much as possible.

"In fishing streamers and bucktails, the type of water also should be considered. When it is of medium depth with deep pockets, or when it is turbulent, fairly large flies can be used. Violent action should be given to them; even slapping them down to attract attention.

"When waters are quieter or shallower, a sparser, more subdued, more natural fly is likely to be more effective, and the action given to it should be gentler. In deep, quiet pools and in lakes or ponds it often is necessary to let the fly sink very deep and to retrieve it slowly, by inches.

"Some of my patterns such as the *Silver Darter*, *Golden Darter*, *Gray Smelt*, and *Ghost Shiner*, when tied in small sizes, often will take rising trout when they won't take a dry fly. Of course many anglers won't use streamers or bucktails in low, clear water, but I find them effective. It is important to cover the water thoroughly, because under such conditions trout scatter and lie in unexpected places. In summer fishing over sophisticated trout a very slight rod or line action imparts considerable motion to the fly. But keep it working in the water, rather than in the air!"

Following in the footsteps of the revered Lew Oatman, a knowledgeable angler from Lancaster, Pennsylvania, named Sam Slaymaker, II, adopted a different but equally sensible approach to the development of exact imitations. Knowing that trout in streams where they spawn have no compunction against devouring their own young, Sam developed three bucktails to imitate their young: the *Little Brown Trout*, *Little Rainbow Trout*, and *Little Brook Trout*. He says:

"My first step was to have two small hatchery fish—a brook and a brown—cast into clear plastic prisms. By manipulating these, the fish's colors could be viewed separately. This made it easier to find materials which would come closest to duplicating each color. The brown's hues appeared less varied than those of the brook, so I started by tying a bucktail to look like a young brown trout. From back to belly the colors had to be dark brown, blending into a lighter brown and finally into a creamlike white. Since the fish's speckles appeared yellow and orange red, these colors had to be lightly mixed with the browns.

"My coloration was achieved by using dark squirrel tail on top, receding into a lighter shade of it mixed sparingly with strands of yellow and reddish orange dyed bucktail. The body was white spun wool wrapped with thin copper wire ribbing which served to promote the quality of iridescence common to fish under water. The cheeks were jungle cock, and the tail came from a breast feather of a ring-necked pheasant."

The *Little Brown Trout* became so successful for taking big brown trout that Sam developed the other two trout patterns. All three did so well that they have been featured in several national magazines and are being manufactured and sold by the Weber Tackle Company, of Stevens Point, Wisconsin, in "streamerette" as well as in larger sizes.

Since one of the best baits for brook trout is the pectoral fin of a brook trout, it naturally followed that a fly would be developed to imitate it. This was done, evidently entirely independently, by Robert H. Cavanagh, Jr., of Woburn, Massachusetts, and by the Gulline Brothers, Montreal, Canada. Since the two versions are almost identical, only one is shown in the color plates of this book. The *Trout Fin* is so successful as a natural imitative pattern that it deserves mention here. Its description is included in Part II.

Fly dressers who wish to be creative find beautiful effects can be obtained by paying extra attention to color blending in dressing streamers. The top expert in this field is my old friend Austin S. Hogan, a scholarly artist and angler from Cambridge, Massachusetts, who is one of the best fly dressers I know. Some of his fly bodies are of spun fur, or dubbing, which he carefully dyes and mixes to obtain the color tones desired to imitate whatever baitfish he has in mind. The wings of his flies often are composed of different colored pairs of neck hackles chosen and laid on for the color effect they will have when viewed together. Mixed colors of hair often enhance the final result. One of his cleverest tricks is to split saddle hackles either by removing all of the top or all of the bottom fibers from the quills, usually of the outside pair. For example, to imitate a banded silver minnow, he uses a wing of white saddle hackles outside of which, on each side,

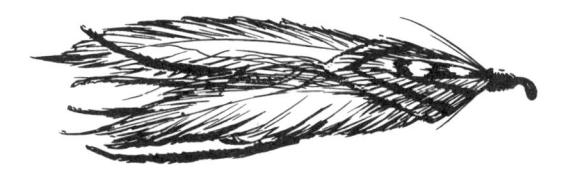

FIG. IX-5

CHIEF NEEDAHBEH'S "BIPLANE" STREAMER
(Viewed from top)

is a badger or cochy-bondhu hackle with the bottom herl stripped off to provide a darker upper half and a very dark medial line, with the white of the inside feathers showing below. Examples of two of his color-blended flies are shown in the color plates.

Very few "flat-wing" streamers have been developed, but the idea is such an intriguing one that this may be due to lack of experimentation. (The *Cowee Special* streamer is a good example, and is described in Part II.) In streamers of the "flat-wing" type the wing is tied in at right angles with the bend of the hook. To gain proper action the feather (or feathers) must be symmetrical and straight, and they must be tied in at almost a perfect right angle with the ribs exactly in line with the hook. Advocates of this type of fly feel that it gives a fluttering, open-and-shutting action very intriguing to fish. It also provides more of a three dimensional appearance that may be more noticeable when viewed from underneath.

A combination of the orthodox and the "flat-wing" types is found in the *Nine-Three* streamer, where one set of feathers is laid on flat and another set is laid on upright over them. The *Nine-Three* streamer (see Part II) is so popular in Maine that the variation in type must have something to recommend it.

My old friend, Chief Needahbeh, of Maine's Penobscot tribe, swears by a very unusual type which he calls a "Biplane" streamer (Figure IX-5). This is both a "flat-wing" and a "splayed-wing" creation for which the Chief says the big trout and landlocked salmon of Maine's Moosehead Lake have a distinct passion. He dresses the body in the orthodox manner and adds a bit of bucktail and/or peacock herl which is splayed at an angle of about 15 degrees on both sides of the hook. He adds two neck hackles applied flat and splayed in the same manner, and frequently adds a fairly large "shoulder" to both top and bottom of the fly. (To splay a hair or feather wing the thread is wound in a figure eight between each half of the divided wing and the hook.)

Needahbeh sometimes wants these flies to float. He says: "On choppy waters I wanted a streamer that would ride the surface and hop from one wave to another. After casting it out I let it float a minute or so and then retrieve it with various jumpy motions. A dip into a fly floating preparation makes the fly stay on the surface for a longer period of time. It acts like a surf board and it certainly takes fish too!"

Needahbeh was an angler who developed his own ideas for catching Maine's big trout and landlocked salmon—and he was a complete master of the sport. He loved to fish along the big lake when it was too rough for other boats to venture out. "That's when we catch the big old whoppers!" he would say—and we proved it many times. He showed me the trick of "chumming" with broken fresh water clam shells or white pebbles tossed, a few at a time, in the boat's wake while trolling. They seemed to attract salmon, and he was sure of it. Sometimes he used broken sugar wafers with equally good results. He believed that odors would attract or repel fish, and thus never handled terminal tackle with gasoline, motor oil, or other "bad" odors on his hands. Sometimes he dipped his bucktails and streamers in the oil remaining in a sardine can, and considered this very good medicine indeed.

Splayed wing streamers and bucktails have long since passed from the experimental class. They are frequently used in fresh water fishing and are common and popular for salt water use, as is illustrated by the *Gordon Dean* and *Joe Brooks* flies in Figures VIII-1 and 3. Their active, fluttering action is especially valuable where there is little or no current to aid the angler in working the fly. The first fisherman to my knowledge who ever used splayed-wing flies was Theodore Gordon, who incorporated the idea in some of his famous *Bumblepuppies* which, as discussed in Chapter II, he mentions in 1903 as having used "some years ago."

A variation of the splayed wing type is found in bucktails with

Fig. IX-6

ARTHUR C. MILLS, JR.'S "LIFE ACTION" BUCKTAIL

orthodox wings but with splayed shoulders or cheeks, such as the "Life Action" bucktail (Figure IX-6) originated by Mr. Arthur C. Mills, Jr., of the historic New York City tackle shop of William Mills and Son, in 1932 or 1933. In this fly, each of the two shoulders are made up of two or three breast feathers superimposed and curving outward to give more lifelike gill action to the fly.

Both splayed and flat-wing methods of dressing are used with marabou streamers, as well as the usual concave placement of the feathers, to enhance the action of the marabou wings in the water (see *Silver Garland Marabou* and *Ballou Special* marabou streamers in Part II).

A popular type of streamer in Australia, New Zealand, England and certain other countries, and one for which I should think we would find greater use here, is the "Matuku." Major Theodore Brun, of Melbourne, gave me a sample of it when I was in that city during the war and in 1964 Mr. Hector Sodersten, of New Zealand, sent me a complete set. The wings (usually four hackles) of Matuku streamers are laced to the body after being tied in. This evidently is done with a separate thread, tied in with the tinsel, or can be done with the tinsel itself. The thread (if used) follows the tinsel and is tied over the upright feathers whose fibers are separated in the correct places to allow the thread or tinsel to pass between them. This makes a very secure wing which cannot become twisted under the bend of the hook. Both hook and wing are of conventional streamer fly lengths. Since the Matuku is a type rather than a pattern, this principle of tying down the wing can be used in wide variety.

Nearly all methods for applying body dressings are explained in

FIG. IX-7

THE MATUKU TYPE STREAMER

fly tying manuals so it should not be necessary to repeat them here. An exception is the Garland body developed by Mr. E. H. Rosborough, of Chiloquin, Oregon, who is one of the leading professional fly tiers in the Northwest. His *Silver Garland Marabou* (see Part II), in its many color combinations, is a famous fly for big fish in both fresh and salt water, from coast to coast. The distinctiveness of the fly is in the body, which is made of Christmas tree tinsel whose many filaments reflect light very much as do the scales of a fish. The body is rather difficult to apply unless one knows how. For instructions on how to do it Mr. Rosborough referred me to a short article written by Mr. A. J. McClane, Fishing Editor of *Field and Stream* magazine, which is as follows:

"In regard to wrapping the Garland body, tie in at least one-fourth inch of the body material with heavy nylon working thread and have a good thread base under it, well lacquered and dried. Otherwise the body material will skid around the shank of the hook. It is best to use a core of long fibered Scotch wool, well saturated with lacquer, under the tinsel. The wire core of the tinsel sinks into the wool somewhat, eliminating any possibility of skidding later. Fold it back as you go and you will end up with the body better tapered than if you shear it afterward.

"If you desire to make a quantity of these bodies, mix a thinned pint of clear Duco lacquer and immerse all of the bodies in it for ten minutes. Drain off the excess on heavy waxed paper and then hang them in an open oven on wire bars. Two slow burners are sufficient to dry them but be sure that the door is partly open. After thorough drying, bend all filaments to the rear and you have a tarnish and

Notes on Types and Dressings

rust-proof body for fresh or salt water use. Don't leave the Garland body exposed to the light until after lacquering as sunlight will tarnish it badly."

Another important method of dressing bodies has been developed for weighted flies by Mr. Peter J. Schwab, of Yreka, California, who uses them in his famous *Queen Bess, Princess, Brass Hat, Van Luven, Bellamy, Wood Pussy,* and *Paint Brush* bucktails, as described in Part II. The wire bodies of these flies provide an ideal amount of weight to sink them in fast rivers, yet not such an excess of it that would make them logy in action or difficult to cast. He described the method in the July 1946 issue of *Sports Afield* magazine which I have been permitted to quote.

"The importance of using the correct hook cannot be overemphasized. Hook and wing lengths must be correctly proportioned. The standard light wire hooks which answer so well for bass and minor trout have no place on a steelhead river, where they must be very strong. The Limerick bend, in the lengths and weights specified below, has the fewest faults, but even here I should like to see the depth of penetration increased on all sizes smaller than the number 2.

"For the two-winged bucktails I use the following: size 1/0 Limerick, standard wire; size 2 Limerick, 2X strong; size 4 Limerick, 3X strong and, rarely, size 6 Limerick, 3X long and 3X strong. For three-winged bucktails (and often for two-winged) I use 1/0 Limerick, standard wire and shank; size 2 Limerick, 3X long and 2X strong; size 4 Limerick, 3X long and 3X strong. Ball-eyed hooks are better for bucktails and streamers than tapered eye hooks because they are heavier, stronger and larger, sinking better and allowing better knotting to the leaders. Get them 'TDE' (turned down eye) of course.

"In the all-wire bodied flies, the bodies are made of copper, brass, silver or gold wires, in diameters to match size of hook; i.e., ·018 inch wire for size 6 hooks, ·023 inch wire for size 4 hooks, and ·028 inch wire for sizes 2 and 1/0 hooks. All wires must be soft. Where the pattern calls for tinsel, wool or floss (silk) covered bodies over wire cores, use the next size smaller wire. Otherwise the fly will be too fat to be pleasing and too heavy for nice casting.

"Prepare the hook with a tightly spaced winding of size A sewing

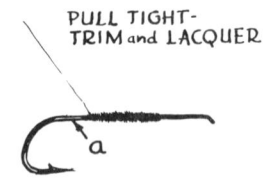

1. Preparing the hook

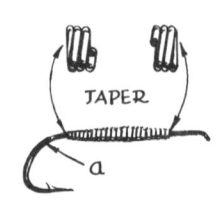

2. Applying wire body and tapering ends

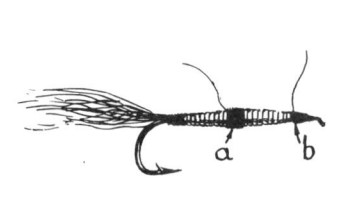

3. Making silk winding for rear wing of 3-wing fly

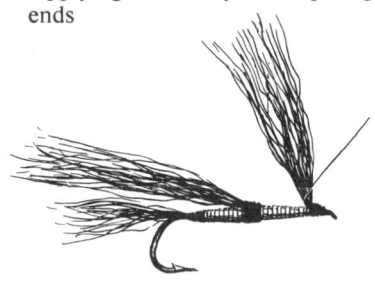

4. Method of raising wing on 2-wing and 3-wing flies

5. Completed 3-wing (Note the "spike" type throat)

6. Completed 2-wing fly (Both are the "Brass Hat" pattern)

FIG. IX-8

METHOD OF DRESSING PETER J. SCHWAB'S
WIRE BODIED BUCKTAILS

silk as shown in drawing 1 in Figure IX-8. (The 00 and smaller sizes of tying silks are too small.) Finish with whip fastening. Lacquer and dry for at least half an hour while you prepare additional hooks. This preparation is necessary to prevent slippage of the wire body.

Notes on Types and Dressings

"Grasp end of wire with small pliers or fingers of left hand, bend over hook at 'a' (drawing 1), and pull tightly with right hand which is holding spool of wire. Wind forward in close, tight coils, starting on the bare hook, three-sixteenths inch above the bend and going forward over the lacquered foundation and over the bare hook again to within one-quarter inch of the eye. You won't think these minute details redundant after you have tied a few!

"Use small cutting pliers to cut off surplus wire. Press loose ends into close contact with body coils and with an ignition file (or other small file having rounded, smooth edges) file the burrs and rough ends of the wire, down to a slight taper as shown in drawing 2 (Figure IX–8). Burnish the body with any convenient tool. Wipe body with clean cloth. Flow with thin water-clear lacquer to prevent tarnish with age. Dry.

"Make a few turns with size A sewing silk over bare hook at 'a' (drawing 2). Make half-hitch. Lacquer. Attach tail and wind tightly with enough silk to build up to diameter of wire body. Saturate with lacquer.

"(For three-winged bucktails only.) First apply close winding of silk thread over center of body, making a band about one-eighth inch wide as shown in 'a' (drawing 3). Lacquer. Tie on the rear wing, trimming butts of hair closely with curved manicure scissors. Saturate butts with lacquer and finish with a narrow band of windings as in drawing 4. Lacquer, dry and proceed as in next paragraph.

"(For both two-winged and three-winged bucktails.) Prepare end of hook, using enough size A sewing silk to close eye of hook at one end and to pull a tapered jam against wire body at other end as shown in 'b' (drawing 3). Lacquer copiously.

"Tie in hackle (throat) if called for by pattern. If no hackle is wanted, proceed as in next paragraph. Where hackle is required, fasten in by butt end; run silk back to thread clip at *left* of hook; wind hackle back towards bend in close coils, catch with thread, break off hackle tip, then wind thread forward *through* the hackles and fasten at front with half-hitch, thus securing a hackle tie which will stand much rough usage and chewing by the fish before it will come loose. Lacquer.

"Tie in base color of hair, always the *lightest* of the several colors to be used. To prevent matting of hair in a solid bunch flat against body of fly, after first catching the hair in position, take a turn of silk around the hair alone as shown in drawing 4 (Figure IX-8). Now pull the thread tightly forward, thus raising the hair until it stands in a round tuft at an angle of nearly 45 degrees above the hook. Holding the thread tightly, start the next turn diagonally over butts of hair to keep the wing elevated while you complete the winding. After another turn or two of silk, make a couple of tight half-hitches, trim off butts of hair, saturate with lacquer and finish the tie. Lacquer and allow to dry before applying final top wing. (If a spike is to be used, lacquer and tie the spike in while lacquer is still wet: finish off with whip tie, lacquer again and dry. The spike is tied in in the same way as the base color of hair.)

"Tie in top color of wings. To prevent the two colors from blending, make the same kind of turn around the top hair by itself as was suggested for the base color of hair. This time, however, you will find that after fastening the hairs of the top wing your left fingers will be unable to raise the top wing hairs without also lifting a few of the base hairs beneath. It looks like a tangled mess but it isn't. The colors still are separated at their bottoms.

"Tilt the wing forward with your left fingers; poke a needle into the bottom open spaces between the two colors and hold it there. Now open your left fingers, releasing the hair. Pass the needle upwards and presto! the wing colors are separated again.

"Tie in jungle cock, chatterer or other overlays to suit your taste, or tie off without them. Lacquer. The fly is finished."

In addition to Mr. Schwab's instructions as given above and the instructions for dressing each individual fly as explained in Part II, the following comments are contained in letters from him to the author:

"The only significant change (in this series of bucktails) has been the substitution of hair tails for feather tails, using gray squirrel in the *Queen Bess*, black hair or skunk in the *Wood Pussy*, and dyed polar bear hair of proper color in all other patterns. The hairs named outlast feathers and are equally effective.

"Originally, only *Paint Brush* was tied in the three-winged style, followed by *Brass Hat* and others, but during the past three seasons

Notes on Types and Dressings

(this letter was written in 1949) *all* patterns are tied in *both* two-wing and three-wing styles. A simplified *Paint Brush* in the two-wing style, with the rear bright red wing eliminated, has been popular.

"The most popular three-wing patterns are *Queen Bess, Brass Hat* and *Paint Brush*. For steelhead I only use them myself after the season is well under way, when big fish have arrived and the water is high, cold and often clouded. For the most part, during early and mid-season and in high altitudes or some distance from salt water, the two-wing patterns are much more used and more easily cast.

"It is important that all wire bodied bucktails should be polished with liquid metal polish immediately after tying, as even polished wires lose their lustre by opening of the surface as they are wound around the small shank of the hook. 'Bon Ami' on a piece of wet turkish toweling is excellent and is easily scrubbed off in running water. Without scrubbing, some of the abrasive will remain between the coils of wire and is sure to cloud the finish after lacquering. After polishing, scrubbing and drying over heat, the wire bodies are lacquered with thin, colorless lacquer or head 'cement' to prevent tarnish. This is all done, of course, before tails and wings are added.

"Unquestionably, the most *killing* material is the crinkly hair of eastern white tailed deer in natural and dyed shades, gray squirrel or black bear. Unfortunately, deer hair doesn't last long (in steelhead fishing). The most *lasting* flies, though lacking in much of the lively action of those tied with deer tail hair, are tied with gray squirrel, polar and black bear hair. Long, thin polar bear hair has a *much* better action than the short, thick polar bear hair used by most professionals for production reasons.

"The most effective bucktails are those tied with long, rakish, lightly dressed wings. They are far more effective than when tied with short wings in the orthodox 'hair fly' style.

"Spikes (beards, pectoral fins or torn gills—call them what you will) are usually omitted. They have a tendency to spoil the swimming action, particularly in the two-wing patterns, and if the fly shows the slightest tendency to swim sideways instead of on an even keel the spikes are promptly snipped off or are thinned to a very few hairs.

"Historically, with the single exception of the *Princess*, I have been using all of these patterns and many, many more since about

1926 but always with unweighted bodies, usually of tinsel. The only *new* things about the patterns are the wire bodies, the tying technique and the careful selection of the *best* patterns, involving the elimination of the unnecessary patterns, however beautiful or effective they might be at times when the fish would grab anything thrown at them. This work was done on the Klamath River in 1945 and 1946, where it is imperative to use flies that will sink well, excel in swimming action and cast easily. The first flies were of tinsel, floss or dubbing, dressed over wire cores. The fish soon tore the coverings off, whereupon the plain, uncovered wire proved to be more effective than the covered wire on all three of the counts just given. I had the help of George Bellamy and Bobbie Dunn, with whom I fished every day for not less than three months in 1945 and through most of 1946.

"I have a seemingly uncontrollable habit of tying my wings a trifle shorter than they should be for greatest effectiveness. The wings should always extend beyond the bend one-half the length of the shank. These bucktails are tied to imitate minnow action; not insects.

"Don't be fooled by the apparent uprightness of the wings. In water, under the influence of the current, or manipulation of the angler, the wings quickly fall down and the bucktail assumes the slender, rakish form of a minnow. The wings are tied upright in the first place so they won't later fall so low as to mask the glitter of the body. Every effort has been made to secure greatest visibility."

I have quoted these instructions and comments of Mr. Schwab in considerable length because he explains clearly and concisely how to dress a *securely tied fly*, whether it be a bucktail in one of the Schwab patterns or something else. He has spent more days astream than most of us do in an entire lifetime. His patterns, whether tied in the weighted form or not, are excellent fish takers for virtually all species of fish in all parts of the country. They are basic color combinations, valuable both in fresh water or in salt. In my humble estimation, Peter J. Schwab is one of the greatest anglers of all time and I am deeply grateful for the detailed assistance he has given to me to make this book as complete as it is. In Chapter II I referred to the high wing type flies, of which the Schwab patterns are examples, as "fast water flies" because in my opinion it requires fast water (or extremely energetic manipulation) to draw the wing down to present a minnow-

Notes on Types and Dressings

like effect, as opposed to what I have termed the "low wing flies," of which the *Edson Tigers* are examples. I sent Mr. Schwab a copy of the manuscript of Chapter II. He took violent issue with my segregating bucktails and streamers into these two types. With all deference to Pete Schwab I am taking the liberty of leaving the manuscript unchanged. It is true that the high wing on these flies prevents masking the glitter of the body, but I must leave it to the judgment of other anglers to determine the pertinency of their relative suitability for fast or for slow water.

Mr. C. Jim Pray, of Eureka, California, has adapted radio tube pins to the making of metal bodies for streamers and bucktails. These pins are cylindrical in shape, with ends drawn together sufficiently so that the pins can be opened and clamped around a hook. The fly dresser is restricted somewhat by the types of pins which are available, but they make very simple bodies which are indestructible and which have enough weight to sink the fly readily. The bucktail shown in Figure IX-9 is equipped with one of these bodies.

This bucktail also has a bead head which Mr. Pray calls an "Optic." The heads of Optic bucktails are made from open metal beads, available in one-eighth, three-sixteenth and one-quarter inch diameters, which can be clamped just behind the eye of the hook and painted as suits the angler. Mr. Pray prefers the one-quarter inch size for his steelhead flies, applied usually to hooks which are No. 4 in length with a 1/0 bend, 4X strong, with hollow point and tapered eye in the Limerick pattern. I believe that these are made for him by O. Mustad and Son, of Oslo, Norway.

Jim Pray's Optic bucktails are famous for their ability to take big steelhead and salmon. The principal patterns are these:

Black Optic: A body of gold oval tinsel with black hackle throat, black hair wing and a black bead head with yellow iris and black pupil.

Red Optic: A body of silver oval tinsel with a red hair wing over which is a small amount of yellow hair. The bead head is black with a yellow iris and black pupil.

Orange Optic: A body of silver oval tinsel with red hackle throat, orange hair wing and a black bead head with white iris and red pupil.

Fig. IX-9

C. JIM PRAY'S "OPTIC BUCKTAIL" (with clamped metal body)

Cock Robin Optic: A body of silver oval tinsel with orange hackle throat, ground squirrel or badger hair wing and a black bead head with yellow iris and black pupil.

Mr. Pray has written to me these comments about his Optic bucktails:

"Briefly, I brought out the Optic in the fall of 1940, just getting in on the first of the winter run of steelhead. In the June, 1941, issue of *Field and Stream* appeared a four column article about what this fly did in its maiden swim in the Eel River. Since that time the *Red Optic* has taken more big steelhead trout than any other single pattern of fly. By actual tabulation there have been more than 500 steelhead taken with it which weighed over eleven pounds, and thousands under that weight.

"During November, when the winter run of fish start coming into the Eel River, there is a period when both they and the silver salmon hang around Cock Robin Island before coming up into the pools out of the tidewater. We already had found the *Silver Demon* productive there, so I took it and worked it into an Optic, christening it the *Cock Robin Optic* because it was particularly good in that section of the river. After the fish get up into the pools, where wading is done almost exclusively, the *Red Optic* is supreme, although the *Orange Optic* also is a favorite.

"I think it is well to advise people that the Optic principally is a fly for slow moving pools where large fish are resting. Even in Alaska, Frank Dufresne found this so. In the fast riffles of the Klamath I am certain that it is no better than its color combination because the

Notes on Types and Dressings

fly moves so fast that the fish do not have a clear look at the large head and the bulging eye."

Mr. Peter J. Schwab has this to say about Jim Pray's Optic bucktails:

"I like them because they look so quaint and comical. On the Eel River the *Red Optic* is practically a *must*. It beats them all, at least two to one, and it does it so consistently as to rule out the last element of pure luck or coincidence."

The history of the painted eye on the head of a fly goes back at least until 1934, when Mr. W. H. Hobbs, of Derby, Connecticut, found them very effective and gave the idea to the tackle firm of Cook, Newton and Smith, Inc., of New Haven, Connecticut, who also made them under the name of "Optic" bucktails. These do not have the bead head. Bead head flies are popular also in salt water, as has been noted in Chapter VIII where the Gordon Dean Bead Head streamers were discussed.

The catalogs of the celebrated English firm of Hardy Brothers for many years have shown streamers and bucktails with tiny spinning "propeller" blades affixed between the head and the eye of the fly. Similar propellers are available in the United States (from Herter's, of Waseca, Minnesota, for example) which can be slipped over the point and barb of the hook and slid up to the eye. These propellers should revolve against a metal bearing surface which can be made by building up eight or ten superimposed turns of flat metal tinsel tied off against the head of the fly. A sample of this addition to bucktails and streamers, as made by the Elm Sporting Goods Co., of Westfield, Massachusetts, is shown in Figure IX–10.

If the angler desires his fly to dive and wobble erratically he can add to its head a wiggling disc, which is a small metal scoop or cup tied in by its metal shank under the head as shown in Figure IX–11. Glass eyes, metal cheeks, metal shoulders and similar embellishments contribute to the unusuality of streamer and bucktail patterns if the fisherman desires to deviate from the orthodox to the extent of using them.

Fishing any sort of a fly in weeds, among lily pads or in very shallow water can be extremely annoying. It always has seemed to me that whenever an especially promising cast is made in such a spot

Fig. IX-10

BUCKTAIL EQUIPPED WITH SPINNING PROPELLER ATTACHMENT

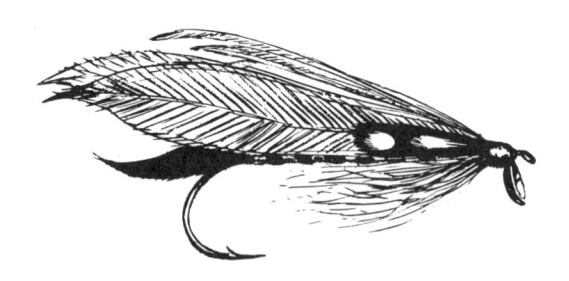

Fig. IX-11

STREAMER EQUIPPED WITH WOBBLING DISC OR CUP

the fly is bound to catch in aquatic growth, or at least to pick some up on the hook, which of course prevents us from catching the best fish of the day!

In addition to the wire weed-guard, one type of which is shown in Figure VIII-1, I like to dress a few "Upside down" flies as shown in Figure IX-12. These are made in exactly the same manner as orthodox streamers or bucktails, except that the fly is tied with the bend of the hook pointing up, rather than down. The dressing is applied to both sides of the hook. It must be sufficient in stiffness and quantity to protect the point from catching on weeds when the feathers or hair are wet and matted down.

An excellent example of such a fly for bass, and certain other fresh

FIG. IX–12

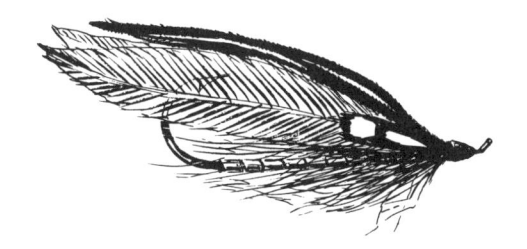

WEEDLESS STREAMER OR "UPSIDE DOWN" FLY

FIG. IX–13

STROUD'S "OZARK" (WEEDLESS) BUCKTAIL

and salt water fish, is Mr. Paul D. Stroud's *Ozark Bucktail*, as shown in Figure IX–13. Mr. Stroud writes of his origination as follows:—

"This fly is an offshoot of Dr. Hoag's *Hair Basser* which was a great fly in many ways but which lacked several things I tried to include in the *Ozark Bucktail*. It needed to be streamlined and tied more securely on the hook. I also changed the rudder to make it travel with the hook point up. In the past twenty years the *Ozark Bucktail* has taken all types of gamefish from the noble bluegill to the leaping tarpon. It is tied in sizes 8 to 8/0 in many combinations of buck and skunk tail hair. It is not tied to be weedless, but due to the fact that it travels upside down it is semi-weedless. It is effectively fished with or without a spinner."

Mr. Stroud's method of dressing the *Ozark Bucktail* is explained in the book FLY TYING, by William Bayard Sturgis.

Mylar is a thin metal-like plastic available in sheet form or as braided mylar tubular cord. In thinnest sheet form, in silver color,

1. Tie in Tail
(if required)

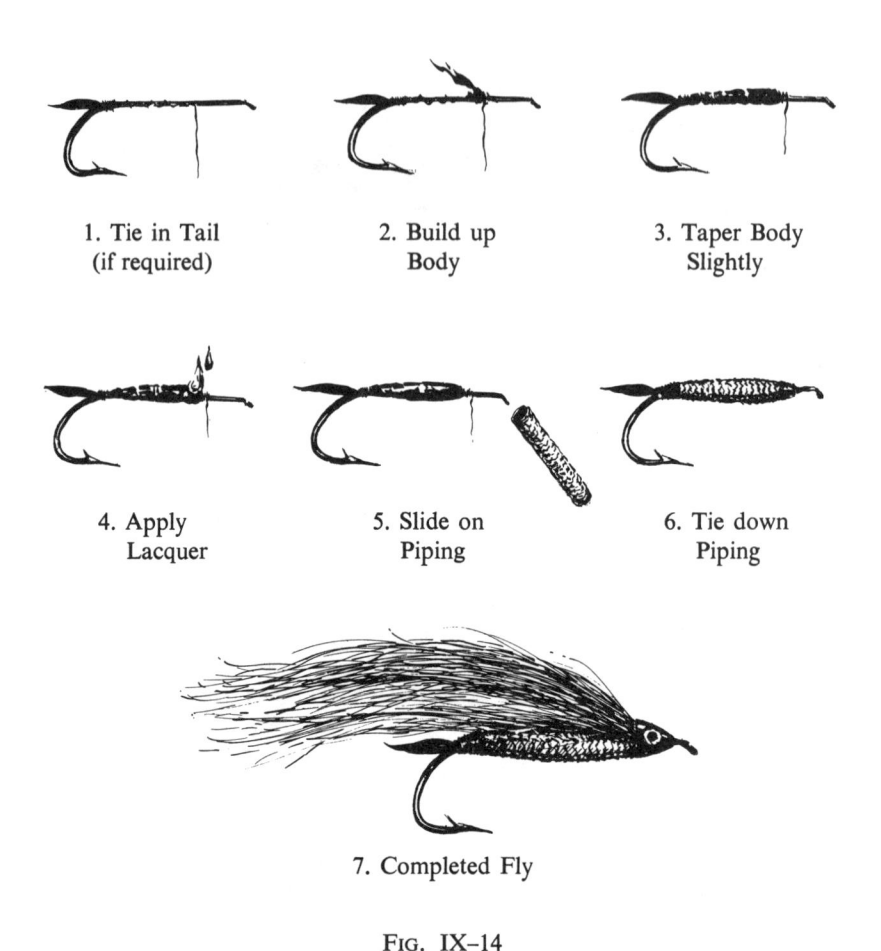

2. Build up
Body

3. Taper Body
Slightly

4. Apply
Lacquer

5. Slide on
Piping

6. Tie down
Piping

7. Completed Fly

Fig. IX-14

DRESSING BODIES WITH MYLAR TUBULAR CORD

it attracted considerable attention in 1963 and 1964 for dressing the sides of streamers and bucktails to provide more flash than is possible by winding the hook shank with tinsel. It was cut in strips not over one-quarter inch wide (depending on the size of the fly), with the rearward end then cut to a point or a curved shape. Two similarly cut sections were tied in at the front end, parallel to the hook shank, in a similar manner to the application of jungle cock cheeks.

Notes on Types and Dressings

When this book is published, mylar cheeks may have been forgotten. As this is written, suitable mylar is difficult to obtain. In my opinion, this embellishment usually provides too much flash, is perishable when chewed by fish, and is less desirable than the braided tubular cord which is used as a body covering. In any event, flies with mylar used as cheeks are illustrated in Figure VIII-4 and at the bottom of Color Plate I.

I am indebted to Arthur W. Fusco, Medford, Massachusetts, for the following description of the application of braided mylar tubular cord for use in streamer or bucktail bodies. Evidently the silver-like cord is used commercially as a trimming. Art Fusco is a fellow member of the United Fly Tyers Club, of Boston, and is the regional authority on the subject.

"When you are mounting piping on a single long shank streamer hook, the hook shank should be built up with either curon, chenille, or wool, preferably curon because it forms a neater body and is extremely easy to work with. Removing the cotton core from the piping is a simple process. After you have measured the proper length and have it cut, hold one end of the piece between thumb and forefinger of one hand and compress or peel the outer shell down toward the stationary end with the other hand. This exposes the core material, which then can be removed and discarded.

"If the pattern calls for a tail, it should be tied in before the body is built up. After building up the body and before sliding on the piping, put a few drops of lacquer on the front end of the filler material. This facilitates sliding the piping over it. Then slide the piping over the hook eye so the built-up body passes through the piping. Tie down the piping fore and aft with winding thread to make neat tapered ends, completing with a whip finish. Give the body and windings two coats of lacquer, either tinted or clear.

"Some fly dressers, instead of building up the body as above, insert a wooden match stick, cut to proper length, inside the tube to fill out the body. A section or two of lead wire could be used if it is desirable to have the fly weighted.

"This is an easy way to apply a secure body, and the result is almost identical to the appearance of a small baitfish.

"The method used to apply piping as a body material on tandem hooks is a trifle more complicated, but the finished product is well worth the effort. The connecting link between tandem hooks should be a relatively strong and flexible material such as Sevenstrand stainless steel leader material. This connecting wire is first attached to the rear tandem hook by placing the wire on top of the hook shank and winding 2/0 nylon thread tightly and closely over it from eye to bend of hook. Lacquer this first layer of thread liberally and, while it is still wet, wind the thread closely and evenly again up the shank to the eye. Whip finish, lacquer again, and set it aside to dry. The trick here is to attach several of them in this manner, so that by the time you have finished tying the last one the first one has dried, with no time wasted.

"Measure and cut a piece of piping to the desired length; remove the core, and slide it over the wire from the front or unattached end. (The wire passes through the center of the piping.) You may tie the tail end of the piping down now, or wait until the front hook has been attached and tie them both down. Either is satisfactory. The front hook is attached to the wire in the same manner as the rear hook. It is easy to hold the piping back out of the way while doing this.

"Now, bend the wire to conform to the shape of the front hook (the wire will extend around the bend of the hook, out beyond the point and parallel to the shank of the front hook past the eye). Naturally the piping will bend around with the wire also. Slip the piping on over the point and up around the bend until you estimate enough piping has passed beyond the hook point to cover the shank of the front hook. Allow the wire to straighten out, and with a little assistance the point of the hook will push through the piping. Slide the piping on up to cover the shank and tie it down at the eye.

"Tinting the piping body is accomplished by using a mixture of fountain pen ink and clear lacquer. The most convenient method is to purchase a small bottle of clear fingernail polish (the type with built-in applicator brush attached to the cap). Add several drops of ink to it; shake well, and it will stay thoroughly mixed. Buy a bottle for each color you intend to use.

"The bodies of tandem flies need not be built up as we did with the single hook flies. Two coats of lacquer on the piping make it hard and durable." A fly so dressed is shown in Figure VI–1.

Notes on Types and Dressings

In storage or in use, the joining material between the front and rear hooks of trolling flies sometimes becomes kinked. When kinked, they are difficult or impossible to straighten, which decreases or cancels their effectiveness. Paul Kukonen has a remedy for this, one which also makes it possible to detach the rear section of the fly and add a new one when desirable.

"Do not use gut, monofilament, nylon, nor any other of the plastic line and leader materials for joining the hooks," he says. "These may warp. A material which won't warp is Sevenstrand stainless steel wire, in tests of from forty to ninety pounds." We have used his method and we recommend it. He explains it as follows:

"Cut a piece of the wire about three-and-a-half or four inches long. Fold it, leaving one end about one-quarter inch longer than the other. Pass the open ends through the eye of the rear (dressed or undressed) hook from the rear and loop the wire over the hook shank. Pull the wire tight and wind the hook behind the eye with 2/0 tying thread of the same color as the body, thus tightly securing the hook in place on the looped wire.

"Make a thread body on the forward hook by winding the thread closely from front to rear. Apply lacquer. Lay the doubled wire on the hook and wind closely and tightly forward until the shorter of the two lengths of wire is covered. This should be about one-quarter inch from the eye. Bend back the single wire tightly toward the rear and tie it down firmly with close windings backward and forward. Apply lacquer. It is now impossible to pull the hooks apart. Proceed to dress the fly as usual.

"If the rearward hook needs replacing for any reason, merely cut the windings of thread which lash it down and push the looped wire back and around the hook, thus freeing the hook from the loop. Attach a new dressed or undressed hook in the reverse manner."

Attempts to impart maximum action into streamer and bucktail patterns have resulted in the splayed-wing style discussed in Chapter VIII and illustrated there in Figures VIII–1 and VIII–3 and also in the patterns based on Joe Brooks' series of "Blondes" which seem to be a development of the Homer Rhode, Jr. *Tarpon Bucktail* illustrated in Figure VIII–3. The point should be stressed that these are by no means confined to salt water uses. Splayed-wing types make very

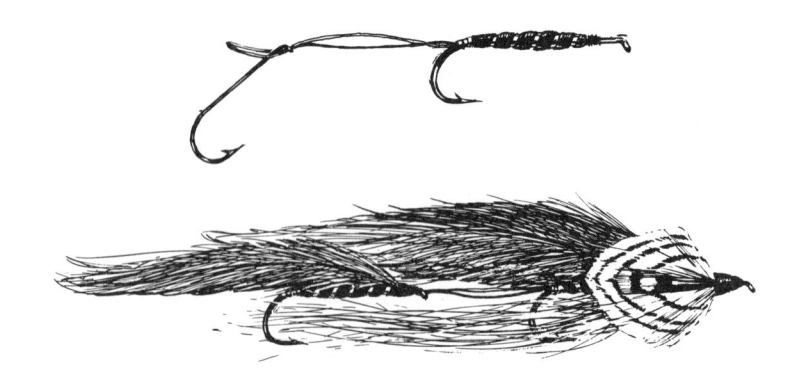

FIG. IX-15

A WIRE LINKAGE FOR TANDEM FLIES

successful steelhead patterns and are becoming increasingly prominent in other areas of fresh water angling.

A case in point is the *Engells Splaywing Coachman*, which was top fly for Atlantic salmon in many areas of the Cains and Miramichi Rivers in New Brunswick in 1965. It has a tail of a very small bunch of red hackle fibers, a body of rusty peacock herl (with one turn in front of the wing) and a divided wing of white impalla or goat hair extending no longer than the tail and splayed upward and outward at an angle of about 20 degrees. The fly is dressed on 2X or 3X long salmon hooks in sizes from No. 6 to No. 10, the larger sizes usually being more appropriate for high water. Occasional dressings are on double hooks, more to make the fly ride evenly and steadily in the current than to increase its hooking and holding ability. Every action of rod and current makes the splayed wing pulsate, or "breathe," thus giving intense action to the fly. The author feels that this type should be used more often (both with hair and with hackle wings) for trout, bass, and other fresh water game fish.

A second type of "breather" fly is the series of Joe Brooks' "Blondes," one of which is illustrated in Plate V and which were described in the December, 1963, and June, 1965, issues of *Outdoor Life*. A bunch of bucktail is tied in over the bend of the hook. The body is dressed with silver tinsel, forward of which is a single upright

Notes on Types and Dressings 205

wing of another bunch of bucktail so applied that the wing is splayed upward at an angle of about 45 degrees. Hook sizes usually are 1/0 and 3/0, with 5/0 being used for big tarpon. The *Strawberry Blonde* has a forward wing of red and a rearward wing (or tail) of orange. The *Platinum Blonde* is all white; the *Honey Blonde* all yellow; and the *Black Blonde* all black. A *Pink Blonde* pattern has both wings of pink bucktail, and an *Argentine Blonde* one has a medium blue forward wing and a white rearward wing (or tail). The upward wing is pulled down by rod or current action and, continually recovering, actively pulsates while being fished. The "Blondes" are highly productive for most species of salt water game fish all along the eastern coast and should be used more extensively in its northern section than they are as this is being written. In smaller sizes they should do well for many fresh water species.

In Chapter VIII we noted that flies of the "Blonde" type had been used most successfully (especially in salt water fly fishing) for several decades prior to the publicity which was given to them in the early 1960's. The high wing, also discussed in connection with the Schwab patterns and others, and illustrated by the "Orange Steelheader" and the "Bellamy," for example, in Plate VIII gives pronounced action in fast or turbulent water or when fished very actively, plus affording complete freedom from fouling the hook. A type of fly such as this, so popular with and so productive for so many eminent anglers, should suggest to the rest of us that a lot more can be done with it to help us to hook more fish.

While the above six "Blonde" patterns are favorites of Joe Brooks, and other very similar patterns are equally popular with knowledgeable anglers in the southwest and northwest, let us stress the point that the ingenuity of the angler or fly dresser can be given very wide latitude in formulating similar and perhaps even better variations. For example, color combinations (with hair wings) described under the "Silver Garland Marabou" streamer in Part II should be effective. So should the combinations given for Pacific salmon flies on page 113. They should be effective for many species of salt water fish everywhere and, in suitable sizes, for various fresh water species as well.

Given these productive color combinations, and knowing that we can adapt almost any bucktail to the type, we also can make variations in body dressings to suit the kind of fish we plan to catch. We can make the fly sink quicker by substituting for the tinsel body the type of Schwab wire bodies described on pages 190 to 195, or we can use bodies of mylar tubular cord, as described on pages 200 to 203. The latter can be made into top-water flies by inserting a trimmed match stick as part of the underbody, or can be made into a fast-sinking fly by using a section or two of lead or copper wire instead. Experimentation is part of the fun of fly fishing, especially when we use such sound experience as a basis.

It was stated, perhaps too quickly, that one of the main reasons for this type of fly is because its structure prevents the wing from fouling itself under the bend of the hook. As noted in the designs for Florida salt water fishing in drawings VIII-1 and VIII-3, this is rather standard. It also is very necessary. Fish almost never take a foul-winged fly. Anglers usually have but one chance to cast to an individual fish. In tarpon, permit and in bonefishing, for example, they may travel for miles and may stalk big fish for days before spotting a real prize. Thus they intend to take no chances of using a fly whose wing, in casting, may wrap itself under the bend of the hook.

The same principle again should be recalled in flies for fresh water uses. In conventional streamer and bucktail patterns the hook should be long, and the wing should not extend too far beyond the bend of the hook, in order to prevent fouling.

Without getting into too much detail, beginners in angling could be reminded of two hints which, if ignored or forgotten, may make the correct selection and presentation of the fly relatively ineffectual. Before the fly is attached to the leader its hook should be inspected for needle-point sharpness. Even new hooks may need touching up with a stone or (for large hooks) a file. Use occasionally blunts or bends the point, and even almost imperceptible rust impairs hooking ability. Thus, the experienced angler always carries a small whetstone or a file (or both) and uses them perhaps even more often than is necessary.

Secondly, leaders always should be straight. If waves or coils exist in them, they can be removed by pulling them between a doubled small piece of rubber (such as a square cut from an inner tube) which is held between thumb and forefinger to provide sufficient friction.

Notes on Types and Dressings

Finally, while straight (non-offset) hooks always have been traditional in fly dressing, the relatively new double-offset hooks (the "*Eagle-Claw*" design) may have better hooking and holding qualities. The single-offset hook (offset, or kirbed, to one side only) usually causes a fly to ride unevenly, and thus almost entirely is ignored in fly dressing. But the double-offset hook (offset *both* to the right and to the left) allows the fly to ride balanced and on an even keel. This type, always most popular in bait-fishing, also is worthy of experimentation in dressing various types of streamers and bucktails.

We shall consider Part II of this book in the nature of an appendix, because certainly it is more to be referred to than read. Even though the angler does not wish to dress his own flies, and even if he has no great interest in checking the authenticity of patterns, what is to come may contain bits and pieces of streamer fly and bucktail lore which may be worthy of attention.

When STREAMER FLY FISHING IN FRESH AND SALT WATER was written in 1950, it contained over 200 patterns considered to be standard at that time. The dressing instructions were taken from flies in the author's collection which were tied by their originators, or (in a few cases where such originals were not available) they were taken from flies known to be accurate and authentic copies. The author attempted to explain the dressings in such detail that fly tyers could copy them accurately from the script without ever having seen the actual flies. Thus, over the years, the former book became coveted by fly dressers as well as by anglers and collectors, and often has been referred to as the "Hoyle" of the subject.

Helen Bates pondering her husband's avocation, circa 1940.

Wallace Stevens, Helen Bates, and "Shang" Wheeler observing Bruce Bates cleaning his first salmon, circa 1942. *(Photograph by the author)*

Notes on Types and Dressings

As a case in point, a fellow member of the United Fly Tyers Club, of Boston (Mr. Robert H. Cavanagh, Jr., of Woburn, Massachusetts) dressed every fly described in the former book without having seen the actual originals. When this laborious task was completed, he told me about it and showed me the mounted collection. We compared each of his copies with my originals, and both of us were surprised and very pleased to note that he had been able to make accurate and faithful reproductions without any exceptions of importance.

"When you write the new book," he said, "I hope there won't be too many new patterns. I'd hate to do that job almost all over again!"

Well, I'm afraid I have news for my good friend, Bob Cavanagh. In the ensuing fifteen years most of the flies in the former book have remained standard and popular patterns, and thus have a firm place in the new one. But many became forgotten, or nearly so, in favor of newer and better patterns. Due to space limitations and the desire to exclude unessential material, these have been eliminated, and many new and currently standard patterns have taken their places. So if Bob wants to maintain a complete collection, I'm afraid he has more work to do! Very pleasant and relaxing work, we both might add, and work made much easier by the addition of the color plates.

STREAMER FLY TYING AND FISHING, as well as its preceeding volume, is the culmination of a great many happy years devoted to the study of these fur and feather imitations of baitfish which are renowned for catching more and bigger game fish. The wealth of beautiful flies, and the reasons for dressing them the way they are, is a subject of great fascination to many fishermen. Actually, any angler's fly book need not contain very many patterns, if they are intelligently chosen. They need not be elaborate and expensive examples of the fly dresser's art, even though such are a great pleasure to own and to use.

Of all that this book contains, the very essence of its teaching is to suggest that the angler select patterns of a size and type similar to the prevalent baitfish; that he select them in accord with his judgment of weather and water conditions and with regard to the species of fish he is seeking. Once he's selected it, he should fish his fly as the baitfish swims, in waters shallow or deep, as their temperatures dictate, and in places where game fish should be located at the time. If the fly is selected and fished with these simple principles in mind, it is safe

210   Tackle and Tactics

to assume that the angler has an equal or better chance of hooking his fish than if he had used any other type of lure.

While all the patterns given in Part II could not be illustrated in the eight color plates, 119 of the most important ones will be found there. After the names of flies which are described in Part II, there appears the Roman numeral of the color plate number in which they are included.

The author in camp, circa 1938.

PART TWO

The History and Dressing of Famous Patterns

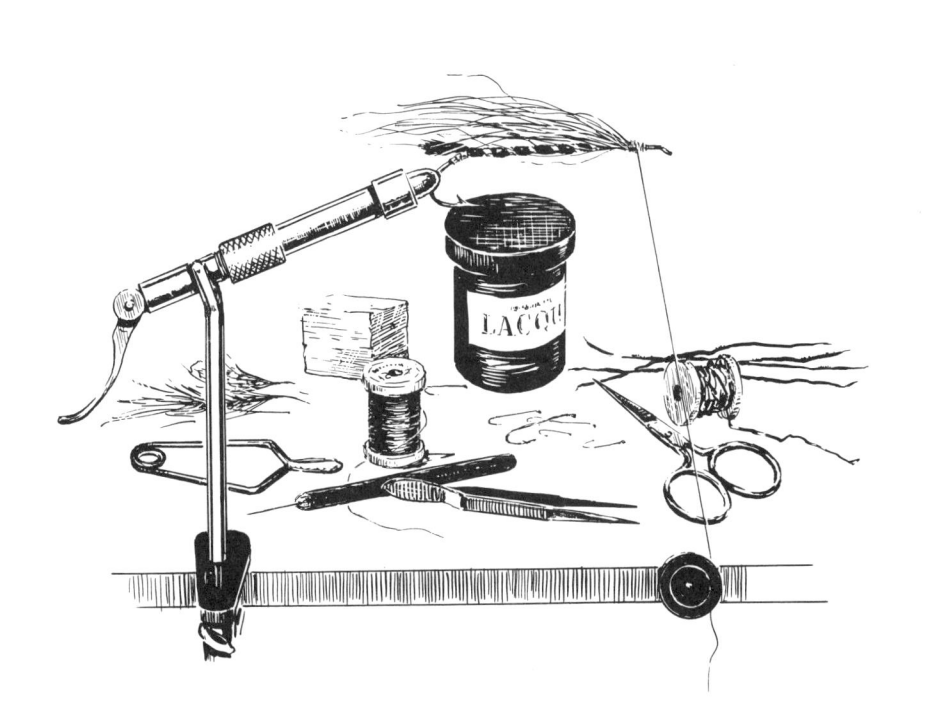

Anglers who fish with streamer flies and bucktails often complain that it is usually difficult, and sometimes nearly impossible, to purchase authentic patterns dressed as the originators of the flies intended them to be. It is difficult because the majority of professional and amateur fly dressers are unable to locate correct patterns or formulas for their guidance. In spite of their good intentions, many of the more complicated flies they produce bear no more than a general resemblance to the originals; and when they are copied by others, the errors are further compounded.

A well-known professional came to see me a while ago with several samples of the famous *Supervisor*, the *Edson Dark Tiger*, and the *Gray Ghost*. An angler had ordered two dozen each of these flies with the stipulation that they be dressed faithfully in accordance with the correct patterns. The professional had purchased samples in three leading stores. Finding that they varied widely in appearance, he consulted the few books available containing dressing formulas. These only added to his confusion, because the instructions were too brief to allow flies to be tied accurately from them, or the books he consulted were not in agreement with each other.

I produced for him samples of the three flies which had been given to me by the originators of the patterns. I called his attention to individualities which the originators insisted were most important, but with which few fly dressers were familiar. He copied the flies exactly as they should be, told his customer why he knew that they were correct, and has enjoyed a considerable increase in business from this gentleman and his friends ever since.

Obviously, it is as easy to dress flies properly as it is to do them improperly. In an attempt to aid other anglers and fly tiers in producing correct patterns, there follow the detailed dressings of more than 200 well-known streamer flies and bucktails. I have stated in the Introduction to this book that the majority of the descriptions have been taken directly from flies in my own collection, given to me by the originators of the patterns themselves. Quite obviously, these dressings can be accepted without question. To identify them, the words "As dressed by the originator" follow the instructions; or in cases where the originator did not tie his own flies but sent me samples approved by him, the words "As dressed for the originator" are included.

Unfortunately, flies from such impeccable sources could not be obtained in every instance. In such cases I have described the most authentic dressings obtainable and have stated the sources from which they were obtained, so that fly tiers and anglers may judge for themselves the degree of their authenticity. In every case I have attempted to describe the flies in such detail that they can be duplicated faithfully without additional assistance.

It is expected that fishermen will call me to account for what they consider to be sins of omission or commission in the choice of patterns contained in this book. I have tried to include all of the famous flies, as well as many which are less well known but which enjoy noteworthy regional or historic prominence. Anglers who observe the omission of certain patterns may find them to be sectional favorites which are adaptations of older flies listed herein under other names.

There are historical facts connected with many of the well-known flies which seem to be of unusual interest. Who invented the first acknowledged pattern of a distinctive streamer fly or bucktail? Which of at least six claimants actually designed the *Black Ghost*? Which of the many Cains River patterns were tied by their originators, and which are the inspirations of others? Who designed each well-known fly; when, and for what types of fish? Where it has been possible to

Famous Patterns

set down correct information of general interest I have attempted to do so, in the belief that many of these flies possess backgrounds which should be preserved. Fortunately, a large number of the originators of the historic patterns have been friends and fishing companions of mine. Some of the facts with which they have endowed this book have not been published previously.

Many readers will question the inclusion of certain designs, saying that they properly should be termed neither bucktails nor streamers. There is no sharp dividing line between bucktails and hair flies, or between streamers and what are commonly termed wet flies. Neither is there any sharp line between "good" flies and "bad" flies. There are many, originally dressed as small wet flies, which are now accepted in the categories of bucktails and streamers. I have included all of them which seem to be of general interest, at the same time eliminating many others which would have cluttered the book with too many needless variations. Some of those included defy all the rules of sensible fly dressing. No angler in his right mind would want to use them in place of the many excellent patterns which this book also contains. I would have been well content to have discarded such flies, but in doing so, I would have been influenced too greatly by my own opinion. If the flies are well known and seem to be separate entities unto themselves, they have been included, regardless of my personal feelings in the matter.

The descriptions of these flies comprise the part of this book which follows. In certain cases specific flies have two or more names. These may be located by consulting the index.

ALASKA MARY ANN BUCKTAIL (PLATE VIII)

Head: Black
Tail: A very small bunch of red hackle fibers or red hair
Body: Dressed rather full with ivory or light tan silk
Ribbing: Medium flat silver tinsel (optional)
Wing: A small bunch of white polar bear hair extending to the end of the tail
Cheeks: Jungle cock, rather short

(As dressed by the originator)

This Alaskan bucktail, originated by Mr. Frank Dufresne, well-known writer and former member of the U. S. Fish and Wildlife

Frank Dufresne's sketch of the Kobuk Hook

Service, had its beginning in a fishing lure used by the Kobuk Eskimos. Mr. Dufresne describes it in a letter to the author as follows: "I saw it first along the Kobuk River in Kotzebue Sound, Alaska, back in 1922. It was being used by the Eskimos, attached to a length of black whalebone line to haul out most anything in the river—Dolly Vardens, Arctic char, sheefish, pike, and grayling. They made it by carving a small piece of ivory roughly into the shape of a minnow, driving a cooper's nail through it and bending it to form a barbless hook. Then they tied on a smidgin of polar bear hair, and on the barbless hook they fastened a very small red corner from the mouth of the guillemot bird.

"That was the Kobuk Hook. I came down out of that country with several of them. They were killers, believe me. When I had lost all of them but one, I decided to tie another along more conventional lines. Using a No. 8 long-shanked hook I wound on some ivory colored silk for a body, tied on a wing of polar bear hair and added a wisp of red-dyed hair for the tail. To simulate the black whalebone eye, inset in some of the original Kobuk Hooks, I used jungle cock.

"The thing had no name until a friend of mine used it in Southeastern Alaska in a stream where rainbows, cutthroats, Dolly Vardens and salmon all abounded. He beat the heck out of me with my own creation, and, when he said 'Man, this catches 'em all; the whole Mary Ann of 'em,' the name was born.

Famous Patterns

"The Weber Tackle Company has been tying it for years and showing it in their catalog. It is tied in several different color combinations, but this is the correct one. Out West and in Alaska you see it all over the place. It's a bucktail, of course, and seems to work best when and where trout are hitting either whitefish or salmon fingerlings."

ALEXANDRA STREAMER (PLATE II)

Head: Black
Tail: A fairly long but rather narrow section of a red goose or swan wing feather
Body: Medium embossed silver tinsel
Ribbing: Narrow oval silver tinsel
Throat: A wide black saddle hackle wound on as a collar and separated at the top to accommodate the wing
Wing: A fairly large bunch of bright green peacock herl. The herl should be so selected as to be very green and very fine. The wing extends beyond the tail of the fly

(As dressed by Fin, Fur and Feather, Ltd.)

Evidently this fly originated as a trout fly in England. In 1929 Mr. Frier Gulline, of Fin, Fur and Feather Ltd., of Montreal, adapted it as a streamer fly. It has proved to be one of the best flies of this type for trout and bass in Canada. This pattern evidently was adapted from the Hardy Bros. *Demon* streamer. The dressings are identical, except that the *Demon* has a throat of light blue hackle and the tail is red wool instead of a section of red feather. In England, this fly is favored for salmon, sea trout, and inland trout.

ALLIE'S FAVORITE STREAMER (PLATE IV)

Head: Black, with red band
Tag: Three or four turns of narrow silver tinsel
Body: Red silk, dressed very thin
Ribbing: Narrow flat silver tinsel
Throat: A very small bunch of white bucktail extending beyond the barb of the hook, under which is a small bunch of orange hackle fibers, with a very small bunch of black hackle fibers under this
Wing: Five or six strands of bright green peacock herl as long as the wing, over which are two orange saddle hackles with a black saddle hackle of the same length on both sides of these
Cheeks: Jungle cock, fairly long

(As dressed by the originator)

Originated by Mrs. Carrie G. Stevens, of Madison, Maine, and named in honor of Mr. Allie W. French, of Willimantic, Connecticut, who preferred this fly for fishing in the famous Upper Dam Pool in the Rangeley section of Maine.

ANSON SPECIAL BUCKTAIL

Head: Black
Tag: Three or four turns of medium flat silver tinsel
Tail: A very small bunch of red hackle fibers
Body: Wound with peacock herl, moderately thin
Ribbing: Medium flat silver tinsel
Throat: A few turns of a red hackle, tied downward. The hackle is sparse and rather long
Wing: A small bunch of white bucktail, extending slightly beyond the tail
Shoulders: Each a whole tip of a barred black and white teal flank feather, one-third as long as the wing
Cheeks: Jungle cock, two-thirds as long as the shoulder

(As dressed by Mr. Herbert L. Howard)

Originated by Mr. Anson Bell, an old-time logger in the lumber camps of Maine and particularly on the Magalloway River in Maine and New Hampshire. This dressing is copied from an original given by Mr. Bell to Mr. Howard. The fly is popular for all species of trout, particularly in New England and New York State.

ASHDOWN GREEN STREAMER (PLATE VIII)

Head: Black
Tail: A section of red duck or goose wing feather, rather long and thin
Body: Maroon wool, dressed medium heavy and picked out slightly
Ribbing: Narrow oval gold tinsel
Throat: A maroon saddle hackle, tied on as a collar and then tied downward. The hackle is rather long and enough turns are made to make it fairly heavy
Wing: Two matched sections of white goose or swan wing feathers, extending slightly beyond the tail

(As dressed by Fin, Fur and Feather, Ltd.)

This is an old West Coast pattern originated by Mr. Ashdown H. Green, a famous ichthyologist of British Columbia. Mr. H. L. Gulline, of the famous tackle store of Fin, Fur and Feather Ltd., in Montreal, reports having used this as a trout fly as early as 1889 on the Cowichan River in British Columbia. It was adapted as a streamer in 1939 by Mr. Frier Gulline and as such is a popular trout streamer in Eastern Canada.

ATOM BOMB (YELLOW) (Plate VIII)

Head: Black, with white painted eye with red pupil with black dot in center
Hook sizes: 1/0 to 6, 3X long
Tail: The tips of two bright yellow saddle hackles, half the length of the hook, tied in upright
Body: Silver mylar tubular cord
Throat: A small bunch of brown hackle fibers, rather long
Wing: Bright yellow marabou, over which is a very small bunch of white bucktail, over which are six fibers of peacock herl, all extending to the end of the tail

(As dressed by Mr. E. H. Rosborough)

This is a prominent northwestern pattern evidently originated by George and Helen Voss, of Portland, Oregon. The *Atom Bomb* can be dressed in several color combinations. The *Gray Atom Bomb* differs from the above only in the wing and tail. The tail is the tips of two brown hackles. The wing is a very small bunch of white bucktail, over which is gray marabou, over which is a very small bunch of brown bucktail. All are of the same lengths as in the *Yellow Atom Bomb*.

AUNT IDER STREAMER

Head: Black (sometimes with red painted eye with white center)
Body: Medium flat silver tinsel
Ribbing: Narrow oval silver tinsel
Throat: Five or six strands of peacock herl, under which is a small bunch of white bucktail, both nearly as long as the wing
Wing: A small bunch of yellow bucktail, over which are four grizzly saddle hackles
Shoulders: Each a Ripon's silver pheasant body feather, not over one-third as long as the wing
Cheeks: Jungle cock

(As dressed by Mr. Gardner Percy)

Originated by Mr. Frank Congdon of Middletown, Connecticut, and named for Mrs. Congdon.

BALI DUCK STREAMER

Head: Black
Tag: Narrow flat gold tinsel. The tag is rather long, extending part way down the bend of the hook
Tail: Fifteen or twenty strands of a golden pheasant tippet. The tail is rather long
Butt: Two turns of black chenille
Body: Medium embossed silver tinsel. Just behind the throat is a forward butt of about four turns of peacock herl
Ribbing: Medium flat silver tinsel, extending between the two butts
Throat: Two turns of a brown hackle, tied downward. The hackle should be very soft and the throat sparsely dressed
Wing: Two Bali duck feathers (sometimes called "Yanosh"), tied so that the bright and glossy surfaces are on the outside with the bends of the feathers exactly alike. The wing extends beyond the tail by a distance equal to the length of the tail
Cheeks: Jungle cock

(As dressed by Mr. Earl Leitz)

Originated by Mr. Arthur Bates, of Sault Ste. Marie, Michigan, and named by Mr. Ray Bergman, who fished with Mr. Bates and Mr. Leitz in 1948. This is one of several flies designed for taking the large rainbows (called "Soo" trout) of the St. Mary's River at the outlet of Lake Superior. Since the trout in these rapids are large, these flies usually are dressed on No. 2 hooks.

BALLOU SPECIAL STREAMER (PLATE VII)

Head: Black
Tail: One or two short golden pheasant crest feathers curving downward
Body: Medium flat silver tinsel
Wing: About a dozen hairs of red bucktail slightly longer than the tail, over which are two white marabou feathers of the same length tied on flat (at right angles with the hook)
Topping: About a dozen strands of peacock herl as long as the wing
Cheeks: Jungle cock

(As dressed by the originator)

Originated in 1921 by Mr. A. W. Ballou of Litchfield, Maine (formerly of North Dighton, Massachusetts), after several years of experimentation in attempting to find a type of feather which would give greater action than the hackles usually used on streamer flies.

The fly first was used at the mouth of the Songo River on Sebago Lake, in Maine, to catch the landlocked salmon which run up the river in the spring to spawn. The *Ballou Special*, often called by other names, is considered by many anglers to be one of the best and most successful imitations of the smelt. Mr. Ballou says: "When I first got it up they called it the *Powder Puff*. I tied hundreds, and I mean hundreds, of marabou streamers with all types of dressings, and I had my marabou feathers dyed all colors. Finally I got down to three; the one I call the *Ballou Special*, another one tied with a red tail and a special light blue-green bucktail in place of the red bucktail, and one tied with a yellow body and some light blue bucktail under the marabou, without a tail. All have peacock herl topping and jungle cock cheeks."

Mr. Ballou is given credit for having originated the marabou streamer. His first ones were dressed on long shanked single hooks, and this form of dressing usually is preferred by other anglers. Later he dressed them on short shanked double hooks. He prefers the first method for use when smelt are running upstream, and the second method when they are returning downstream after spawning. Smelt going upstream follow the banks, while on their return they form in schools and keep to the channel of the river. Thus, Mr. Ballou finds greatest success in fishing the fly in the direction in which the smelt are running, casting upstream with the double hooked fly when the smelt are running downstream and allowing the fly to sink and work in the current as it is being retrieved. Anglers fishing for landlocked salmon in the spring and early summer when the smelt are running, feel that the migrations of the smelt govern the location and activity of the salmon, just as surely as fly hatches govern the feeding habits of trout.

BARNES SPECIAL STREAMER

Head: Red
Tail: Two very short jungle cock body feather tips
Body: Medium flat silver tinsel
Ribbing: Narrow oval silver tinsel
Throat: Several turns of a white saddle hackle, tied on as a collar after the wing has been applied. The hackle is rather long and full

Wing: A small bunch of red bucktail, over which is a very small bunch of white bucktail, over which are two yellow saddle hackles flanked on each side by a barred gray Plymouth Rock saddle hackle. The bucktail is nearly as long as the hackles

(As dressed by Mr. Gardner Percy)

This fly was adapted from the *Hurricane* streamer by C. Lowell Barnes, a guide at Sebago Lake, Maine, who added the yellow hackles between the Plymouth Rock hackles. The fly is a favorite in the Sebago Lake area.

BARTLETT'S SPECIAL STREAMER (Plate II)

Head: Black
Tail: A very short golden pheasant crest feather, curving upward and clipped flat at the end
Body: Black silk, dressed rather thinly and tapered at both ends
Ribbing: Narrow flat silver tinsel
Throat: A small bunch of yellow hackle fibers
Wing: Four white saddle hackles
Topping: A golden pheasant crest feather as long as the wing and following its curve. Over this is a very narrow section (about three fibers) of a dark blue swan tail or wing feather as long as the wing and so curved as to follow its conformation

(As dressed by The Weber Tackle Co.)

This fly was originated by Mr. Arthur Bartlett of Presque Isle, Maine. It is essentially a *Black Ghost* with the topping added. This dressing was obtained from Mr. Edward C. Wotruba, President of The Weber Tackle Company, of Stevens Point, Wisconsin, who obtained it from Mr. Bartlett.

BATTENKILL SHINER (Plate VI)

Head: Black   Hook size: No. 8 – No. 6, 6X long
Tail: A very small bunch of gray hackle fibers
Butt: A few turns of red floss
Body: Tapered white floss
Ribbing: Flat silver tinsel, over body only
Throat: A small bunch of gray hackle fibers
Wing: Two medium blue saddle hackles on each side of which is a silver badger saddle hackle, all extending to the end of the tail
Cheeks: Jungle cock, rather short

(As dressed by Mr. Keith Fulsher)

Famous Patterns

This fly is an imitation of shiners common to the Battenkill River, in Vermont. It was copied by Keith Fulsher from an original given to him by the famous angler and fly dresser, Lew Oatman, of Shushan, New York.

BAUMAN BUCKTAIL

Head: Black (red painted eye with white center is optional)
Tail: A section of a barred wood duck or mandarin duck feather
Body: Orange silk, dressed thin (or gold tinsel)
Ribbing: Narrow flat gold tinsel (if a gold tinsel body is used, use oval gold tinsel)
Throat: A bunch of red hackle fibers
Wing: A small bunch of white bucktail over which is a small bunch yellow bucktail
Topping: A bunch of six or eight peacock sword fibers, one-half as long as the wing
Cheeks: Jungle cock

(As dressed by The Weber Tackle Co.)

Originated by Mr. Arthur Bartlett, of Presque Isle, Maine, and named for Mr. Art Bauman of The Weber Tackle Company, of Stevens Point, Wisconsin.

BELKNAP

Head: Yellow (000 silk)   Hook size: No. 8 (2811S Allcock)
Tail: A small bunch of crimson hackle fibers
Body: Six layers of No. 14 flat narrow gold tinsel, lacquered
Wing: A very small bunch of the white tip hair from a genuine calf or fox tail extending to the end of the tail, over which is a very small bunch of the same hair half as long as the first one
Topping: Two narrow sections of gray mottled mallard body feather, not quite as long as the wing
Cheeks: Jungle cock, rather short

(As dressed by the originator)

Originated by Ray Salminen, of West Acton, Massachusetts, to imitate minnows in the Sandwich, New Hampshire area. This fly is popular for stream fishing for brook, brown and rainbow trout.

BELL SPECIAL STREAMER

Head: Black
Body: Medium flat silver tinsel
Throat: Three or four scarlet hackle tips of moderate length
Wing: A small bunch of white ostrich herl, over which is a very small bunch of brown ostrich herl. Both are of the same length and the brown is half as much as the white
Topping: Four or five strands of peacock herl. (This is not called for in the original dressing but later was added by Mr. Bell)
Cheeks: Jungle cock (optional)
(As dressed by Mr. Herbert L. Howard)

Originated by Mr. Anson Bell, of Pittsburg, New Hampshire, who was a logger in the lumber camps of Maine. The original sample of this pattern was obtained by Mr. Howard from Mr. Bell, and was used in the paintings of flies in Ray Bergman's book TROUT. The fly is popular for taking all species of trout, particularly in New York State and in New England.

BELLAMY BUCKTAIL (PLATE VIII)

Head: Black
Tail: A section of a red goose wing feather, wide and long. (Subsequently Mr. Schwab found that a tail of a small bunch of red polar bear hair, rather long, was superior to the feather tail because of its added permanence. This should now be considered the standard dressing)
Body: Wound with copper wire, as shown in the instructions on page 191
Wing: A small bunch of white bucktail, over which is a small bunch of brown hair from a bucktail dyed yellow. The wing extends to the end of the tail. In applying the two parts of the wing, turns of thread are taken under the bucktail to raise the wing to an angle of about 40 degrees
Throat: (Dressed as a "spike" as explained in the above reference.) A small bunch of California gray squirrel (ground squirrel) tail hair. This is generally omitted. A brown hackle applied as a collar may be used, but this also is omitted from the latest versions of Mr. Schwab's dressing
(As dressed by the originator)

Originated by Mr. Peter J. Schwab, of Yreka, California, whose comments on this fly, as printed in the June, 1946, issue of *Sports Afield* magazine, are: "This bucktail is the great favorite of George B. Bellamy, who was largely responsible for its creation. We had been using shot to get our light bucktails deep enough and were having

Famous Patterns

the usual troubles with cut and snarled leaders, awkward, difficult casting and poor action of the lures. George bemoaned the fact that we had no weighted flies. I agreed and, luckily having an ample stock of assorted wires, went to work. The first fly actually tied was a *Van Luven*, with red wool body over a copper wire core. I believe that all bucktails should have a darker topping over a lighter wing, and a yellow dyed bucktail happened to be before me. I cut a lock of hair from the dark portion of the yellow tail, topped it over the white hair of the *Van Luven*, and christened it the *Bellamy*. It was an instant success. Its action in the water was fascinating, and the steelhead jumped to the attack. Their sharp teeth soon tore the red wool covering from the body, but they hit the bare copper wire just as eagerly. I tied up a few without the red wool, and the bucktail continued to be successful through September, October, November, and December. George likes it with the brown hackle. I like it better without. The fish don't care which way it is served just so they can get it."

Although the *Bellamy* was developed as a steelhead fly for the Klamath River, in California, it is equally good as a trout and bass fly in other parts of the country.

BI-BUCK BUCKTAIL

Head: Black
Tail: A small section of a red duck, goose or swan wing feather
Body: Medium flat silver tinsel
Ribbing: Narrow oval silver tinsel (optional)
Wing: A small bunch of white bucktail, over which is a small bunch of brown bucktail
Cheeks: Jungle cock

(As dressed by Fin, Fur and Feather, Ltd.)

This fly is the always popular and easily dressed brown and white bucktail in its most accepted dressing. It is called the *Bi-Buck* in Canada. The wing can be of several other color combinations and in almost any variety of hair. Brown and yellow, red and yellow, yellow and white, black and white, or red and white are among the most popular combinations. The darker color in a two-color bucktail is dressed over the lighter color.

BIG DIAMOND STREAMER

Head: Black
Tail: A narrow section of a red duck wing feather
Body: Medium flat silver tinsel
Ribbing: Narrow oval silver tinsel (optional)
Throat: A very small bunch of greenish-blue bucktail, nearly as long as the wing. Under this is a very small bunch of guinea hen body feather fibers, as long as the shoulder. (Another version of the dressing calls for a very small bunch of white bucktail, nearly as long as the wing, instead of the above)
Wing: Two bright yellow saddle hackles with a golden badger hackle of the same length on each side
Horns: Each a section (two strands) of a red swan feather, nearly as long as the wing
Shoulders: Each the tip of a brown barred mandarin duck body feather, one-third as long as the wing
Cheeks: Jungle cock (optional)

Originated by Mr. Frank Congdon of Middletown, Connecticut, and named for a section of the Connecticut Lakes country in Northern New England. This dressing is as given to The Weber Tackle Company by Mr. Congdon.

BINNS STREAMER   (Plate II)

Head: Black
Tail: A section of a red and of a white duck or goose wing feather, rather long and thin
Body: Medium flat silver tinsel (sometimes yellow wool is used)
Ribbing: Narrow oval silver tinsel
Throat: Two or three turns of a red and a white saddle hackle, tied on mixed together as a collar and then tied downward
Wing: In two matched pairs, each a section of a white goose wing married between two sections of yellow goose wing, the three sections being equal in width. The wing is slightly longer than the tail
Shoulders: Guinea hen breast feathers, one-third as long as the wing
(As dressed by the originator)

Originated by Mr. Frier Gulline, of Fin, Fur and Feather Ltd., for Mr. J. Binns of Montreal, in 1937. It was originally tied as a trout fly and was adapted as a streamer in 1940.

BLACK AND WHITE STREAMER (PLATE II)

Head: Black   Hook size: No. 6, 4X long
Tail: A very small bunch of crimson hackle fibers
Body: Narrow flat silver tinsel
Throat: A few pink bucktail hairs slightly longer than the hook, mixed with a very small bunch of crimson hackle fibers not over half as long as the hair
Wing: Four white saddle hackles, on each side of which are two jet black saddle hackles, all of the same length, about half again as long as the hook. All the fibers on the bottom of the black hackles are stripped off to provide a black upper half and a white lower half of the wing
Shoulders: Jet black mallard body feather on each side, one-third as long as the wing
Cheeks: Jungle cock

(As dressed by the originator)

This streamer was originated by Austin S. Hogan, of Fultonville, New York, to provide high contrast when viewed against dim evening light. It is a good example of Austin Hogan's color blending technique, in this case done by stripping the lower sides of outside hackles to allow the lower parts of the inside hackles to show.

BLACKBIRD BUCKTAIL

Head: Black
Tag: A few turns of narrow flat gold tinsel
Tail: A bunch of black saddle hackle fibers, rather long
Body: Black wool, fairly fat
Ribbing: Narrow oval gold tinsel
Throat: A bunch of black saddle hackle fibers, very long
Wing: A bunch of the guard hairs from a black bear, extending to the end of the tail
Cheeks: Jungle cock, rather long

(As dressed by Mr. William Reynolds)

Adapted by Mr. William Reynolds of Sturbridge, Massachusetts, from the *Shenandoah Fly*, which is dressed in an identical manner, except that the body is tied with black chenille, full and fat, and the gold tinsel and jungle cock are eliminated. A wiggling disc or small spinner usually is used on the *Shenandoah Fly*, which is a favorite for bass. The *Blackbird* bucktail is well recommended for all species of trout, particularly in the Pennsylvania and Ozark regions, where it seems to imitate the Madtom or perhaps the polliwog. The Madtom, or Stonecat, is a food fish found under rocks in the fast water of large rivers, where it is the prey of bass and trout—big brown trout, particularly. Small sizes are preferable late in the season.

BLACK DEMON BUCKTAIL (Plate VIII)

Head: Black
Tail: Two medium width sections of a barred wood duck or mandarin duck feather, both sections being matched to curve upward, and rather long
Body: Thinly wound with narrow oval gold tinsel, several turns of which are taken below the tail to act as a tag. On extra long shanked hooks flat gold tinsel and gold ribbing may be used
Throat: Several turns of an orange saddle hackle, applied as a collar and tied back but not gathered downward. The hackle is glossy and stiff; of moderate length
Wing: A medium sized bunch of black bear hair, extending to the end of the tail. (A feather wing is less often used and usually then only on the short version of the fly. It is two strips of black goose wing curving upward. These may be splayed outward and extend between the end of the hook and the end of the tail)

This is the steelhead dressing of the *Black Demon*. For additional notes see *Cains River Black Demon Streamer*.

BLACK GHOST STREAMER (Plate VII)

Head: Black
Tail: A small bunch of yellow hackle fibers
Body: Of black silk, dressed rather heavily and tapered slightly at both ends
Ribbing: Medium flat silver tinsel
Throat: A small bunch of yellow hackle fibers
Wing: Four white saddle hackles
Cheeks: Jungle cock

(As dressed by the originator)

The *Black Ghost* is one of the relatively few Maine streamer flies which have enjoyed national acceptance by anglers throughout the United States. In Maine waters, nearly every fisherman will acknowledge it to be one of the most productive, especially for landlocked salmon and squaretail trout. Its popularity has caused its origination to be misunderstood and, in some cases, to be misrepresented.

The fly was originated by Mr. Herbert L. Welch, of Mooselookmeguntic, Maine, in 1927, and was first tied under his direction at the Boston Sportsmen's Show in the spring of that year by Nellie

Famous Patterns 229

Newton, a fly dresser of the Percy Tackle Company, of Portland, Maine, which had an exhibit there. Its dressing of black and white makes the reason for its name rather obvious.

Evidently Nellie Newton took a great interest in promoting the fly, as this letter to the author from Mr. A. W. Ballou, one of Maine's expert and old-time anglers from Litchfield, Maine, will testify. He says: "On my trips to Maine it was my custom to stop at the Percy Tackle Shop in Portland, and to spend several hours having dressed new types of streamer flies which I had developed during the winter. On one of these stops in 1927 Mr. Percy asked Nellie Newton, one of his fly dressers, to work with me. Nellie tied a fly with a black body and several white feathers and said it was called the *Black Ghost*. I didn't think much of it.

"I went on from Percy's to Thompson's Camps at the mouth of the Songo River (on Sebago Lake). I had been there ten or twelve days when one morning I pushed the boat out into the river and anchored it there. I hooked into a beautiful trout and had him up to the boat several times, but finally lost him. Just then a Mr. Merritt from Connecticut came along in his boat with his guide. He had seen me with the fish on and shouted that it looked like a Pierce Pond trout. Just then he cast his fly about three feet from my boat and hooked a large fish. When he landed it he pulled up to my boat to use my scales. It was a nice five and one-half pound trout and the fly was still in his mouth.

"When I stared at the fly, Mr. Merritt said, 'Do you want a copy of this fly, Mr. Ballou?' I said I didn't, but asked him where he got it. He said he stopped the day before at a place in Portland where they tied flies and bought half a dozen, but that he didn't think the fly had a name. I said it had a name all right and that it was a *Black Ghost*; the same fly that Nellie had tied for me. After telling her that I didn't think much of it, and then seeing Mr. Merritt catch a five and one-half pound trout right under my boat with it, I swore I never would use one of those darned *Black Ghosts* as long as I lived, and I never have.

"As you know, it turned out to be one of the best streamers that ever was developed. I think Mr. Merritt gave it a big start by giving samples away."

The evidence is that Nellie Newton also gave away many *Black Ghosts* that year. Guides and sportsmen duplicated them, which contributed to the erroneous impression that the fly was invented by several people at about the same time. In checking up on the matter, I wrote to Gardner Percy. He replied: "With regard to the *Black Ghost* streamer fly, Herbie Welch was the originator of the pattern. Nellie Newton tied the fly for Herb at the Boston Sportsmen's Show back in 1927 when we had a display booth there."

In addition to its success with other fish, the *Black Ghost* is an excellent pattern for spring salmon when tied with a white bucktail wing and a throat and tail of golden pheasant crest. Both the feathered original and the bucktail adaptation are favorite flies for landlocked salmon, and for bass as well as for most species of trout. Mr. Welch considers it to be most successful in the early spring or in the late fall.

The *Phoenecia* bucktail is an adaptation of the *Black Ghost* bucktail formerly popular among Catskill anglers who fished the Esopus River in New York State between the portal and Ashokan Dam. It is identical with the *Black Ghost* except that it is ribbed with gold tinsel, has a tail of a double section of dark yellow wool, and no throat. This area produces brown and rainbow trout.

The *Rogers Knight* has enjoyed considerable editorial attention in the New England area. It was originated (if the word should be used in this case) by Edward W. Rogers of Manchester-By-The-Sea, Massachusetts, and differs from the *Black Ghost* only by having a wing of rusty bronze dun saddle hackles, preferably with very dark medial lines.

BLACK GORDON BUCKTAIL

Head: Black
Tag: Thinly dressed with three or four turns of red silk
Body: Black wool yarn thinly dressed at rear and shaped larger toward head
Ribbing: Narrow flat silver tinsel
Throat: A medium sized black hackle; three or four turns tied on as a collar and then tied downward
Wing: A small bunch of black or dark brown bucktail tied on as a steelhead wing, rather high, on a large steelhead hook 2X long

(As dressed by Mr. Don C. Harger)

Famous Patterns

This fly was originated by Mr. Clarence Gordon, a well known guide and steelhead angler of the North Umpqua Lodge on the Umpqua River of Oregon. It is especially good for summer run steelhead on the upper reaches of Oregon's coastal rivers.

BLACK LEECH STREAMER

Head: Black   Hook sizes: No. 2 to No. 8, 3X to 6X long
Tail: A very small bunch of scarlet hackle fibers, a little longer than the gap of the hook
Body: Wound rather heavily with peacock herl
Throat: A black saddle hackle wound on as a collar and tied downward
Wing: Four jet black saddle hackles, the two on one side being back to back with the two on the other side, to provide a splayed wing slightly longer than the tail

(As dressed by Mr. E. H. Rosborough)

This is a popular northwestern pattern which is especially productive for trout in lakes where leeches are present. This fly should not be confused with another called the *Leech Streamer*, which consists of a heavy maroon body and a throat of a small bunch of black hackle fibers. The wing is two maroon saddle hackles, over which are two black saddle hackles. All four feathers are tied on flat (at right angles with the hook) so that the two black hackles are on top.

BLACK NOSED DACE BUCKTAIL   (Plate I)

Head: Black
Tail: A fine piece of red yarn, very short
Body: Medium flat silver tinsel
Ribbing: Fine oval silver tinsel
Wing: A small bunch of white polar bear hair or bucktail, over which is a small bunch of black bear hair or black hair from a skunk's tail, over which is a small bunch of brown bucktail. The black hair is a little shorter than the brown and the white. Care should be taken to use small bunches of hair so that the fly will not be overdressed

(As dressed by the originator)

Originated by Mr. Arthur B. Flick, of Westkill, New York, to imitate the baitfish commonly called the "Black Nosed Dace," as described in his book STREAMSIDE GUIDE TO NATURALS AND THEIR IMITATIONS (G. P. Putnam's Sons, New York). Mr. Flick advised that the fly be dressed on hook sizes, 4, 6, 8, or 10, the smaller sizes being preferable late in the season. When the small sizes are tied, Chinese or Mexican deer tails will be found suitable, because the hair is softer than the hair of the white-tailed deer. Mr. Harold N. Gibbs, the noted salt water fly fisherman of Barrington, Rhode Island, has found this fly, in larger sizes, with a red throat added, to be excellent for taking striped bass.

BLUE DEVIL STREAMER (PLATE IV)

Head: Black, with red band
Tag: A few turns of narrow flat silver tinsel
Body: Thinly dressed with black silk
Ribbing: Narrow flat silver tinsel
Throat: A small bunch of white bucktail, extending beyond the barb of the hook, under which is a small bunch of orange hackle fibers
Wing: Six or eight strands of bronze peacock herl, over which are two orange saddle hackles flanked on each side by a dark blue saddle hackle, slightly shorter. The peacock is as long as the orange hackles
Shoulders: Light brownish-gray feathers from the breast of a partridge
Cheeks: Jungle cock, rather short
(As dressed by the originator)

This is one of the earliest streamer fly patterns originated by Mrs. Carrie G. Stevens, of Madison, Maine, for eastern brook trout and landlocked salmon. It was first used at Upper Dam Pool, in the Rangeley Lakes section of Maine in 1923.

BLUEFISH BUCKTAIL

Head: Black, with white painted eye with red pupil
Body: Medium flat silver tinsel
Throat: A few strands of red hackle fibers
Wing: A bunch of light blue capra (Asiatic goat) hair with some of the underfur left in. Bucktail may be substituted. The wing is very long
Shoulders: Jungle cock breast feathers, one-fourth as long as the wing
(As dressed by the originator)

Originated by Mr. Frank B. Gibbs, of Rumford, Rhode Island. This fly is for night use and is taken by bluefish only when it is fished very slowly. The action of the current is all that is needed. A very long shank hook is used, and the fly is tied with the head an inch or

Famous Patterns

more back on the shank of the hook, so that the sharp teeth of the bluefish will not come in contact with the leader.

BLUE MARABOU STREAMER (PLATE III)

Head: Black   Hook size: No. 8 to No. 1/0, 6X long
Tail: A very small bunch of red-orange hackle the length of the gap of the hook
Body: Wound with gray floss
Ribbing: Flat gold tinsel
Throat: A small bunch of grass-green polar bear hair, as long as the hook
Wing: A small bunch of white polar bear hair extending to end of tail. Over this are two light-blue marabou feathers slightly longer than the polar bear hair
Shoulders: On each side, a badger saddle hackle almost as long as the wing
Cheeks: Jungle cock, short

(As dressed by the originator)

This fly was originated by Mr. Paul Kukonen, expert professional fly dresser and casting champion of (110 Green Street) Worcester, Massachusetts, for landlocked salmon and brook trout. It is similar to the *Supervisor* and the *Spencer Bay Special*, except that Mr. Kukonen thinks the addition of marabou and polar bear hair makes it more effective. He has caught many hundreds of salmon and trout on the fly in New England, Canada, and Labrador, including a seven-and-a-half pound brook trout in Pierce's Pond, Maine. The fly in smaller sizes is excellent for brown and rainbow trout. Dressed as a tandem fly, on 6X long No. 2 or No. 1 hooks, it is excellent for trolling on the surface or for deep (wire line) trolling in summer.

BOB WILSON STREAMER

Head: Yellow
Tail: A very short golden pheasant crest feather, curving upward. The feather usually is trimmed to even the end
Body: Copper wire or embossed copper tinsel, dressed very thin
Throat: A few turns of a black hackle wound on as a collar and tied downward. The throat is long and sparsely dressed
Wing: Two matching sections of barred wood duck or mandarin duck feathers, fairly narrow and long, extending just beyond the tail

(As dressed by Mr. Herbert L. Howard)

This fly originated in Scotland as a wet fly in about the year 1890. It was first tied by Mr. Robert Wilson, who used it as a boy in Scotland. He later lived in Old Greenwich, Connecticut, where he adapted the fly to a streamer in the early 1920's. Mr. Wilson was a close friend of Mr. George Fraser and of Mr. Howard. He used this fly in lively competition with Mr. Fraser and his *Fraser* streamer, but neither could decide which fly was better than the other.

BOBBY DUNN BUCKTAIL

Head: Black
Tail: A section of a red goose wing feather, wide and long. (Subsequently, Mr. Schwab found that a tail of a small bunch of red polar bear hair, rather long, was superior to the feather tail because of its added permanence. This should now be considered the standard dressing)
Body: Wound with copper wire, as shown in the instructions on page 191
Wing: A small bunch of white polar bear hair, over which is a small bunch of red polar bear hair. A few strands of dark brown bucktail may be put over this, but it is omitted on the standard pattern. The wing extends to the end of the tail. In applying the two parts of the wing, turns of thread are taken under the bucktail to raise the wing to an angle of about 40 degrees. Bucktail may be substituted for the polar bear if desired
Throat: (Dressed as a "spike," as explained in the above reference.) A small bunch of red polar bear hair. This is generally omitted

(As dressed by the originator)

This is one of a series of steelhead flies originated by Mr. Peter J. Schwab, of Yreka, California, principally for fishing on the Klamath River. It is primarily influenced by the nationally successful *Parmacheene Belle* colors, and was named for Mr. Bobby Dunn, a noted California angler and fishing companion of Mr. Schwab.

BOLSHEVIK STREAMER

Head: Black
Tail: The tip of a golden yellow neck hackle
Body: Medium flat silver tinsel
Throat: A small bunch of light brown bucktail, nearly as long as the wing
Wing: A red saddle hackle on each side of which are two dark ginger furnace hackles with a very pronounced black stripe
Cheeks: Jungle cock

(As dressed by the originator)

Famous Patterns

Originated by Mr. Fred B. Fowler of Oquossoc, Maine, in 1925. This fly is preferred for late fall fishing for both squaretail trout and landlocked salmon in Maine.

BONBRIGHT STREAMER (PLATE V)

Head: Black
Tail: Two very narrow and rather long sections of a red and a white duck wing feather, the red and the white of each section being married together. The colors of each of the two sections are reversed. A very short golden pheasant crest feather is added. The two married sections and the golden pheasant crest feather are of the same length and all curve upward
Body: Of medium flat silver tinsel, built up slightly toward the head. (The fresh water version is thin and not built up)
Ribbing: Fine oval silver tinsel
Throat: A small bunch of white hackle fibers of medium length
Wing: Four white neck hackles, rather long
Horns: Each a single fiber from a blue mackaw tail feather, two-thirds as long as the wing
Shoulders: Each a golden pheasant crest feather nearly as long as the wing. Outside of this is a red duck breast feather with a solid edge, one-fourth as long as the wing. The red shoulders are dressed high so as not to conceal the body and throat but to conceal all the front of the wing. The throat joins the underside of the red shoulder on both sides
Checks: Jungle cock, set in the center of the red shoulders
(As dressed for the originator)

This fly is a development of the *Colonel White*. The augmented pattern was dressed about 1925 on the instructions of Mr. G. D. B. Bonbright, president of the Seaboard Airline Railway, to Mr. Steward Slosson, a fly dresser for Abercrombie and Fitch Company, of New York City. Mr. Bonbright used the fly for tarpon fishing in Florida and made it famous due to the large numbers of tarpon and other salt water fish taken with it. He preferred 4/0 hooks for tarpon and insisted that the heads of the flies be soaked in duPont cement and then black lacquered.

The *Bonbright* streamer, which had its genesis as one of Maine's earliest landlocked salmon flies, was readapted to Maine fishing by Mr. L. Dana Chapman, a tackle dealer of Boston, who gave the Percy Tackle Company an order for some of these flies dressed for fresh water fishing. Mr. Percy renamed it the *Dana*. It also has been called the *Ross McKenney*, as discussed in Chapter II.

BRASS HAT BUCKTAIL

Head: Black
Tail: A very small bunch of yellow dyed polar bear hair, very long (yellow dyed bucktail may be substituted). Early dressings called for "yellow or red goose, preferably yellow." Mr. Schwab now prefers the hair tail
Body: Wound with yellow brass wire (see instructions on page 189)
Wing: A small bunch of white bucktail, over which is a small bunch of yellow bucktail topped with a very few hairs of black bucktail or skunk. The wing extends to the end of the tail. In applying the two parts of the wing, turns of thread are taken under both the white and the yellow bucktail to raise the wing to an angle of about 40 degrees. In the three-winged pattern the rear wing is white bucktail (dressed on a very long shanked hook) and the lower part of the front wing is yellow bucktail, dressed fairly full, with the upper wing brown bucktail dyed yellow or an extremely small bunch of black bucktail or skunk. The brown bucktail dyed yellow is Mr. Schwab's choice
Throat: (Dressed as a "spike" as explained in the above reference.) A small bunch of yellow bucktail. This is generally omitted, particularly in the two-wing dressing

(As dressed by the originator)

The weighted dressing, as explained in the above reference, is a later improvement, succeeding the unweighted gold tinsel version. Of this fly, Mr. Schwab says: "I would hate to go steelhead fishing without this pattern in both two-winged and three-winged versions. Its only rival is the *Queen Bess*. When the day is dark or the river is high or murky, I bend on a *Brass Hat*, knowing it will be seen.

"When the day is dark but the water is clear and low, I use the *Brass Hat* in the two-winged version, tied to sizes 2 or 4 Limerick hooks, 2X and 3X strong respectively, on the standard shank. When the day is dark and/or the river is high or murky, I try a three-winged *Brass Hat*, tied on a size 2 Limerick, 3X long and 2X heavy. As a three-winged bucktail it is the perfect companion to the deeper-hued *Paint Brush*. It has everything—flashing, swimming, darting action."

Mr. Schwab originated this fly for use on the Klamath River, in California, but it is an excellent bucktail for all fresh water game fish in other parts of the country. Its color scheme should recommend it for salt water fishing also.

Famous Patterns

BROOK TROUT (PLATE VI)

Head: Olive green, painted white underneath
Tail: A very small bunch of white hackle, over which is a very small bunch of black hackle, over which is a larger bunch of rich orange hackle, all as long as the gap of the hook. The three colors should not be blended, and the orange should be as much as the black and white together. The three imitate the color scheme of a brook trout's fin
Body: The rear three-fourths is white floss, with the forward one-fourth salmon pink floss, tapered quite full
Ribbing: Medium flat gold tinsel
Throat: The same as the tail, and of same length
Wing: Two grizzly saddle hackles, on each of which is an olive-green hackle. The green hackles are painted with three alternating very small yellow and scarlet dots along the quill
Cheeks: Jungle cock, eye only

(As dressed by the originator)

This beautiful imitation of a small brook trout was originated by the famous angler Lew Oatman, of Shushan, New York, for use in waters where large brook trout are accustomed to feed on small ones. The fly has had outstanding success, especially in Quebec and in California lakes where eastern brook trout were planted. It is also effective for rainbow trout and other species. (An original of the fly, dressed by Mr. Oatman, is illustrated in Plate VI.)

BROOKS BLONDE PATTERNS (PLATE V)
(See Chapter IX.)

BROWN FALCON BUCKTAIL

Head: Black
Tag: Two turns of medium embossed silver tinsel
Butt: Red silk, rather wide
Body: Medium embossed silver tinsel, butted just behind the head with red silk
Wing: A fairly large bunch of white bucktail, over which is a fairly large bunch of yellow bucktail
Shoulders: A brown saddle hackle on each side, nearly as long as the wing
Cheeks: Jungle cock

(As dressed by Mr. Gardner Percy)

This fly is one of the most popular for black salmon in New Brunswick. It is very similar to Hardy Brothers' *Smelt*, which was the original of the pattern. Since black salmon flies are fished usually in very high water, and since weighted flies are not allowed, streamers and bucktails for this type of fishing must be very heavily dressed in order to make them sink. All black salmon streamers are dressed on No. 2 or 4 long shanked hooks.

BROWN GHOST STREAMER

Head: Black
Tag: A few turns of narrow flat silver tinsel
Body: Dark brown silk
Ribbing: Narrow flat silver tinsel
Throat: Four or five strands of bright green peacock herl, under which is a very small bunch of white bucktail, both slightly longer than the hook, beneath which is a golden pheasant crest feather as long as the shoulder and curving upward
Wing: A golden pheasant crest feather slightly longer than the hook and curving downward, over which are four medium brown saddle hackles
Shoulders: Teal body feathers, dyed brown, nearly half as long as the wing
Cheeks: Jungle cock

(As dressed for the originator)

This is a copy of the famous *Gray Ghost* streamer in a different color, as originally adapted by Mr. Gardner Percy, of Portland, Maine, to obtain a successful streamer predominantly brown in color. It has proved to be excellent, particularly for large brown trout.

BUCKTAIL SILVER STREAMER

Head: Black
Body: Medium flat embossed silver tinsel
Throat: The tip of a very short golden pheasant crest feather dyed red
Wing: A very small bunch of white bucktail over which are two creamy white badger hackles of the same length as the bucktail
Cheeks: Jungle cock, very short

(As dressed by the originator)

This is one of a series of three streamers originated by Mr. Ray Bergman of Nyack, New York, in 1933. These flies should be dressed sparsely in small sizes. They are excellent for all species of trout. A popular adaptation of this fly is made by applying the bucktail as a throat and leaving off the throat called for above. In this adaptation, medium flat silver tinsel is used on the body, which is ribbed with oval silver tinsel.

Famous Patterns

THE BUMBLEPUPPY (PLATE VII)

This historic fly, originally tied both as a bucktail and as a streamer, evidently is the first of all the modern patterns of this type. Originated by the famous Theodore Gordon, creator of the popular *Quill Gordon* and father of the American dry fly, the *Bumblepuppy* actually is not one fly but rather several related patterns as developed by Mr. Gordon over many years prior to his death in 1915. As described on pages 16, 17, 40, 41, 42, and 331 of THE COMPLETE FLY FISHERMAN (The Notes and Letters of Theodore Gordon), by John McDonald (Charles Scribner's Sons, New York), the fly is dressed as follows:

Head: Red or yellow chenille, or black, plain varnished
Tag: Silver and red silk
Tail: Scarlet ibis, two mated feathers, back to back and quite straight on hook
Butt: Red or yellow chenille
Body: White silk chenille dressed full; not thin
Ribbing: Medium flat silver tinsel
Throat: Badger; large, long and lots of it
Wing: White hair from deer, white bear or goat, over which are strips of white swan or goose
Shoulders: Widgeon feathers, as long or longer than the badger
Cheeks: Jungle cock, tied low (in line with the hook)

In Mr. Gordon's letters he states that he has "used the *Bumblepuppy* most successfully for pike, salmon, striped bass, and other game fish." Probably the rather elaborate dressing which Mr. McDonald quotes was not the one to which Mr. Gordon refers, because it certainly is not the final version as developed by Gordon over the years, as the following will show.

In a letter to the author, Mr. Roy Steenrod, of Liberty, New York, game warden friend and fishing companion of Mr. Gordon, says, "The *Bumblepuppy* meant to Mr. Gordon any fly to which there was no name. He tied many of them. I called on Herman Christian, a fly tier friend of Gordon's, and we are both of the opinion that the fly I have tied and am sending to you was the favorite and the one of which he often spoke as having taken so many fish with in the lakes of Rockland County, New York. I know that Gordon was tying these

Joe Bates

Famous Patterns

flies as early as 1880." Mr. Steenrod's version of Gordon's favorite *Bumblepuppy* is as follows:

Head: Black
Tail: A dozen rather long fibers from a red hackle feather
Body: White chenille
Throat: About two turns of a red and a white neck hackle, to make a very long but not heavily dressed collar
Wing: A very small bunch of white bucktail, extending slightly beyond the tail of the fly
Shoulders: Four sections of a brown turkey tail feather; two for each shoulder. Each two are matched with the concave sides together to give the appearance of a single feather. They are tied on rather high, like the wings of a wet fly, but the two shoulders splay out to make a "V" when viewed from the top. The shoulders are nearly as long as the bucktail

Mr. Herman Christian, of Neversink, New York, who fished with Gordon over a long period of years, differs slightly with Mr. Steenrod in the dressing of the *Bumblepuppy*, particularly in the fact that the Christian version does not have splayed shoulders. Instead, the brown turkey feather is used as a wing, as described in the following dressing:

Head: Black
Tail: A small bunch of red hackle fibers, rather long
Body: White wool or chenille, rather heavy
Ribbing: A single strand of red wool yarn
Throat: About two turns of a red and a white neck hackle, mixed to make a very long but not heavily dressed collar
Wing: A bunch of white bucktail, extending slightly beyond the tail of the fly. The lower half of the bunch of bucktail is clipped off at about half its length after it has been tied in. Over the bucktail is a wing of two long but narrow matched sections of a brown turkey tail feather, extending as far as the beginning of the tail

Note: The early *Bumblepuppies* were tied on regular wet fly hooks, usually in size 4 or 6. This version is dressed on a long shank streamer fly hook, size 2 or 4. Long hooks were not available during Mr. Gordon's lifetime.

The above evidently is the *Bumblepuppy* preferred by Theodore Gordon. In using it, Mr. Christian found that better results were obtained by dressing the body with white chenille, without the red wool ribbing. In letters to the author he says:

"Mr. Gordon made me lots of flies and when he got sick I started to make them but never thought I would do so for the public. Mr. Gordon made me a lot of *Bumblepuppies*—perhaps twenty different kinds. But the one I made was the only one that was any good. It is a killer. A friend of mine was fishing in Moose River (Maine) a few years back and caught his limit of big native trout and (landlocked) salmon every day with the *Bumblepuppy*, while his friends didn't catch any. Another man caught a brown trout in the Delaware River on the *Bumblepuppy* while fishing for bass. It weighed thirteen pounds and nine ounces. I have caught many, many bass on it, so it is a real good fly for big fish. I have also caught walleyed pike on it. I am sending you a fly like Mr. Gordon made for me (with the red ribbing) and one like I make (with the white chenille but no ribbing). Mr. Gordon almost always put a stripe on the body, either gold, silver, or copper tinsel or some kind of wool. I don't like the stripe and never have had much luck with Mr. Gordon's *Bumblepuppies* which had stripes on them. I think my version is the best one. Of course, I made it for bass but there have been lots of big fish caught on it all over the country, including big trout of all kinds, and salmon."

Thus it would seem that the "twenty kinds of *Bumblepuppies*" tied from time to time by Theodore Gordon were a progressive attempt by him to arrive at what he thought was the ideal pattern. Since Mr. Gordon's research was cut short by his untimely death, evidently Mr. Christian's adaptation should be considered as the final version and as such it should be accepted. Quite obviously, Theodore Gordon was far in advance of his time in developing streamers and bucktails, since his early work compares favorably with that of others done decades later. Added to his fame as "the father of the American dry fly" should be equal fame for having originated the modern streamer fly and bucktail.

CAINS RIVER STREAMERS

This series of flies is credited to Mr. Fred N. Peet, a famous amateur distance fly casting champion and angler of Chicago, Illinois. While it is true that Mr. Peet originated several of these patterns, it also is true that he did not design all of them and that their rather individual style of dressing was in use several years before

Famous Patterns

Mr. Peet tied the first of the series for use in New Brunswick's Cains River in 1924. It is also true that additional patterns have been developed in Cains River style by other anglers and have been included in this set. For example, in Mr. William Bayard Sturgis' book FLY TYING he includes the *Gold Demon*, *Black Demon*, and *Silver Demon*, the first of which evidently was brought to this country from New Zealand in 1933 or 1934 by the great fly fisherman, Mr. Fred Burnham. This fly gained much of its American popularity through the efforts of Mr. C. Jim Pray, of Eureka, California, generally conceded to be the greatest expert on steelhead flies who ever lived. The *Black Demon* and *Silver Demon* were originated by Mr. Pray to complete this set of three, and are discussed further under those flies. I shall include them in the Cains River series because they are frequently considered to belong there, although Mr. Pray also ties them as steelhead bucktails with a somewhat different dressing.

One of the best informed authorities on the genesis of the Cains River patterns is Mr. Oscar Weber, of The Weber Tackle Company of Stevens Point, Wisconsin, who was a friend and angling companion of Mr. Peet. Mr. Weber wrote the author as follows: "Mr. Peet originated the *Highlander*, *Kidder*, *Miramichi*, *Peet's Masterpiece*, and the *Cains River Streamer*. *Herman's Favorite* was designed by Mr. Raymond E. Herman, of Chicago, Illinois. *Roaring Rapids* was designed by a Colorado angler whose name I am unable to supply. *Allen's First Choice*, *Allen's Last Chance*, *Dunk's Special*, *Aleck's Wonder*, and *Wade's Choice* were designed by myself. *Allen's First Choice* and *Allen's Last Chance* were named for Mr. Harry Allen, who used to lease the Cains River and who furnished equipment and guides for the Cains River trip. *Aleck's Wonder*, *Wade's Choice*, and *Dunk's Special* were named for three guides who worked for Mr. Allen."

Originally tied for taking Atlantic salmon, the Cains River series also is good for trout (including steelhead), bass and many other species of fish. Since these famous and beautiful patterns are regarded by many anglers and fly dressers as being collectors' items I shall include the dressings of twenty-one of the most important patterns.

All these flies are distinguished by having barred mandarin or wood duck tails about three-eighths of an inch wide and three-fourths of an inch long, occasionally with other feathers added. All have double-wound medium flat tinsel bodies (which should be well lacquered). In connection with the bodies, Mr. Pray states: "Peter Schwab (who knew Fred Peet personally) contends, and I subscribe to the same theory, that Fred Peet did tie quite a few of these flies with bodies other than flat silver or gold tinsel. The *Cains River Steelhead Streamer*, for example, is tied with a chenille body although the original might have had a beige or tan yarn or silk body. I can't say for sure."

In the Cains River patterns the wings usually are of four hackles, the two in the middle frequently being of a different color from the two on the outside. Jungle cock cheeks are used on all the flies. The jungle cock is rather long; about three-fourths of an inch on flies of conventional size (with two-and-a-half-inch wings). The shoulder hackles are added *last*, tied on as a collar *over* the butt of the wing and the jungle cock. The hackles are of moderate width, fairly heavily dressed, and usually are of two different colors; most often not mixed. The second color is wound toward the head and is concentrated at the head after the first color has been tied down.

The dressings given here are as tied by Mr. C. Jim Pray, taken from patterns tied by him especially for this book. The author realizes that there may be different conceptions of the proper dressings of the Cains River patterns but considers that these done by the expert hand of Mr. Pray are as authoritative as any which can be obtained. Many of these patterns originally were tied for The Weber Tackle Company, of Stevens Point, Wisconsin, whose founder, Mr. Oscar Weber, has testified as to their correctness.

Proper colors are important if these flies are to be dressed as Mr. Peet liked them. In this regard, Mr. Peter Schwab writes: "The beautiful blue which Fred preferred can be easily described if you know artist's water color paints. It is the rich French blue, a very full color and warm for a blue. He never used the washed out, cold (but purest of all blues) cobalt, similar to the *Silver Doctor* blue. Fred's red is hard to describe except that it is also full and rich, decidedly on the order of warm scarlet. Fred's yellow is a full rich golden yellow, glowing, on the order of cadmium yellow." These comments may indicate to fly dressers the tones preferred by Mr. Peet in other colors.

Famous Patterns

On all Cains River streamers all wing hackles are of the same length. When a two-color collar is called for, the rear color should be twice as heavily dressed as the forward color. Two or three turns of tinsel should be taken around the bend of the hook below where the tail is tied in. The heads are varnished black. Mr. Pray used regular number two sproat hooks, although the flies may be dressed on hooks 2X or 3X long. Nearly all the series are similar in design. An example is included in Color Plate II.

For simplicity, the above information will not be repeated in the dressings which follow:

(CAINS RIVER) ALECK'S WONDER STREAMER

Tail: Two sections of a barred wood duck feather with a thin section of a French blue goose wing feather of the same length between
Body: Medium flat gold tinsel
Wing: A scarlet saddle hackle with a rich yellow saddle hackle on each side and a French blue saddle hackle on each side of this
Cheeks: Jungle cock
Collar: A few turns of a scarlet saddle hackle with a few turns of a French blue saddle hackle ahead of this

(CAINS RIVER) ALLEN'S FIRST CHOICE STREAMER

Tail: Two sections of a barred wood duck feather
Body: Medium flat silver tinsel
Wing: Two French blue saddle hackles with a cream badger saddle hackle on each side
Cheeks: Jungle cock
Collar: A few turns of a scarlet saddle hackle with a few turns of a rich yellow saddle hackle ahead of this

(CAINS RIVER) ALLEN'S LAST CHANCE STREAMER

Tail: Two sections of a barred wood duck feather
Body: Medium flat silver tinsel
Wing: Two French blue saddle hackles with a gray Plymouth Rock saddle hackle on each side
Cheeks: Jungle cock
Collar: A few turns of a gray Plymouth Rock saddle hackle with a few turns of a French blue saddle hackle ahead of this

CAINS RIVER STREAMER

Tail: Two sections of a barred wood duck feather
Body: Medium flat silver tinsel
Wing: Two French blue saddle hackles with a beige saddle hackle on each side
Cheeks: Jungle cock
Collar: Several turns of a beige saddle hackle

CAINS RIVER STEELHEAD STREAMER

Tail: Two sections of a barred wood duck feather
Body: Dressed fairly heavily with very pale grey or cream chenille
Wing: Four golden badger neck hackles
Cheeks: Jungle cock
Collar: A few turns of a rich yellow saddle hackle with a few turns of a scarlet saddle hackle ahead of this
Note: This dressing is an adaptation of Mr. C. Jim Pray, of Eureka, California, for steelhead fishing and should be dressed on a heavy number one hook, very short. The fly is especially successful on California's Klamath River.

(CAINS RIVER) DUNK'S SPECIAL STREAMER

Tail: Two sections of a barred wood duck feather
Body: Medium flat silver tinsel
Wing: Two magenta saddle hackles with a French blue saddle hackle on each side
Cheeks: Jungle cock
Collar: A few turns of a magenta saddle hackle with a few turns of a French blue saddle hackle ahead of this

(CAINS RIVER) HERMAN'S FAVORITE STREAMER

Tail: Two sections of a barred wood duck feather
Body: Medium flat gold tinsel
Wing: Two scarlet saddle hackles with a medium brown saddle hackle on each side
Cheeks: Jungle cock
Collar: Several turns of a medium brown saddle hackle

(CAINS RIVER) HIGHLANDER STREAMER

Tail: Two sections of a barred wood duck feather
Body: Medium flat silver tinsel
Wing: Two emerald (Highlander) green saddle hackles with a gray Plymouth Rock saddle hackle on each side

Famous Patterns

Cheeks: Jungle cock
Collar: A few turns of an emerald green saddle hackle with a few turns of a gray Plymouth Rock saddle hackle ahead of this

(CAINS RIVER) KIDDER STREAMER

Tail: Two sections of a barred wood duck feather
Body: Medium flat gold tinsel
Wing: Two dark chocolate brown saddle hackles with a gray Plymouth Rock saddle hackle on each side
Cheeks: Jungle cock
Collar: Several turns of a dark chocolate brown saddle hackle

(CAINS RIVER) MIRAMICHI STREAMER (PLATE II)

Tail: Two sections of a barred wood duck feather with a thin section of a medium blue goose wing feather of the same length between
Body: Medium flat gold tinsel
Wing: Two magenta saddle hackles with a medium blue saddle hackle on each side
Cheeks: Jungle cock
Collar: A few turns of a magenta saddle hackle with a few turns of a medium blue saddle hackle ahead of this

(CAINS RIVER) PEET'S MASTERPIECE STREAMER

Tail: Two sections of a barred wood duck feather with a thin tip section of a French blue goose feather half as long on each side
Body: Medium flat gold tinsel
Wing: Two French blue saddle hackles with a cream badger saddle hackle on each side
Cheeks: Jungle cock
Collar: A few turns of a dark chocolate brown saddle hackle with a few turns of a French blue saddle hackle ahead of this

(CAINS RIVER) RAINBOW STREAMER

Tail: Two sections of a barred wood duck feather
Body: Medium flat gold tinsel
Wing: Two French blue saddle hackles with a golden yellow saddle hackle on each side
Cheeks: Jungle cock
Collar: A few turns of a rich yellow saddle hackle *mixed* with a few turns of a scarlet saddle hackle

(CAINS RIVER) ROARING RAPIDS STREAMER

Tail: Two sections of a barred wood duck feather with a thin section of a scarlet goose wing feather of the same length between
Body: Medium flat silver tinsel
Wing: Two scarlet saddle hackles with a rich yellow saddle hackle on each side
Cheeks: Jungle cock
Collar: Several turns of a French blue saddle hackle

(CAINS RIVER) SCOTCH LASSIE STREAMER

Tail: Two sections of a barred wood duck feather
Body: Medium flat silver tinsel
Wing: Two French blue saddle hackles with a rich yellow saddle hackle on each side
Cheeks: Jungle cock
Collar: A few turns of a magenta saddle hackle with a few turns of a French blue saddle hackle ahead of this

(CAINS RIVER) SILVER DOCTOR STREAMER

Tail: Two sections of a barred wood duck feather
Body: Medium flat silver tinsel
Wing: Two medium brown saddle hackles with a gray Plymouth Rock saddle hackle on each side
Cheeks: Jungle cock
Collar: A few turns of a French blue saddle hackle with a few turns of a gray Plymouth Rock saddle hackle ahead of this

(CAINS RIVER) SILVER GRAY STREAMER

Tail: Two sections of a barred wood duck feather
Body: Medium flat silver tinsel
Wing: Two bright orange saddle hackles with a grey Plymouth Rock saddle hackle on each side
Cheeks: Jungle cock
Collar: Several turns of a gray Plymouth Rock saddle hackle

(CAINS RIVER) WADE'S CHOICE STREAMER

Tail: Two sections of a barred wood duck feather with a thin section of a French blue goose wing feather of the same length between
Body: Medium flat silver tinsel
Wing: Two gray Plymouth Rock saddle hackles with a scarlet saddle hackle on each side and a rich yellow saddle hackle on each side of this
Cheeks: Jungle cock

Famous Patterns

Collar: A few turns of a gray Plymouth Rock saddle hackle *mixed* with a few turns of a rich yellow saddle hackle

(CAINS RIVER) WILKINSON STREAMER

Tail: Two sections of a barred wood duck feather
Body: Medium flat silver tinsel
Wing: Two medium brown saddle hackles with a gray Plymouth Rock saddle hackle on each side
Cheeks: Jungle cock
Collar: A few turns of a magenta saddle hackle with a few turns of a French blue saddle hackle ahead of this

(CAINS RIVER) BLACK DEMON STREAMER

Tail: Two sections of a barred wood duck feather
Body: Medium flat gold tinsel
Wing: Four jet black saddle hackles
Cheeks: Jungle cock
Collar: Several turns of an orange saddle hackle

(CAINS RIVER) GOLD DEMON STREAMER

Tail: Two sections of a barred wood duck feather
Body: Medium flat gold tinsel
Wing: Two medium brown saddle hackles with a gray Plymouth Rock saddle hackle on each side
Cheeks: Jungle cock
Collar: Several turns of an orange saddle hackle

(CAINS RIVER) SILVER DEMON STREAMER

Tail: Two sections of a barred wood duck feather
Body: Medium flat silver tinsel
Wing: Four gray Plymouth Rock saddle hackles
Cheeks: Jungle cock
Collar: Several turns of an orange saddle hackle

The three *Demon* streamers described above, as tied in the Cains River style, were adapted or originated by Mr. C. Jim Pray, of Eureka, California, and the dressings are from originals tied by him. Regarding them he wrote the author: "At the time William Sturgis published his book FLY TYING he included in the Cains River series three flies which of course Fred Peet never could have seen. He figured they would work up nicely in the Cains River style. Two of them were my own concoctions and one of them was the original *Gold Demon*. The *Gold Demon* was the original of the *Demon* flies, orange hackles seeming to suggest a demon. The original fly was usually a conventional size 6 with a flat gold body, yellow golden pheasant crest tail, brown barred mallard feathers for a wing and with jungle cock cheeks and an orange throat. In streamers there have been many materials offered to take the place of the brown mallard feathers, which are not long enough for streamers. The *Gold Demon* was very popular during its early arrival here (in California) and in Oregon.

"Late in 1935 or 1936 I brought out the *Silver Demon*, with silver rope tinsel body, barred wood duck tail, orange throat, and a wing of barred gadwall feathers. This fly originally contained no jungle cock checks. In its first year on the Eel and Klamath Rivers my shop records show that the *Silver Demon* outsold the *Gold Demon* by 1,300 to 300. It still is a very standard number for steelhead trout on all coast streams.

"Along in 1937 a black fly was popular in the Orleans area of the Klamath River, and about that time I brought out the *Black Demon*. Originally I tied it with a silver body, no tail, orange throat, and a black bucktail wing. Since that time other tiers have incorporated a wood duck tail, and some have used gold for the body, so you may find it with a gold body and a wood duck tail. Probably it is better that the tail is the same as the *Silver Demon*. I am merely giving you the correct history."

CAMPEONA STREAMER (Plate II)

Head: Red
Tag: Four or five turns of narrow silver tinsel
Tail: Two very narrow but rather long sections of a red duck wing feather
Butt: Three turns of fine white chenille
Body: Bright medium green wool, applied as dubbing, pulled out loosely, especially on the underside of the body, after the ribbing has been applied. The body is not heavily dressed.
Ribbing: Medium flat silver tinsel
Throat: Three or four turns of a dark red hackle, rather long and gathered downward. The body is fuzzed out nearly to the tip of the throat

Famous Patterns

Wing: A fairly large bunch of peacock herls of equal length, extending slightly beyond the tail
Shoulders: Each the tip of a teal body feather, covering the peacock and about one-third as long as the wing

(As dressed by Mrs. Elizabeth Greig)

This fly originated in Chili and is widely used in South America. The pattern was sent to Mrs. Greig, famed New York City dresser of salmon flies, for duplication for South American customers. Mrs. Greig has found it successful on New York State streams for all trout.

CANDLEFISH BUCKTAIL (Plate V)

Head: Black, usually with white painted eye and black pupil
Body: Medium flat silver tinsel. (If no ribbing is used, embossed tinsel is preferable)
Ribbing: Medium oval silver tinsel (optional)
Wing: A very small bunch of white polar bear hair, over which is a very small bunch of pale green* polar bear hair, over which is a very small bunch of pale blue* polar bear hair. These three bunches make up the lower third of the wing. The middle third is a small bunch of medium red polar bear hair. Over this is a very small bunch of pale blue polar bear hair, over which is a very small bunch of pale green polar bear hair. As an optional topping a very small bunch of French blue (or violet) polar bear hair may be added. If this topping is not added, the two colors marked with an asterisk may also be eliminated. All the colors of hair are of the same length, extending well beyond the end of the hook

(As dressed by Mr. Roy A. Patrick)

This fly, which originated in the Puget Sound area of the Pacific Northwest, was designed to imitate the candlefish, a prominent baitfish for coho (silver) salmon. It is the result of studies made by anglers there to obtain a combination of colors which would closest approximate those of the candlefish. Prominent among these anglers were Mr. Roy A. Patrick, Mr. Letcher Lambuth and Mr. Zell E. Parkhurst, all of Seattle, Washington. The fly is one of the few standard patterns, and one of the most successful for fly fishing for coho salmon.

"THE CARTER FLY" BUCKTAIL

Head: Black
Tail: About a dozen tips of polar bear hairs dyed bright golden yellow. The tail is rather long

Body: Wound with scarlet chenille of moderate thickness
Ribbing: Narrow oval gold tinsel
Throat: Several turns of a scarlet saddle hackle, applied as a collar and tied back but not gathered downward. The hackle is stiff, glossy and of moderate length
Wing: A medium sized bunch of glossy black bear hair, extending to the end of the tail

(As dressed by the originator)

Originated in the spring of 1938 by Mr. C. Jim Pray, of Eureka, California, and named in honor of Mr. Harley R. Carter, of Berkeley, California. The fly is especially popular on the Klamath and Rogue Rivers for steelhead fishing. For additional notes on Mr. Carter, see *Carter's Dixie* bucktail.

CARTER'S DIXIE BUCKTAIL (Plate VIII)

Head: Black
Tail: About a dozen tips of polar bear hairs dyed bright golden yellow. The tail is rather long
Body: Wound thin with narrow oval gold tinsel. Several turns of tinsel are taken below the tail, around the bend of the hook, as a tag, before the tail is tied in
Throat: Several turns of a scarlet saddle hackle, applied as a collar and tied back but not gathered downward. The hackle is stiff, glossy, and rather long
Wing: A medium sized bunch of white bucktail, extending to the end of the tail. White polar bear often is substituted and two strips of white goose may be used if a feather wing is desired

(As dressed by the originator)

Originated by Mr. C. Jim Pray, of Eureka, California, who writes of the fly as follows: "I tried this first in 1934 and Harley R. Carter used it that year both on the Klamath, in the Orleans area, and on the Rogue River. Harley Carter played guard on the Stanford football team in the period of Andy Smith's California Wonder Team along in the 1920's. I believe he also was Intercollegiate Heavyweight Boxing Champion during that period. The first time I saw him was on the great Big Bar Riffle below Orleans. We were all using waders, except Harley, and I remember that it was chilly. Harley had sneaked up for a day's fishing on his way North and had forgotten his waders. When I first saw him he was up to his arm pits in the cold water fly fishing with nothing on but a pair of pants, a shirt and an ordinary

Famous Patterns

pair of shoes. He stayed there for several hours until he had caught quite a few nice steelhead. I shivered in my waders watching him. Verily, he was quite a man! It was at this time that I christened this fly, which then had no name, in honor of Harley Carter. Along in 1938 Harley decided that he wanted a black hair fly of some sort and that was how the *Carter Fly* came into existence. Although Harley used both flies, he favors the *Carter Fly* much more than this earlier *Carter's Dixie*. Many other anglers have adopted the *Carter's Dixie*, and evidently it is here to stay."

CHAMP'S SPECIAL STREAMER

Head: Black
Tail: A short section of red wool or silk floss
Body: Medium flat silver tinsel
Ribbing: Narrow oval silver tinsel (optional)
Throat: A very small bunch of white bucktail, under which are four or five peacock herls, both as long as the wing
Wing: An extremely small bunch of yellow bucktail (for which two golden pheasant crest feathers sometimes are substituted) as long as the hackles, over which are four grizzly saddle hackles

This fly was originated by Mr. Frank Congdon, of Middletown, Connecticut, and was named for his wife. The dressing is as given to The Weber Tackle Company, of Stevens Point, Wisconsin, by Mr. Congdon.

CHAPPIE STREAMER (PLATE VIII)

Head: Orange
Tail: The tips of two long and narrow Plymouth Rock hackles. The hackles are as long as the body (dressed on a regular hook) and may be placed back to back if desired
Body: Medium thick, of orange wool
Ribbing: Orange silk thread (to make a smooth, tight body)
Throat: Two or three turns of a Plymouth Rock hackle tied on as a collar and not tied downward. The throat is sparse but as long as the body
Wing: The tips of two long and narrow Plymouth Rock hackles. The wing extends nearly to the end of the tail and is dressed very high on the hook. The hackles may be placed back to back if desired

(As dressed by the originator)

This fly was originated by Mr. C. L. (Outdoor) Franklin, of Los Angeles, California, for steelhead and cutthroat trout fishing. It was described in the November 1949 issue of *Field and Stream*, which commented as follows:

"During the 1947 season Mr. Franklin nailed 163 steelhead of over three pounds and sixteen salmon of from fifteen to thirty-seven pounds using this mottled wing streamer exclusively. To tie the *Chappie* properly, you have to select the right hackle feathers for the wing and tail. Unless they are long and narrow they won't flutter. Some tiers place the feathers back to back (turned out). In Los Angeles several fly merchants sell it with a money back guarantee. If you fish it slow and deep with slight jerks and don't get a fish you get your money back. To date there have been no refunds. This is a very popular fly in the coastal states."

Mr. Franklin is a familiar figure on the steelhead riffles of the Klamath and is regarded as one of the West Coast's most experienced anglers. In a letter to the author, he says:

"I have used the *Chappie* for over twenty-five years with unfailing success; in fact, it is the only fly in my fly box year after year and I believe Pete Schwab will bear me out when I say that I hook and land more fish with the *Chappie* than any other fisherman on the Klamath River.

"It was introduced to me by a small chap on the Snake River just outside of Yellowstone Park. This chap was catching two-and-a-half to three pound cutthroats on almost every cast while I, with my expensive tackle, could not get a single one. Upon my asking what he called the fly, he replied that he didn't know the name and that it was 'just a bunch of feathers.' I went to my car, where I had a supply of materials, and improved the outline of the fly. I named it *Chappie* after the young chap who gave it to me. I have sent samples of it all over the country, and everywhere the result has been the same. It takes black bass, tarpon, salmon, steelhead, rainbow trout and even bluegills and crappie. The method of use is to allow plenty of time for the fly to sink and then to retrieve it *very* slowly. This has worked even on the famous golden trout."

CHESAPEAKE BAY SHAD FLY   (Plate V)
(See Chapter III, page 67.)

Famous Patterns

CHIEF NEEDAHBEH STREAMER (Plate II)

Head: Black
Tag: Narrow flat silver tinsel
Tail: A section of red duck or goose wing feather
Body: Red silk. (The original version, as dressed by Chief Needahbeh, has a red hackle "throat" one-third of the way forward on the body. A similar effect could be obtained by palmering a red hackle, but it was not done in this case. The purpose of the "throat" evidently was to give greater action to the fly)
Ribbing: Narrow flat silver tinsel
Throat: A red saddle hackle tied on as a collar after the wing has been applied. It is dressed rather full
Wing: A red saddle hackle on each side of two yellow saddle hackles
Cheeks: Jungle cock, rather short

(As dressed by the originator)

Originated by Chief Needahbeh of the Penobscot tribe of Indians, of Greenville, Maine, who also dressed this fly without a tail or secondary throat, and with orange hackles in the wing instead of red. Chief Needahbeh says that this later version is especially good on dark days and that both flies are good for smallmouth and largemouth bass, as well as for the trout and landlocked salmon for which the fly originally was intended.

COACHMAN STREAMER

Head: Black
Tag: Three or four turns of narrow flat gold tinsel (optional)
Body: Wound fairly heavily with peacock herl
Throat: A small bunch of brown hackle fibers
Wing: Four white saddle or neck hackles

(As dressed by Capt. Sumner Towne)

This is one of the many streamers and bucktails which have been taken from trout fly patterns. It is usually tied in the smaller sizes. White bucktail may be substituted for the hackles.

COCK ROBIN BUCKTAIL (Plate III)

Head: Black   Hook sizes: All sizes, 5X long
Body: Rear half is yellow wool; forward half is red wool, slightly tapered
Butt: Narrow flat silver tinsel
Ribbing: Narrow flat silver tinsel, continued from butt

Throat: A small bunch of red hackle fibers or red hair, mostly extending to barb of hook
Wing: A very small bunch of orange-red hair (bucktail, polar bear, ringtail or impalla) over which is a very small bunch of white hair, over which is a very small bunch of orange-red hair, to form a triple wing extending slightly beyond the bend of the hook
Cheeks: Jungle cock (on larger sizes only)

(As dressed by Mr. Kenneth Botty)

Mr. Paul Kukonen, who obtained this pattern from Mr. Joseph Kvitsky, of Westfield, Massachusetts, says: "Tapered bucktail or polar bear hair should be used in the larger sizes, and the short hairs in each bunch should not be pulled out. Ringtail or impala (calf) is better in the smaller sizes. The fly originally was tied for spring salmon, but we have found it extremely effective in many areas for brook trout, lake trout, and smallmouth bass."

COLONEL BATES STREAMER (PLATE IV)

Head: Red, with black band
Tail: A small section of a red duck or swan wing feather
Body: Medium flat silver tinsel
Throat: A small bunch of dark brown saddle hackle fibers
Wing: Two yellow saddle hackle feathers with a slightly shorter white saddle hackle feather on each side
Shoulders: Gray mallard feathers, nearly half as long as the wing
Cheeks: Jungle cock

(As dressed by the originator)

Originated by Mrs. Carrie G. Stevens, of Madison, Maine, during the Second World War and named for Colonel Joseph D. Bates, Jr., of Longmeadow, Massachusetts. With regard to this fly, Mrs. Stevens writes that it is second only to her famous *Gray Ghost* in popularity among her customers. It is highly favored for landlocked salmon and for smallmouth bass at all times, and for all species of trout particularly under conditions of discolored water. Dressed on salt water hooks, it is successful for striped bass, baby tarpon, bonefish, weakfish and for many other salt water species.

Mr. Frank Mooney, of the Andover (Massachusetts) Fly Fishers Club, says: "This beautiful streamer has been so consistently successful for me that if I had to settle for one streamer pattern I would be content with the *Colonel Bates*. This confidence is shared by many good fishermen. We use it chiefly for trout and tie it in the smaller sizes, 10's, 12's and 14's. In these small sizes we make two small variations, using mallard breast feathers for the shoulders and a small bunch of red hackle fibers for the tail. We have difficulty finding teal in the smaller sizes, and we think mallard gives a nice appearance, being not so strongly marked as the teal. When we tie the larger sizes we stay with the original pattern."

COLONEL FULLER STREAMER

Head: Black
Body: Medium flat silver tinsel
Ribbing: Narrow oval silver tinsel
Throat: A small bunch of golden yellow hackle fibers
Wing: Four golden yellow saddle or neck hackles. Marabou of the same color is substituted in some version of this fly. In this case, the two marabou tips may be applied flat on top of the hook or they may be placed back to back. Both of these methods of dressing give better action than tying them on with the concave sides together. The fly also may be dressed as a bucktail, using either polar bear hair or bucktail dyed golden yellow
Shoulders: Each the tip of a red goose or turkey body feather extending one-third the length of the fly. These feathers should be very wide, and the outside edges should be a pronounced line, rather than fringed

(As dressed by Mr. Gardner Percy)

This fly was adapted to the streamer and bucktail family by Mr. Gardner Percy. It was taken from the bass fly of the same name, originated by Mr. John Shields, of Brookline, Massachusetts, in 1894, and named in honor of Colonel Charles E. Fuller, of Boston, Massachusetts. Being predominantly yellow, it is an excellent pattern for spring salmon, landlocked salmon, bass, and all species of trout, particularly under conditions of discolored water. Its brightness makes it less successful in clear water, except for landlocked salmon and bass, when a fly of less pronounced yellow color, such as the *Colonel Bates*, usually is more resultful. These colors of yellow and red are among the best for salt water game fish, as well as for many fresh water species.

COLONEL WHITE STEAMER

Head: Black
Body: Medium flat silver tinsel
Ribbing: Narrow oval silver tinsel
Throat: A small bunch of white hackle fibers
Wing: Four white neck hackles
Shoulders: Each the tip of a red goose or turkey body feather, one-third as long as the wing and with a pronounced edge

(As dressed by Mr. Gardner Percy)

This fly is nearly identical to the *Ordway* streamer, except for the method of applying the wing. (See notes under *Ordway* streamer). This adaptation of the several red and white streamer flies is attributed to Mr. William Burgess of Maine, who called it the *Rooster's Regret*, although it is not of the *Rooster's Regret* type. When it was placed in the list of patterns of the Percy Tackle Company, of Portland, Maine, it was renamed as above, evidently due to its similarity to the *Colonel Fuller*. It is an excellent salt water pattern.

CORONATION BUCKTAIL (Plate V)

Head: Black, usually with white painted eye with black pupil. (The heads on many coho flies are made purposely large to imitate the heads of baitfish)
Body: Medium flat silver tinsel
Ribbing: Medium oval or embossed silver tinsel. (This is optional but is preferred by many anglers in order to give greater light reflection)
Wing: A bunch of white polar bear hair, over which is a bunch of bright red polar bear hair, over which is a bunch of medium blue polar bear hair. The three bunches are of the same quantity and length, extending well beyond the end of the hook. Usually the fly is dressed rather heavily. Single hook flies are tied on number 2/0 or 3/0 long shanked hooks, usually with ringed eyes so that a spinner may be attached for trolling. For other methods of dressing this fly see page 109.

(As dressed by Mr. Roy A. Patrick)

Few coho (or silver salmon) flies have become standardized in their dressings. In addition to this one, the *Candlefish* bucktail and the *Herring* bucktail are shown in this list of patterns. The *Coronation* bucktail was originated for coho salmon fishing by a group of anglers in the Puget Sound area of the Pacific Northwest and is one of the best known patterns for that type of fishing.

COSSEBOOM SPECIAL BUCKTAIL (Plate III)

Head: Red
Tag: Three or four turns of medium flat silver tinsel
Tail: A small bunch of fibers of medium olive-green silk, of moderate length, cut off flat
Body: Medium olive-green silk, dressed moderately thin
Ribbing: Medium flat silver tinsel
Throat: A light greenish-yellow hackle, wound on as a collar after the wing has been applied. The hackle is fairly long and medium heavy, and is not tied downward
Wing: A small bunch of gray squirrel tail hair, slightly longer than the tail of the fly

(As dressed by Mr. Herbert L. Howard)

Originated by Mr. John C. Cosseboom, the angler and poet from Providence, Rhode Island, while fishing on the Margaree River for bright salmon when they would not take other flies. At the time, this fly proved successful and later was famed as one of the best all-around flies for bright salmon, especially on Anticosti Island, in the St. Lawrence area. The fly is popular in Nova Scotia, Newfoundland, New Brunswick, and Quebec and also has been used successfully in Scotland, England, Norway, Finland, and Iceland. It is a favored trout fly in many other foreign countries, where it is dressed on long shanked hooks in sizes from 5/0 to 12. The original had a body of green rayon.

COWEE SPECIAL STREAMER (Plate III)

Head: Black
Tail: A section of a red goose feather, wide, short and pointing upward
Body: Thinly wound with medium flat gold tinsel
Throat: A wide and short section of a red goose feather, tied on vertically
Wing: A very small bunch of yellow bucktail with a single pintail duck side feather on top. The pintail feather extends to the end of the tail and is tied flat against the hook, horizontal rather than vertical and curling downward slightly on each side

(As dressed by the originator)

This fly was originated in 1938 by Mr. Stanley Cowee of Springfield, Massachusetts, for brook trout and rainbow trout fishing in New England. The flat wing opens and shuts in action to imitate a swimming minnow. The fly is especially popular for rainbow trout and is a favorite of many New England anglers, including the author. Usually it is tied in the smaller sizes, particularly in sizes 6 and 8 on 3X long hooks.

CRANE PRAIRIE SPECIAL STREAMER

Head: Black Hook sizes: This is a tandem fly with the No. 6, 3X long, trailer hook pointed upward and joined to the No. 2, 3X long, forward hook as closely as possible. It often is dressed on gold hooks.
Tail: The tips of four grizzly hackles, long enough to cover the rear hook. (The dressing is on the forward hook only)
Body: Wound with heavy light orange chenille
Ribbing: Oval gold silver tinsel
Throat: A very wide grizzly hackle wound on as a collar
Wing: The tips of six large neck hackles, the three on each side applied back to back with the three on the other side to provide a splayed wing. The wing extends to the end of the tail

(As dressed by Mr. E. H. Rosborough)

This fly is popular in the Crane Prairie region of Oregon. (The vast Crane Prairie Reservoir empties into the Deschutes River and is famous for big brown trout.) There is an optional body dressing of peacock green chenille twisted together with peacock herl. This has no added ribbing.

CUPSUPTIC STREAMER

Head: Black
Tail: A small bunch of yellow hackle fibers
Butt: Made in three parts, which take up one-third of body. Rear quarter of butt is peacock herl, middle half is white silk, and forward quarter is peacock herl
Body: Red silk
Ribbing: Narrow flat silver tinsel, over red silk only
Throat: A small bunch of yellow hackle fibers
Wing: Two dark red saddle hackles with a bronze furnace saddle hackle on each side
Shoulders: Each a gray saddle hackle, two-thirds as long as the wing
Cheeks: Jungle cock

(As dressed by the originator)

Famous Patterns

Originated by Herbert L. Welch, Oquossoc, Maine, and named for Cupsuptic Stream, a famous trout water in the Rangeley section of Maine.

CUT LIPS STREAMER (PLATE VI)

Head: Black   Hook size: No. 2 to No. 8, 4X long
Tail: A small bunch of blue dun hackle fibers
Body: Lavender floss or wool, slightly shaped
Ribbing: Medium narrow flat silver tinsel
Throat: A small bunch of blue dun hackle fibers
Wing: A pair of olive-green saddle hackles, on each side of which is a dark blue dun saddle hackle, all extending slightly beyond the tail
Cheeks: Jungle cock

(As dressed by the originator)

This is one of the famous imitator patterns originated by the late Lew Oatman, of Shushan, New York. The fly imitates the Cut Lips minnow; a very dark one that is found on New York's Ausable River, some parts of Vermont's Battenkill, and in many other trout streams, especially around rapids and falls. Mr. Oatman liked it tied in the larger sizes.

DAMSEL STREAMER

Head: Black
Tail: The tips of three strands of peacock herl, of conventional length
Body: Rear half: peacock herl; front half: bright red wool
Ribbing: Narrow oval gold tinsel, over the peacock half of the body only
Throat: (Tied on after adding the wing and shoulders.) An English partridge hackle tied on as a collar
Wing: Two matched sections of metallic turkey wing feathers, extending as long as the tail
Shoulders: About six strands of a peacock sword feather on each side, one-half as long as the wing

(As dressed by Fin, Fur and Feather, Ltd.)

This fly was originated by Mr. Andrew Barr, of Montreal, about 1939. It is one of the most popular Canadian streamers for trout, bass, and landlocked salmon, especially very early in the season, as soon as the ice has left the lakes.

DICK'S KILLER BUCKTAIL

Head: Black
Tag: Narrow flat gold tinsel, very long
Tail: About fifteen strands of a golden pheasant tippet, rather long
Body: Wound fairly heavy with peacock herl
Wing: A bunch of yellow bucktail, short enough so that it will not catch under the hook. An extra long shanked hook is used
Topping: A very small bunch of strands from a wood duck or mandarin duck breast feather, nearly as long as the wing
Shoulders: Each a section of a red turkey feather, rather slim but nearly as long as the wing
Cheeks: Jungle cock, two-thirds as long as the shoulders

(As dressed by the originator)

Originated by Mr. Dick Eastman, of Groveton, New Hampshire, in 1928. Mr. Eastman writes to the author: "I started tying flies in 1928 when I was camp manager at Idlewild on Second Connecticut Lake. One fly I tied was a yellow bucktail like the one enclosed and it worked very well. Later in the summer some guests had a fly called the *Lake George*, which also proved to be a good fish taker, with peacock herl body and a red wing. I experimented by putting the best parts of the two flies together and got a fly with a peacock herl body, golden pheasant tippet tail and yellow bucktail wing topped with wood duck, red turkey shoulders and jungle cock cheeks. This fly proved to be a real killer of trout, so I named it *Dick's Killer* and have tied more than 1,000 of this pattern.

"Later on that year, Bill Edson, who was camping at First Connecticut Lake, came to Idlewild and I went fishing with him. When he left, I gave him a couple of *Dick's Killers*. Some time after he wrote me a letter in which he said, 'Your *Dick's Killer* works as well on rainbows and brown trout on the Westfield River as it did around Second Connecticut Lake.' After that, Edson promoted and tied the *Light Tiger*. Then he originated the *Dark Tiger*.

"These flies work very well here and in the Laurentide Park and other sections of Canada. They take (landlocked) salmon on the Connecticut lakes. I have tied *Dick's Killer* with yellow, red, and black heads. Probably the ones I gave Edson had yellow heads." (See comments under *Edson Light Tiger Bucktail* and *Edson Dark Tiger Bucktail*.)

DR. BURKE STREAMER (Plate II)

Head: Black
Tail: About fifteen peacock sword fibers, more bunchy and longer than usual
Body: Medium flat silver tinsel, somewhat thicker than normal, since it must be built up to compensate for the bulge of the tail
Ribbing: Narrow oval silver tinsel
Throat: A bunch of yellow hackle fibers, rather long
Wing: Four white saddle hackles
Cheeks: Jungle cock

(As dressed by the originator)

This fly was originated by Dr. Edgar Burke, of Jersey City, New Jersey, who writes to the author that it was "first devised and used on Kennebago Stream, in Northwestern Maine, in 1927. It was designed as a dusk fly for large squaretail trout, and proved highly effective. Its name was given to it by my then guide, Frank Savage, of Bemis, Maine."

Dr. Burke was as famous as an artist and an angler as he was as a surgeon. He has enjoyed a generation or more of fishing on Maine's famous trout and landlocked salmon waters. It was he who so beautifully illustrated the trout flies in Mr. Ray Bergman's well-known book TROUT. Another of Dr. Burke's originations is the *Family Secret* streamer described later on.

DR. MILNE STREAMER

Head: Black
Tag: Four or five turns of narrow gold tinsel
Tail: One or two very short golden pheasant crest feathers, curving upward
Body: Wound with yellow chenille
Wing: A very small bunch of black bear hair as long as the tail, over which are four gray neck hackles extending well beyond the tail
Topping: A thin section of red swan or goose wing feather as long as the jungle cock
Shoulders: Each a brown mallard breast feather, nearly two-thirds as long as the wing
Cheeks: Jungle cock, of medium length

(As dressed by the originator)

This well-known Maine streamer fly is popular for taking landlocked salmon. It was originated by Mr. Bert Quimby, of South Windham, Maine, as the result of suggestions made to him by Dr. Douglas M. Milne of South Portland, Maine, for whom the fly was named.

DR. OATMAN (PLATE VI)

Head: Black   Hook sizes: No. 6 to No. 2
Tail: A small bunch of white hackle fibers, as long as the gap of the hook
Body: The rearward two-thirds is white floss; the forward one-third is red floss. The body is slightly tapered
Ribbing: Narrow flat gold tinsel
Throat: A small bunch of yellow hackle fibers, slightly longer than the red section of the body
Wing: Four white saddle hackles, extending slightly beyond the tail
Cheeks: Jungle cock, fairly short

(As dressed by the originator)

This fly is one of the famous series originated by Lew Oatman of Shushan, New York, around 1953. It was named for his father who was a country doctor.

DON'S DELIGHT STREAMER (PLATE IV)

Head: Black, with red band
Tail: A small bunch of red hackle fibers
Body: Medium flat gold tinsel
Throat: A small bunch of white hackle fibers
Wing: Four white saddle hackles
Shoulders: Each a golden pheasant tippet, extending one-third as long as the wing
Cheeks: Jungle cock

(As dressed by the originator)

Originated by Mrs. Carrie G. Stevens, of Madison, Maine, and named for Mr. Donald Bartlett of Willimantic, Connecticut. The fly has been a local favorite at Upper Dam Pool, in Maine, for many years.

Famous Patterns

DOT EDSON STREAMER

Head: Silver
Body: Medium flat silver tinsel with two narrow strips of pale blue flat tinsel tied in, one on each side, before the body is wound. The two strips are pulled forward and are tied at the head after the body is wound, so that they extend along both sides of the body
Throat: White bucktail as long as the hook, with a very small bunch of red hackle fibers beneath, tied in very short
Wing: Four silver grey saddle hackles
Shoulders: Each a Ripon's silver pheasant body feather, one-fourth as long as the wing
Cheeks: Jungle cock, very short

(As dressed by the originator)

Originated by Mr. William R. Edson of Portland, Maine, and named by him for his wife. This fly was tied to imitate a smelt and should be dressed very sparsely.

DUSTY STREAMER

Head: Black
Tag: Four or five turns of narrow flat silver tinsel
Body: Black silk, dressed very thin (red silk was used on the original version)
Ribbing: Narrow flat silver tinsel
Throat: Six strands of peacock herl, under which is a very small bunch of white bucktail, both as long as the wing. Under this is a short golden pheasant crest feather curving upward. (This has been eliminated in the most recent version)
Wing: Four barred Plymouth Rock neck or saddle hackles, with very pronounced black and white bars
Cheeks: Jungle cock

(As dressed by the originator)

Originated by Mr. Bert Quimby, of South Windham, Maine, especially for taking landlocked salmon in the spring. The fly first was used on Moosehead Lake, in Maine.

EDSON DARK TIGER BUCKTAIL (Plate VII)

Head: Yellow
Tag: Three or four turns of narrow flat gold tinsel
Tail: The tips of two extremely small yellow neck hackles, back to back
Body: Wound with fine yellow chenille
Throat: The tips of two extremely small red neck hackles (to simulate gills)

Wing: A small bunch of the brown hair from a bucktail dyed yellow, extending just beyond the end of the hook. (An important element in dressing this fly, which is often overlooked, is that the wing must be short enough so that it will not catch in the bend of the hook when the wing becomes turned under the hook when the fly is being fished)
Cheeks: Jungle cock, extremely short. (Use eye only)
(As dressed by the originator)

This is one of the most famous of all bucktail flies for trout, landlocked salmon, bass and many other species of game fish. It was originated by Mr. William R. Edson, of Portland, Maine, in 1929 as a companion fly to the *Edson Light Tiger Bucktail*. An extra long shank hook is used, usually 5X long. Mr. Edson prefers a Sproat in sizes from 4 to 10. Gold metal cheeks sometimes takes the place of the jungle cock on flies which Mr. Edson has dressed. He considers that the gold eye gives a better flash in the water. Jungle cock often is used by other fly dressers because the gold eyes are difficult to obtain.

EDSON LIGHT TIGER BUCKTAIL (PLATE VII)

Head: Black. (This fly is tied with black thread rather than with yellow thread because the black does not show when applying the peacock body. Many of Mr. Edson's early versions were dressed with yellow lacquer over the black head, but this no longer is considered necessary)
Tag: Three or four turns of narrow flat gold tinsel
Tail: A section of a barred wood duck or mandarin duck feather long enough to show two black bars
Body: Wound with peacock herl, several strands being twisted with the thread while they are being applied. The body is fairly full; the number of strands depending upon the size of the fly
Wing: Yellow bucktail, short enough so that it will not catch under the hook. The ends should be fairly even
Topping: The tips of two extremely small red neck hackles, not over one-third as long as the wing. (A section of red duck wing feather was used in the early versions)
Cheeks: Jungle cock, extremely short. (Use eye only. See notes under *Edson Dark Tiger Bucktail* on hooks and use of optional gold metal cheeks)
(As dressed by the originator)

This companion fly to the *Edson Dark Tiger Bucktail* was originated by Mr. William R. Edson, of Portland, Maine, in 1929. Its origination possibly was influenced by the *Dick's Killer Bucktail*, as is noted in the comments on that fly. Both the *Light* and *Dark Tigers* generally are conceeded to be among the most successful flies for all species of fresh water game fish, and particularly for trout and landlocked salmon. Care should be taken that the wing is not overdressed and that it is tied close to the body to give maximum streamlined effect. The author prefers to dress the topping with a section of red duck wing feather rather than with the two red hackle tips. If the hackle tips are used, they should be applied flat, one over the other, to form a narrow "V" on top of the fly.

EMERSON HOUGH BUCKTAIL

Head: Black
Tail: About fifteen tips of light reddish-brown bucktail hairs of various lengths; the longest being about an inch
Body: Of brown deer body hair tied on as a hair body, loose and rough. The body is almost spherical in shape and is clipped to enhance its roughness
Wing: A bunch of dark brown bucktail not over once and a half as long as the hook and not quite as long as the end of the tail. The width of the body will make the wing cock up at an angle of nearly 45 degrees

(As dressed by Mr. Peter J. Schwab)

The *Emerson Hough* bucktail was originated by Indian guides in the Canadian Northwest. Samples of it were brought back from that territory just prior to 1920 by Mr. Hough, an accomplished angler and angling writer of Chicago, Illinois. This fly which bears his name is unusual in its type of body dressing, being very similar to a deer hair bass bug in appearance. In clipped deer hair body flies of this type, such as the *Algoma** bucktail, the hair of the body should be loose and reasonably sparse. This dressing is from an original given by Mr. Hough to Mr. Peter J. Schwab, who writes about it as follows: "Emerson Hough and Fred Peet, who used the fly a great deal, insisted that the important thing, never to be overlooked, was to keep the fly looking *rough*. According to them it should never be tied with the solid fullness so often seen in lures with buckhair bodies, and in my limited experience with the fly I agree with them. I never thought

---

* The *Algoma Bucktail* has a trimmed body of gray caribou or deer hair, clipped to a uniform fat cigar shape. The tail is a long, thin section of a Lady Amherst pheasant tail feather curving upward. The throat is a small bunch of fibers from a fiery brown hackle, rather long. The wing is a bunch of mixed gray and brown bucktail over a smaller amount of white bucktail, both extending to the end of the tail.

it dainty enough to throw at such beautiful fish as trout, but I have used it a lot for bass and panfish, all of which seem to show a preference for the rough body." The fly usually is dressed on a regular length hook, preferably in size 6.

ESOPUS BUCKTAIL

Head: Black
Tail: Of bright red bucktail, cut off sharply, one-third as long as the wing. A good sized bunch of bucktail is used to give the effect of a paintbrush when cut off
Body: Medium gold or silver tinsel. The body is first filled in with wool to enlarge it before adding the tinsel. This fat body is designed to give a large, shiny area. Regular length hooks are used, so that the body and the tail are of the same length
Wing: In any of the following color combinations—
Black over white bucktail
Brown over white bucktail
Red over white bucktail
The wing is one half longer than the body and tail combined. It is raised to an angle of 45 degrees from the body to show the body more clearly and to give more action in the water. The wing is rather fully dressed

(As dressed by William Mills & Son)

This fly is very similar in shape to western steelhead flies. It was originated by William Mills and Son, of New York City, and originally was tied with a yellow tail. Since 1935 the red tail has been standard. This fly is very successful for large brown trout (and other species of trout) on the Esopus River of New York State, for which it is named. A more popular version of the *Esopus* bucktail is shown in this book as the *Bi-Buck* bucktail.

FAMILY SECRET STREAMER

Head: Black
Tail: Between ten and twenty peacock sword fibers, depending on size of hook. The tail is long and very bunchy
Body: Medium flat silver tinsel. The body is somewhat thicker than normal since it must be built up to compensate for the bulge of the tail
Ribbing: Narrow oval silver tinsel
Throat: A bunch of guinea hen hackle fibers, rather thick and long
Wing: Four white saddle hackles
Cheeks: Jungle cock

(As dressed by the originator)

Originated by Dr. Edgar Burke, of Jersey City, New Jersey, who wrote to the author: "This is really a modification of the *Dr. Burke Streamer* and in my own opinion is a more universally useful pattern. First used in 1928 for landlocked salmon, it proved spectacularly successful and the best catches of big salmon and trout I have ever made were due to it. It is a good pattern for virtually all fresh water game fish, bass included, and it is particularly effective for large brown trout." (See notes under *Dr. Burke Streamer*.)

In explanation of its name, Dr. Burke says: "During a sterile spell on the upper Kennebago River (in Maine), when none of the rods then on the stream had been doing anything for days, I had enjoyed excellent fishing. I was fishing the famous Island Pool when another angler, accompanied by his guide, appeared on the footpath, obviously much disappointed to find the pool already occupied. The guide, whom I knew well, called out to me, 'Do you mind if we watch you fish for awhile, Doctor?' I, of course, assented. I was taking one good fish after another. This, in view of the prevailing non-productiveness of the river, was too much for the guide. Unable to contain himself, he yelled out, 'For Pete's sake, Doctor, what fly are you using?' In a bantering tone I called back, 'That's a family secret, Jim!' Whereupon my own guide, Dick Grant, seized my arm and said, '*There's* the name for your fly!' and so it has been, ever since. The little incident narrated above, to the best of my recollection, was in 1928."

FRASER STREAMER

Head: Black
Butt: Two turns of "dirty-orange" chenille, in imitation of an egg sack
Body: Of bright green wool, medium thick, not shaped and not picked out
Ribbing: Very fine oval silver tinsel
Wing: Four white neck or shoulder hackles
Shoulders: Each a narrow, short yellow neck hackle, extending two-thirds the length of the wing, dressed high to show the lower part of the wing
Cheeks: Jungle cock

(As dressed by Mr. Herbert L. Howard)

Originated by Mr. George Fraser, of Edinburgh, Scotland, who learned fly fishing by poaching on Scotch rivers, particularly on the waters of the Tay River on the estate of Lord Dewar. Later, Mr. Fraser fished all over the world and was partial to this fly for all types of game fish. He used it on the Esopus River, in New York State, and in many other states and countries. The dressing is from an original given to Mr. Howard by Mr. Fraser.

GALLOPING GHOST STREAMER

Head: Black
Tag: A few turns of medium embossed silver tinsel
Tail: A section of a red duck or goose wing feather
Body: Of orange silk, dressed fairly thin
Ribbing: Medium embossed silver tinsel
Throat: A bunch of orange-red hackle fibers, rather long
Wing: Two Bali duck (Yanosh) shoulder feathers, extending beyond the tail
Cheeks: Jungle cock, fairly short

(As dressed by the originator)

Originated by Mr. Bert Quimby, of South Windham, Maine. This fly is very similar to the *Jesse Wood* Streamer, which is a much older pattern.

GASPERAUX BUCKTAIL

Head: Black
Body: Medium embossed silver tinsel
Ribbing: Medium oval silver tinsel
Wing: A bunch of yellow bucktail over which is a bunch of red bucktail
Cheeks: Jungle cock

(As dressed by the originator)

This fly is essentially a red and yellow bucktail. It was originated by Mr. George T. Richards and Mr. Charles M. Wetzel, entomologist and author of PRACTICAL FLY FISHING, who writes the author as follows: "This fly was designed while salmon fishing in New Brunswick with Julian Crandall, Bob Becker and Nick Kahler. It is named 'Gas peraux' for the small baitfish of that name which inhabit the river. Everyone took many salmon on it and it proved to be the most popular fly on the stream."

GEES-BEAU STREAMER

Head: Black
Tail: Two narrow sections of an orange swan or goose wing feather, curving upward

Famous Patterns

Body: Rear half is medium flat silver tinsel dressed thin; front half is yellow wool picked out to make it fuzzy
Ribbing: Narrow oval silver tinsel over both sections of body
Throat: A bunch of yellow hackle fibers, rather long
Wing: Four white saddle hackles
Shoulders: Two matched sections of orange swan or goose wing feathers, fairly wide, nearly half as long as the wing and dressed high curving downward and covering the tops of the wing hackles
Cheeks: Jungle cock

(As dressed by Mr. Gardner Percy)

Originated by Mr. Charles Phair, a famed angler and fly dresser of Presque Isle, Maine. There are two other flies with similar names, one of them being the *Jessabou* streamer, which also is attributed to Charlie Phair. This fly is dressed with a thin body of flat silver tinsel, a throat of brown hackle fibres, a wing of four brown neck hackles, a topping of peacock herl as long as the wing, and with jungle cock cheeks. It is probable that these two flies originally may have been a single pattern with a single name and that the second dressing and name is an adaptation of the first. A third fly, very similar to the *Gees-Beau* is the *Jazz Boa* streamer, to which this comment also applies.

GENERAL MACARTHUR STREAMER (PLATE IV)

Head: Red or blue (Mrs. Stevens ties it with three bands of red, white, and blue thread, but this is more than most fly dressers will wish to attempt)
Tail: A small bunch of red hackle fibers of medium length
Body: Medium flat silver tinsel
Throat: A very small bunch of dark blue hackle fibers, under which is a very small bunch of white hackle fibers, with a very small bunch of red hackle fibers under this; all of the same length
Wing: Two white saddle hackles, on each side of which is a light blue saddle hackle, with a Plymouth Rock saddle hackle on each side of this. All six hackles are of the same length, reaching just beyond the tail
Cheeks: Jungle cock

(As dressed by the originator)

Originated by Mrs. Carrie G. Stevens, of Madison, Maine, during the Second World War and named in honor of General Douglas MacArthur. Although the fly was designed from a patriotic point of view, rather than because the colors suited accepted angling stan-

On the way to McNally's, circa 1909.

This photograph is inscribed "Ross McKinney, Joe Bates and Engineer 'Thibodeau'—logging railroad from Chesuncook Lake to Eagle Lake, Maine," circa 1935.

272

dards, the fly has proved very successful for trout and landlocked salmon in Maine waters. The colors resemble those in the famous *Supervisor* streamer, and the fish evidently are under the impression that they resemble the coloration of a smelt.

GHOST SHINER (PLATE VI)

Head: Same color as wing   Hook size: No. 8, 4X long
Tail: A few fibers from a light green hackle
Body: Wound with white floss, tapered
Ribbing: Medium flat silver tinsel
Throat: A small bunch of fibers from a white hackle, as long as the gap of the hook
Wing: A sparse bunch of summer (European) sable tail hair, as long as the tail. (This is quite a silky hair, very light brown or tan in color)
Cheeks: Jungle cock, tied in short
(As dressed by the originator)

This is one of the natural imitation patterns originated by the famous angler, Lew Oatman, of Shushan, New York. It imitates the baitfish of the same name. It also is similar to the straw-colored minnow, the pearl minnow, and the emerald minnow. It is a clear water fly and can be tied down to very small, sparse sizes. It is one of a group which have done well under difficult conditions in England. In the smaller sizes it may be fished to resemble a darting nymph, or small fry. (The dressing and comments are from notes given to the author by Mr. Oatman.)

GIBBS STRIPER BUCKTAIL (PLATE V)

Head: Black, with tiny yellow painted eyes with red pupils
Body: Narrow flat silver tinsel
Throat: A small bunch of red hackle fibers, rather long
Wing: A bunch of capra (Asiatic goat) hair with some of the underfur left in. (White bucktail may be substituted)
Shoulders: A section of dark blue nazurias (swan wing feather) one-half as long as the wing. This should be tied in so that it will lie midway of the wing, to make a stripe down the middle of the wing
Cheeks: Each a short barred teal body feather, one-third as long as the shoulder. (Ball duck or guinea hen breast feathers may be substituted)
(As dressed by the originator)

Originated by Mr. Harold N. Gibbs of Barrington, Rhode Island, to represent a silverside, which is a forage fish of the smelt family. This is a favorite fly for striped bass and other salt water game fish. It also is successful for smallmouth bass, landlocked salmon and other fresh water species. For salt water use it should be dressed on a 1/0 or 3/0 non-corrosive regular length hook.

In 1965, Mr. Gibbs sent the author an improved version of this fly, saying, "After a bass or two had been taken on the old *Gibbs Striper* the blue swan shoulders were reduced to only four or five blue hairs. So we replaced this with blue capra or bucktail to form a triple wing of white over blue over white. The bright hooks don't need to be bound with tinsel, but we do put a silver tinsel body on black or bronze hooks. We prefer short shanked hooks and rather short wings (about twice as long as the hook)."

Mr. Gibbs also sent the author a similar version tied by Al Brewster, a professional fly dresser of Riverside, Rhode Island. In this one the upper white wing is eliminated to provide a blue over white wing. The head has yellow painted eyes with red pupils. Mr. Brewster says, "This variation is intended to imitate baitfish such as shad, white perch, butterfish, pogeys, and alewives. Flies used here in July have wings two-and-a-half-inches long. By October they are increased to a full five inches. This is an extremely successful fly."

GOLDEN DARTER (PLATE VI)

Head: Black   Hook sizes: No. 10 to No. 6, 6X long
Tail: A very small section of mottled turkey wing quill, no longer than the gap of the hook
Body: Wound with clear yellow floss, slightly tapered
Ribbing: Medium narrow flat gold tinsel
Throat: A very small tip of a jungle cock body feather, no longer than the gap of the hook, and pointed downward
Wing: Two golden-edged badger saddle hackles, slightly longer than the tail. (Use four hackles on large sizes)
Cheeks: Jungle cock, rather short

(As dressed by the originator)

This is another imitative pattern originated by Lew Oatman, of Shushan, New York. In sending the author this authentic dressing, Mr. Oatman said, "This fly imitates the *Black Nosed Dace* in a spare

Famous Patterns

pattern. It is a running mate to the *Silver Darter*, and I use it in water that is somewhat discolored. The *Silver Darter* is best in clear water."

GOLDEN ROGAN BUCKTAIL (Plate II)

Head: Black, with a painted red band, narrow, at the back of the head

Tag: Four or five turns of fine silver wire, begun at the bend of the hook, forward of which are several turns of red silk, dressed thin, about three times as long as the silver

Tail: A golden pheasant crest feather, fairly long and curving upward. Above this is the tip of a section of a barred wood duck feather showing a black, white and black band only, very thin and half as long as the golden pheasant

Butt: Three or four turns of a black ostrich herl

Body: Consists of four butts of black ostrich herl, including the one above, equally spaced with the forward butt at the head of the fly. The spaces between are wound thinly with fine gold wire. Just ahead of the rear butt, and just behind the three forward butts, is a "throat" of about twelve strands of fine gold wire or the finest oval gold tinsel (called "French Twist"). The ends of these four "throats" are cut in a graduated manner so that the rear "throat" extends to the barb of the hook and each forward "throat" is slightly longer

Wing: A small bunch of golden badger hair with the black band in the middle, as long as the tail of the fly

Topping: Two golden pheasant crest feathers, dyed red, curving downward to meet the tip of the tail

(As dressed by the originator)

The *Golden Rogan* bucktail is not to be confused with the *Golden Rogan* salmon fly, as illustrated in *Fortune Magazine* for June, 1948, since the two dressings are entirely different. Both flies were originated by Mr. Alex Rogan, of New York City, generally considered to be one of the two greatest American dressers of salmon patterns (the other being Mrs. Elizabeth Greig, also of New York City). Alex Rogan came by his extraordinary ability naturally, since his father was a celebrated Irish fly dresser and his uncle, Michael Rogan, was one of the most influential salmon fly tiers in history. It is not unusual, therefore, that the *Golden Rogan* bucktail (and the *Rogan Royal Gray Ghost* shown elsewhere in this book) should be influenced strongly by the artistry of salmon flies in the superbly delicate and detailed workmanship of its dressing. Few anglers will go to the expense, or the labor, of acquiring flies of this sort for fishing, but many will delight in owning them or in attempting to dress them because, like the more complicated salmon flies, they are the summit of perfection and beauty in the fly tier's art.

GOLDEN SHINER (Plate VI)

Head: Black   Hook size: No. 10 to No. 6, 6X long
Tail: A very small bunch of orange fibers from the base of an orange hackle or from the base of an orange goose or swan nashua feather. The tail is as long as the gap of the hook
Body: Wound with white floss, slightly tapered
Ribbing: Medium flat gold tinsel
Throat: A small bunch of white bucktail, below which is a wisp of the tail material
Wing: A small bunch of clear yellow bucktail topped with four peacock herl tips, all slightly longer than the tail
Shoulders: On each side, a gray-blue dun saddle hackle, as long as the wing
Cheeks: Jungle cock, rather short

(As dressed by the originator)

This is one of the imitative patterns designed by the late Lew Oatman of Shushan, New York. In sending the dressing to the author, Mr. Oatman said, "This fly is designed for largemouth bass in lakes where the Golden shiners have these rich colors. In some waters the Golden shiner has a washed-out faded appearance, but in some northern lakes they are brilliant. This is one of the best patterns for largemouths, in my experience. I have had good luck with this and with the *Yellow Perch* even when the lake was working by fishing the streamer two or three feet deep and moving it slowly so it sinks just below the concentration of pollen which occurs near the surface. At such times, the strike is very deliberate and may feel as though the hook had caught."

GOLDEN SMELT (Plate VI)

Head: Black   Hook sizes: No. 6 to No. 2, 6X long
Tail: A very few black-ended tippets from a Golden pheasant body feather, as long as the gap of the hook
Body: The rearward two-thirds is wound with yellow floss; with the forward one-third wound with pink floss. The body is slightly tapered
Ribbing: Medium narrow flat gold tinsel
Throat: A small bunch of yellow hackle fibers, tied in fairly short
Wing: Two light green saddle hackles, on each side of which is a golden badger saddle hackle, all extending slightly beyond the tail
Cheeks: Jungle cock, tied in fairly short

(As dressed by the originator)

Famous Patterns

Originated by Lew Oatman, of Shushan, New York, about 1953, to imitate the baitfish of the same name.

GOLDEN WITCH STREAMER (Plate IV)

Head: Black, with red band
Tag: Four or five turns of narrow flat silver tinsel, beginning over the point of the extra long shanked hook
Body: Dressed very thin with orange silk
Ribbing: Narrow flat silver tinsel
Throat: A very small bunch of white bucktail extending beyond the barb of the hook, under which is a small bunch of barred Plymouth Rock hackle fibers
Wing: Four or five strands of peacock herl as long as the hackles, over which are four barred Plymouth Rock saddle hackles
Shoulders: Each a golden pheasant tippet, one-third as long as the wing
Cheeks: Jungle cock, rather short
(As dressed by the originator)

Originated by Mrs. Carrie G. Stevens, for taking trout and landlocked salmon in Maine lakes. This is one of the earliest of the Maine streamer flies and is one of the popular patterns for casting and trolling.

GOVERNOR AIKEN BUCKTAIL (Plate III)

Head: Black
Tail: A section of barred wood duck or mandarin duck body feather
Body: Medium flat silver tinsel
Ribbing: Narrow oval silver tinsel
Throat: A bunch of white bucktail extending just beyond the hook, under which is a small section of red swan or goose wing feather nearly half as long as the bucktail
Wing: A bunch of lavender bucktail
Topping: Five or six strands of peacock herl, as long as the wing
Cheeks: Jungle cock
(As dressed by Fin, Fur and Feather, Ltd.)

This fly was named in honor of Governor (since Senator) George D. Aiken, of Vermont. It is not one of the most popular bucktails in New England, but is very popular in Canada for landlocked salmon and for rainbow trout, particularly in the Lake Memphremagog area, where it is called the *Smelt* streamer, and is considered to very accurately imitate the coloration of a smelt. The Canadian dressing is the same as the American, except that the wing has a very small bunch of yellow bucktail under the lavender, with a small bunch of white bucktail under the yellow. A gray mallard shoulder is substituted for the jungle cock cheek. The fly often is tied in tandem.

GOVERNOR BRANN STREAMER

Head: Black
Tail: A narrow section of a red duck wing feather, rather long
Body: Medium flat silver tinsel
Ribbing: Narrow oval silver tinsel
Throat: A very small bunch of dark brown bucktail, nearly as long as the wing. (The throat is not used in the latest patterns tied by Mr. Quimby, but is used in the patterns of several other fly dressers)
Wing: Four olive green saddle hackles on each side of which is a brown game cock hackle having a black middle stripe. All six feathers are of the same length
Cheeks: Jungle cock

(As dressed by the originator)

Originated by Mr. Bert Quimby, of South Windham, Maine, and named for a former Governor of the State of Maine. The fly originally was tied and presented to the Governor on the occasion of his visit to the Boston Sportsman's Show during his term of office. It is a popular pattern for trout and particularly for large brown trout.

GRAND LAKER STREAMER (PLATE III)

Head: Black
Tag: Three or four turns of narrow flat gold tinsel
Body: Medium thin, wound with black silk
Ribbing: Narrow flat gold tinsel; two pieces tied in together and wound in opposite directions to give a diamond effect
Throat: A very small bunch of brown bucktail, nearly as long as the wing, or a small bunch of very long light brown hackle fibers
Wing: Four medium brown saddle hackles. The outside two may be slightly shorter than the two in the center
Cheeks: Jungle cock

(As dressed by Mr. Benn Treadwell)

This fly is a development of the flies of the *Rooster's Regret* type discussed in Chapter Two. Flies of this type originated on Grand Lake Stream, in Maine, about 1910. In discussing the *Grand Laker,*

Famous Patterns

Mr. Benn Treadwell, old-time guide of Grand Lake Stream, writes: "I cannot claim to be the originator; in fact, I do not think any one person can claim that honor, since the *Grand Laker* is the result of the combined ideas of many of our guides. In its original form it was very crude, consisting of two brown hackles tied on a short hook with thread. As time passed, one guide and then another would add to the pattern. Then someone started using the long shank hook and dressed the fly as it appears today. It is probably the first, and certainly the best known, of our local flies."

GRAY GHOST STREAMER (PLATE IV)

Head: Black, with red band
Tag: Narrow flat silver tinsel
Body: Dressed very thin with orange silk
Ribbing: Narrow flat silver tinsel
Throat: Four or five strands of peacock herl, under which is a very small bunch of white bucktail, both extending beyond the barb of the hook. The peacock is as long as the wing and the bucktail only slighter shorter. Under these is a golden pheasant crest feather as long as the shoulder and curving upward
Wing: A golden pheasant crest feather curving downward, as long as the hackles. Over this are four olive-gray saddle hackles
Shoulders: Each a Ripon's silver pheasant body feather, one-third as long as the wing and very wide
Cheeks: Jungle cock

(As dressed by the originator)

This famous fly was originated by Mrs. Carrie G. Stevens, who describes its origination in a letter to the author as follows: "At the time my *Gray Ghost* was originated, Wallace Stevens (who is a fishing guide) and I were living at our camp at Upper Dam, Maine (which is only a short distance from the famous Upper Dam Pool). On the first day of July in 1924 I had the inspiration of dressing a streamer fly with gray wings to imitate a smelt and I left my housework unfinished to develop the new creation. It was a much cruder job than those I have tied since then, but it had two hackle feathers for a wing and an underbody of white bucktail, to which I added several other feathers which I thought enhanced its appearance and its resemblance to a baitfish.

"Then I felt impelled to try the new fly in the pool and soon was casting with it from one of the aprons of the dam into the fast water. In less than an hour I hooked and landed a six-pound, thirteen-ounce brook trout which I entered in the *Field and Stream* Fishing Contest. The entry won for me second prize and a beautiful oil painting by Lynn Bogue Hunt, awarded for showing the most sportsmanship in landing a fish. Because the trout was such a nice one and was caught on a new fly I had made, it caused much excitement and resulted in my receiving many orders for flies. Soon I found I was in the fly tying business. My first flies left much to be desired. I found that with too much hair and only two feathers the fly would ride bottom up in the water, but by using less hair and four feathers the trouble was corrected. For want of something better I used chicken breast plumage which I dyed myself to make the shoulders. I used a small feather with black spots for the cheeks because I did not know then about the beautiful jungle cock and other imported feathers I am using today.

"The *Gray Ghost* was one of my early fancy patterns and is the most popular streamer used today. My next most popular pattern was originated during the war. It is the *Colonel Bates* and was named for you, as you know. The *Gray Ghost* was designed to represent a smelt and is especially good for early season fly fishing in waters where fish feed on smelt and similar baitfish. Mr. Frank Bugbee, President of a bank in Willimantic, Connecticut, named the fly. He made semi-annual trips to Upper Dam until his death several years ago. I suppose the reason the fly has enjoyed so much popularity is because all the fly tiers are making it and it is used more extensively than most other patterns.

"I have never used a vise; have never seen anyone tie a fly and no one has ever seen me tie one. I have never read or had any fly tying instructions. I was several years perfecting my flies and was not satisfied until they were right in every detail. My first flies were tied on regular hooks. I did not use the extra long shanked hooks until a couple of years after the *Gray Ghost* was originated."

Mrs. Stevens' patterns have the feminine touch of being dressed more for beauty of color and detail than because the combinations are chosen for their allure to fish. Her *Gray Ghost* is conceded by

Famous Patterns

nearly every fisherman to be one of the nation's first ten most resultful streamer flies for taking trout or landlocked salmon. Her patterns are such exquisite examples of the fly dresser's art that more of them are retained as collector's items than are used for actual fishing. As an accomplished fly dresser who learned the art unaided, Mrs. Stevens is conceded to be one of the truly great in American fly tying. The *Gray Ghost* was the first of the several flies of the so-called "Ghost Family" which followed it, such as the equally famous *Black Ghost* (which was a true origination, rather than an adaptation) and the *Green Ghost*, *Lady Ghost*, *White Ghost* and several others of lesser importance.

Mrs. Stevens has now ceased dressing flies and has given her self-taught art to others. Since she deserves a permanent place in the history of fly dressing, her methods are explained in Chapter IX. A few very slight variations will be noted there in the way she dresses the famous *Gray Ghost*.

GRAY SMELT   (PLATE VI)

Head: Gray   Hook size: all sizes, 6X long
Tail: A golden pheasant crest feather, about as long as the gap of the hook, and curving upward
Body: Wound with white floss, slightly tapered
Ribbing: Medium flat silver tinsel
Throat: None
Wing: Two light green saddle hackles, outside of which are two blue dun saddle hackles, one on each side. The wing is half again as long as the hook
Cheeks: Jungle cock

(As dressed by the originator)

Originated by Lew Oatman of Shushan, New York. In a letter to the author about this fly, Mr. Oatman says, "This fly was designed to imitate the white and silver flash and gray green of the natural smelt. It has been very effective for trout and in 1953 took one of the rare Marston trout in Quebec. When tying larger sizes for landlocked salmon, care should be taken to emphasize its slenderness. While a smelt may look quite dark to us viewing it from above, the paler colors of this pattern may look more natural to the salmon striking from an angle below the fly. It also is excellent when used as a trolling streamer."

GREEN BEAUTY STREAMER (Plate IV)

Head: Black, with red band
Tag: Four or five turns of narrow flat silver tinsel
Body: Dressed thin with orange silk
Ribbing: Narrow flat silver tinsel
Throat: An extremely small bunch of white bucktail extending beyond the barb of the hook, under which is a golden pheasant crest feather as long as the shoulder and curving upward
Wing: Five or six strands of bright green peacock herl, over which are four olive-green saddle hackles. The herl is as long as the hackles
Shoulders: Wood duck or dyed mallard side feathers of a varigated brown color, one-third as long as the wing
Checks: Jungle cock

(As dressed by the originator)

Originated by Mrs. Carrie G. Stevens, for taking trout and landlocked salmon in Maine waters. The fly also has been used successfully for Atlantic salmon.

GREEN DRAKE STREAMER

Head: Black
Tag: Four or five turns of narrow flat gold tinsel
Tail: A very small bunch of black hackle fibers
Butt: Two or three turns of peacock herl (four or five strands twisted)
Body: Dressed thin of yellowish-brown silk
Ribbing: Black silk thread
Throat: A small bunch of light brown hackle fibers, as long as the shoulders
Wing: Two olive-green saddle hackles, outside of which are two medium brown saddle hackles, one on each side
Shoulders: Each a teal body feather dyed yellow, one-third as long as the wing
Cheeks: Jungle cock, fairly long

(As dressed by the originator)

This is one of several streamer patterns which were inspired by trout flies of the same name. This adaptation was originated by Mr. Gardner Percy of Portland, Maine.

GREEN GHOST STREAMER

Head: Black
Tag: Three or four turns of narrow flat silver tinsel
Body: Dressed thin with orange silk

Famous Patterns

Ribbing: Narrow flat silver tinsel
Throat: Five or six strands of peacock herl, under which is a small bunch of white bucktail, both extending beyond the barb of the hook
Wing: Six medium green saddle hackles
Topping: A golden pheasant crest feather, as long as the wing and following its curve. (This sometimes is omitted)
Shoulders: Each a Ripon's silver pheasant body feather, one third as long as the wing
Cheeks: Jungle cock

(As dressed by the originator)

This fly was originated by Mr. Bert Quimby, of South Windham, Maine, for taking trout and landlocked salmon in Maine lakes. Its origination was influenced by the popularity of the *Gray Ghost* streamer, which it imitates very closely except for the color of the wing. Streamer flies with green wings (such as the *Nine-Three* streamer) are very successful on Maine lakes since their color is similar to that of smelt, which is widely taken by trout and salmon, especially during the spring migratory runs of this important baitfish.

GREEN KING STREAMER

Head: Black
Body: Medium flat silver tinsel
Wing: A small bunch of white bucktail, over which are two olive-green and two gray Plymouth Rock neck hackles, with the green hackles outside. The bucktail is as long as the hackles
Cheeks: Jungle cock

(As dressed by the originator)

This fly is an adaptation of the better known *Nine-Three* streamer with the Plymouth Rock hackles used instead of the two black hackles. The adaptation was made by Mr. Gardner Percy in the belief that it more closely imitated the coloration of a smelt.

A streamer very similar to the *Green King* is the *Green's Pot* (often called the *Green Spot*), which is dressed with four dark green saddle hackles and a very small bunch of bright green bucktail over the white bucktail. The body usually is ribbed with narrow oval silver tinsel.

GREYHOUND STREAMER (PLATE IV)

Head: Red, with black band
Tag: Four or five turns of narrow flat silver tinsel, beginning above the point of a 5X long hook
Tail: A small bunch of red hackle fibers, extending to the end of the hook
Body: Dressed thin with red silk
Ribbing: Narrow flat silver tinsel
Throat: Six or seven strands of peacock herl, under which is an extremely small bunch of white bucktail, both extending beyond the hook. Under this is a small bunch of red hackle fibers
Wing: Four light gray saddle hackles
Shoulders: Each a Jungle cock body feather extending one-third the length of the wing
Cheeks: Jungle cock, fairly short

(As dressed by the originator)

Originated by Mrs. Carrie G. Stevens. This fly usually is dressed on an extremely long shanked hook, or on tandem hooks, and ordinarily is used for trolling.

GREY PRINCE STREAMER (PLATE II)

Head: Black
Tail: A short golden pheasant crest feather, curving upward
Body: Medium flat embossed silver tinsel
Ribbing: Narrow oval silver tinsel
Throat: A badger saddle hackle tied on as a collar and then tied downward
Wing: Four matched sections of pearl mallard feathers, extending slightly longer than the tail
Cheeks: Jungle cock

(As dressed by the originator)

This fly was originated in 1947 by Mr. B. A. Gulline, of Fin, Fur and Feather, Ltd., of Montreal. It is popular in Canada as a trout and bass streamer.

GREY SQUIRREL SILVER STREAMER

Head: Black
Body: Medium embossed silver tinsel
Throat: The tip of a very short golden pheasant crest feather dyed red
Wing: A very small bunch of grey squirrel tail hair over which are two grey Plymouth Rock saddle hackles of the same length as the squirrel hair
Checks: Jungle cock, very short

(As dressed by the originator)

This is one of a series of three squirrel tail streamers originated by Mr. Ray Bergman of Nyack, New York, in 1933. These flies should be dressed sparsely in small sizes. They are excellent for all species of trout. When the author visited the Gunnison River in Colorado in 1948, the most popular streamer fly on the stream was this one. There it is called the *G. J. Streamer* and is erroneously attributed to a local fisherman who must have acquired it when Mr. Bergman visited the Gunnison. A well-known angler on the Gunnison River says of it: "We have found it best suited for rainbows early in the season. It is also good in high water or for an evening fly for all species of trout."

GRIZZLY KING STREAMER

Head: Black
Tag: Three or four turns of narrow flat gold tinsel
Tail: Two narrow sections of a red duck wing feather, matched and curving upward
Body: Dressed thin of green silk
Ribbing: Narrow flat gold tinsel
Throat: A small bunch of gray Plymouth Rock hackle fibers
Wing: Four gray Plymouth Rock saddle hackles
Shoulders: Each a teal body feather, one-third as long as the wing

(As dressed by the originator)

This fly was inspired by the trout fly of the same name and was originally dressed by Mr. Gardner Percy, of Portland, Maine.

GRIZZLY PRINCE (PLATE I)

Head: Black   Hook sizes: All sizes, 4X long
Tail: A very small bunch of stripped orange hackle fibers
Body: Wound with flat silver tinsel
Throat: A very small bunch of white bucktail extending slightly beyond the bend of the hook. Under this is a very small bunch of stripped orange hackle fibers as long as the gap of the hook
Wing: Select two pairs of white saddle hackles and lay them on the hook, extending to the end of the tail. Prepare four grizzly saddle hackles (2 pairs) of the same size as the white hackles, selecting wide feathers for the purpose. Strip all fibers from the bottom halves of the grizzly hackles. Lay two of these stripped hackles on each side of the white hackles so as to cover the upper half of the white saddle hackles, thus allowing the bottom halves of the white hackles to show
Shoulders: On each side, a wood duck body feather covering the forward third of the wing
Cheeks: Jungle cock

(As dressed by the originator)

Originated by Austin S. Hogan, of Fultonville, New York, famous for his art of color blending to obtain natural baitfish effects, as discussed in Chapter IX. This fly is a general baitfish imitation for waters with medium visibility. It is of special note as an example of the two-color effect obtainable by stripping the fibers from either the top or the bottom of hackles.

HAGEN SANDS BONEFISH FLY   (PLATE V)

Head: Black, built up, with yellow eyes and black pupils   Hook sizes: 1/0 and 1, stainless steel or nickel
Body: None
Wing: A fairly large bunch of white bucktail with the underfur retained, tied on top of the hook and extending beyond the barb. Over this are two yellow neck hackles outside of which are two gray barred rock hackles, all of the same length, slightly longer than the hook. The feathers are tied in as splayed wings curving outward and upward for a "breather" effect

(As dressed by the originator)

This fly was originated in 1949 by Mr. Hagen R. Sands, of Key West, Florida, to imitate both a small minnow and a small mantis shrimp. With it, Mr. Sands took a record bonefish weighing fourteen pounds, four ounces. Mr. Sands wrote the author: "This is a consistent producer on the bonefish flats and has been used to catch large tarpon, permit, and numerous other fish. The fly is best fished by holding the rod parallel with the water and using the strip and pause method. The line should be stripped in nearly two feet at a time."

HARLEQUIN STREAMER   (PLATE II)

Head: Black
Tail: A section of a red swan or goose wing, rather long and thin
Body: Medium flat silver tinsel
Ribbing: Narrow oval silver tinsel
Throat: A badger hackle tied on as a collar and then tied downward
Wing: Two long matched sections of goose or swan wing feathers, each section being married from equal parts of black, dark blue and white, with the black at the top and the blue in the middle. The wing is slightly longer than the tail

(As dressed by the originator)

This fly was originated by Mr. B. A. Gulline, of Fin, Fur and Feather, Ltd., for Mr. W. A. Newman of Montreal, in 1932. It repre-

Famous Patterns

sents a Chub minnow, which has a bluish stripe down its side. It is one of the popular flies for trout in Canada. It is a member of the famous *Trout Fin* series; the other two flies in the series being the *Trout Fin* in orange and in red.

HELEN BATES STREAMER

Head: Black
Tag: Four or five turns of narrow flat gold tinsel
Tail: A very short golden pheasant crest feather, curving upward
Butt: Two or three turns of bright red silk
Body: Narrow flat gold tinsel, palmered fairly thickly from butt to head with a brown saddle hackle, with which the fly is built up at the throat
Wing: Four dark brown furnace hackles
Topping: A golden pheasant crest feather, as long as the wing and following its curve
Cheeks: Jungle cock

(As dressed by the originator)

This fly, originated by Mr. William Reynolds, a nationally known fly dresser of Sturbridge, Massachusetts, was named in honor of Mrs. Joseph D. Bates, Jr., of Longmeadow, Massachusetts. It is a favorite for all species of trout in the Eastern United States throughout the year, and especially for large brown trout.

HERB'S GHOST BUCKTAIL

Head: Black
Tag: A few turns of medium flat silver tinsel
Tail: A very short golden pheasant crest feather
Body: Of orange silk, built up very slightly
Ribbing: Medium flat silver tinsel
Throat: A few turns of a yellow hackle tied downward. The throat is rather long but sparsely dressed
Wing: A very small bunch of white bucktail, over which is a very small bunch of dark brown bucktail, both extending slightly beyond the tail
Shoulders: On each side, a yellow saddle hackle as long as the wing. Over this is an orange hackle, half as long as the wing and extremely fine. These two orange hackles are deep orange or orange-red in color, and are taken from high on the neck so that they are extremely narrow. They are set above the yellow hackles, almost to give the appearance of horns
Cheeks: Jungle cock

(As dressed by the originator)

This fly was originated by Mr. Herbert L. Howard with the assistance of Mr. Herbert Gerlach of Ossining, New York, a friend of whose had taken many bright salmon on the Miramichi River in New Brunswick with a similar fly when others failed. This fly is popular also on the Restigouche River and in other New Brunswick waters for both black and bright salmon. It has the appearance of a streamer, although it is not always dressed as such. The fly is not an adaptation because little was remembered of the fly which inspired it. The *Herb's Ghost* first was tied at Jack Russell's Camp on the Miramichi, and was so resultful that it immediately became popular. Originally it was tied on a wide gape salmon hook with a 2X short shank, although the proper hook now is a Number 2 long shank Limerick. When an augmented fly is called for, Mr. Howard considers this and the *Grizzly King* the best, tied even as large as on 4/0 and 5/0 hooks.

HERRING BUCKTAIL   (PLATE V)

Head: Black, usually with white painted eye and black pupil
Body: Medium flat silver tinsel. (If no ribbing is used, embossed tinsel is preferable)
Ribbing: Medium oval silver tinsel (optional)
Wing: A very small bunch of white polar bear hair, over which is a very small bunch of pale green polar bear hair, over which is a middle band of a bunch of polar bear hair of gun metal gray. Over this is a very small bunch of dark green polar bear hair, with a very small bunch of dark blue polar bear hair over this

(As dressed by Mr. Roy A. Patrick)

This is a companion fly to the *Candlefish* bucktail, and is a scientifically designed pattern made to imitate the Herring, a common baitfish for coho (silver) salmon. The fly is used extensively in the Puget Sound area of the Pacific Northwest and is one of the few standard patterns for coho fishing. It was designed from the angling experiments of a group of Puget Sound anglers, notably Mr. Roy A. Patrick, Mr. Zell E. Parkhurst and Mr. Letcher Lambuth, all of Seattle, Washington. For hook sizes and other data on coho fly fishing, see pages 110 to 115.

HORNBERG SPECIAL STREAMER   (PLATE I)

Head: Black   Hook size: No. 6, regular
Body: Wound with flat silver tinsel

Wing: Two barred gray mallard breast feathers one and one-half inches long, between which are the very narrow tips of two yellow neck hackles as long as the mallard and nearly concealed by it. These cover the shank of the hook, and are stroked to a point at their ends by applying a small amount of laquer to them, rubbed between thumb and forefinger. The width of the feathers (for above size of hook) is at least a quarter of an inch, with the yellow hackles narrower. (An easy way to apply the mallard is to strip the lower sides of the feathers from the quills)
Cheeks: Jungle cock, fairly long
Throat: Four or five turns of a grizzly hen neck hackle wound on dry fly style as a collar after wing and cheeks have been applied. (This dressing should be fairly wide and heavy. The wing should not be applied too far forward, to accommodate it.)

(As dressed by The Weber Tackle Company)

Mr. Ed Wotruba, president of Weber Tackle Company, Stevens Point, Wisconsin, wrote the author: "This was the idea of retired Conservation Warden Frank Hornberg when he was on active duty in Portage County. We helped him develop it, and tied the first one for commercial sale. I think he had in mind to simulate a small minnow, which this fly does nicely when fished wet. It is also very effective when dressed and fished dry. It is primarily a trout fly but takes panfish very readily. This is an authentic sample of the original pattern."

This fly, called the *Hornberg* in the East, is considered "a great new fly." In the eastern version no lacquer is added to the tips of the wing. Some variations use yellow hair instead of the yellow hackles, and teal instead of the mallard. The fly often is fished dry until it sinks, whereupon it is fished as a streamer.

HURRICANE STREAMER

Head: Black
Tail: Two jungle cock feathers, small and short
Body: Medium flat silver tinsel
Ribbing: Narrow oval silver tinsel
Throat: Eight or ten peacock sword fibres
Wing: A very small bunch of red bucktail, over which is a very small bunch of white bucktail, with two Plymouth Rock saddle hackles over this. The bucktail is as long as the hackles

This fly is sometimes known as the *Wonder* streamer. It was originated by Mr. Fred B. Fowler, of Oquossoc, Maine, in 1925. In Maine it is considered especially productive for taking landlocked salmon in the early spring. It is often tied with tandem hooks and used as a trolling fly.

IMPROVED GOVERNOR STEELHEAD BUCKTAIL
(PLATE VIII)

Head: Black
Tail: A very small bunch of red hackle fibers, rather long, tied in forward of the red silk and gold ribbing, after they have been applied
Body: Rear third: red silk, ribbed with narrow oval gold tinsel. (This is in effect a tag, since the tail is tied in forward of it. Mr. Pray prefers a heavy hook with a number 1 bend, very short.) Front two thirds: dark green chenille. (The usual dressing for the *Improved Governor* calls for peacock herl over padding, but the chenille gives the same effect and is more permanent, since steelhead tear peacock herl badly)
Throat: Mahogany (red-brown) hackle tied on as a collar, long, stiff and full
Wing: Dark brown wolverine hair, very long. (The regular dressing calls for a section of a dark mottled brown wing feather of a hen ringneck pheasant, woodcock or turkey.) A hair wing is preferable in the steelhead version. Dark brown bear hair may be substituted if wolverine is not available
Cheeks: Jungle cock, dressed high and rather long. (This is not called for in the regular dressing)

(As dressed by the originator)

The *Improved Governor* is an adaptation of the *Governor* fly which originated in England prior to 1850. There are several variations of the fly, including the *Improved Governor* and the *Governor Special*. This steelhead version of this fly was originated by Mr. C. Jim Pray of Eureka, California, a famous fly dresser and steelhead angler of the West Coast. It is particularly effective on the Klamath and Eel Rivers of California.

IRIS No. 1 BUCKTAIL

Head: Black, with painted red band at rear
Body: Medium flat silver tinsel
Ribbing: Very fine oval silver tinsel or silver wire
Wing: A very small bunch of dark red polar bear hair, over which is a very small bunch of bright yellow polar bear hair, over which is a very small bunch of pale green polar bear hair, with a very small bunch of light blue polar bear

Famous Patterns

hair over this. All bunches are of the same length and must be extremely small so that the fly will not be overdressed. (Bucktail may be substituted for the polar bear hair, if desired)
Cheeks: Jungle cock

(As dressed by the originator)

This fly, originated by Mr. Preston J. Jennings, of Brooklyn, New York, is typical of a series devised by him on the theory that minnows best can be imitated with flies dressed in spectrum colors. Another of Mr. Jennings' flies, shown in this book, is the *Lord Iris Streamer*.

JANE CRAIG STREAMER (Plate VII)

Head: Black
Body: Medium flat silver tinsel
Throat: A small bunch of white hackle fibers
Wing: Six white saddle hackles
Topping: Seven or eight strands of bright green peacock herl, as long as the wing
Cheeks: Jungle cock

(As dressed by the originator)

This is one of the earliest and best known of the Maine streamers. It was originated by Mr. Herbert L. Welch, of Mooselookmeguntic, Maine, and named in honor of Jane Craig, a vaudeville actress of the team of Dalton and Craig, which toured the Keith Circuit when this fly was originated in about 1923. Mr. Welch later dressed the fly with yellow hackles and named it the *Yellow Jane Craig*. The white version was dressed to imitate a smelt. The yellow adaptation was designed to give the fly greater visibility on dark days or in discolored water. Mr. Welch considers saddle hackles vastly superior to the heavier neck or shoulder hackles because they make a more streamlined fly and give better action in the water.

JEAN BUCKTAIL

Head: Black
Tail: A very small bunch of orange bucktail tips or orange hackle fibers
Body: Medium flat gold tinsel
Throat: Two or three turns of a yellow hackle, dressed downward, rather long and sparse

Wing: A small bunch of blue-gray bucktail, over which is a small bunch of orange bucktail, with a small bunch of blue-gray bucktail over this. The bunches must be extremely small so that the fly will not be overdressed. They are of the same length and extend slightly beyond the tail
Shoulders: Each a very small jungle cock body feather, one-third as long as the wing
Cheeks: Jungle cock, half as long as the shoulder

This fly originated in British Columbia or in the northwestern United States, where it is popular for all species of trout. The dressing is from an original given to Mr. Herbert L. Howard, of New Rochelle, New York, who gave it to Mr. Ray Bergman for his popular book TROUT.

JESSE WOOD STREAMER (PLATE I)

Head: Black
Tail: A narrow section of a red duck wing feather, rather long
Body: Medium embossed or oval silver tinsel. (In the early versions, the body was wound with fine silver wire)
Throat: A furnace hackle tied around the hook and bunched downward. The hackle should be short and used only in part to make the throat thinly dressed. (In the earliest version of this fly, a sample of which was presented to the author by Mr. Arthur C. Mills, Jr., of William Mills and Son, the throat is dressed much longer and heavier than recommended here, and the hackle is almost black at the front, shaded to dark brown at the rear)
Wing: Two Bali duck shoulder feathers, extending just beyond the tail. The upper halves of these feathers should be light brown in color, and the lower halves jet black. (This feather sometimes is called "Yanosh," which is a misnomer given to it as a joke. The name, however, is widely used)
Cheeks: Jungle cock, fairly short

This fly was originated by Mr. Jesse Wood, of Warwick, New York, in 1926 to imitate a minnow. As a customer, he worked with Mr. Ray Bergman in developing the fly when Mr. Bergman was a salesman with William Mills and Son, of New York City. This is the dressing which is personally approved by Mr. Bergman. Mr. Wood preferred the tandem hook dressing but the fly is correctly tied with either single or tandem hooks. The fly also was dressed for Mr. Wood by Mr. Frier Gulline, of the firm of Fin, Fur and Feather, Ltd., of Montreal, in 1929. The dressing is the same, but in Canada the fly usually is known as the *Demon* streamer.

Famous Patterns

JOSSY SPECIAL BUCKTAIL

Head: Black Hook sizes: No. 8, 4X long
Body: Wound with white chenille
Ribbing: Two or three twisted strands of peacock herl
Wing: A fairly small bunch of brown bucktail half again as long as the hook. On each side of this is a white saddle hackle of the same length as the hair and applied to splay outward

(As dressed by Mr. E. H. Rosborough)

This pattern was originated by Mr. W. E. Jossy, of River Forest Place, Oregon. It is especially popular on Oregon's Deschutes River, which is famous for steelhead fishing. (In applying peacock herl wound on as a body or ribbing, twist the strands of peacock herl with a section of similarly colored thread for added strength.)

KELLY BILL BUCKTAIL

Head: Red
Tail: A section of orange wool, short but rather heavy
Body: In two parts. The rear half is medium flat gold tinsel. The front half is orange wool of medium thickness
Ribbing: Medium flat gold tinsel. (The wool part of the body may be applied so that the ribbing is an extension of the rear half of the body)
Throat: About two turns of a black hackle, tied downward. The throat is fairly long and rather sparse
Wing: A small bunch of gray squirrel tail hair, extending just beyond the tail
Cheeks: Jungle cock, fairly short

(As dressed by the originator)

Originated in 1925 by Mr. Herbert L. Howard from a suggestion given to him by Mr. Bill Kelly (usually called "Kelly Bill"), of the Cranberry Lake region of the Adirondack Mountains, in New York State. Mr. Kelly insisted that an orange and gold fly with a gray wing was the best fly for all species of trout. The fly has proved productive in the East and should be equally so in the West for steelhead and other varieties of trout.

KENNEBAGO STREAMER

Head: Black
Tail: A small bunch of orange hackle fibers
Butt: Made in three parts, which take up one-third of body. Rear quarter of butt is peacock herl, middle half is pale blue silk, and forward quarter is peacock herl

Body: Medium flat gold tinsel
Ribbing: Medium oval silver tinsel, over gold only
Throat: A small bunch of orange hackle fibers
Wing: Two dark red saddle hackles with a golden badger saddle hackle on each side
Cheeks: Jungle cock

(As dressed by the originator)

Originated by Mr. Herbert L. Welch, of Oquossoc, Maine, and named for Kennebago Stream, a famous trout and landlocked salmon water in the Rangeley section of the state of Maine.

LADY DOCTOR BUCKTAIL (Plate VII)

Head: Black
Tag: Three or four turns of narrow flat gold tinsel
Tail: The tips of two moderately long and very small yellow neck hackles back to back
Butt: Two or three turns of bright red silk
Body: Thinly wound with bright yellow silk
Ribbing: Narrow flat gold tinsel. Just ahead of the tinsel is palmered a yellow hackle, tapering larger toward the head. The balance of the usable part is wound on as a throat
Throat: A small bunch of yellow hackle fibers, if the remainder of the palmered hackle (tied downward) is not sufficient
Wing: A small bunch of white polar bear hair over which is a smaller bunch of black bear hair, both extending just beyond the tail
Topping: Two jungle cock feathers tied closely back to back over the wing. They should be half as long as the wing
Shoulders: Each a red dyed breast feather with a sharp outside edge one-third as long as the wing and tied straight along hook

This beautiful and productive fly was originated in 1926 by Warden Supervisor Joseph S. Stickney, of Saco, Maine. Originally it was tied in small sizes to imitate a bee, but it now is more popular dressed as a bucktail, even though it seems to lack a logical reason for being such. The fly was named by Mr. Stickney for his wife, a well-known physician, of Saco, Maine. Since Mr. Stickney did not dress his own flies the majority of them were made for him by the Percy Tackle Company, of Portland, Maine. The dressing described here is from a fly presented by Mr. Stickney to the author, who was one of his fishing companions for many years.

The *Lady Doctor* is famous as a trout, bass and landlocked salmon fly under conditions when a bright pattern is needed. In 1934

Mr. Gardner Percy dressed a variation of it, called the *Adeline*, which is identical except that it lacks the black part of the wing and the red shoulders. This fly is included in the set of small trout bucktail patterns sponsored by the Cape Cod Trout Club, of Massachusetts. Both the *Lady Doctor* and the *Adaline* are excellent for all species of trout when tied as ordinary wet flies in small sizes. The author has used them successfully for cutthroat trout and steelhead.

LADY GHOST STREAMER (Plate III)

Head: Black
Body: Medium flat silver tinsel
Ribbing: Narrow oval silver tinsel
Throat: Six or seven peacock herl fibers, under which is an extremely small bunch of white bucktail, both as long as the wing. Under this is a fairly short golden pheasant crest feather, curving upward
Wing: A golden pheasant crest feather, as long as the wing and curving upward, over which are four golden badger saddle hackles
Shoulders: Each a Reeves pheasant body feather, showing a golden-brown base and a black edge. The feathers are one-third as long as the wing
Cheeks: Jungle cock, long enough to touch the black outside band of the shoulder

(As dressed by the originator)

This very popular imitation of a minnow was originated by Mr. Bert Quimby, of South Windham, Maine, one of his state's best known and most experienced guides and fly dressers. The original version of the fly differs somewhat from this new dressing, in that it has a tail of a few strands of golden pheasant tippet and a body of red silk ribbed with narrow flat silver tinsel. In this dressing the two golden pheasant crest feathers are lacking and the Reeves pheasant shoulders have a white base and a wide dark red-brown outside band.

LEECH STREAMER (Plate I)

Head: Black
Body: Dressed moderately heavily of maroon wool
Throat: A bunch of black hackle fibers
Wing: Two maroon saddle hackles over which are two black saddle hackles. The four feathers are tied on flat (at right angles with the hook) with the black feathers on top, and they are somewhat longer than usual

(As dressed by the originator)

This fly was originated by Mr. Frier Gulline, of Fin, Fur and Feather, Ltd., in the early 1930's. Since it is dressed to imitate a leech (commonly called a "bloodsucker" in many parts of the United States) the red feathers and wool must be a very dark blood red. The fly is very popular in Canada for both trout and bass, since the leech is a favorite item of their diet in many northern lakes. The fly must be fished very deep and very slowly, in the gradual undulating motion of a leech rather than with the darting motion of a minnow. It is especially productive early in the season.

LEITZ BUCKTAIL

Head: Black
Tag: Narrow flat gold tinsel. The tag is rather long, extending part way around the bend of the hook
Tail: The tips of two red hackles, rather long and splayed outwardly
Butt: Two turns of black chenille
Body: Medium embossed silver tinsel. Just behind the throat is a forward butt of four turns of black chenille
Throat: Two turns of a red hackle, tied downward. The throat is rather sparsely dressed
Wing: A bunch of white bucktail, over which is a bunch of black and red bucktail mixed equally. The wing extends to the end of the tail and is rather fully dressed
Cheeks: Jungle cock, rather long

(As dressed by the originator)

Originated by Mr. Earl Leitz, of Sault Ste. Marie, Michigan, and named in his honor by Dr. Marks of the same city, who took a prize rainbow trout on this fly in 1947. This is one of several flies which were originated for taking the large rainbows, or "Soo" trout, of the St. Mary's River at the outlet of Lake Superior. Since the trout in these rapids are large, these flies usually are dressed on Number 2 hooks.

LITTLE BROOK TROUT BUCKTAIL (Plate I)

Head: Black   Hook sizes: No. 12 to No. 2, 6X long
Tail: A very small bunch of bright green bucktail under or over which is a section cut from bright red floss, both slightly longer than the gap of the hook
Body: Wound with cream-colored spun fur
Ribbing: Narrow flat silver tinsel
Throat: A very small bunch of bright orange bucktail, the same length as the tail

Famous Patterns

Wing: Of four very small separated bunches of hair, each extending slightly beyond the tail. A very small bunch of white bucktail over which and blending into it is a very small bunch of bright orange bucktail. Over this is a very small bunch of bright green bucktail, topped by a very small bunch of barred badger hair

(As dressed by the originator)

This fly and the two which follow were originated by Samuel R. Slaymaker II, of Gap, Pennsylvania, to imitate trout fry as mentioned in Chapter III and discussed in Chapter IX. The three flies are manufactured for sale by the Weber Tackle Company, of Stevens Point, Wisconsin, both in regular sizes and small "streamerette" size. As previously discussed, they have exceptional records for taking trout in waters where trout fry exist, and are almost equally useful for many other species.

LITTLE BROWN TROUT BUCKTAIL (Plate I)

Head: Black   Hook sizes: No. 12 to No. 2, 6X long
Tail: A very small breast feather, with the dark center removed, from a ringneck pheasant. The feather is as long as the gap of the hook, and curves upward
Body: Wound with white spun wool
Ribbing: Copper wire. (Narrow flat gold tinsel may be substituted)
Throat: None
Wing: Of four very small separated bunches of hair, each extending slightly beyond the tail. A very small bunch of yellow bucktail over which is a very small bunch of reddish-orange bucktail, slightly blended. Over this is a very small bunch of medium dark squirrel tail topped and slightly blended with a very small bunch of dark brown squirrel tail
Cheeks: Jungle cock

(As dressed by the originator)

Originated by Samuel R. Slaymaker II, of Gap, Pennsylvania, as described in the preceding pattern.

LITTLE RAINBOW TROUT BUCKTAIL (Plate I)

Head: Black   Hook sizes: No. 12 to No. 2, 6X long
Tail: A small bunch of bright green bucktail, slightly longer than the gap of the hook
Body: Wound with pinkish-white fur
Ribbing: Narrow flat silver tinsel
Throat: A very small bunch of pink bucktail, as long as the tail

Wing: Of four very small separated bunches of hair, each extending slightly beyond the tail. A very small bunch of white bucktail over which is a very small bunch of pink bucktail, slightly blended. Over this is a very small bunch of bright green bucktail topped and slightly blended with a very small bunch of natural badger hair
Cheeks: Jungle cock

(As dressed by the originator)

Originated by Samuel R. Slaymaker II, of Gap, Pennsylvania, as described under *Little Brook Trout*.

LORD DENBY STREAMER

Head: Black
Tail: About six or seven fibers from a golden pheasant tippet, medium long
Body: Medium flat silver tinsel
Throat: Two turns of a red saddle hackle mixed with one turn of a light blue saddle hackle, applied as a collar and then tied downward. The throat is dressed sparsely, with the hackles of medium length
Wing: A light blue saddle hackle between two Plymouth Rock saddle hackles, extending slightly beyond the tail
Cheeks: Jungle cock, small and rather short

(As dressed by the originator)

Originated by Mr. Robert E. Coulson, of Lyon and Coulson, Inc., of Buffalo, New York, in 1924. Mr. Coulson was an angling writer who used the pen name of "Breems Forrest." The *Lord Denby* Streamer, as well as the *Saguenay* and *St. Ignace*, were designed for taking the large eastern brook trout on the Nipigon River in the Nipigon district of Ontario. It was named for Lord Denby, who fished the river with Mr. Coulson.

LORD IRIS STREAMER (PLATE VII)

Head: Black
Tail: In two matched sections; each a married section of swan or goose wing feathers, red, blue, and yellow, with the red at the top. Each completed married section is narrow but rather long
Body: Medium flat silver tinsel
Ribbing: Narrow oval silver tinsel
Throat: A yellow hackle tied on as a collar and then tied downward
Wing: Four ginger furnace hackles
Shoulders: Each a matched section of red, blue and yellow swan or goose wing, married together with the red at the top. The shoulder is dressed along the top of the wing and is two thirds as long, but rather narrow
Cheeks: Jungle cock

(As dressed by Fin, Fur and Feather, Ltd.)

Famous Patterns

This fly is one of those originated by Mr. Preston Jennings, of Brooklyn, New York, supposedly to imitate the colors of minnows as they appear by the breaking down of light passing through a prism.

MacGREGOR BUCKTAIL

Head: Black
Tag: Two or three turns of medium flat silver tinsel
Tail: A very short golden pheasant crest feather
Body: Wound with "dirty-orange" chenille
Ribbing: Medium flat silver tinsel
Throat: A very small bunch of grizzly hackle fibers, rather long
Wing: A medium sized bunch of grey squirrel tail hair, as long as the tail
Cheeks: Jungle cock, fairly short

This fly was given to Mr. Herbert L. Howard, of New Rochelle, New York, by Mr. George Fraser of Edinburgh, Scotland. Copies of it were given by Mr. Howard to the author and to Mr. Ray Bergman for his well-known book TROUT. Its originator is unknown. The fly is popular for all species of trout and is also valuable for both bright and black Atlantic salmon.

MAD TOM (Plate VI)

Head: Black   Hook sizes: No. 2 or No. 4, regular length
Tag: Several turns of medium flat silver tinsel wound down onto the bend of the hook
Tail: Two bunches of marabou fibers. First, a small short bunch of white. Above that is a longer bunch of tobacco brown extending about an inch and a half beyond the bend of the hook
Body: First wrap the hook shank with white floss. Then, just ahead of where the tail is tied in, tie on a bunch of black marabou fibers which top the full length of the tail. Then tie in the end of a thick black chenille rope and wind back and forth, finally tying off at the head. This is built up to represent the thick shoulder of the natural catfish
Wing: (Evidently) None
Throat: A black hackle with fibers about an inch long, wound on as a collar. These fibers should be coarse so, when wet and sticking together in clusters, they resemble the whiskers of a catfish

(As dressed by the originator)

This is an unusual pattern originated by the famous angler and fly dresser Lew Oatman, of Shushan, New York. The above dressing was given to the author in a letter written by Mr. Oatman to him prior to his death. Since the author has never seen the pattern, the dressing is given in Mr. Oatman's words. (The comment about the wing is the author's, who also presumes that the instructions regarding the black marabou could have been included in the dressing for the tail.) In Mr. Oatman's letter he said, "This pattern is not intended to be an exact imitation of any one species of catfish, but rather a general pattern resembling several such as the Mad Tom, Stone Cat, Tadpole Cat, and all the little bullheads and cats having the characteristic thick shoulder, tapering body, and generally dark appearance."

MAGOG SMELT BUCKTAIL

Head: Black, with tiny yellow painted eye with black pupil
Tail: A very small bunch of teal body feather fibers
Body: Medium flat silver tinsel
Throat: A very small bunch of red hackle fibers
Wing: A very small bunch of white bucktail, over which is a very small bunch of yellow bucktail, over which is a very small bunch of violet bucktail
Topping: Five or six strands of peacock herl
Shoulders: Each a teal body feather, one-third as long as the wing

(As dressed by Mr. Harold N. Gibbs)

This fly was originated by Mr. Frier Gulline, of Fin, Fur and Feather, Ltd. It was first used for taking landlocked salmon in the Memphremagog Lake area near the border of Quebec Province and Vermont. Mr. Edward A. Materne, of East Providence, Rhode Island, obtained a sample and dressed duplicates on Number 1 hooks for striped bass. It is particularly successful for smallmouth bass, landlocked salmon, and striped bass, as well as for several other varieties of fresh and salt water game fish. Mr. Harold N. Gibbs, of Barrington, Rhode Island, and Mr. Materne, both famous salt water fly fishermen, gave the fly its original popularity in the United States.

MALE DACE STREAMER (PLATE VI)

Head: Black Hook sizes: No. 12 to No. 4, 4X long
Body: Wound with very pale cream floss, slightly tapered
Ribbing: Medium narrow flat gold tinsel
Throat: A very small bunch of rich orange hackle fibers, about as long as the gap of the hook

Famous Patterns

Wing: Two olive green saddle hackles, on each side of which is a golden edged badger hackle. All are of the same length, extending slightly beyond the bend of the hook, and all should be slender
Cheeks: Jungle cock, tied in short

(As dressed by the originator)

This is another of the natural imitation patterns by Lew Oatman of Shushan, New York. In his notes he says, "This fly imitates the male Black Nosed Dace in spawning season. These little fellows are very common in our trout streams, and this pattern has just enough color under such conditions."

MARABOU PERCH STREAMER (Plate I)

Head: Green, built up to match body, and painted with large yellow eyes with red pupils
Body: Of silver mylar tubular cord, painted on sides with green vertical bands and with a red band just behind the eye
Throat: A bunch of white marabou fibers extending to barb of hook
Wing: A yellow marabou feather, over which is an olive green marabou feather. Over this is a topping of several strands of peacock herl, all extending slightly beyond the bend of the hook

(As dressed by the originator)

Originated by Arthur Fusco of Medford, Massachusetts, to imitate a small yellow perch, which is a favorite food for game fish living in lakes and ponds. Mr. Fusco is an expert in dressing flies with mylar bodies. His method is described in Chapter IX.

MASCOMA STREAMER (Plate III)

Head: Black   Hook sizes: No. 10 to No. 4, 4X long
Tail: A very small golden pheasant crest feather, curving upward
Body: Two or three layers of flat gold tinsel (to build up the body)
Ribbing: Oval gold tinsel
Throat: A very small bunch of orange hackle fibers about half as long as the hook
Wing: About seven hairs of polar bear or bucktail in each of the following colors: yellow, blue and red. These can be mixed. Over this on each side is a section of bronze mallard wing with the tips curving slightly upward. All these elements are of the same length; slightly longer than the hook. (Teal or mallard can be substituted for the bronze mallard)
Cheeks: Jungle cock, preferably of light color and tied in very short

(As dressed by Mr. Paul Kukonen)

This fly (of unknown origin) began as a salmon fly in New Brunswick and has been very successfully adapted as a trout streamer; especially productive with the mallard or teal wing in discolored water and with the bronze mallard wing in clear water.

McGINTY BUCKTAIL

Head: Black
Tail: Two rather wide and long sections of a red duck or goose wing feather
Body: Dressed full, of black and yellow chenille, alternating two or three turns each to provide three black and two yellow bands. A regular length hook should be used
Throat: Two or three turns of a brown hackle, rather long
Wing: A bunch of brown bear hair, extending to the end of the tail
(As dressed by the Author)

The *McGinty* bucktail is an adaptation of the trout fly of the same name. Although originally dressed in small sizes to imitate a bee, it has become a well-known bucktail pattern, particularly in the West and Middle West. The history of the fly cannot be determined. It is popular for trout and bass.

MICKEY FINN BUCKTAIL
(Illustrated as a streamer in Plate VII)

Head: Black
Body: Medium flat silver tinsel
Ribbing: Narrow oval silver tinsel
Wing: A very small bunch of yellow bucktail, over which is a very small bunch of red bucktail, with a bunch of yellow bucktail equal in size to the first two bunches over this. (In dressing this fly correctly, it is important to note that the lower yellow band and the red band are of the same size, but that the upper yellow band is about twice the size of the lower)
(As dressed by Mr. John Alden Knight)

Jungle cock cheeks are not called for on the official version, although they frequently are used. In Canada, the fly is dressed with feathered wings, by adding to the tinseled body a long but narrow tail of a section of a red goose feather, a yellow hackle throat and a wing, extending to the end of the tail, of married sections of yellow, red and yellow goose wings. The wing is a double wing and is long but narrow. The *Mickey Finn* also can be dressed as a marabou

Famous Patterns 303

streamer by substituting for the wing, two yellow marabou tips and by adding shoulders of red saddle hackles, as long as the marabou. Jungle cock cheeks also are added in this dressing.

This fly was an unnamed and relatively unknown pattern until Mr. John Alden Knight, angler and author of Williamsport, Pennsylvania, popularized it in his writings. The story of its introduction is quoted from letters to the author from the principals. Mr. Knight says: "In the spring of 1932, when I was living in Rye, New York, I was invited to fish the waters of a trout club a short distance out of Greenwich. My host, Junior Vanderhoff, gave me a small bucktail which he had found most effective for catching stocked squaretail trout from this little stream (the Mianus River). It delivered the goods that day; in fact, it was the only fly that did so.

"I learned from Mr. Vanderhoff that this fly was one of a series of six small bucktails in various color combinations which were at one time put out by William Mills and Son. Then, the fly was known only as the *Red and Yellow* bucktail. I used the fly for a couple of years quite successfully.

"In 1936 I had occasion to go to Toronto, Canada, on business, and there I met the late Frank Cooper, of the firm of Larway, Temple and Cooper, and his friend, Gregory Clark. Mr. Cooper and a friend of his took me as a guest to the Mad River Club, where we fished for native squaretail (by 'native' I mean the unstocked variety). The club members had been taking these fish, not without a little difficulty, by the greased-line method with small salmon flies. I showed them the one pattern of (what later was to be called) the *Mickey Finn* that I had with me but they were not impressed. Finally I prevailed on one of them to give the fly a trial.

"On the first cast I cautioned the angler to let the fly sink three or four feet below the surface before starting the retrieve. He did so, rather lackadaisically, and then started the fly across the pool in short, well-spaced jerks. On the second cast, fished in this way, he hooked a two-pounder. I used the fly on the Mad River that afternoon and with it managed to hook and release about seventy-five trout; a feat which was unheard of on the part of a guest in those waters.

"On the way home we christened the fly the *Assassin*. Later that year it was rechristened by Gregory Clark, noted feature writer and war correspondent who was with the *Toronto Star*. He called it the *Mickey Finn*.

"In the fall of 1937 I made an arrangement with *Hunting and Fishing* Magazine and with The Weber Tackle Company to write a story about the *Mickey Finn* for *Hunting and Fishing*. The Weber Company took a full column advertisement in that issue and featured the fly and yours truly in it. The magazine appeared on the news stands when the Sportsmen's Show was on in New York. In the space of two days not a single copy of *Hunting and Fishing* Magazine could be found on the New York news stands. I suppose that the name and the flashy colors struck the public fancy. In any event the fly tiers at the show were busy for the entire week tying *Mickey Finns*. Each night bushel baskets of red and yellow bucktail clippings and silver tinsel were swept up by the cleaning crew at Grand Central Palace, and by Friday of that week not a single bit of red or yellow bucktail could be purchased from any of the New York supply houses. It was estimated that between a quarter and a half million of these flies were dressed and distributed during the course of that show. How accurate that estimate is I have no way of knowing but I do know that almost everybody encountered in the aisles had a *Mickey Finn* stuck in his hatband.

"During the next few months the entire facilities of the Weber company were stretched to the breaking point in their frantic efforts to keep up with *Mickey Finn* orders. One outfit in Westchester actually saved itself from bankruptcy proceedings by specializing intensively in the manufacture of *Mickey Finns*. As matters now stand, it is a difficult thing to find any angler on any stream anywhere who has not at least one *Mickey Finn* in his kit. The 'Mary Pickford' trophy for the prize brook trout taken annually in Ontario was won for the next two consecutive seasons with *Mickey Finn* flies. I still use the fly and find it to be a consistent fish-getter."

Mr. Gregory Clark, mentioned by Mr. Knight in the letter above, adds this: "A day or two after I named the fly the *Assassin* I recollected a story that recently had been published in *Esquire* Magazine about how Rudolph Valentino had been killed by Mickey Finns administered to him by the resentful waiters of New York and Hollywood and I rechristened the fly the *Mickey Finn*. All we did up here

Famous Patterns

was to make it respectable and legitimate and to give the nameless waif an honest name."

MILLER'S RIVER SPECIAL BUCKTAIL (Plate III)

Head: Black Hook sizes: No. 12 to No. 4, 4X long
Tail: Five or six golden pheasant tippet fibers extending only slightly beyond bend of hook
Body: Wide flat gold tinsel
Ribbing: Oval gold tinsel
Wing: A very small bunch of yellow polar bear hair or bucktail, over which is a very small bunch of black polar bear hair or bucktail, both extending just beyond end of the tail
Shoulders: Each a golden pheasant red side feather extending half as long as the wing and tied in horizontally so the lower part acts as a throat, with the upper part no higher than the wing
Cheeks: Jungle cock, light colored and tied in short

(As dressed by the originators)

This very attractive fly was originated by Mr. Paul Kukonen and the late Henry Scarborough of Worcester, Massachusetts, and is named for the river in the northern part of the state. While favored as a brook trout and landlocked salmon fly, it is especially suitable for brown trout in stream or river fishing. Mr. Kukonen (a famous fly dresser) says, "Select the brightest colored shoulder feathers and peel the sides to the correct size. Tie both sides in together by making three turns of thread around the quills and pulling them into place until the feathers just start to crush. Tie the jungle cock in short if the fly is to be cast; long if to be trolled only."

MINNOW STREAMER

Head: Black Hook sizes: No. 6 to No. 10, 3X long
Tail: A small bunch of fibers from a cock ring-necked pheasant's tail, half as long as the hook
Body: Wound with magenta floss, slightly tapered
Ribbing: The ribbing is narrow flat silver tinsel, and is wound on starting at the middle of the body and going forward. (Thus, the ribbing should be tied in before the body is applied)
Wing: Two sections of fibers from a cock ring-necked pheasant tail, extending to the end of the tail

(As dressed by Mr. E. H. Rosborough)

This is a popular northwestern pattern.

MIRACLE MARABOU STREAMERS (Plate I)

This series of five imitative patterns was originated by Mr. Bob Zwirz, of Connecticut (proprietor of The Anglers Cove, Inc., 478 Third Ave., New York City), and by Mr. Kani Evans, of New York, over a period of several years prior to 1963 in an effort to copy closely the five most important species of minnows common to waters in the northern states. The use of mylar is important in the series, to provide flash along the sides rather than along the belly of each pattern. The series was introduced by Mr. Zwirz in an article in the March, 1963 issue of *Field and Stream* and in other publications.

The five flies are dressed, using size 000 white silk thread, on 4X long shanked hooks in sizes from No. 8 to No. 2. All have fully built-up heads painted with clear lacquer and tinted with colors in the dressing instructions which follow. Rather large white or cream-colored eyes with black pupils are painted on the heads. Bodies are of spun fur in colors specified in the dressings, tapered full toward the head of the fly and picked out on the sides with a dubbing needle, the picked-out hairs then being stroked backward toward the tail.

The wings are of whole marabou feathers in colors as noted. Each feather is wetted, preferably by running it through the lips before placing it on the shank of the hook. The mylar is cut in strips slightly less than one-quarter inch wide (depending on size of the fly); tied in horizontally on each side of the wing, extending slightly beyond the bend of the hook and cut on the lower sides toward the ends to taper upward gradually to a point. Wings are slightly longer than the mylar. Throats and tails are a small bunch of fibers stripped from saddle hackles, slightly longer than the gap of the hook. If the mylar does not cling to the marabou wing, it can be brushed on the inside *lightly* with clear head cement. For purposes of simplicity these general instructions are given for all the flies and are not repeated in the individual dressings. The five patterns are as dressed by the originators.

BLACKNOSE DACE

Head: Top half, brown; lower half, white
Tail: Cream or very light ginger
Body: Antique white

Famous Patterns

Throat: Same as tail
Wing: Two whole antique white marabou feathers, over which are two whole light drab (olive toward brown tone) marabou feathers
Mylar: Silver, with upper third painted black, the paint extending from the tip to the painted eye. (Use black "Magic Marker" pencil, or lay a narrow (wetted) strip of black saddle hackle just over the mylar)

The blacknose dace is a small member of the Dace family vitally important as a bait for trout. It is widely distributed from the St. Lawrence southward through Georgia and westward to the Mississippi in the more northerly latitudes. It is exceedingly common in small, clear brooks and prefers moving water but avoids the very fast riffles which harbor its cousin, the longnose dace.

BLUEBACK SHINER

Head: Top half, medium blue; lower half, white
Tail: White
Body: White angora
Throat: Pale cream or very light ginger
Wing: Two whole white marabou feathers, over which is a Silver Doctor blue marabou feather, over which is an American flag blue marabou feather. These are topped with a few short fibers of medium green marabou at the head of the fly
Mylar: Silver

This shiner also is called *River Bait* and *Spottail Shiner*. Two other members of the Notropis group, the *Emerald Shiner* and the *Satin Fin Shiner*, also have a good deal of blue coloring. Though these shiners are found mainly in lakes, and especially in the larger bodies of water, they spend enough time in rivers and streams to be of great importance to trout and salmon fishermen. Members of the bluebacked group are distributed widely from James Bay (in Canada) southward through the Great Lakes and the Mississippi River system down through South Carolina. They are abundant throughout their range and are of great value as natural forage for various fresh water game fish.

GOLDEN SHINER

Head: Yellowish, painted with clear lacquer
Tail: Pale yellow

Body: Pale yellow angora
Throat: Orange
Wing: Two pale maize marabou feathers, over which are two medium olive marabou feathers, all extending to the end of the tail of the fly
Mylar: Gold

This shiner is best known as a bait for largemouth and smallmouth bass and pickerel. Fundamentally it is a warm water species inhabiting ponds, lakes and slow moving stretches of broad rivers. Occasionally it grows to lengths of ten or twelve inches. It is widely distributed from Manitoba eastward to New Brunswick and southward all the way to Florida.

LONGNOSE DACE

Head: Top half, olive; lower half, white
Tail: Cream or very light ginger
Body: Palest green or antique white angora
Throat: Orange
Wing: Two whole pale maize marabou feathers, over which are two medium drab olive marabou feathers, all extending to the end of the tail
Mylar: Gold, with the upper third painted black, as described in pattern for the *Blacknose Dace*

This minnow, called the "rock minnow" in some localities, is one of the most important of baitfish. It is a lover of fast water and usually is less than four inches in length, but sometimes grows to six inches. It is a relative of the blacknose dace (*Rhinichthys attratulus*), but likes faster water than the blacknose. The longnose dace is one of the most widely distributed minnows in North America, ranging from coast to coast in the latitude of the Great Lakes and southward through North Carolina and then down to northern Mexico.

SILVER SHINER

Head: Top half, drab olive; lower half, white
Tail: Two-thirds white and one-third pale olive, mixed
Body: White angora
Throat: Same as tail
Wing: Two whole white marabou feathers, over which are two whole dark olive marabou feathers, all extending to the end of the tail of the fly
Mylar: Silver

Famous Patterns

This shiner is a stream dweller requiring moving water. It is plentiful in most trout streams and sometimes is mistaken for "brook silversides." It ranges widely from Quebec to Saskatchewan and southward to the Gulf of Mexico. There are several subspecies, but all with the same general coloration. Many of these subspecies move into clear lakes in large schools, but streams are their primary home.

MONTREAL STREAMER

Head: Black
Tail: A long and narrow section of a red duck wing feather
Body: Medium flat silver tinsel
Ribbing: Narrow oval silver tinsel
Throat: A bunch of magenta hackle fibers
Wing: Four magenta saddle hackles
Shoulders: Each a section of a brown turkey tail feather, of medium width and one-third as long as the wing

(As dressed by Mr. Gardner Percy)

This pattern was adapted from the trout fly of the same name. There are several accepted dressings for it, no one of which can be considered authentic. Another popular dressing is— Tail: scarlet impala or a small bunch of scarlet hackle fibers. Body: scarlet silk, medium thick. Ribbing: narrow oval silver tinsel. Wing: fox squirrel tail.

MOOSE RIVER STREAMER

Head: Black
Body: Medium flat silver tinsel
Wing: A very small bunch of white bucktail, nearly as long as the hackles, over which are four golden badger neck hackles
Topping: Six or seven strands of peacock herl, as long as the wing
Shoulders: Each a golden pheasant tippet, one-third as long as the wing

(As dressed by the originator)

Originated by Mr. George Munster, of Rockwood Station, Maine, in 1932 and first used on the Moose River, in Maine. Although this is a standard Maine streamer pattern, its popularity has spread to the Northwest where it is one of the few Maine streamer patterns used for all species of western trout.

MORNING GLORY STREAMER (Plate IV)

Head: Red, with black band
Body: Red silk, dressed thin
Ribbing: Narrow flat silver tinsel
Throat: White bucktail extending just beyond barb of hook, beneath which is a black silver pheasant crest feather and then a very small bunch of blue hackle fibers, both as long as the shoulders
Wing: A black silver pheasant crest feather as long as the saddle hackles and curving downward over which are four bright yellow saddle hackles
Shoulders: Each a red mackaw body feather, one-third as long as the wing
Cheeks: Jungle cock

(As dressed by the originator)

Originated by Mrs. Carrie G. Stevens, of Madison, Maine.

MUDDLER MINNOW (Plate I)

Head: Black (red, for weighted flies) Hook sizes: No. 12 to No. 1, 3X long
Tail: A small section of natural turkey wing quill, slightly longer than the gap of the hook
Body: Wound with flat gold tinsel
Wing: A moderately large bunch of gray squirrel tail hair, on each side of which is a fairly large section of a mottled turkey wing feather tied on nearly as long as the bucktail, extending to the end of the tail and pointing upward at about a 30 degree angle
Shoulders: Natural deer body hair, spun on to surround the hook, flattened and clipped short at front and tapering longer backward, leaving a small part as long as possible. (Use care when applying the wing to leave room at the head for the clipped deer hair shoulders. This can be dressed rather heavily, perhaps using two or three spinnings of the hair)

(As dressed by the originator)

This very famous fly was originated on the Nipigon River in Northern Ontario, Canada, by Don Gapen, of the Gapen Fly Company, Anoka, Minnesota. He was trying to imitate the Cockatush minnow that inhabits the Nipigon watershed. This is a flathead type of minnow that lives under rocks in stream water. In parts of Wisconsin these are called "muddlers." The Indians of the Nipigon area spear them at night with a straightened hook or a table fork, using lighted birch bark as a torch to see by, since the muddlers come from under the rocks only at night.

Mr. Gapen wrote the author, "When the *Muddler Minnow* is fished under water, it represents a minnow. In the smaller sizes and

Famous Patterns

fished very slowly, it represents a nymph very well. In the grasshopper season you can float them to represent this trout food. I have used them floating during May Fly time with great success. I have caught the following fish with them: all trout, all bass, crappies, sunfish, snook, bonefish, and redfish (channel bass). Also, at times I have taken walleyes, pike, grayling, bonita, jacks, and even sharks."

The success of the *Muddler Minnow* influenced the development of a similar pattern by Dan Gapen called *The Thief* and described in this section. It also has influenced many variations. The underwing occasionally is dressed with mixed black and white calf tail hair, and the spun hair at the head sometimes is of antelope, caribou, or other animals.

Dan Bailey, of Dan Bailey's Fly Shop, in Livingston, Montana, has had success with combining the above pattern with marabou. He dresses the body with silver tinsel chenille, often with a red tail. The wing is white, yellow, gray, brown, or black marabou extending half again as long as the hook, and topped with ten or more strands of peacock herl. His clipped deer hair body is the same as the *Muddler Minnow* except with a longer clipped head.

While the *Muddler Minnow* is a famous fly for many species of fish, we should note that it is especially effective for smallmouth bass, particularly during times of low water. At such times it is fished on or very near the surface, as one would fish a dry fly to rising trout. This method can be alternated by retrieving it in short jerks which cause a wake on or near the surface.

MYLAR BODIED BUCKTAILS (Plates I, V and VIII)
(See Chapter IX.)

NIMROD BUCKTAIL

Head: Black
Body: Medium flat silver tinsel
Ribbing: Narrow oval silver tinsel
Throat: A very small bunch of yellow bucktail, as long as the wing
Wing: A small bunch of medium green bucktail, over which is a small bunch of black bear hair or black bucktail of the same length
Cheeks: Jungle cock

(As dressed for the originator)

This bucktail was originated by Mr. Henry S. Beverage, former Fishing Editor of the Portland (Maine) *Press-Herald*, and was dressed for him by Mr. Bert Quimby, well-known fly dresser of South Windham, Maine. The fly is preferred for landlocked salmon early in the season.

NINE-THREE STREAMER (Plate III)

Head: Black
Body: Medium flat silver tinsel
Wing: A small bunch of white bucktail extending beyond the end of the hook (or hooks, if in tandem), over which are three medium green saddle hackles *tied on flat*, over which are two natural black hackles tied on upright. All hackles and the bucktail are of the same length
Cheeks: Jungle cock

(As dressed by the originator)

Originated by Dr. J. Hubert Sanborn, of Waterville, Maine, to imitate a smelt, which is the favorite baitfish of landlocked salmon and trout in many Maine lakes. This is one of the most popular Maine streamer flies; named the *Nine-Three* because Dr. Sanborn's first salmon caught with it weighed nine pounds and three ounces. The fly is often dressed on tandem hooks, joined by gut, and is used for trolling. It is also dressed on long shanked hooks in small sizes for trout. Of it, Dr. Sanborn says: "I designed the *Nine-Three* to imitate a smelt as it looks in the water, with dark back, lighter below, and with silver belly and jungle cock eyes. The fly looks rough, but when wet it forms together evenly. The green feathers are tied on flat instead of edgewise which gives the fly a motion in the water that the others don't have. I have told many commercial fly tiers about this but nobody will tie it this way because it looks rough. We fellows believe it the best fly year round for trout, togue, salmon, perch, and bass. I have also caught Atlantic salmon on it."

NORWEGIAN MOUSTACHE BUCKTAIL

Head: Red
Tail: About a dozen strands of golden pheasant tippet of moderate length. (The tail usually is omitted)
Body: Medium flat gold tinsel, thin at rear and shaped very slightly toward head. (Lead fuse wire may be applied under the tinsel to weight the fly)

Ribbing: Fine round gold wire
Throat: Three or four turns of a bright orange hackle of medium width
Wing: A divided or splayed wing with the right side light brown bucktail and the left side white bucktail. Each of the two bunches of bucktail extends just beyond the end of the tail, separated at an angle of about 30 degrees from each other and dressed rather high on the hook, which is large and heavy, usually 2X long

(As dressed by Mr. Don C. Harger)

Originated in 1942 by Ex-governor Morley Griswold, of Nevada for fishing on the Umpqua River in Oregon. The fly was named for a Norwegian gardener who wore a white moustache which was stained brown on one side by tobacco juice. In 1946 Mr. Griswold took a twenty-eight pound steelhead on Oregon's Deschutes River with this fly. At the time it was the largest steelhead ever taken with an artificial fly. The dressing is very similar to other successful steelhead flies, such as the *Silver and Orange,* except for the rather unusual separated colors in the two sides of the splayed wing.

ORANGE STEELHEADER BUCKTAIL (PLATE VIII)

Head: Black
Tail: A small bunch of polar bear hair, dyed hot orange, rather long
Body: Wound with silver wire of at least 22 gauge over a foundation of black thread, size B. Both thread and wire should be lacquered (see instructions on page 189)
Wing: A bunch of light orange polar bear hair over which is a bunch of hot orange polar bear hair, both extending to the end of the tail. The thread is passed under each of the two bunches before tying the head, in order to raise and separate the hair

(As dressed by the originator)

Originated by Mr. Fred A. Reed, of Nevada City, California. This fly is one of the most popular for steelhead in the Northwest and is also used extensively on inland lakes and streams for all varieties of western trout. Mr. Reed dresses it on a 1/0, 2/0 or 3/0 hook, 2 or 3X heavy, 1 or 2X long. When tied as a triple wing fly an additional wing of hot orange is tied in midway of the hook, which in this case has an extra long shank. Bucktail may be substituted for the polar bear. An easier way to dress the body than to use silver wire is to use three amp lead fuse wire covered with silver tinsel. This method is less permanent than that of using the silver wire.

ORDWAY STREAMER

Head: Yellow
Body: Medium flat silver tinsel
Throat: A small bunch of white bucktail, slightly longer than the hook
Wing: Four white neck hackles, the two of each pair curving outward to make a "V"
Shoulders: Each a red goose body feather, about one-third as long as the wing and curving outward to allow greater action to the wing

(As dressed for the originator)

This fly is almost identical to the *Colonel White*, the main difference being in the splayed dressing of the feathers to give the fly greater action in the water. In this it is very similar in construction to many salt water streamer flies and, if dressed on non-corrosive hooks, would be an excellent salt water pattern. It was designed by George T. Ordway, of Franklin, New Hampshire, and was tied and named for him by the Percy Tackle Company, of Portland, Maine. Both the *Ordway* and the *Colonel White* seem to have influenced the *Bonbright* streamer, which is the most elaborate pattern in this color combination.

OWL EYED OPTIC (Plate VIII)
(See page 118)

PAINT BRUSH BUCKTAIL

Head: Black
Tail: A very small and very long bunch of dark red bucktail
Body: Wound with silver wire, or with copper wire covered with medium flat silver tinsel (see instructions on page 189)
Wing: A small bunch of yellow bucktail, over which is a small bunch of bright red bucktail topped with a few hairs of brown bucktail dyed red. The wing extends to the end of the tail. In applying the two parts of the wing, turns of thread are taken under both the yellow and the red bucktail to raise the wing to an angle of about 40 degrees. In the three-wing pattern the rear wing is bright red bucktail (dressed on a very long shanked hook) and the lower part of the front wing is yellow bucktail, dressed fairly full, with the upper wing dark red bucktail. All three wings extend to the end of the long tail. Polar bear hair may be substituted for the bucktail if desired
Throat: (Dressed as a "spike" as explained in the above reference.) A small bunch of yellow bucktail. This generally is omitted, particularly in the two-wing dressing

(As dressed by the originator)

Originated by Mr. Peter J. Schwab, of Yreka, California, in 1927. This is one of a series of steelhead flies listed in the comments on the *Princess Bucktail*, and in notes on page 192.

PARMACHEENE BEAU STREAMER   (Plate II)

Head: Black
Tail: Two tiny sections of red and white swan wing feathers, married together with the red at the top, Both are rather long, thin, and curve upward. (A section of barred wood duck or mandarin duck body feather occasionally is substituted)
Body: Medium flat silver tinsel
Ribbing: Narrow oval silver tinsel
Throat: One red and one white neck hackle wound on mixed as a collar and gathered downward
Wing: Four white saddle hackles. (The same wing often is used as called for in the *Parmacheene Belle* streamer. In this case, the shoulders and horns called for here are eliminated)
Horns: Each a single strand from a red macaw tail feather, nearly as long as the wing
Shoulders: Married red and white sections of right and left goose wing feathers, alternating white, red and white. The shoulder is one-half as long as the wing and the three married sections are equal in width
Cheeks: Jungle cock

(As dressed by the author)

A bucktail wing frequently is used in dressing this fly, as described under the *Parmacheene Belle* streamer. The *Parmacheene Beau* is a popular adaptation of the *Parmacheene Belle*.

PARMACHEENE BELLE STREAMER   (Plate VII)

Head: Black
Tail: Two tiny sections of red and white swan wing feathers, married together with the red at the top. Both are rather long, thin, and curve upward
Butt: Three or four turns of peacock herl (optional)
Body: Wound with dark yellow wool, picked out slightly and shaped larger toward the head
Ribbing: Narrow oval silver tinsel
Throat: One red and one white neck hackle wound on mixed as a collar and gathered downward
Wing: Two wings, one each from right and left swan wing feathers. Each wing is composed of three married sections equally wide, white, red and white, extending just beyond the tail
Cheeks: Jungle cock (optional)

(As dressed by Fin, Fur and Feather, Ltd.)

Many dressers dispense with the difficulty of marrying the wing feathers by putting on white wings and adding a strip of red on the outside. Bucktail wings are a later version composed of a very small bunch of white bucktail, over which is a very small bunch of red bucktail, with a very small bunch of white bucktail over this. The fly is identical with the trout fly of the same name except that it is dressed as a streamer. It was originated prior to 1890 by Mr. Henry P. Wells, of Providence, Rhode Island, and was named for Parmacheene Lake and the Parmacheene Club, in the Rangeley section of Maine. A similar fly, dressed with a silver body, is known as the *Parmacheene Beau*.

The *Parmacheene Belle*, when dressed as a bucktail, is excellent as a steelhead fly on Washington, Oregon, and California rivers. In the Eel River of California, and on many others, it is popular for chinook salmon and for silver salmon as well as for steelhead. The hook used is a heavy iron, size 1, 2X short. The tail is a small bunch of mixed red and white bucktail. The body and throat is as given above, with the throat long and fully dressed. The wing, in the steelhead version, is a very small bunch of red bucktail, over which is a very small bunch of white bucktail, over which is a very small bunch of red bucktail, all of equal length and very long, extending slightly beyond the end of the tail. Since the hook used is very short, part of the body may be applied as a tag, extending part way down the bend of the hook, before the tail is added. Jungle cock cheeks are not called for in the pattern but many anglers think that they enhance the value of the fly.

The *Delaware* streamer, a variation of the *Parmacheene Belle* which was originally called the *Seth Brown*, is a smallmouth bass fly first used in the headwaters of the Delaware River, in New York State. It has a gold tinsel tag, red wing section tail, red chenille butt, heavily dressed yellow chenille body ribbed with oval gold tinsel, white hackle wing, red wing section shoulders and a throat of a wide red hackle palmered fairly heavily after the wing and shoulders have been applied.

PINK LADY BUCKTAIL
Head: Red. (Use red thread in tying)
Tag: Three or four turns of medium flat gold tinsel

Famous Patterns

Tail: Seven or eight golden pheasant tippet fibers
Body: Of pink wool, dressed medium thick and shaped slightly larger toward head. The wool is not picked out. (Silk may be substituted)
Ribbing: Medium flat gold tinsel
Throat: A small bunch of yellow hackle fibers, rather long
Wing: A very small bunch of blue-grey bucktail, over which is a very small bunch of brown bucktail. Both extend slightly beyond the tail
(As dressed by Mr. Herbert L. Howard)

This is an adaptation of the *Pink Lady* dry fly originated by Mr. George M. L. LaBranch, of New York City. The fly is used considerably for brown and rainbow trout in the waters of central and northern New York State.

PLYMOUTH STREAMER

Head: Black
Tail: A section of a red duck, goose or swan wing feather, narrow and long
Body: Medium flat silver tinsel
Ribbing: Narrow oval silver tinsel (optional)
Throat: A Plymouth Rock hackle applied as a collar and separated to accommodate the wing
Wing: Four Plymouth Rock saddle hackles
(As dressed by Fin, Fur and Feather, Ltd.)

This is one of the simplest of the streamers. The body dressing is standard for many similar patterns having different throats and wings.

POLAR CHUB BUCKTAIL (Plate I)

Head: Painted brown on top, pale green underneath   Hook sizes: All sizes, 4X long
Tail: A fairly large bunch of white polar bear hair, nearly half as long as the hook
Body: Prepare a slightly tapered floss base and coat it with heavy lacquer. While this is wet, wind the body with large silver oval tinsel. Lacquer this and let it dry before applying the wing
Wing: Three small bunches of polar bear hair, each extending to the end of the tail; white, over which is olive green, over which is dyed brown (or brown bear hair)
Cheeks: Jungle cock, short and wide
(As dressed by the originator)

This fresh water or (on stainless steel or nickel hooks) salt water fly was originated in 1955 by E. H. (Polly) Rosborough, a prominent angler and professional fly dresser of (Box 36) Chiloquin, Oregon. Mr. Rosborough previously had originated the popular *Silver Garland Maribou* patterns, but feels that this fly is easier to cast. It represents several types of baitfish; particularly small chubs (roaches). It is a popular bucktail for many species of game fish both in fresh and in salt water.

PRINCESS BUCKTAIL

Head: Black
Tail: A small bunch of "hot orange" polar bear hair, very long
Body: Wound with brass or gold plated wire (see instructions on page 189, and notes below)
Wing: A small bunch of yellow polar bear hair, over which is a small bunch of "hot orange" polar bear hair. In applying the two parts of the wing, turns of thread are taken under both bunches of polar bear hair to raise the wing to an angle of about 40 degrees. (Bucktail may be substituted for polar bear hair in this dressing.) The wing extends to the end of the tail

(As dressed by Mr. Peter J. Schwab)

This is one of a series of wire bodied steelhead flies popularized by Mr. Peter J. Schwab, of Yreka, California. The set includes the *Bellamy*, *Bobby Dunn*, *Brass Hat*, *Paint Brush*, *Princess*, *Queen Bess*, *Van Luven*, and *Wood Pussy*; all originated by Mr. Schwab except for this one, which is attributed to Mr. Charles H. Conrad, of San Francisco, California. The *Princess* was named for Mr. Schwab's granddaughter, Ginnie Lobb. Mr. Schwab says of it, "The *Princess* was tied to meet the demand for a bucktail of predominantly orange hue, but note that the orange is 'hot orange' which is about two-thirds yellow and one-third red, and that yellow is used on the under wing. It is a beautiful fly whether tied with polar bear hair or bucktail. Although it usually is tied with a brass or gold plated wire body I like it best when the wire is covered with plain gold tinsel and ribbed with oval gold tinsel. Mark my words and see if some 'inventor' doesn't come along and give the fly a colored floss body and introduce it as his very own 'killer.' It is pretty with almost any kind of body."

Famous Patterns

QUEBEC STREAMER

Head: Black
Tail: A short golden pheasant crest feather, curving upward
Butt: Three or four turns of bright yellow silk
Body: Maroon wool, medium thick and picked out slightly
Ribbing: Narrow oval gold tinsel
Throat: A maroon saddle hackle tied on as a collar and then gathered downward
Wing: Two matched sections of purple goose or swan side feathers, covered by two matched sections of bronze mallard side feathers, all slightly longer than the tail

(As dressed for the originator)

This fly was originated by Mr. Alexander Learmonth, of Montreal, in 1931 and dressed for him by Mr. Frier Gulline, of Fin, Fur and Feather, Ltd., of Montral. It is one of the most popular flies for trout and bass in Canada, and it is used frequently for landlocked salmon.

QUEEN BEE STREAMER

Head: Black
Body: Medium flat silver tinsel
Throat: A small bunch of red hackle fibers
Wing: A small bunch of yellow bucktail, over which is a small bunch of white bucktail, with four medium brown saddle hackles over this. The bucktail and the hackles are of the same length, extending beyond the barb of the hook
Cheeks: Jungle cock

(As dressed by the originator)

Originated by Dr. J. Hubert Sanborn, of Waterville, Maine, for trolling for squaretail trout in Maine lakes. The fly usually is tied on tandem hooks. With it, Dr. Sanborn has taken many large trout, including one of seven pounds which qualified him for Maine's famous "The Big One That Didn't Get Away Club."

QUEEN BESS BUCKTAIL

Head: Black
Tail: A small bunch of California gray squirrel, rather long, showing the black bar and white tip
Body: Wound with silver wire, or with copper wire covered with medium flat silver tinsel (see instructions on page 191)

Wing: A small bunch of yellow bucktail, over which is a small bunch of California gray squirrel. The wing extends to the end of the tail. In applying the two parts of the wing, turns of thread are taken under the bucktail and under the squirrel to raise the wing to an angle of about 40 degrees

(As dressed by the originator)

This is one of a series of wire bodied steelhead flies originated by Mr. Peter J. Schwab, of Yreka, California, and is the one which he considers his favorite for taking steelhead on the Klamath River. He named it in honor of his wife. The fly usually is dressed in the double-wing version above described. In the three-wing dressing a longer shank hook is used and the rear wing is yellow bucktail with the front wings as given above. The addition of a throat of golden pheasant tippet is optional. Detailed notes on the dressings and use of these steelhead bucktails, as evolved by Mr. Schwab after many years of experience, are given on pages 189 to 195. He considers them of national value in taking all species of trout. His comments, as taken from his article in the June, 1946 issue of *Sports Afield* magazine are: "Previously I tied it with flat silver tinsel over a thinly padded body with a tail of barred wood duck and a spike (this differs from a throat, as explained in the reference) of small paired golden pheasant tippets. In this combination it is still more beautiful. If I were limited to one bucktail it would be the *Queen Bess*. It is a highly successful lure for trout and bass everywhere. The only changes made in the original pattern were the substitution of wire for the yarn padding immediately upon the discovery of the added value of this feature; the substitution of the dyed goose tail after I ran out of barred wood duck; and the omission of the spike after I ran out of pheasant tippets! Just so we gave the fish that seductive flash of silver, yellow and gray they were fully satisfied.

"We renamed the fly on the Klamath River last October 22nd when five of us made big catches with it, including a ten-pounder landed by Queen Bess (my wife) herself. It had previously proven itself the full equal and the one possible superior of the *Van Luven* as an all-purpose, all-weather fly. Use it on dark days or bright days, in clear or murky water. If the fish will strike at all, they will strike the *Queen Bess*."

After the above was printed, Mr. Schwab, in a letter to the author, says: "The only significant change has been the substitution of hair

Famous Patterns

tails for feather tails, using gray squirrel in *Queen Bess*. The hairs outlast feathers and are equally effective."

QUEEN OF WATERS BUCKTAIL

Head: Black
Tag: Fine gold tinsel
Tail: A small bunch of guard hairs from the tail of a cottontail rabbit
Body: Wound smoothly with orange wool, palmered from tail to head with a light brown saddle hackle which is built up at the throat
Wing: A bunch of guard hairs from a brown or Kodiac bear over which is a small bunch of guard hairs from the back of a cottontail rabbit. The rabbit hair should be one-third as long as the bear hair when the fly is dressed
Checks: Jungle cock

(As dressed by the originator)

This fly is excellent for all eastern species of trout and bass all season through. Smaller sizes are preferable later in the year. There are several versions of the *Queen of Waters* bucktail, all inspired by the trout of the same name. This one is by Mr. William Reynolds, a prominent fly dresser, of Sturbridge, Massachusetts.

RAILBIRD STEELHEAD BUCKTAIL (PLATE VIII)

Head: Black
Tail: An Amherst pheasant crest feather, very long. (A small bunch of claret or scarlet hackle fibers may be substituted. Yellow is used on some variations)
Body: Of claret wool, fairly thin, palmered with claret hackle, medium thick and fairly long. (This fly usually is dressed on a heavy number 1 hook, very short)
Throat: A yellow hackle tied on as a collar, moderately heavily dressed and as long as the palmered claret hackle
Wing: A small bunch of grey fox tail hair, very long, extending beyond the tail
Cheeks: Jungle cock, dressed high and rather long

(As dressed by Mr. C. Jim Pray)

Originated by Mr. John S. Benn, an Irish fly dresser who emigrated to California. This popular pattern was first tied about 1900 with wings of railbird flight feathers, for which barred sprig or gadwall (taken from under the wings of the bird) later were substituted. The fly always has been famous for taking steelhead and many other species of western trout, particularly on the Eel and Klamath rivers.

The above variation, adapted by Mr. C. Jim Pray, is now more popular than the earlier versions with feathered wings, and is used successfully from California to Alaska.

The early pattern of the *Railbird Steelhead* fly is as given above except that the wing is dressed with black and white barred teal flank feather strips instead of the gray fox. Although there is reason to believe that the above historical facts are true, Mr. A. J. McClane, Fishing Editor of *Field and Stream* magazine, writes about the *Railbird Steelhead* as follows: "One of the old-time patterns developed in or about 1915. As with many good patterns, its conceptions came about through pure chance. Jim Hutcheson, a steelhead veteran of long standing, was fishing the Breakwater Pool on the Eel River, taking some nice steelhead on a fly called the *Kate*. Several friends working the same piece of water were doing very badly, and they asked Jim what fly he was using. Being in a Puckish frame of mind, he replied that the fly was a 'railbird,' local argot that referred to people who sat in front of the cigar store. He passed out samples and one fellow who wanted some extras sent the fly to Martha Benn (a San Francisco tier of that period). Fly tying materials were hard to get in those days, so Martha improvised, making the fly as near to the original as she could. It was none too close, so she dubbed it the *Humboldt Railbird*. The *Railbird* has been changed many times since, but this dressing is still standard.

"There is a popular California variation of the *Railbird* originally tied by Mr. C. Jim Pray, for Mr. Fred Bair of Klamath Lodge, which is dressed as follows: *BAIR'S RAILBIRD* — Body: flat silver tinsel; Tail: claret or wine hackle tip; Throat: yellow hackle (eight or ten turns); Wings: barred black and white teal flank; Cheeks: jungle cock."

RAY BERGMAN BUCKTAIL

Head: Black
Body: Medium embossed silver tinsel
Throat: A very small bunch of red hackle fibers, rather short
Wing: A very small bunch of white polar bear fur over which is a very small bunch of pale yellow bucktail. The wing is sparsely dressed
Shoulders: Each the tip of a red body feather from a macaw, one-third as long as the wing

(As dressed by the originator)

Originated by Mr. Ray Bergman, of Nyack, New York, in 1925. He says of it: "At the time we called all flies of this type streamers. It would be termed a bucktail now. I do not consider this fly of any particular interest except that it was one of the early ones." The fly often is known as the *R. B. Streamer.*

RAYMOND STREAMER

Head: Black
Tag: Narrow flat gold tinsel
Tail: A short golden pheasant crest feather, curving upward
Body: Wound moderately thin, with bronze silk
Ribbing: Narrow flat gold tinsel
Throat: A small bunch of fairly long strands from a dark red feather from the body of a golden pheasant
Wing: A very small bunch of brown bucktail over which is a pair of wings stripped from a barred brown feather of a mallard. The wings are narrow and should be nearly as long as the bucktail
Topping: A golden pheasant crest feather long enough to curve over the tips of the bucktail and meet the tail of the fly
Cheeks: Jungle cock

(As dressed by the originator)

Originated by Mr. William Reynolds, of Sturbridge, Massachusetts, for taking Atlantic salmon on the Miramichi River. This fly also is excellent for brown and rainbow trout. Small sizes are best for late season fishing. It is named for Mr. Warren G. Raymond, of Boston, Massachusetts.

RED FIN STREAMER (PLATE VI)

Head: Black   Hook sizes: No. 8 and No. 6, 6X long
Tail: A very few fibers of bright red marabou, cut off vertically above end of bend of hook
Body: Wound with pink floss, slightly tapered
Ribbing: Flat gold tinsel
Throat: A very few fibers of bright red marabou, cut off vertically to be same size as the tail
Wing: Two black saddle hackles, on each side of which is a golden badger saddle hackle, all of same length and extending slightly beyond the tail
Cheeks: Jungle cock, small and short

(As dressed by the originator)

This is another of the natural imitation patterns of the late Lew Oatman, of Shushan, New York. It was not included in the notes given to the author by Mr. Oatman, but was provided by Mr. Keith Fulsher, of Eastchester, New York, who was a close friend of Lew's and a collector of his original patterns. Mr. Fulsher says, "Lew Oatman was trying to catch the colors of the Red Fin shiner. Like many of Lew's patterns, it takes advantage of the lateral stripe offered by the badger saddle hackles. I think the fly was originated about 1952. Originally the tail and throat were made very long with red marabou; the throat extending beyond the hook bend and the tail streaming far out behind. Later, Lew clipped both tail and throat short and preferred this later style."

REDHEAD BUCKTAIL   (PLATE III)

Head: Red   Hook sizes: No. 12 to No. 8, 4X long
Tail: The tip of a small Amherst pheasant crest feather, about as long as the gap of the hook, and curving upward
Body: Medium flat gold tinsel
Ribbing: Medium oval gold tinsel
Wing: A very small bunch of white capras hair (Asian goat), over which is a very small bunch of red squirrel tail hair. The wing is dressed sparsely

(As dressed by the originator)

Originated by Mr. A. I. Alexander III, of Andover, Massachusetts, who says, "This resembles a multitude of small baitfish in our local trout waters, and is for casting with a light, delicate rod in small water. Small streamers and bucktails have a good record of hooking fish with me. There are no short strikes, as there can be with the big No. 2 and No. 4 patterns. When a fish grabs a small fly, he has hold of the iron."

RED HORSE STREAMER   (PLATE VI)

Head: Black   Hook sizes: No. 8 and No. 6, 6X long
Tail: The tips of two yellow hackles, on each side of which is an orange hackle, all of same length and very short
Body: Wound with white wool, slightly tapered
Ribbing: Oval silver tinsel
Throat: The same as the tail
Wing: Two olive-green saddle hackles, on each side of which is a gray blue dun saddle hackle; all of the same length and extending well beyond the tail
Cheeks: Jungle cock

(As dressed by the originator)

Famous Patterns

This is another pattern by Lew Oatman, of Shushan, New York. Mr. Oatman says, "This pattern was designed for bass in waters where the Red Horse sucker is common. There are many rivers, in Colorado for instance, where trout feed on them."

RED PHANTOM STREAMER (PLATE VIII)

Head: Black bead head with white eye with black pupil
Tail: A very small bunch of red hackle fibers
Body: Wound with bright red wool shaped heavier toward the head. The wool is not picked out
Ribbing: Medium flat silver tinsel
Wing: A bunch of strands from a white marabou feather extending just beyond the tail of the fly

(As dressed by the originator)

Originated by Mr. E. H. (Polly) Rosborough, of Chiloquin, Oregon, in 1948. This marabou streamer is considered to be one of the best flies for steelhead and is excellent for bass and squaretail trout as well. The white marabou wing makes it extremely active and visible in the most turbid of waters. The body can be weighted if desired.

RED SQUIRREL GOLD STREAMER

Head: Black
Body: Medium embossed gold tinsel
Throat: The tip of a very short golden pheasant crest feather dyed red
Wing: A very small bunch of fox squirrel tail hair over which are two honey badger hackles of the same length as the squirrel tail hair
Cheeks: Jungle cock, very short

(As dressed by the originator)

This is one of a series of three streamers originated by Mr. Ray Bergman in 1933. These flies should be dressed sparsely in small sizes. They are excellent for all species of trout.

RELIABLE STREAMER

Head: Black   Hook sizes: No. 10 to No. 6, 4X long
Tail: A very small bunch of orange-red hackle fibers tied in over the tip of the barb of the hook and extending slightly beyond the bend
Butt: Two turns of flat gold tinsel. (This is continued for the ribbing)

Body: Wound with red chenille
Ribbing: Flat gold tinsel
Throat: A very small bunch of orange-red hackle fibers
Wing: A very small bunch of natural cream colored polar bear hair extending just beyond the end of the tail. Over this on each side is a fairly wide wing, of the same length as the hair, cut from a golden pheasant tail feather (or feathers). This conceals most of the hair, and slants upward slightly

(As dressed by the originator)

Originated by Mr. Paul Kukonen, professional fly dresser and fly casting champion of Worcester, Massachusetts. Mr. Kukonen says, "This fly originally was tied with sections of turkey wing feather(s). It imitates nothing, but is exceptionally good for casting or trolling for trout, especially after the water cools off in September and October. The wing sections are matched rights and lefts, from a fourth to half an inch wide, depending on the size of the fly." Several turkey wing flies are dressed similarly in various color combinations, such as *Stewart's Hawk*, which is included in these patterns.

ROGAN ROYAL GRAY GHOST STREAMER (PLATE II)

Head: Black
Tag: Four or five turns of fine silver wire, begun at the bend of the hook, forward of which are several turns of light yellow silk, dressed thin, about three times as long as the silver
Tail: A moderately long golden pheasant crest feather, curving upward, over which is a golden pheasant crest feather dyed red and cut off to one-half the length of the one below
Butt: Four or five turns of a black ostrich herl. The butt is moderately heavily dressed
Body: Dressed very thin with orange silk
Ribbing: Narrow oval silver tinsel, rather widely spaced
Throat: Five peacock herls extending to the tip of the tail, below which is a very tiny bunch of white polar bear hair of the same length, with a long golden pheasant crest feather below this, curving upward with the tip touching the tip of the tail of the fly
Wing: Four gray shoulder hackles extending to the tip of the tail
Topping: Two golden pheasant crest feathers, both laid on as one, extending to the tip of the tail to balance the throat feather. The curves of these feathers should match the curve of the wing
Shoulders: Each a section of a barred wood duck feather wide enough to cover the wing and one-third as long

(As dressed by the originator)

Famous Patterns

The *Rogan Royal Gray Ghost* is a glorification of the *Gray Ghost* described elsewhere in this book. This adaptation is the work of Mr. Alex Rogan, the renowned salmon fly dresser of New York City and is an attempt by him to enhance the beauty of the famous *Gray Ghost* by making it as nearly like a salmon fly as possible and still having it remain technically a streamer. This fly is dressed on a 5X long Limerick hook. Mr. Rogan, also dresses the *Rogan Royal Gray Ghost* as a salmon fly by using a salmon hook and making the fly somewhat shorter. In this version, horns of blue macaw and cheeks of blue chatterer are added, with a few strands of a teal body feather added to the tail. The wood duck shoulder is longer, extending two-thirds the length of the wing. The head is wound with several turns of black ostrich herl, the tip of the head being painted red. Added comment about Mr. Rogan is included in data on the *Golden Rogan* bucktail.

ROSE OF NEW ENGLAND BUCKTAIL

Head: Black
Tag: A few turns of narrow embossed silver tinsel
Tail: One or two very short golden pheasant crest feathers, curving upward
Butt: Two turns of red wool
Body: Medium embossed silver tinsel. Just behind the head is another butt of red wool of the same size as the butt at the rear
Ribbing: Narrow oval silver tinsel
Wing: A tiny bunch of yellow bucktail, over which is a tiny bunch of red bucktail, over which is a tiny bunch of yellow bucktail, with a tiny bunch of brown bucktail over this. All four bunches are of the same size. Care should be taken not to have the fly over-dressed
Cheeks: Jungle cock

(As dressed by Judge Lee Parsons Davis)

This fly was originated by Mr. Everett Price, a guide on the Miramichi River in New Brunswick. It was introduced by Judge Lee Parsons Davis, of White Plains, New York, who writes the author: "The above dressing is in accordance with the original patterns, with some refinements which do not change the pattern. While I did not originate the fly, I do claim to have introduced it to the fly fishing fraternity, and many years ago I got Abercrombie and Fitch Company to catalog it. I discovered it while fishing in the early spring on the

Miramichi River, near Doaktown, with Howard Lyons as guide. We were not having luck with the streamer flies at hand. One morning he took me into a barber shop run by Doris O'Donnell in Doaktown. Doris was quite a character. He weighed about 300 pounds. At the time of my introduction he had a customer half shaved in the barber's chair. Lyons asked him to tie a *Rose of New England* for me. He left the customer to shift for himself while he tied two of them rather roughly. When I asked him what I owed him he replied, 'If you don't catch any fish today you don't owe me anything. If you do, fifty cents will square it.' I caught many fish that day on that fly and have used it constantly ever since. Tied on Number 12 hooks, it is as successful for trout as the larger sizes are for salmon."

ROXY'S FOX SQUIRRELTAIL

Head: Black
Tail: A very small bunch of fibers from a mandarin duck breast feather
Body: Wound very thin with red silk
Ribbing: Narrow flat silver tinsel
Throat: A medium brown saddle hackle tied on as a collar and then gathered downward. The hackle is as long as the shoulder and rather sparsely dressed
Wing: A small bunch of fox squirrel tail hair
Shoulders: Each a white duck breast feather, about one-third as long as the wing

(As dressed by Lyon and Coulson, Inc.)

This fly was originated by Mr. Roxy Roach, of Tawas City, Michigan, who died in 1947. (See notes under *Roxy's Gray Squirreltail*.)

ROXY'S GRAY SQUIRRELTAIL

Head: Black
Tail: A very small bunch of fibers from a mandarin duck breast feather
Body: Wound very thin with olive-yellow silk
Ribbing: Narrow flat gold tinsel
Throat: A narrow section of a red duck wing feather about one-third as long as the wing, over which is a Plymouth Rock saddle hackle tied on as a collar and then gathered downward. The hackle should be as long as the duck feather and should be sparsely dressed
Wing: A small bunch of gray squirrel tail hair
Shoulders: Each a white duck breast feather, about one-third as long as the wing

(As dressed by Lyon and Coulson, Inc.)

Famous Patterns

This pattern was originated by Mr. Roxy Roach, of Tawas City, Michigan. Mr. Roach was recognized as one of the most skillful anglers on Michigan's Au Sable River. He developed the *Roxy's Gray Squirreltail* and the *Roxy's Fox Squirreltail* for taking the large brown trout for which the lower reaches of this river are famous. He made these bucktails both weighted and unweighted in several sizes up to size 2, always dressed on long shanked hooks.

ROYAL COACHMAN STREAMER (Plate II) and BUCKTAIL (Plate VIII)

Head: Black
Tail: A narrow but long section of a bright red duck or goose wing feather
Butt: A few turns of green peacock herl
Body: Wound very thin with scarlet silk
Throat: A fairly long brown hackle wound on as a collar and gathered downward
Wing: Two matched sections of white swan wing feathers extending slightly beyond the tail

(As dressed by Fin, Fur and Feather, Ltd.)

This streamer is an adaptation of the trout fly of the same name; for generations one of the best and most historic of English wet and dry fly patterns. The dressing given above is the most popular one for the waters of eastern Canada. The fly is less popular in the eastern United States than on western coastal rivers, where most anglers include it (or a very similar pattern) as one of the most productive for steelhead, cutthroat and all other species of large trout. This dressing occasionally is varied by shaping the body fatter toward the head and adding a ribbing of narrow oval silver tinsel. A tail of half a dozen strands of a golden pheasant tippet may be substituted for the section of red duck wing. Four white saddle hackles or a bunch of white polar bear, bucktail or other white hair often is used instead of the swan wing sections (which are preferred rather than duck or goose because of their longer length).

The *Royal Coachman* used on western rivers nearly always is a bucktail rather than a streamer. Most of the western patterns call for a shorter hook than do the eastern versions and a second butt of peacock herl (sometimes both butts are of black chenille) usually is added behind the throat. The bucktail wing often is twice as long as the hook and is heavily dressed. Normally there is no ribbing. The tail is composed of a small bunch of red hackle fibers rather than a section of wing feather. Many anglers consider it important to add jungle cock cheeks. In 1937 a Washingtonian named Jack Wallenschlaeger began using narrow strips of chamois for the tails of the *Royal Coachman* and the *Yellowhammer* and called them *Shammytails*. This variation is popular for all trout in the Northwest and in British Columbia. There, *Royal Coachman* streamers are preferred for crappie and bass, but the bucktail patterns are almost universally used for trout.

That the *Royal Coachman* is adapted to midwestern waters, as well as to those in the East and West, is indicated by a letter from Mr. Harold H. (Dike) Smedley, nationally known writer, angler and distance fly caster, who writes the author: "Michigan's one-and-only is the *Royal Coachman* in streamer or bucktail patterns. The trout in Michigan streams react favorably to it in all sizes and materials and no one ever has used a fly that did any better. Michigan fishermen are quite well satisfied with it."

RUSSELL'S FANCY BUCKTAIL

Head: Black
Tag: Four or five turns of medium embossed silver tinsel
Tail: A golden pheasant crest feather, rather long and curving upward
Body: Medium embossed silver tinsel
Ribbing: Narrow oval silver tinsel
Throat: A very small bunch of white bucktail, extending to the barb of the hook
Wing: A very small bunch of white bucktail, over which is a very small bunch of yellow bucktail, both as long as the tail
Cheeks: Jungle cock, rather short

(As dressed by Judge Lee Parsons Davis)

This fly, also called the *Yellow Peril* bucktail, is named for Mr. Jack Russell of Russell's Camps, on the Miramichi River, in New Brunswick. It is one of the well-known flies for black salmon and, in Maine and Canada, is a favorite for landlocked salmon. Elsewhere, it is good for bass and pond-fish. It originated on the Miramichi River, and has been used there extensively since 1920.

Famous Patterns

SAGUENAY STREAMER

Head: Black
Tail: About six or seven fibers from a golden pheasant tippet, medium long
Body: Medium embossed gold tinsel
Throat: A yellow saddle hackle tied on as a collar and then gathered downward. The throat is dressed sparsely and is of medium length
Wing: A yellow saddle hackle between two Plymouth Rock saddle hackles. They should be thin and should extend slightly beyond the tail
Cheeks: Jungle cock, small and rather short

(As dressed by the originator)

Mr. Robert E. Coulson, of Lyon and Coulson, Inc., of Buffalo, New York, originated this fly in 1924. The *Lord Denby* and the *St. Ignace* make up a set of three patterns which were designed for taking the large eastern brook trout on the Nipigon River in the Nipigon district of Ontario. This one was named for one of Mr. Coulson's Indian guides.

ST. IGNACE STREAMER

Head: Black
Tail: About six or seven fibers from a golden pheasant tippet, medium long
Body: Medium flat gold tinsel
Throat: A honey badger hackle, tied on as a collar and then tied downward. The throat is dressed sparsely and is of medium length
Wing: Three honey badger hackles. They should be thin and should extend slightly beyond the tail
Cheeks: Jungle cock, small and rather short

(As dressed by the originator)

This fly was originated by Mr. Robert E. Coulson, of Lyon and Coulson, Inc. in 1924. The *Lord Denby* and the *Saguenay* complete a set of three which were designed for taking the large eastern brook trout on the Nipigon River. The *St. Ignace* was named for St. Ignace Island at the mouth of the Nipigon River around whose shallow shores large trout frequently are found in substantial numbers.

SANBORN STREAMER (PLATE II)

Head: Black
Tag: Four or five turns of narrow flat gold tinsel
Body: Medium thick, wound with black silk

Ribbing: Narrow flat gold tinsel
Throat: A small bunch of bright yellow hackle fibers
Wing: Four bright yellow neck hackles
Cheeks: Jungle cock

(As dressed by the originator)

Designed by Mr. Fred Sanborn, of Norway, Maine, and originally tied for him by Mr. Gardner Percy of the Percy Tackle Company, of Portland, Maine. This fly essentially is the *Black Ghost* dressed in yellow and gold rather than in white and silver. It is one of the favorites in Maine for trout and landlocked salmon. Many anglers also consider it an excellent bass fly.

SANDERS STREAMER

Head: Black
Body: Narrow flat silver tinsel
Wing: A very small bunch of white bucktail extending well beyond the hook, over which are four grizzly saddle hackles, slightly longer than the bucktail
Cheeks: Jungle cock

(As dressed by the originator)

This fly is closely related to the primitive and haphazard early streamers of the *Rooster's Regret* type discussed in Chapter II. It originally was tied to order by the Percy Tackle Company, for Sanders Brothers Store, leading outfitters in Greenville, Maine, for the backwoods fishing country of the Mooshead region of Maine.

SATIN FIN STREAMER (PLATE III)

Head: Black   Hook sizes: No. 10 to No. 2
Tail: A very few fibers of yellow marabou, cut off vertically just beyond the bend of the hook
Body: Wound with white silk floss, slightly tapered
Ribbing: Flat medium silver tinsel
Throat: A very few fibers of yellow marabou, cut off vertically to the same length as the tail
Wing: Two blue saddle hackles, on each side of which is an orchid saddle hackle, all of the same length and extending slightly beyond the tail
Cheeks: Jungle cock, small

(As dressed by the originator)

This beautiful streamer was originated by Keith C. Fulsher, of Eastchester, New York, as a trout and bass fly. Mr. Fulsher says,

Famous Patterns

"This was originated in 1957 to imitate the Satin Fin minnow (*Notropis whipplii*) found in many streams and lakes in New York and surrounding states. This is a valuable food for trout, bass, and other game fish and is not uncommon in warm waters. I wanted a fly with the bluish purple coloring found not only in the Satin Fin itself but also in many other species of baitfish. The dominant yellow fins are particular to the Satin Fin, and this use of marabou for fins is very effective; adding not only color but also action to the fly. This is intended to represent the Satin Fin in its breeding colors."

SCALED SHINER STREAMER
Head: Black
Tail: A very small bunch of black hackle fibers with a smaller bunch of white hackle fibers over these
Body: Fairly heavily dressed with olive-green silk. The body is tied loosely enough so that the ribbing will sink into it slightly to give the appearance of scales
Ribbing: Heavy black thread; two pieces tied in at the tail and criss-crossed above and below the body to provide a scale effect
Throat: An extremely small and a very short bunch of red hackle fibers
Wing: Four black hackles, extending to the end of the tail and dressed rather high on the hook for greater action in the water
Cheeks: Jungle cock, very short

(As dressed by the originator)

This fly was originated by Mr. Don Shiner, of Nescopeck, Pennsylvania, who writes about it as follows: "I couldn't recall just how many times I've had good fortune with this pattern, but it works well in this section of Pennsylvania. It is one of my favorites for trout and bass. I also tie this with a gold body, ribbed with the same black tying thread. This makes a good pattern for lake fishing when there are golden shiner minnows in the water."

SHANG'S FAVORITE STREAMER (Plate IV)
Head: Black, with red band
Body: Wound thinly with red silk
Ribbing: Narrow, flat silver tinsel
Throat: A very small bunch of white bucktail extending beyond barb of hook, under which is a small bunch of grey hackle fibers
Wing: Four or five strands of green peacock herl, on each side of which are two grizzly saddle hackles. The hackles, peacock and bucktail all are of the same length

Shoulders: Each a red duck breast feather extending one-third the length of the wing. The two red feathers should cover the bases of the four grizzly hackles and they should have very pronounced outside edges
Cheeks: Jungle cock, not quite as long as the shoulders

(As dressed by the originator)

This fly was originated by Mrs. Carrie G. Stevens, the famed fly dresser of Madison, Maine, and was named in honor of Hon. Charles E. (Shang) Wheeler, former state senator of Stratford, Connecticut, and at one time amateur champion duck decoy maker of the United States. Mr. Wheeler spent many summers at Upper Dam, on Mooselookmeguntic Lake, in the Rangeley section of Maine, where Mrs. Stevens had her summer camp, and assisted Mrs. Stevens with suggestions for dressing many of her flies.

SHANG'S SPECIAL STREAMER (PLATE IV)

Head: Black, with red band
Body: Flat silver tinsel
Throat: A small bunch of white bucktail extending slightly beyond the barb of the hook
Wing: Four or five strands of green peacock herl, over which are two complete jungle cock neck feathers, one on each side of the herl. The herl, jungle cock and bucktail all are of the same length
Shoulders: Each a red duck breast feather one-third as long as the wing. The red feathers are wide and have a decided edge
Cheeks: Jungle cock, half as long as the shoulders

(As dressed by the originator)

This fly was originated about 1930 by Mrs. Carrie G. Stevens, and was named in honor of Hon. Charles E. (Shang) Wheeler, who gave her the idea for the fly and who used it successfully for the big eastern brook trout in the famous Upper Dam Pool in the Rangeley section of Maine. The fly is most popular in sizes 6 and 8.

SHUSHAN POSTMASTER BUCKTAIL (PLATE VI)

Head: Black   Hook sizes: No. 6 to No. 10, 6X long
Tail: A very small section of a brown mottled turkey feather, as long as the gap of the hook
Body: Wound with light yellow floss, slightly tapered
Ribbing: Flat gold tinsel

Famous Patterns

Throat: A few fibers from a duck wing quill, dyed bright red and as long as the tail
Wing: A small bunch of fox squirrel tail hair, extending to the end of the tail
Cheeks: Jungle cock, small and short

(As dressed by the originator)

This bucktail was originated by Lew Oatman, of Shushan, New York, about 1953 and named for the postmaster of the town, who was one of Lew's favorite fishing companions on the Battenkill River, which flows from Vermont into New York State.

SILVER DARTER STREAMER (PLATE VI)

Head: Black   Hook sizes: No. 4 to No. 12, 2X to 6X long
Tail: A very small section from a silver pheasant wing quill, slightly longer than the gap of the hook
Body: Wound with white floss, slightly tapered
Ribbing: Medium narrow flat silver tinsel
Throat: Two or three fibers of a peacock sword feather, reaching about half way to the point of the hook and curving toward it
Wing: Two white edged badger saddle hackles, extending slightly beyond the end of the tail
Cheeks: Jungle cock, small and short

(As dressed by the originator)

This is another of Lew Oatman's patterns. In sending it to the author he said, "This imitates the Cayuga minnow and is very effective for brook, brown, and rainbow trout. It does well in heavily fished streams throughout the season, even in low, clear water, and does equally well in wilderness areas. I often have taken trout with it when I couldn't seem to pick a dry fly rising trout would strike. It should be a very slim fly in the water, and I like to use the slenderest hackles available."

SILVER DEMON BUCKTAIL

Head: Black
Tail: A very small bunch of orange hackle fibers of moderate length
Body: Thinly wound with narrow oval tinsel, several turns of which are taken below the tail to act as a tag. On extra long shanked hooks, flat silver tinsel and silver ribbing may be used
Throat: Several turns of an orange saddle hackle applied as a collar and tied back but not gathered downward. The hackle is glossy, stiff and of moderate length

Wing: A medium sized bunch of badger hair extending slightly beyond the end of the tail. (Ground squirrel tail hair may be substituted and is to be preferred over gray squirrel because it is stiffer and more wiry. In the feather winged version, sections of barred gadwall feathers are used. The two matched sections are fairly narrow and curve upward, extending between the end of the hook and the end of the tail)

(As dressed by the originator)

This is the steelhead dressing of the *Silver Demon* and is very similar to the *Silver and Orange* bucktail described a little further on. For additional notes, see *Cains River Silver Demon* streamer.

SILVER GARLAND MARABOU STREAMER (Plate V)

Head: Black (Large black optic heads with white eyes and red, black or orange pupils often are used)
Body: Of special silver tinsel, as described below
Wing: Two matched white marabou feathers, considerably longer than the hook
Topping: Four greenish-blue ostrich herls, over which are four black ostrich herls
Shoulders: Four yellowish-green ostrich herls on each side. All the ostrich herl is as long as the marabou
Cheeks: Jungle cock, rather long

(As dressed by the originator)

This unusual type of dressing was originated by Mr. E. H. (Polly) Rosborough, of Chiloquin, Oregon, in 1936. The *Silver Garland* is one of the most famous and most productive of all marabou streamers, due principally to the unusual construction of the body. The body is fairly fat and heavy, dressed with tinsel (over a weighted body if desired) which is formed into a chenille-like fringe similar to Christmas tree tinsel, as described on page 188. This provides a brushlike metal body which should be lacquered to keep it bright. The value of the body is due largely to the added flash of reflected light which this type of tinsel provides. This makes the fly especially productive in high or discolored waters.

Silver Garland Marabous can be dressed with copper tinsel bodies, although the silver is more popular. The one described above is recommended for large trout especially, and particularly in chub-infested waters. The fly is tied with a large variety of wing color combinations, some of which are as follows:

Famous Patterns

For Trout and Steelhead

1. White marabou wing with black ostrich herl topping
2. White marabou wing with black over olive-green ostrich herl topping
3. Hot orange marabou wing with black ostrich herl topping
4. Hot orange marabou wing with black over white ostrich herl topping (Numbers 3 and 4 are especially recommended for steelhead)
5. An all black marabou wing with peacock herl topping

For Bass and Other Spiney-rayed Fish

6. Yellow marabou wing with black ostrich herl topping
7. White marabou wing with royal blue ostrich herl topping
8. White marabou wing with seal brown ostrich herl topping

For Chinook, Silver, Landlocked, Atlantic Salmon and All Other Salt Water Fish Which Feed on Herring and Smelt

9. White marabou wing with royal blue over *Silver Doctor* blue ostrich herl topping

(The Incredible) SILVER MINNOW (Plate I)

Head: Built up to minnow-head shape with 00 nylon thread, painted silver. Small painted black eyes, with yellow dot in center

Tail: A small bunch of gray stripped mallard herl or grizzly hackle

Body: Wound tightly with lead wire. The wire body is covered and tapered with silk floss of any color. This is covered completely by a double overlay of embossed flat silver tinsel

Throat: A small bunch of long crimson rooster hackles, the longest ones extending to the point of the hook

Wing: A very small bunch of while bucktail, over which is a very small bunch of blue (dyed) impala hair. Over this is a gray mallard flank feather tied on flat on top of the hair so that it surrounds all of the hair. The elements of the wing extend half again as long as the hook. Recommended hook size is No. 6, 2XL

Procedure: Tie the tail material onto the shank of the hook just ahead of the barb. Wrap the shank with lead wire, leaving it bare for 1/8th inch at the end and 1/4th inch back from the eye. This will provide for a tapered body. Silk floss is wound on to give an underlay for a smooth wrap of silver tinsel. Double-wind the tinsel overlay, starting from the eye, wrapping spirally to the tail and returning to the eye. The hair is sparsely tied in as above. The mallard flank feather is laid on top of the hair and folded in at the sides. Do this so the feather won't flare out at the sides. Tie in the red rooster throat. Finally, wind on a full head of thread. Lacquer the head three times. Then apply two coats of silver paint. Paint on eyes as above.

This fly was dressed by Maury Delman, prominent outdoor writer from Flushing, New York, as tied by its originator, Al Giradot, of Detroit, Michigan. In an article in the March, 1965, issue of *Sports Afield*, Maury says, "Properly fished, the *Silver Minnow* is the quintessence of deadliness. In Labrador I coaxed landlocked salmon from their white water lies when all other flies failed completely. In Iceland the fly evoked hard strikes from sea trout. Manitoba's heralded God's River gave up lunker brook trout in heavy water. It has given me furious action from smallmouths and educated trout in eastern streams—and even walleyes. When Al first tied the fly he did not weight the body, so the streamer momentarily floated, requiring vigorous stripping in to sink it. He wanted a minnow mimic that would travel the route of natural bait. By adding the lead and tinsel, he got precisely what he wanted."

SILVER MINNOW BUCKTAIL (Plate V)

Head: Red. The head is properly dressed by adding a hollow brass bead painted red with a small yellow eye with a red pupil
Body: Medium flat silver tinsel over a thin padding of a base of fine wire
Ribbing: Medium oval silver tinsel
Throat: A few fibres of a red hackle, of medium length
Wing: A very small bunch of white bucktail, over which is a small bunch of gray squirrel tail hair of the same length
Topping: Four or five strands of peacock herl as long as the wing
(As dressed by Mr. Don C. Harger)

This fly originated in British Columbia, where it was tied to imitate sea-run baitfish, particularly the candlefish and the smelt. It is particularly effective in estuaries and salt chucks in Washington and British Columbia rivers for searun cutthroat, silver salmon and for steelhead. The fly is dressed in several variations in the sections where it is most used, but this basic dressing usually remains the same. Some anglers eliminate both the bead head and the throat. Others eliminate the gray squirrel part of the wing and use a greater amount of peacock

Famous Patterns

herl. The fly is almost identical with several eastern dressings, and its similarity in appearance to a baitfish should make it universally successful.

SILVER AND ORANGE BUCKTAIL

Head: Black
Body: Medium embossed silver tinsel. The originator prefers to dress the fly on a 2X short turned down ball-eye hook with 4X head, with size B lacquered thread. The tinsel is tied in close to the eye, wrapped back to the bend of the hook, lacquered, and then wrapped back to the start of the tie
Throat: Several turns of a hot orange hackle. The throat is as long as the hook and rather heavily dressed
Wing: A bunch of Kashu pine squirrel tail hair tied over the collar of hot orange hackle. (Kashu pine squirrel tail is of a very pale ginger color with a white tip.) The wing is slightly longer than the hook

(As dressed by the originator)

Originated by Mr. Fred A. Reed, of Nevada City, California. This is primarily a steelhead fly for northern California and Oregon, but it also is popular for all other species of trout. The wing may be tied with bucktail of a similar color. The fly is also very successful if the wing is left off entirely.

SILVER SALMON STREAMER

Head: Black
Tail: The tips of two bright yellow saddle hackles, very thin and of moderate length
Body: Dressed very thin with medium yellow silk
Ribbing: Medium flat silver tinsel
Throat: Applied as a collar; several turns of a bright yellow saddle hackle of moderate width, separated at the top to accommodate the wing
Wing: Four thin white saddle hackles
Cheeks: Jungle cock of moderate length, dressed high

(As dressed by the originator)

This fly was originated by Mr. Horace P. Bond, of Bangor, Maine, for fishing for landlocked salmon and squaretail trout in Maine lakes. Since it usually is used for trolling it normally is dressed on a very long hook. Another very similar Maine streamer is the *Silver Ghost*, which has a body of flat silver tinsel ribbed with oval silver tinsel but which otherwise is identical to this one. The *Silver Ghost* was first tied by Mr. Gardner Percy, of Portland, Maine, in a desire to try the *Black Ghost* streamer with a silver body.

SILVER TIP BUCKTAIL (Plate III)

Head: Black, with a fine red lacquered ring at the base   Hook sizes: No. 6 and No. 8, 4X long
Tail: A strand of bright red wool, cut off above the bend of the hook
Body: Four to six strands of fine gold oval tinsel tied in together and wrapped solidly up the hook shank. (The body should be fairly thin)
Wing: A small bunch of silver tip grizzly bear hair extending slightly beyond the end of the tail. (The hair should be well marked with a dark brown base and light amber tips. The wing should be sparsely dressed)
Cheeks: Jungle cock, very small and short
(As dressed by the originator)

Originated by Keith C. Fulsher, of Eastchester, New York. Mr. Fulsher says, "This fly was originated in 1955, and two things are dominant about it. The bright yellow tinsel, put on in this fashion, provides many little reflecting surfaces to make the fly glitter brightly in the water. The silver tip grizzly hair with the light translucent tips gives the impression of a little minnow's tail flicking as it swims. The fly is designed to imitate general species of baitfish. The name comes from the wing material used. The red added to the head provides a flash of gill coloring. This is an early season fly for discolored water. It has been successful throughout the Northeast and Middle West. It is a good salmon fly when dressed on salmon wet fly hooks, with a collar of sparse yellow hackle added."

SKYKOMISH SUNRISE BUCKTAIL

Head: White
Tag: Three or four turns of narrow flat silver tinsel
Tail: A very small bunch of red hackle fibers, over which is a very small bunch of yellow hackle fibers, rather long and not mixed
Body: Fairly heavily wound with red chenille
Ribbing: Narrow flat silver tinsel
Throat: Three or four turns each of a red and a yellow hackle, wound on mixed as a collar and not tied downward. The hackles are fairly wide
Wing: A small bunch of white polar bear hair, slightly longer than the tail and dressed fairly high on the hook. The hook should be 2X long
(As dressed by the originator)

Mr. George McLeod of Seattle, Washington, originated this fly in 1938, and named it for the Skykomish River in northern Washington. In the opinion of many Washington anglers this fly is more successful than all of the other patterns combined for steelhead and cutthroat trout. Mr. McLeod has taken several summer-run steelhead of over twenty pounds each on it.

SOO FLY BUCKTAIL

Head: Black
Tag: Narrow flat gold tinsel. The tag is rather long, extending from above the tip of the barb part way down the bend of the hook
Tail: The tips of two red hackles, rather long and splayed outwardly
Body: Rear two-thirds is medium embossed silver tinsel. Front third is wound with peacock herl
Throat: Two turns of a red hackle, applied as a collar and gathered downward
Wing: A bunch of yellow bucktail, over which is a bunch of black and red bucktail, mixed equally. The wing extends to the end of the tail and is rather sparsely dressed so that it will sink rapidly
Cheeks: Jungle cock

(As dressed by the originator)

Originated by Mr. Earl Leitz, of Sault Ste. Marie, Michigan, for taking the large rainbows, or "Soo" trout, in the rapids of the St. Mary's River at the outlet of Lake Superior. Since these trout are large, these flies usually are dressed on Number 2 hooks. Mr. Ray Bergman, who has fished with Mr. Leitz, stated in his columns in *Outdoor Life* that the *Soo* fly is dressed in various ways and he gives the following dressing as one of the variations—

Butt: Yellow chenille (like an egg sack). (Although Mr. Bergman does not mention it, there probably is a tag of narrow flat gold tinsel, since many of the other flies used in these waters have it)
Tail: Tips of two barred Plymouth Rock hackles, dyed a deep Montreal claret. They should be rather long and splayed outwardly
Body: Medium embossed silver tinsel
Ribbing: Medium flat silver tinsel
Wing: A bunch of claret red bucktail, over which is a bunch of yellow bucktail, over which is a bunch of brownish or faded black bucktail
Cheeks: Jungle cock

Mr. Leitz states that the first dressing is the most popular of the several flies preferred for fishing the St. Mary's rapids. Other popular flies for this purpose are the *Bali Duck* streamer, the *Leitz* bucktail and the *Scotty*. The second dressing given above is very similar to the *Rose of New England*, which also should be a good fly for these waters.

SPENCER BAY SPECIAL STREAMER (Plate III)

Head: Black
Tail: Eight or ten strands of a golden pheasant tippet, long enough to show a black band
Body: Very thin, of medium flat silver tinsel
Ribbing: Narrow oval silver tinsel
Throat: Applied as a collar; a pale yellow hackle forward of which is a small number of turns of a Silver Doctor blue (light blue) hackle, the two being moderately bushy and of average width. The collar is separated at the top to accommodate the wing
Wing: Two light blue saddle hackles with a cream badger neck hackle on each side. The badger hackles have a very pronounced black band, very wide at the butt
Cheeks: Jungle cock of moderate length, dressed high
(As dressed by the originator)

This fly was originated by Mr. Horace P. Bond, of Bangor, Maine, for trolling for landlocked salmon. It was named in honor of Mr. Amory Houghton, owner of the Spencer Bay Camps on Moosehead Lake, in Maine. The fly is a favorite for landlocked salmon and big trout in Maine waters. Usually it is dressed on a very long hook.

SPRUCE STREAMER (Plate VIII)

Head: Black
Tail: Four or five peacock sword fibers, about one-half inch long when dressed on an average sized hook (regular length hooks should be used for this fly)
Body: Rear quarter is red wool, not picked out, but built up toward the peacock. Front three-quarters is wound with peacock herl, rather heavily dressed
Throat: A silver badger hackle, wound on as a collar, fairly bushy, applied after the wing has been put on
Wing: Two silver badger hackle tips, tied on back to back so that they splay out in the form of a "V," extending slightly beyond the tail of the fly
(As dressed by Mr. E. H. Rosborough)

The *Spruce*, listed prominently among northwestern trout patterns, is a fly of the *Improved Governor* type, ascribed to an angler by the name of Godfrey who lived in Seaside, Oregon. It was designed

Famous Patterns

primarily to take the summer and fall runs of cutthroat trout ("harvest" or "blueback" trout) in Oregon streams. The *Spruce* fly probably was made to imitate an insect found in stands of Oregon spruce timber, but it is now considered to be a streamer fly, regardless of the original reason for its dressing. While it is most successful as a cutthroat fly, it also is favored for brown and rainbow trout. Originally, the fly was called the *Godfrey Special* or *Godfrey Badger Hackle*. Regarding this, a California gentleman who knew Mr. Godfrey wrote to the Fishing Editor of *Field and Stream*: "This is a fly I have fished with great success for all trout, including steelhead. I found it especially deadly on Yellowstone cutthroat. I tied the fly for years and called it the *Godfrey Special* after its originator. I began to see a great many of them appearing in Portland, where they were sold for the coastal streams. Fishing Paulina Lake several years ago I met an angler using what I had heard of but had not seen up to that time—a *Spruce* fly. It was the Godfrey badger hackle tip wing fly. This last season, fishing the lower Klamath, a native asked me to tie him a pattern called the *Kamloops*. He had to go to Orich to get a sample. It was the *Godfrey Special*, or *Spruce*. He swore it would take twice as many 'creek' trout (cutthroat) as any other fly."

A variation of the *Spruce Streamer* is the *Spruce Bucktail*, tied with a small bunch of badger hair instead of with a badger hackle wing. The rest of the dressing is the same. A variation known as the *Silver Spruce* is used primarily for brown trout and rainbows, and is identical except that it has a silver tinsel body instead of the red wool and peacock. It first was tied by E. H. Rosborough of Chiloquin, Oregon, at the suggestion of Mr. Al Kellogg, manager of the Meier and Frank Company of Portland, Oregon. This fly, tied with a wing consisting of a small bunch of badger hair, of the same length as the feather wing, is popular on the Nehalem, Trask and Nestucca Rivers of Oregon. White tipped squirrel tail occasionally is substituted for the badger. Then it is known as the *Silver Spruce Badger*.

Another variation is the *Red Spruce*, tied with a red wool body, fairly heavy but not picked out, and ribbed with narrow, flat silver tinsel. Other parts of the dressing are the same as the *Spruce*, except that a red hackle is placed inside the badger hackle on each side of the divided wing. All hackles are of the same length. Regarding it, Mr. E. H. Rosborough, who is famed as a dresser of western flies, wrote the author: "The *Red Spruce* was designed for eastern brook trout. I first saw it at the Meier and Frank Company of Portland, Oregon, in the summer of 1943. I believe it was brought out by a husband and wife combination working under the name of Smith-Ely, of Blue River, Oregon, who at that time furnished most of Meier and Frank's flies. I am responsible for the *Silver Spruce* in both the feather and hair wing versions. A lot of tiers will use golden badger hackle in all of its color variations when the silver is hard to get, but not me! There are too many variations now. The value of the *Red Spruce* is not as high as the others, except possibly for eastern brook trout.

"Although the *Spruce* was tied primarily for large sea-run cut-throat, it does very nicely on steelhead. It is dressed in sizes all the way down to Number 12 for trout fishing. In size 10 on a long shank hook it took many steelhead on the Klamath during the 1946 season. The action of the turned out wings on a slow, jerky retrieve makes it deadly in still water stretches."

STEVENSON'S SPECIAL BUCKTAIL

Head: Red
Tail: A small bunch of guinea hen body feather fibers dyed red
Body: Rear half is medium oval gold tinsel. Front half is wound with black chenille
Throat: A guinea hen body feather applied as a collar and tied back but not gathered downward. The throat is fairly long and rather heavily dressed
Wing: A bunch of fine yellow bucktail, extending to the end of the tail and dressed rather high on a large steelhead hook 2X long
Cheeks: Jungle cock (optional)

(As dressed by Mr. Don C. Harger)

This fly was originated by Mr. Clive N. Stevenson, of Roseburg, Oregon, who has taken a large number of record steelhead with it on several western coastal rivers.

STEWART'S HAWK STREAMER (PLATE III)

Head: Black Hook sizes: No. 6 and No. 8, 5X or 6X long
Tail: A very small bunch of white bucktail, about half the length of the hook shank
Body: Embossed silver tinsel
Throat: A very small bunch of red hackle fibers, about half as long as the hook

Wing: A very small bunch of medium blue polar bear hair or bucktail extending to the end of the tail. On each side and joined over the front are two fairly wide sections of gray-brown and white hawk wing feathers selected for good markings. These are pointed at the ends and extend to the end of the tail. (Since most species of hawks are protected in most regions, turkey wing sections or other large wing feathers of similar color may need to be substituted)
Cheeks: Jungle cock, very small

(As dressed by the originator)

This fly was originated by Austin S. Hogan, of Fultonville, New York, and named for his friend and angling companion Clarence "Cak" Stewart, of Fonda, New York. Mr. Hogan says, "This fly has been used very successfully for smallmouth bass in the north Atlantic states. The wing feathers, selected for softness, move inward and outward on intermittent retrieve. A similar pattern calls for a yellow chenille body with wing of white bucktail covered by sections of white goose or swan wing feathers." (Another similar fly of this type is the *Reliable*, discussed previously.)

SUMMERS GOLD BUCKTAIL

Head: Black
Tail: The tip of a golden pheasant tippet, tied in just below the second black band
Body: Medium flat gold tinsel
Throat: A red hackle feather, tied on as a collar, medium heavy and rather long
Wing: A small bunch of white bucktail, over which is a small bunch of medium brown bucktail, both slightly longer than the tail

(As dressed by Mr. Herbert L. Howard)

Dr. Orrin Summers, of Boundbrook, New Jersey, first tied this fly in 1912 and first used it on the Raritan River, near Nauright, in New Jersey. It is a universally useful bucktail for all fresh water game fish in all parts of the country, including bass and panfish, and for many salt water species as well. It has been used successfully for Atlantic salmon, particularly when an exaggerated fly is needed, in sizes 3/0 and 4/0 or larger.

SUPERVISOR STREAMER (Plate VII)

Head: Black
Tail: A thin section of red wool, rather short
Body: Medium flat silver tinsel

Ribbing: Narrow oval silver tinsel (optional)
Throat: A small bunch of white hackle fibers (optional)
Wing: An extremely small bunch of white bucktail, over which are four very light blue saddle hackles. The bucktail is nearly as long as the hackles, both extending well beyond the tail
Topping: Six or seven strands of peacock herl, as long as the wing (optional—see note below)
Shoulders: Each a pale green shoulder hackle, two-thirds as long as the wing and fully as wide. (Correct shoulder hackles are short and stubby, with a creamy-green center and a brighter green edge. They should be extremely pale in color)
Cheeks: Jungle cock

The *Supervisor* usually is considered to be one of the most important of the Maine-type streamer flies, especially for trout and landlocked salmon in waters where smelt exist. The idea for its dressing was conceived by Warden Supervisor Joseph S. Stickney, of Saco, Maine, while fishing at Moose Pond in Maine in 1925. Warden Supervisor Stickney originated it to imitate the finger smelt which the large squaretail (eastern brook) trout were pursuing at the time. The fly is named for Mr. Stickney's title. Since Mr. Stickney did not dress his own flies, he had other dressers make them for him and he gave several of these to the author, who was his annual fishing companion until his death in 1945.

Originally, Mr. Stickney had the *Supervisor* dressed without peacock topping. Later, he added this, calling the fly the *Supervisor Imperial*. This new version was so much more successful than the former one that Mr. Stickney chose to discard the former and to call the *Supervisor Imperial* by its shorter name. He preferred ribbing for dark days or murky water, but thought it too bright for casting on the sunlit clear water of lakes. Some of the flies he used were tied with the white throat and some were not. He preferred the fly sparsely dressed to more closely imitate the conformation of a smelt and he was very particular about the color and shape of the shoulders.

It is probable that this fly was an original creation of Mr. Stickney's, although it may have been influenced (or vice versa) by one of the Hardy Brothers' *Terror* streamers, which were dressed similarly except that the shoulders were of barred gray hackles and there was no peacock, bucktail or jungle cock. In England, the *Terror* streamer is favored for salmon, sea trout and the trout of inland waters.

TAP'S TIP BUCKTAIL

Head: Black (built up to conform to size of body). White eye with black pupil
Hook sizes: No. 4 to No. 8, 2X to 6X long
Body: Silver braided mylar tubular cord (as discussed in Chapter IX)
Wing: Four very small bunches of bucktail: white under green under red under black, all of the same length; half again as long as the hook

(As dressed by the originator)

This simple but effective bucktail is one of the favorites of the famed author, angler, and gunner H. G. "Tap" Tapply, of Lexington, Massachusetts, who is known to every sportsman as one of the editors of *Field and Stream.* It is named for his monthly column in that magazine, "Tap's Tips." It is an excellent fly for trout, land-locked salmon, and smallmouth bass. Tied on non-corrosive hooks, it also is an excellent fly for many species of salt water game fish.

THE THIEF (PLATE III)

Head: Covered with several turns of black chenille   Hook sizes: No. 2 to No. 12, 3X or 4X long
Tail: A small section of red duck wing feather, as long as the gap of the hook, and tied in upright
Body: Wound with silver tinsel
Wing: A bunch of gray squirrel tail hair extending slightly beyond the tail. Over this on each side is a fairly wide section of turkey wing feather as long as the hair

(As dressed by the originator)

This fly is a darker version of the *Muddler Minnow,* and was originated by Dan Gapen of the Gapen Fly Company, Anoka, Minnesota. The fly represents a minnow and was designed to take crappies in lakes and streams in Minnesota where a little darker fly than the *Muddler Minnow* was needed. It first was used in the International Falls area of Minnesota for big black crappies, but was later found to be an excellent fly for all species of trout, especially rainbows.

THOR BUCKTAIL (PLATE VIII)

Head: Black
Tail: A very small bunch of rather stiff orange hackle fibers of medium length

Body: Medium thick, wound with dark red chenille
Throat: Several turns of a mahogany saddle hackle, applied as a collar and tied back but not gathered downward. The hackle should be stiff, glossy and rather long
Wing: A medium sized bunch of white bucktail, extending to the end of the tail. White polar bear hair often is used

(As dressed by the originator)

This fly, one of the most famous of western steelhead patterns, was originated by Mr. C. Jim Pray, of Eureka, California, on Christmas Day of 1936. It is tied both as a bucktail and in the more conventional short pattern. The *Thor* first was used by Mr. Walter Thoreson, of Eureka, California, who took an eighteen pound steelhead with it to win first prize in the 1936 *Field and Stream* Contest (Western rainbow fly division) on the day it first was tied. It was named *Thor* from the first four letters of Mr. Thoreson's name. In 1938, also on Christmas Day, Mr. Gene Sapp, of Ferndale, California, took a seventeen-and-three-quarters pound steelhead with the *Thor* to win *Field and Stream's* first prize for that year also.

Mr. Pray wishes to make it clear that, "Harry Van Luven (see *Van Luven* bucktail) tied a fly very closely resembling this pattern probably earlier than I tied the *Thor*. It was essentially the same except that it had a silk body instead of chenille and it was spiraled with oval silver tinsel. In my shop the *Thor* outsells any other fly for most streams, particularly the Klamath. It has traveled widely through the nation and in Alaska and British Columbia; wherever large fish are to be found."

THUNDER CREEK BUCKTAIL SERIES (Plate I)

(The eight patterns in this unusual series originated by Keith C. Fulsher, of Eastchester, New York, are described (with dressing instructions) in Chapter IX.)

TROUT FIN STREAMER (Plate III)

Head: Black
Tail: A section of a red goose or swan wing feather, long, thin and curving upward
Body: Medium flat silver tinsel

Famous Patterns

Ribbing: Fine silver cord
Throat: A cream badger hackle wound on as a collar and gathered downward. The throat is rather long and of moderate fullness
Wing: Two or four matched sections of married swan or goose wing feathers, fairly soft, in red, black, and white. The lower part of the wing is red, married to black in the middle and white on top. The red is twice as wide as either the black or the white. The wing extends just beyond the end of the tail
Cheeks: Jungle cock, fairly short. (This is optional and usually is not included)

(As dressed by the originator)

There are three streamers in the Trout Fin series; the *Harlequin*, in blue, black and white, the *Trout Fin*, as dressed above, and a second version of the *Trout Fin*, where orange is substituted for the red. All were originated by Mr. B. A. Gulline, of Fin, Fur and Feather, Ltd. The orange and red versions first were tied in 1929 for Mr. B. A. Gulline by Mr. Frier Gulline. The orange version differs from the red version in that it has a throat of red hackle fibers rather than the cream badger. Gold cord occasionally is substituted for the silver as a ribbing, and a few turns of either may be added as a tag. Anglers with whom these patterns are favorites prefer the red version for fishing in Canada, in the belief that it more closely approximates the color of the Canadian trout, which often are called "red trout" because of their high coloration. The orange version usually is used in the United States, where the trout ordinarily are less pronounced in color.

The proportions of the wings are highly important. The red (or orange) should be as thick as both the black and white together, and the black and white should be equal in thickness, so that the married wing is composed of one-half red (or orange), one-fourth black and one-fourth white. Slightly more or less of the red or orange may be used in proportion if the color of the feather is much lighter or darker than normal.

Since a brook trout's fin has been a popular bait for many years, it is natural that others would imitate it in flies. Thus, Robert H. Cavanagh, Jr., of Woburn, Massachusetts, independently developed an almost identical pattern for fishing at Grand Lake Stream, Maine. His version calls for a tag of three or four turns of yellow floss, a tail of a short golden pheasant crest feather, curving upward, a butt of peacock herl and a throat of guinea hen hackle. Other elements are the same. Those with the skill and patience to handle married wings will find this fly so beautiful that it seems a shame even to get it wet. Bob Cavanagh dressed a few for the author several years ago. Two remain in my fly book and, while chewed almost beyond recognition by scores of trout, they still are highly effective.

TROUT PERCH STREAMER (PLATE VI)

Head: Gray-tan, to match the upper wing   Hook sizes: No. 2 to No. 10, 3X long
Tail: A very small bunch of fibers from a blue dun hackle, slightly longer than the gap of the hook
Body: Wound with white floss, slightly tapered
Ribbing: Medium flat silver tinsel
Throat: The same as the tail, and of same length
Wing: A small bunch of summer sable tail hair, extending to the end of the tail. Over this are two fibers of pink dyed ostrich, of the same length. On each side of the hair and ostrich is a chinchilla saddle hackle of the same length
Cheeks: Jungle cock, small and short

(As dressed by the originator)

This is next to the last of the imitator patterns designed by Lew Oatman, of Shushan, New York. He says, "Pike perch will feed heavily on schools of trout perch, especially during the spawning season when these little minnows run towards and into the creeks. This pattern, the *Ghost Shiner*, and the *Silver Darter* are fine when fly fishing for the pike perch."

UMPQUA SPECIAL BUCKTAIL (PLATE VIII)

Head: Red
Tail: A very small bunch of white bucktail of moderate length
Body: The rear one-third is yellow wool or silk; front two-thirds red chenille or wool. The body is shaped more fully toward the head
Ribbing: Narrow oval silver tinsel from tail to head
Wing: A small bunch of white bucktail extending just beyond the end of the tail
Shoulders: Each a narrow strip of a red goose feather laid along the midsection of the wing and nearly as long. A tiny bunch of red bucktail sometimes is substituted for each of the shoulders
Throat: A dark brown hackle tied on as a collar after the wing and shoulder have been applied. The hackle is of moderate length and fullness and is not gathered downward

(As dressed by Mr. Don C. Harger)

Famous Patterns 351

The *Umpqua Special*, sometimes known as the *Rogue River Special*, is claimed by several fly dressers, but seems to have been the result of variations of several old patterns. It contains a body similar to the *Van Luven*, the red and white wing of the *Parmacheene Belle*, the hackles of the *Royal Coachman* and a touch of yellow present in any of a score or more of well-known flies. Prominent in its past is Mr. Clarence Gordon, of the North Umpqua, who is credited with part of its distinctiveness as a pattern. Early in its career a variation of it was known as the *Wharton Red*, tied with an all-red body. Mr. F. D. Colvin had a similar steelhead fly dressed to the order of Mr. Frank Youngquist, of Coos Bay, California, with the same body and a wing of salmon pink and white bucktail. Mr. Colvin later changed the fly to add yellow to the body and substituted yellow for the salmon-pink bucktail in the wing. This is called the *Colvin's Rogue River Special*; one of the many accepted variations. When the description of the pattern was published in *Field and Stream* magazine more than twenty fly dressers sent in supposedly correct versions, no two of which were exactly alike. Regardless of these details, the fly became so successful on the North Umpqua River that it later became best known as the *Umpqua Special*. Anglers on the Rogue River prefer it with small double hooks and jungle cock cheeks and know this adaptation as the *Rogue River Special*. The *Umqua Special* frequently is tied on Number 8 or 10 hooks for low water summer fishing. In its larger sizes it is extremely popular as a steelhead fly, particularly on northern California and Oregon waters.

VAN DE CAR BUCKTAIL

Head: Black
Tail: About a dozen strands of a red saddle hackle, rather long
Body: Medium flat gold tinsel
Ribbing: Medium oval gold tinsel
Throat: A red saddle hackle of moderate length wound on as a collar and tied downward
Wing: A small bunch of fox squirrel tail hair
Cheeks: Jungle cock, fairly short
(As dressed by the originator)

This fly was originated by Mr. Tom Van De Car, of Hutchinson, Kansas. It is a favorite western trout fly, particularly on the Gunnison

River of Colorado. Usually it is dressed in the smaller sizes, such as numbers 6, 8, and 10.

VAN LUVEN BUCKTAIL

Head: Black
Tag: Three or four turns of medium flat silver tinsel. (This is optional and is not used by Mr. Schwab and many other fly dressers)
Tail: A small bunch of red polar bear hair, rather long. (In early dressings a tail of a section of a red goose wing feather, of moderate width and rather long, was used but the hair tail is now considered superior)
Body: Of red silk or wool, fairly thick. This can be applied over copper wire if it is desired to have the fly weighted, as described on page 189.
Ribbing: Narrow oval silver tinsel
Throat: A brown hackle wound on as a collar, fairly long and heavy
Wing: A small bunch of white polar bear hair, extending to the end of the wing. Over this it is optional to place an extremely small bunch of yellow polar bear hair of the same length. Bucktail may be substituted for all polar bear hair called for in this dressing. As in most steelhead flies, two or three turns of thread should be taken under the wing to raise it to an angle of about 40 degrees
(As dressed by Mr. Peter J. Schwab)

This is one of the most popular of all western steelhead flies. Mr. Peter J. Schwab, the famous writer and angler of Yreka, California, wrote about it in the July, 1946, issue of *Sports Afield* magazine as follows: "This fly was named by me during the winter of 1926-1927 after my old friend and steelhead mentor, Harry Van Luven, of Portland, Oregon. It was originally tied on plain hooks as a hair fly with standard short wings, but we found it even better as a bucktail with wings one and a half times the length of the hook. Harry used the white hair from the tail of the western blacktailed deer for the smaller hair fly, but he preferred the longer white hair of eastern deer tails for the bucktail version. He tied six of the "red flies" every night in his little cabin near Ennis Riffle on the Rogue River, and it was the only fly I ever knew him to use. The pattern was evolved by a simple process of elimination starting with the great *Royal Coachman*. Harry first omitted the easily torn peacock herl. Finding this good, he wanted still more red so he added the red tail. Finally after much experimenting, in collaboration with Jack Myers, both men were satisfied and they replaced the white goose wings with wings of white bucktail. Certainly this simple fly is one of the greatest

Famous Patterns

of steelhead and rainbow trout flies, even as its co-authors were two of the greatest fishermen on the west coast. I still use the *Van Luven* as my standard of comparison."

E. H. (Polly) Rosborough of Chiloquin, Oregon, developed a popular adaptation called the *Silver Admiral*, which differs from the *Van Luven* only as follows: The dressing is fluorescent except for hook, tinsel, and head. The throat (tied as a collar) is heavy, long fluorescent bright red hackle. The wing is of white fluorescent polar bear hair slightly longer than the tail. The recommended hook is 1XL-2XS nickel. The *Silver Admiral* is preferred for turbid, roily water, especially for winter steelhead fishing before sunrise and at dusk. For this type of fishing the fly is dressed with an underbody wound with ·015 lead fuse wire.

WARDEN'S WORRY BUCKTAIL (Plate VII)

Head: Black
Tag: Three or four turns of narrow flat gold tinsel
Tail: A narrow section of a red duck or goose wing feather, moderately long
Body: Orange-yellow spun fur or wool applied loosely or picked out to make it fuzzy. The body is of medium fullness
Ribbing: Narrow oval gold tinsel
Throat: Three or four turns of a yellow hackle, wound on as a collar and gathered downward
Wing: A small bunch of light brown bucktail, extending just beyond the end of the tail

This fly was originated about 1930 by Warden Supervisor Joseph S. Stickney, of Saco, Maine, from whose title the *Warden's Worry* took its name. It is a favorite for trout, landlocked salmon, and many other game fish in all sections of the United States. It is often fished behind a spinner for walleyed pike. The dressing is from a fly given by Warden Stickney to the author.

WELCH RAREBIT STREAMER (Plate VII)

Head: Black
Tail: Extremely narrow sections of duck or goose wing feathers in red, yellow and blue plus two strands of a peacock sword feather. All four colors are of equal and normal length, with the blue and yellow married together on one side (with the yellow at the top) and the red and peacock on the other side

Body: Medium flat silver tinsel
Ribbing: Narrow oval silver tinsel
Throat: A small bunch of fibers from a guinea hen body feather
Wing: One wine red (dark red) saddle hackle on each side of which are two white saddle hackles
Topping: Nine strands of bright green peacock herl, as long as the wing
(As dressed by the originator)

This is one of the best known of the Maine streamers. It was originated by Mr. Herbert L. Welch, of Mooselookmeguntic, Maine, to imitate a smelt, which is the principal food fish in many Maine lakes. The name *Rarebit* is often misspelled. Mr. Welch dresses this fly without jungle cock cheeks.

WESLEY SPECIAL BUCKTAIL

Head: Black
Tail: A very small bunch of strands from a golden pheasant tippet
Body: Medium flat silver tinsel
Ribbing: Narrow oval silver tinsel
Throat: A few turns of a black hackle, of medium length gathered downward
Wing: A small bunch of white bucktail, over which is a small bunch of blue-gray bucktail, both slightly longer than the tail
Cheeks: Jungle cock

This is one of the patterns obtained by Mr. Herbert L. Howard of New Rochelle, New York, for Mr. Ray Bergman's book TROUT. It is popular on the Rifle River and in the Ausable River area of Michigan, particularly as a trout fly.

WHITE WATER BUCKTAIL

Head: Black, built up as a bead head, with white eye and black pupil
Tail: A double section of red wool, heavy and fairly short
Butt: Rather large, of black wool
Body: Medium flat silver tinsel. The forward part of the body is composed of a butt of peacock herl about twice as long as the rear butt. Both butts and the body have the same effect as the body of a *Royal Coachman*
Throat: A very small bunch of black hackle fibers, rather long
Wing: A bunch of very dark natural brown bucktail, extending longer than average beyond the tail
(As dressed by the originator)

Famous Patterns

This fly was originated by Mr. Herbert L. Howard, of New Rochelle, New York, for use in the fast streams of Michigan and Wisconsin. The fly is particularly effective in white water, hence its name. It has been used most successfully in Canada for brook trout and brown trout, especially in fast water and in riffles. Since rainbow trout inhabit such waters through preference, the fly is very popular for them on occasions where a dark fly with a flash of red and silver is needed.

WIZARD STREAMER (PLATE IV)

Head: Black, with red band
Body: Thinly wound with red silk
Ribbing: Narrow flat silver tinsel
Throat: A few strands of peacock herl, beneath which is a small bunch of white bucktail, both extending well beyond the barb of the hook. Beneath this is a small bunch of white neck hackle fibers
Wing: Two black saddle hackles with a yellow saddle hackle of the same length on each side. The wing is as long as the peacock and bucktail of the throat
Cheeks: Jungle cock

(As dressed by the originator)

Originated by Mrs. Carrie G. Stevens. This fly is a favorite in Maine waters for trout.

WOOD PUSSY BUCKTAIL

Head: Black
Tail: A small bunch of black skunk hair, very long
Body: Wound with silver wire, or with copper wire covered with medium flat silver tinsel (see instructions on page 189)
Wing: A small bunch of white polar bear hair or white skunk hair, over which is a small bunch of black skunk hair. The wing extends to the end of the tail. In applying the two parts of the wing, turns of thread are taken under both the white and the black hair to raise the wing to an angle of about 40 degrees

(As dressed by the originator)

This fly was originated by Mr. Peter J. Schwab, of Yreka, California, in 1927. This is one of a series of steelhead flies listed in the comments on the *Princess* bucktail, and in notes on page 194. The series is dressed with wire bodies to assist them in sinking in the swift and deep western coastal rivers, such as the Klamath, where they were first used. In either the weighted or unweighted types they are consistently valuable in all parts of the country for all species of game fish.

YELLOW BREECHES STREAMER

Head: Yellow
Body: Medium oval silver tinsel
Throat: The tip of a red hackle tied in vertically; of medium length
Wing: A yellow marabou feather, over which is a bunch of herl from a light brown marabou feather. The bunch of brown marabou is of the same volume and length as the yellow marabou feather
Shoulders: Three herls of a peacock feather on each side, tied in to separate the two colors of the wing. The peacock is of the same length as the wing
Cheeks: Jungle cock

(As dressed by the originator)

This fly was originated by Mr. R. W. McCafferty and Mr. Charles Fox, of Hershey, Pennsylvania, for fishing in Yellow Breeches Creek in Pennsylvania. Mr. McCafferty writes about the fly as follows: "For a number of years I've used marabou streamers of one inch and two inch lengths and find that they take more trout than the longer ones, although the longer ones often cause more excitement in the fish. The *Yellow Breeches* streamer resembles the minnows found in Yellow Breeches Creek, but the fly has been successful in many other places. We also like a *Black Marabou* streamer because of its visibility in dark or dirty water. We have found that the angler can see the *Black Marabou* better than lighter colors under those conditions and so can the fish. In this section we have limestone streams which are always murky. In this milky water the black color almost always is good."

Mr. McCafferty's *Black Marabou* streamer is dressed identical with the *Yellow Breeches*, except that the yellow and brown marabou is replaced by two black marabou feathers.

YELLOW JANE CRAIG STREAMER

Head: Black
Body: Medium flat silver tinsel
Ribbing: Narrow oval silver tinsel
Wing: Four bright yellow saddle hackles
Topping: Six or seven strands of bright green peacock herl, as long as the wing
Cheeks: Jungle cock

(As dressed by the originator)

Famous Patterns

This is a later version of the *Jane Craig* streamer, dressed with hackles instead of white to give the fly greater visibility on dark days or in discolored water. It was originated by Mr. Herbert L. Welch, of Mooselookmeguntic, Maine, in about 1923 and was named for Jane Craig, a vaudeville actress of the team of Dalton and Craig which toured the Keith Circuit of theatres at that time. In addition to the change in colors, this fly differs from the *Jane Craig* in that it has no throat. Also, it is ribbed, while the *Jane Craig* is not.

YELLOW MAY STREAMER

Head: Black
Body: Wound with yellow silk, shaped slightly in the middle
Ribbing: Narrow flat gold tinsel
Throat: A small bunch of yellow saddle hackle fibers, rather long
Wing: Four bright yellow saddle hackles

(As dressed by Mr. Robert J. Stone)

The *Yellow Sally* streamer is identical to the *Yellow May* streamer except that it is not ribbed. Both flies may be dressed with hair wings, although the feathered wings are more common. Both flies were adapted from the trout flies of the same names.

YELLOW PERCH STREAMER (Plate VI)

Head: Black   Hook sizes: No. 1 to No. 6, 3X to 6X long
Tail: A very small bunch of fibers from a yellow hackle about as long as the gap of the hook (Mr. Oatman did not always dress the tail)
Body: Wound with pale cream or amber floss, slightly tapered
Ribbing: Medium flat gold tinsel
Throat: A very small bunch of yellow hackle fibers edged outwardly with four or five orange hackle fibers
Wing: Two grizzly hackles dyed yellow, on each side of which is a yellow saddle hackle, all of the same length and extending slightly beyond the tail (The grizzly hackles should be selected with wide dark bands)
Topping: Several peacock herl, as long as the wing
Cheeks: Jungle cock, rather small

(As dressed by the originator)

This is the last of the excellent imitative patterns originated by the late Lew Oatman, of Shushan, New York. In sending the dressings and fly samples to the author many years ago, Lew wrote about this one, "This fly was designed for largemouth bass which feed on the schools of small perch, and also for some lakes especially in the Westchester (New York) area where rainbow trout have been planted and are known to feed on these little fish. I have found that this streamer and the *Golden Shiner* will take bass during the day when they are not interested in the noisier lures."

YELLOW SQUIRREL BUCKTAIL

Head: Black
Tag: Three or four turns of narrow flat gold tinsel
Tail: A tiny bunch of red saddle hackle fibers
Body: Wound with bright yellow wool or chenille, dressed with moderate fullness
Ribbing: Narrow flat gold tinsel (if chenille is used, oval gold tinsel is preferable)
Throat: A fairly large bunch of soft red saddle hackle fibers, rather long
Wing: A very small bunch of dark blue bucktail, over which is a slightly shorter bunch of gray squirrel tail
Cheeks: Jungle cock

(As dressed by Mr. William Reynolds)

This fly was originated by Mr. Arthur Houle, of Southbridge, Massachusetts. It is popular for eastern brook trout, rainbow trout and bass. In small sizes it is a favorite for panfish.

YERXA BUCKTAIL

Head: Black
Tag: Four or five turns of narrow flat gold tinsel
Body: Yellow wool or dubbing dressed rather full and picked out to make it fuzzy
Ribbing: Narrow flat gold tinsel
Throat: A yellow neck hackle tied on as a collar and then gathered downward to make a full and bushy throat
Wing: A bunch of white bucktail
Cheeks: Jungle cock

(As dressed for the originator)

This pattern was originated by Mr. Jack Yerxa, of Square Lake Camp, Square Lake, Maine, and was named for him by Mr. Gardner Percy, who tied flies for his camp. The fly was first used in 1928 and the original pattern caught over 100 landlocked salmon in Square Lake during that year.

YORK'S KENNEBAGO STREAMER

Head: Black
Tag: Three or four turns of narrow flat silver tinsel
Tail: A very short golden pheasant crest feather, curving upward
Butt: Two or three turns of scarlet silk
Body: Medium flat silver tinsel
Ribbing: Narrow oval silver tinsel
Throat: A small bunch of red hackle fibers
Wing: Four golden badger saddle hackles with a pronounced black stripe. The wing is longer than average
Topping: A small bunch of red hackle fibers
Cheeks: Jungle cock

(As dressed by the originator)

This streamer was originated by Mr. Bert Quimby, one of Maine's most expert streamer fly dressers. He named it for Mr. T. Lewis York, who was the owner of York's Camps on Kennebago Lake, in Maine. It was dressed primarily to imitate the baitfish in Kennebago Lake, and is popular there as a spring fly.

Appendix

This Appendix contains additional background information and patterns for the flies presented in Plates 1–15 not included in the text.

PLATE 3
Original Patterns Dressed by Carrie Gertrude Stevens

As the wife of Rangeley guide Wallace Stevens, Carrie taught herself to tie flies at their cottage in Upper Dam. Her talents as a milliner are evident in both her style and creative use of color. Carrie's early flies were bucktails and were numbered rather than named. Instrumental in the early development of what is now known as the Rangeley style of streamers, Carrie Stevens originated dozens of distinctive patterns and has a permanent place in fly tying history.

ARTULA
Head: Black with red band
Tag: Flat silver tinsel
Tail: Dyed orange hackle (soft)
Body: Orange thread floss
Ribbing: Flat silver tinsel
Throat: A small bunch of white bucktail, extending nearly the length of the wing under which are dyed dark green hackles, followed by brown hackle
Wing: Two dyed chocolate brown saddle hackles followed by two dyed yellow saddle hackles on each side and shorter
Cheeks: Jungle cock

DAZZLER
Head: Black with red band
Body: Medium flat silver tinsel
Throat: Gray squirrel tail, under this is dyed yellow hackle
Wing: Two yellow dyed grizzly saddle hackles
Shoulders: Red dyed duck breast
Cheeks: Jungle cock

F.R.S. SPECIAL
Head: Red with black band
Throat: Red bucktail extending beyond bend of hook, followed by red hackle fibers
Wing: White bucktail

LADY MILLER
Head: Black with red band
Tag: Flat silver tinsel
Body: Black thread floss
Ribbing: Fine flat silver tinsel
Throat: White hackle
Wing: Two dyed orange saddle hackles followed by two white saddle hackles on each side
Shoulders: Jungle cock neck hackle half the length of the wing
Cheeks: Jungle cock

TOMAHAWK
Head: Black with red band
Tag: Flat silver tinsel
Body: Red floss
Ribbing: Flat silver tinsel
Throat: Peacock herl and white bucktail. The peacock is as long as the wing, the bucktail only slightly shorter; under these, blue hackle fibers
Wing: Four medium blue saddle hackles on each side of which is an orange saddle hackle slightly shorter
Shoulders: Golden pheasant green body feather one third as long as the wing
Cheeks: Jungle cock

WILL KETCH
Head: Red with black band
Body: Medium flat gold tinsel
Throat: White bucktail the length of the wing; under this white hackle extending to hook bend
Wing: Two dyed chocolate brown saddle hackles followed by two dyed yellow saddle hackles, outside and shorter
Shoulder: Dyed Silver Doctor blue duck breast feather followed by dyed red duck breast outside and slightly shorter
Cheeks: Jungle cock

173 Main St.
Madison, Me.

Dec. 5th 1949

This method used for salt water flies became well not pull over so easily. Varnish before folding back.

Dear Joe:
In reply to your letter of Nov. 25th. I really dont know what to say or how much I have previously told you but will start from the beginning and tell you how it happened that I originated a new fly that has become so popular. I had tied a few flies previously but they were crude and unattractive and I never became interested in flies or fly fishing. At the time my new fly was originated Mr. Stevens who is a fishing guide and I was living in our Camp at Upper Dam, Me. which is only a short distance from the Upper Dam Hotel and the famous pool for fly fishing. I was fond of outdoor life and spent much time trolling, using worm and live bait. One day in 1924 the first day of July, Mr. Stevens was away for the day — I was busy with my morning camp work when suddenly I had an inspiration — I will make a fly that will resemble a small fish — leaving my work unfinished I was soon busy with my new creation with white hair tied on bottom of hook

for the underpart and two hackle feathers tied on top of hook for the back. The effect was very pleasing. I then continued to finish my camp work when I felt impelled to try out my new fly in the pool. I hastily changed to a more suitable dress and with rod and net was soon fishing with my new fly from one of the aprons of the dam gate house into the fast water. In less then an hour I hooked and landed a 6 lb, 13 oz. brook trout which I entered in Field and Stream Fishing Contest. The event won for me second prize, also a beautiful large oil painting by Lynn Bogue Hunt for showing the most sportmanship in landing a fish. Because the fish was such a nice one an was caught on a new fly I made it cause much excitement and was being talked much about which resulted in my receiving many orders for flies, and soon found I was in the "fly business". My first flies were good but there was much to be desired. They lacked — with too much detail. I have given a true outline of how the fly — "The Rangeley Favorite" — was created and the results that have come from it. I hope it will be helpful to you and you can use any or all of it.

     Sincerely,
     Carrie

Appendix

Plate 4
Shang's White-nosed Pete and Streamers for Upper Dam

JUDGE

Head: Red with black band
Tail: None
Body: Flat silver tinsel
Throat: White hackle fibers
Wing: Grizzly dyed red
Shoulders: None

Following is an excerpt from "Pincushion Pete: The Smartest Trout I Ever Met," an article written by the author that appeared in the February 1947 issue of *Outdoor Life:*

> Sometimes a good fish that can't be caught becomes an obsession to the angler. As I lay awake among the coconut palms in New Guinea and the Philippines, I thought of that big trout many times, and dreamed of the day when I would fish for him again. I wrote to Wallace asking if Pete was still around. A month or two later a package arrived. It contained a photo of Wallace holding the head of Pincushion Pete, mounted under glass, and a framed picture of the famous fish, under which some poetry of doubtful quality was inscribed.
>
> The sight made me very sad—at first. Then a gnawing doubt crept in. I wrote to Shang Wheeler, asking if it were really true that Pete had been caught, and if so, why they had preserved merely the head of such a magnificent fish instead of mounting the whole thing. That fact alone made me suspicious.
>
> In his reply Shang, who also had tried for Pete when I was at Upper Dam, implied, but did not state, that the mounted head of Pincushion Pete was a fake—a fabrication of his own, undertaken to amuse his friends.
>
> He said the last thing he did, before leaving Upper Dam, was to go to the saw mill and look through the trapdoor to see what was in the slack water under the dam. One thing I believe—because I have often been there myself—is his statement that there, calmly fanning their fins in the clear, cold water were Pincushion Pete himself—and two more squaretails just as big! Shang says he is going back, and now that I'm in the States once more, you can bet he won't go alone. I want another crack at Pete!

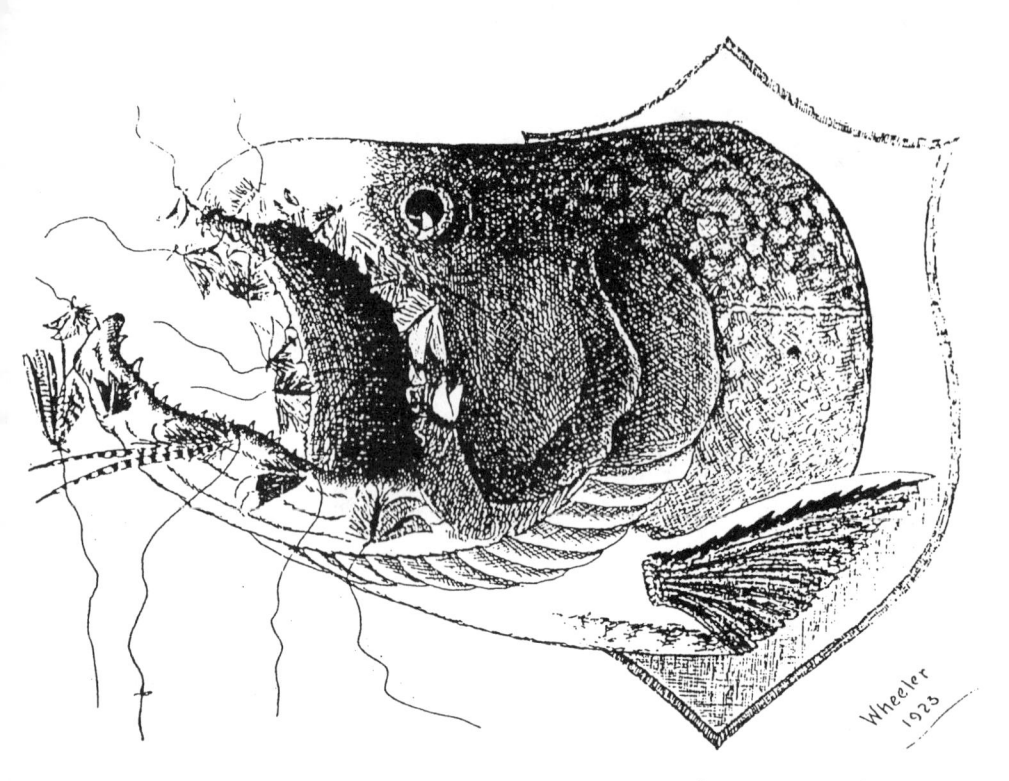

I came to light in 'ninety-six,
  In the "Pool" at Upper Dam.
And while lots of folks think I'm a myth,
  I'm not, for here I am.

I go to the Lake to Summer
  And come back here in the Fall.
I've met fishermen from all over,
  Yes—met and defeated them all.

I've got a collection of tackle,
  Lines, leaders, flies and such.
To me they are trophies of battles,
  And I prize them very much.

I took one from a man named Parish,
  Away back in 'ninety-nine.
Then Dougherty made a donation
  Of fly, leader and piece of line.

I tackled both Morgan and Morton,
  And my souvenirs will show
That I licked them both to a standstill,
  'Though they certainly made me go.

Then I mixed it with "Old man" Barber,
  And wrestled with Calkins too.
The "Old man" fought me the hardest,
  For fishing to Arthur was new.

I had it out with Parker
  And collected from all of the Fairs,
I now have in my collection,
  Flies and leaders that once were theirs.

I next took a crack at Van Dusen,
  And then gave Bugbee a whirl,
But their tackle some was as easy—
  As nuts to a hungry squirrel.

One day I got foul of Tom Miner,
  He gave me a h—l of a chase,
Down over the reef, through the slaughter.
  All over the dog-gone place.

But I've got his "Silver Doctor"
  Hooked fast in my lower jaw.
When the leader broke, Tom also broke
  A part of the Scriptural Law.

I had a tough scrap with Steve Palmer,
  'Twas down in the lower pool.
I tangled his gear in Dougherty's stumps
  And he'll say I'm nobody's fool.

I next ran across Nick Boylston
  And Nick had some "Rooster's Regrets."
I took the first one that he offered
  And it's in my collection yet.

My last real fight was with Wilber,
  For he's a heavyweight too.
When he sat back on his haunches,
  I surely had something to do.

He had a guide named "Gillie"
  Who sat and watched the fun.
I heard him remark—that night in the dark,
  Aint he a "Snuff-colored Son of a gun?"

We neither asked nor gave quarter,
  We fought a square fight and I won.
I finally parted his leader,
  'Though it seemed that I pulled a ton.

I've taken on all comers,
  And I've met some tough ones too.
But they've all gone ashore without me,
  And I'm out here — <u>Ready For You</u>.

Piscatorially yours,
WHITE NOSE PETE.

PLATE 6
Original Patterns Dressed by Bill Edson, with His Fly Wallet

As early as the 1920s, Bill Edson was a fishing companion of the author. Self-styled as a champion fly caster, he frequently appeared at Boston sporting shows. After working for the Montague Rod Company in Massachusetts, Edson moved to Portland, Maine, where he worked in the fishing tackle department of Edwards and Walkers. The originator of many successful patterns, Bill Edson's flies are often distinguished by gold metal "cheeks" that he designed to replace the traditional and costly jungle cock. Most of his flies are tied with inexpensive cotton thread, and the heads are painted black, gray, silver, or yellow.

BILL SPECIAL
Head: Black
Body: Flat silver tinsel
Throat: Small bunch of white bucktail
Wing: Four grizzly saddle hackles
Shoulder: Silver pheasant body feather
Cheeks: Gold metal "Edson" cheeks

DARK EDSON TIGER (SQUIRREL WING)
Head: Black or yellow lacquer
Tag: Flat gold tinsel
Tail: Two yellow saddle hackle tips
Body: Yellow chenille
Wing: Fox squirrel
Throat: Two red hackle tips
Cheeks: Gold metal "Edson" cheeks

EDSON TIGER
Head: Black
Tag: Flat gold tinsel
Tail: A section of barred wood duck
Body: Wound with fine yellow chenille or wool
Ribbing: (Optional, flat silver tinsel)
Throat: A small bunch of red hackle fibers
Wing: Natural brown bucktail or brown hackle
Cheeks: Jungle cock or gold metal "Edson" cheeks

The *Edson Tiger*, dressed with either brown bucktail or brown hackle, is the predecessor to the *Dark Edson Tiger* and the *Light Edson Tiger*. Although Edson used hackle, squirrel tail, or bucktail when tying these early flies, it is the bucktail that has endured. Edson used yellow bucktail for the *Light Edson Tiger* and either red squirrel tail or brown bucktail for the *Dark Edson Tiger*.

GOLD SPRAT #1

Head: Black
Body: Flat gold tinsel
Throat: Small bunch of yellow polar bear and red hackle points
Wing: Two yellow and two orange saddle hackles
Cheeks: Gold metal "Edson" cheeks

GOLD SPRAT #2

Head: Black
Tag: Flat gold tinsel
Throat: Small bunch of yellow bucktail
Wing: Two yellow and two orange saddle hackles
Cheeks: Jungle cock, short

KENNEBAGO SPECIAL

Head: Black
Body: Flat silver tinsel
Throat: Yellow and red hackle tips
Wing: Four furnace saddle hackles
Cheeks: Jungle cock and gold metal "Edson" cheeks

Note: The *Kennebago Special* is remembered as Bill Edson's favorite fly.

OLD FAMILY RECIPE (Also known as the EDSON BELLE)

Head: Black or red thread
Tail: Red hackle tips
Ribbing: Flat gold tinsel
Body: Light yellow wool
Throat: Red hackle tips
Wing: White, red and white bucktail in three equal bunches
Cheeks: Gold metal "Edson" cheeks

This pattern was the "Old Family Recipe" for Guillford and Myrtle Pendexter, who owned a tackle shop in Portland, Maine, that dealt exclusively with Bill Edson flies. They are the grandparents of artist John Swan, also of Portland.

Streamers and Bucktails

photographed by

Michael D. Radencich

THE BUMBLEPUPPY

Theodore Gordon (1854–1915), fisherman, writer, and professional fly tier, evidently named the *Bumblepuppy* with a purpose, for the literal translation is "whist played without rules." Regarded as a fly for which there is no name, there are at least twenty known variations of the *Bumblepuppy*. Gordon would often enclose one such variation when filling orders for his customers. Widely regarded as the father of the American dry fly, some would argue that Theodore Gordon, "the American Walton and Sage of the Neversink," is also the father of the first commercially established American streamer and bucktail.

In addition to the *Bumblepuppy* dressed by the originator, the flies in Plate 1 were tied by Herman Christian and Roy Steenrod, both fishing companions of Gordon.

Originated and Dressed by Theodore Gordon

Dressed by Herman Christian

Dressed by Herman Christian

Dressed by Roy Steenrod

PLATE 1
The Bumblepuppy

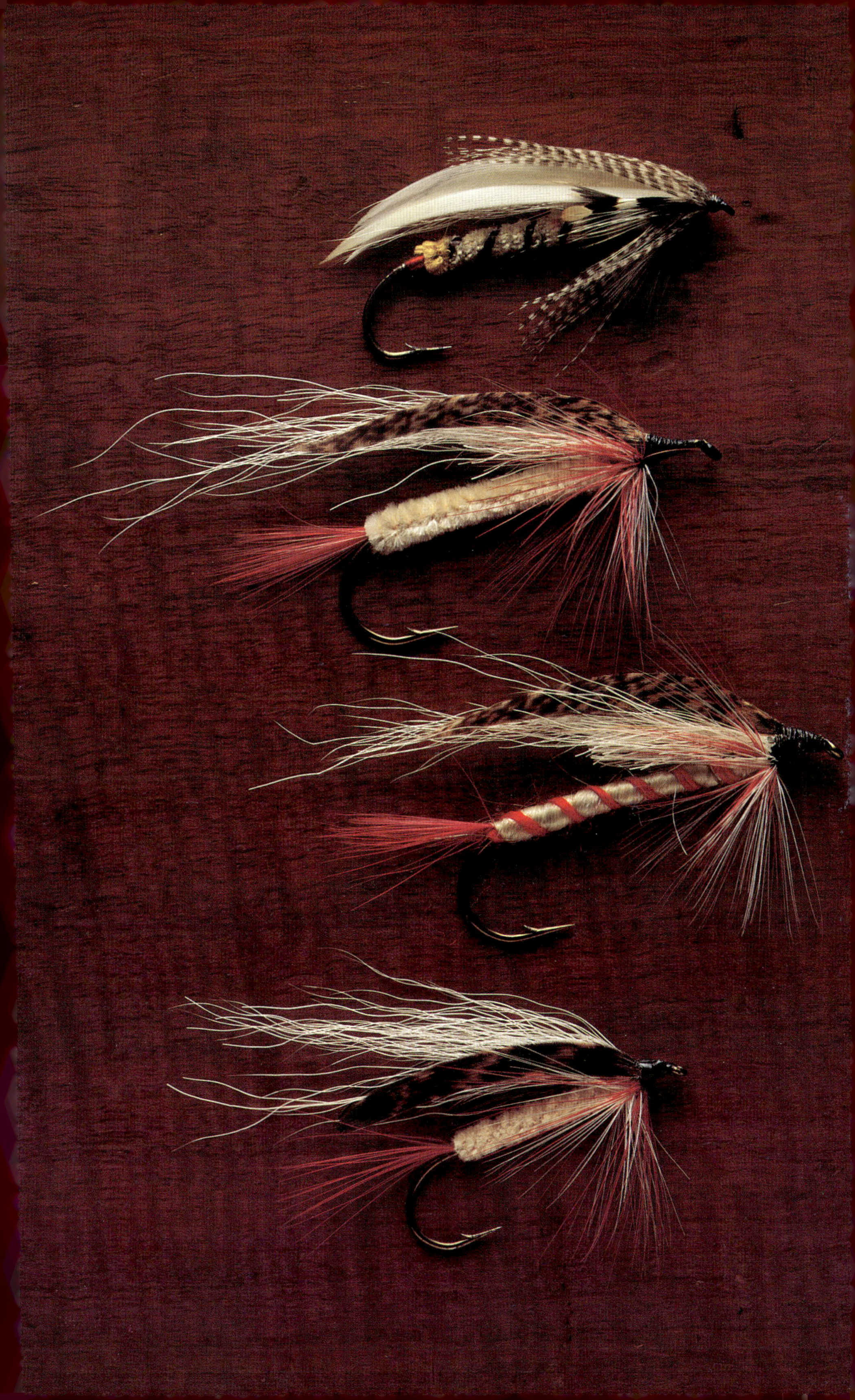

GRAY GHOST
Originated and Dressed by
Carrie Stevens

BLACK GHOST
Originated and Dressed
by Herbert Welch

HORNBERG
Dressed by Robert Cavanagh

SUPERVISOR
Dressed by the author

SPRUCE
Originated and Dressed by E. H.
"Polly" Rosborough

MICKEY FINN
Originated and Dressed
by John Alden Knight

BLACK NOSED DACE
Originated and Dressed by Arthur Flick

MUDDLER MINNOW
Originated and Dressed by Don Gapen

GREEN GHOST
Originated and Dressed by Bert
Quimby

DARK EDSON TIGER
Originated and Dressed by Bill Edson

NINE–THREE
Dressed by Austin Hogan

PLATE 2
Flies That Have Endured

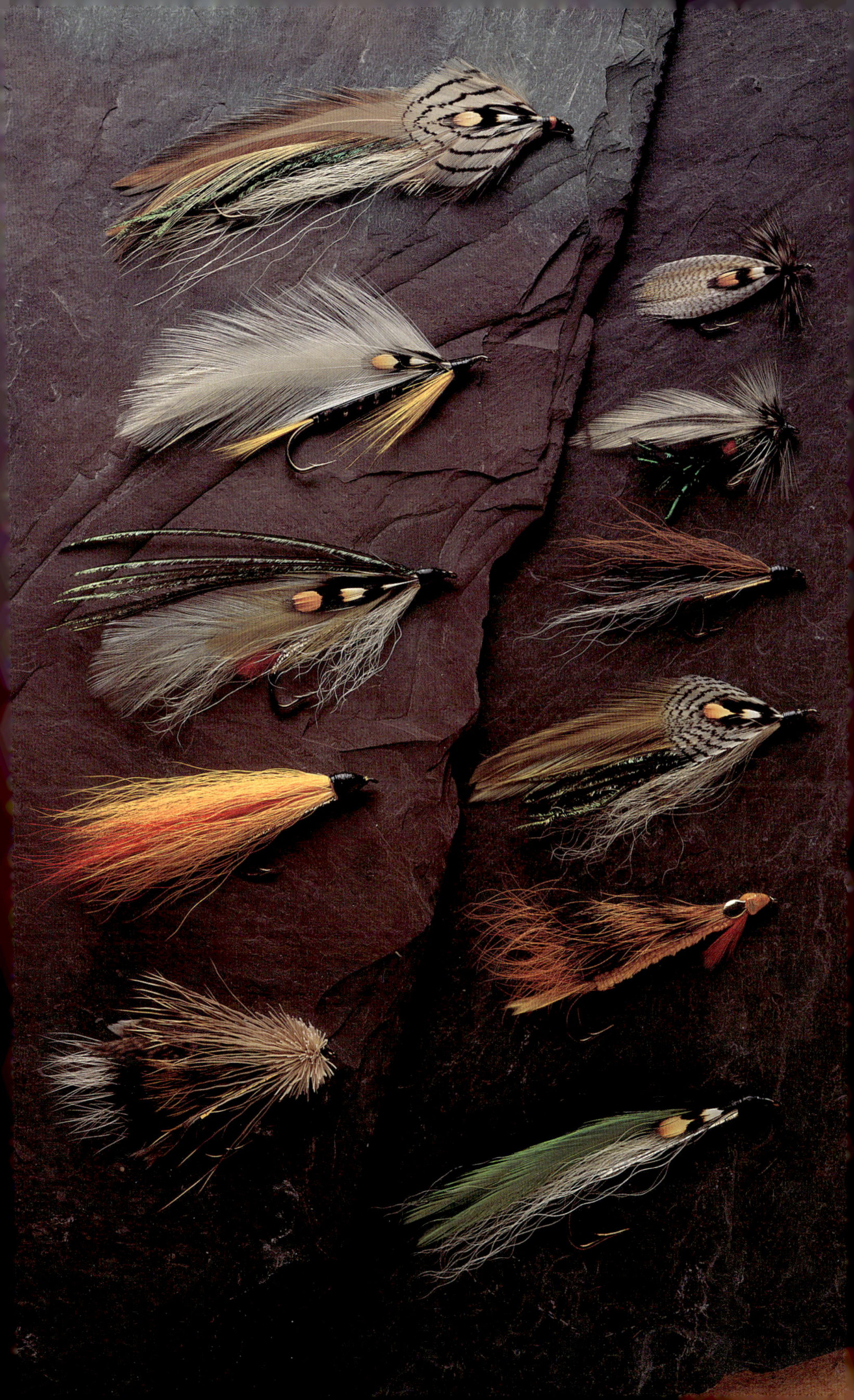

> **Taken July 1-1924**
>
> **The Rangeley's Favorite Trout and Salmon Flies**
>
> Red Spotted Genuine Brook Trout, weighing 6 pounds and 13 ounces, taken at Upper Dam by Mrs. Stevens, on one of her flies.
>
> In ordering, give pattern number and size of hook desired, and address
>
> MRS. CARRIE G. STEVENS,
> Upper Dam, Maine

Carrie Stevens's card with her notation of prize-winning trout.

CARRIE STEVENS

The photograph used for the background of this plate of original Stevens patterns was sent to the author in the 1930s by Carrie Stevens. Inscribed on the back of the photograph in her distinct hand was the notation, "This is where I took the 6 pound, 13 ounce trout."

DAZZLER

GRAY GHOST

TOMAHAWK

ARTULA

F.R.S. SPECIAL

WILL KETCH

LADY MILLER

PLATE 3
Original Patterns Dressed by Carrie Gertrude Stevens

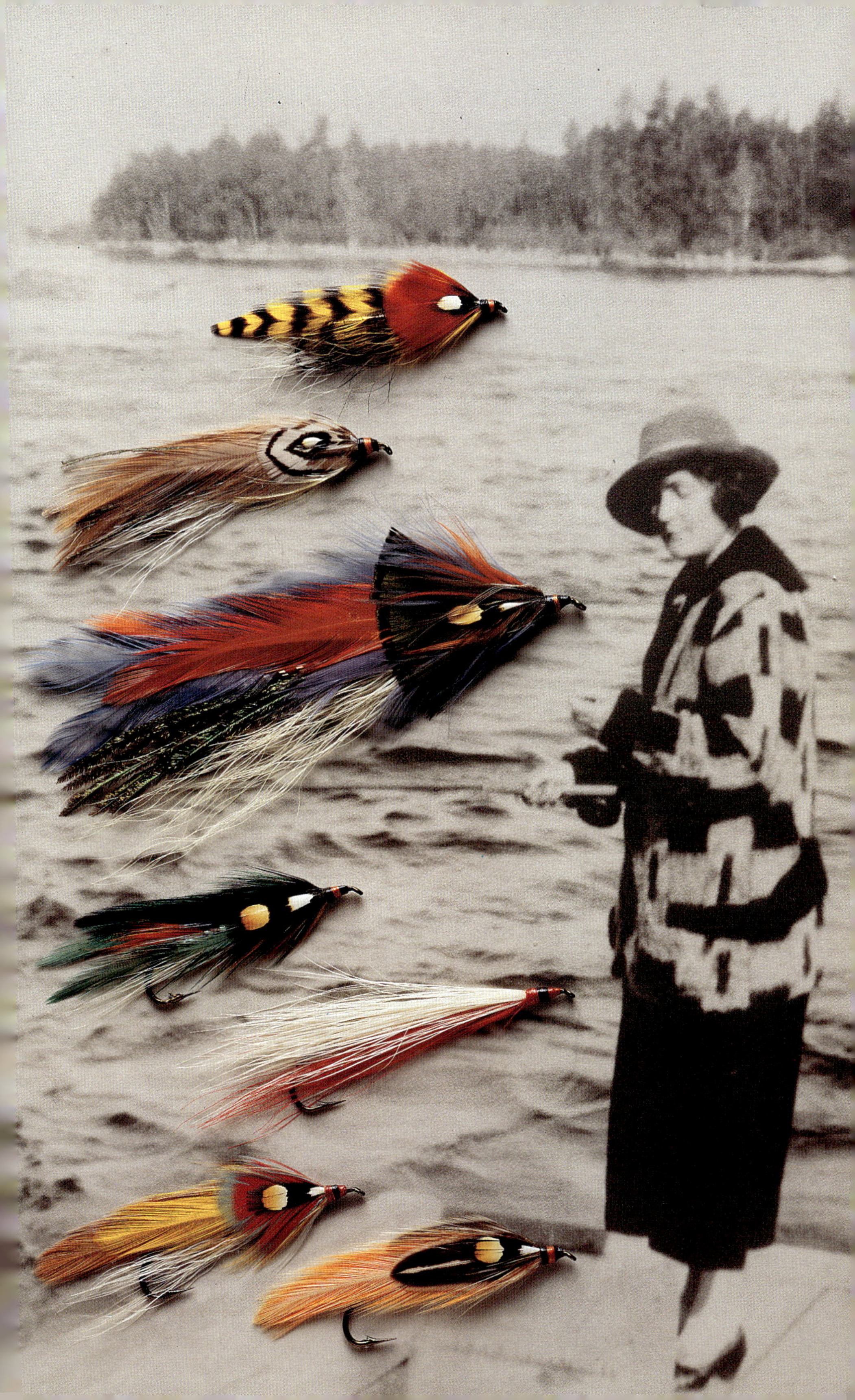

"Shang" Wheeler and Wally Stevens with "White-nosed Pete" artwork and poem *(Photograph by the author)*

CHARLES E. "SHANG" WHEELER

Larger than life in presence as well as talent, Shang Wheeler is recognized as one of the finest amateur decoy carvers in American history. Ever a Connecticut yankee, he enjoyed a number of careers—oysterman, cartoonist, and sporting artist. For hobbies he wove baskets, wrote poems, bred dogs, played football, and boxed. A determining influence on the development of the Rangeley style of streamer flies, he was also an expert sailor and an ardent conversationalist. His spirit was as creative as it was versatile. He is regarded by all who knew him as a fine sportsman and, above all, a fine friend.

The background of Plate 4 is Shang's hand-colored pen-and-ink drawing of "White-nosed Pete," the legendary and elusive trout of Upper Dam Pool.

SHANG'S FAVORITE
Originated and Dressed
by Carrie Stevens

SHANG'S SPECIAL
Originated and Dressed
by Carrie Stevens

JUDGE
Originated and Dressed
by Carrie Stevens

PLATE 4
Shang's White-nosed Pete and Streamers for Upper Dam

Wheeler
1923.

Herbert L. "Herbie" Welch *(Photograph courtesy of The Rangeley Lakes Region Historical Society)*

HERBIE WELCH

Legendary as a Maine guide, Herbert L. "Herbie" Welch was also nationally known as a taxidermist, artist, and fly caster. Early in this century, Herbie was inspired by a 6/0 *Silver Doctor* salmon fly brought to him from England to apply multicolored feathers to reforged hooks in an effort to imitate a smelt. From his shop at Haines Landing at Lake Mooselookmeguntic, he created some of the most elaborate streamers of the era.

The mounted trout in the photograph included in this plate is said to be one of the last that Herbie Welch completed. The six-pound, four-ounce trout was caught by the author in Maine.

KENNEBAGO STREAMER

JANE CRAIG

CUPSUPTIC

WELCH RAREBIT

YELLOW JANE CRAIG

BLACK GHOST

BROOK TROUT VARIATION

PLATE 5

Streamer Flies Originated and Dressed by Herbert Welch

HERBERT L. WELCH
COMPLETE OUTFITTER
HIGH GRADE SPORTING GOODS · EXPERT IN FISH MOUNTING
IN THE HEART OF THE RANGELEY LAKES
MOOSELOOKMEGUNTIC, MAINE

Aug 18-49

...streamer fly is
...yellow)

...if you mention the Bone Fish
correct the spelling of the "Boni...
...ie Smith."
...k with your work
...ers "Herb"

William R. "Bill" Edson

KENNEBAGO SPECIAL

DARK EDSON TIGER
(SQUIRREL WING)

OLD FAMILY RECIPE

UNIDENTIFIED (TRI–COLOR)
BUCKTAIL

UNIDENTIFIED (TEAL WING)
STREAMER

EDSON TIGER (HACKLE WING)

LIGHT EDSON TIGER

GOLD SPRAT #1

EDSON TIGER (BUCKTAIL WING)

GOLD SPRAT #2

DOT EDSON STREAMER

BILL SPECIAL

PLATE 6
Original Patterns Dressed by Bill Edson, with His Fly Wallet

Edson Tied Flies
Pat.
Hook Size
Made by BILL EDSON
PORTLAND, MAINE

NEEDAHBEH'S SHACK
MOOSEHEAD LAKE — GREENVILLE, MAINE
Harford's Point

Unfriendly atmosphere . . . questionable climate . . lousy beds . . . punk food . . . no fuel . . . no running water (hot or cold — dirty or clean) . . . . plenty of mosquitos, blackflies and noseeums . . . ice cold bathing in cold spring-fed lake . . . best of fishing — no trout, no togue, no salmon, no bass, no boats, no canoes, no bait, no outboard motors, no nothing . . . no dull moments . . . plenty of picks, shovels, wheelbarrows, saws and axes for the tired city folk. Come often — bring your own drinking water and papers . . .

Chief Needahbeh in traditional dress *(Photograph courtesy of The Rangeley Lakes Region Historical Society)*

THE CHIEF
Chief Needahbeh (pronounced Ne-DAH-ba) was the proprietor of Needahbeh's Shack, a tackle shop at Moosehead Lake in Greenville, Maine. A Native American Penobscot, he was also known as Chief Roland Nelson and frequently demonstrated his native traditions at sporting shows.

CHIEF NEEDAHBEH
Dressed by Bert Quimby

CHIEF NEEDAHBEH
Originated and Dressed by Chief Needahbeh

PLATE 7
The Chief

salmon
Something
information and
as requested hope
from
me
wishes
Sincerely
thechief.

DUSTY STREAMER

YORK'S KENNEBAGO STREAMER

GALLOPING GHOST STREAMER

WHITE PHEASANT STREAMER

GOVERNOR BRANN STREAMER

LADY GHOST STREAMER

DOCTOR MILNE STREAMER

PLATE 8
Streamer Flies Originated and Dressed by Bert Quimby

Bert Quimby's
STREAMER AND BUCKTAIL FLIES
WINDHAM
BERT QUIMBY
Telephone 35
Tied by
BERT QUIMBY
SIZE 4
LADY GHOST

CAINS RIVER STREAMER

CAINS RIVER ALECK'S WONDER   CAINS RIVER SILVER GRAY

CAINS RIVER SCOTCH LASSIE   CAINS RIVER WILKINSON

CAINS RIVER HIGHLANDER   CAINS RIVER WADE'S CHOICE

CAINS RIVER ROARING RAPIDS

PLATE 9
Cains River Streamers Dressed by C. Jim Pray

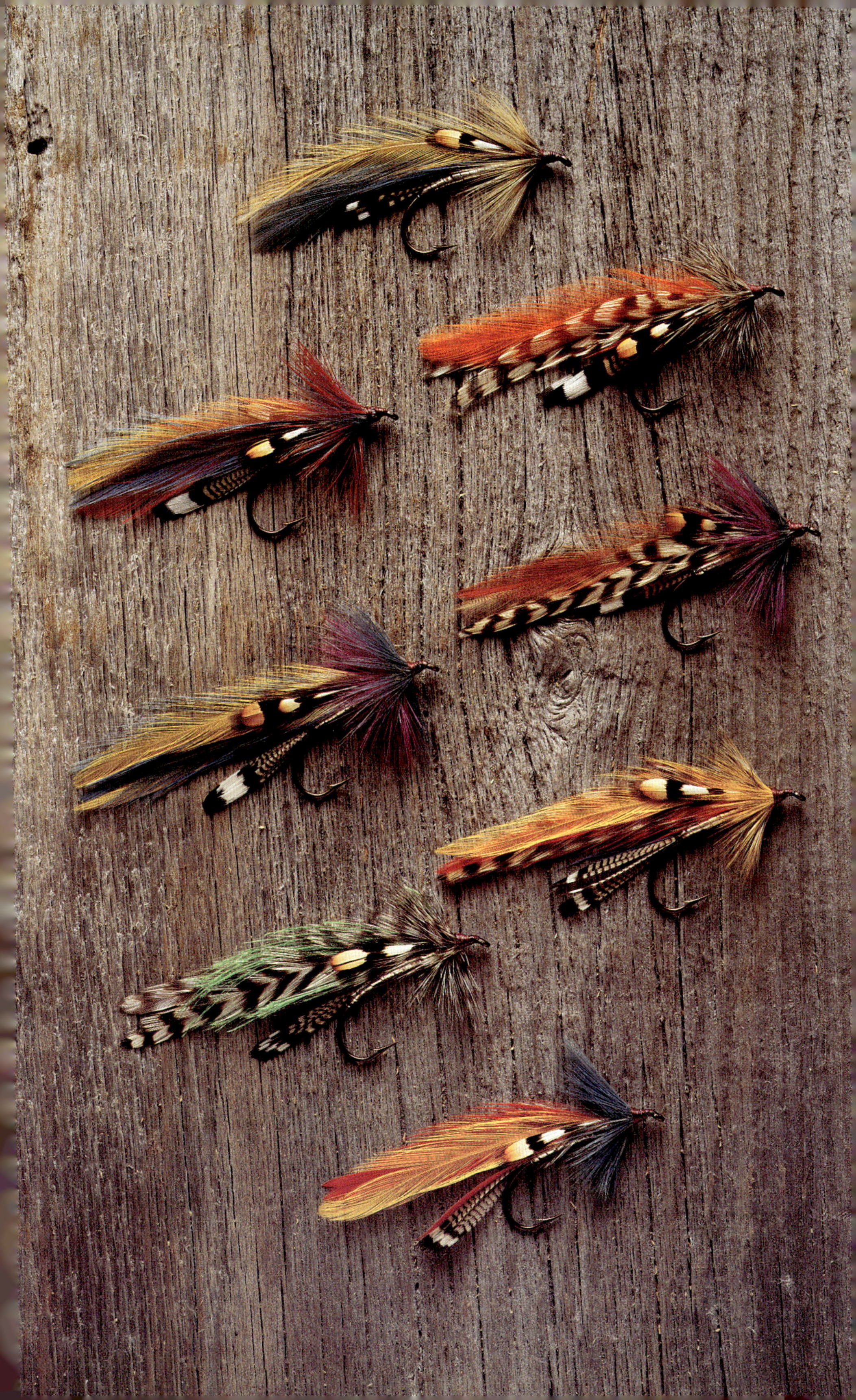

Ray Bergman *(Photograph courtesy of The American Museum of Fly Fishing)*

RAY BERGMAN BUCKTAIL

JESSE WOOD

GREY SQUIRREL SILVER
STREAMER

RED SQUIRREL GOLD STREAMER

BUCKTAIL SILVER STREAMER

PLATE 10
Streamers and Bucktails Originated and Dressed by Ray Bergman

TROUT

RAY BERGMAN
Author of "Just Fishing"

Fly Plates in Full Color Painted by
DR. EDGAR BURKE

Photographs of Fly Tying by
CHARLES F. KRUG

Also Many Diagrams by
IVIN SICKLES

Edgar Burke and Gene Connett

EDGAR BURKE, M.D.

Artist, angler, and surgeon, Edgar Burke spent a generation fishing Maine's trout and landlocked salmon waters. Burke's superb illustrations of trout flies distinguish Ray Bergman's classic work, *Trout*, published in 1938.

The background for Plate 11 is a Herter's pattern page on which Doctor Burke submitted his pattern for the *Family Secret*. Also included in the color plate with two of Edgar Burke's original patterns is his hand-painted card of the *Doctor Burke,* which had been slipped into the author's copy of this book.

DOCTOR BURKE

FAMILY SECRET

PLATE 11
Streamer Flies Originated and Dressed by Edgar Burke, M.D.

n, S...
ly Tying w...
ither method is sa...
s published answer them...
y of the questions as possible.

...eport to GEORGE LEONARD HERTER, 929 3RD AV...
WASECA, MINNESOTA, U.S.A.

S REGARDING THE PATTERN

ttern **"FAMILY SECRET"**

nis name

...was invented by **Edgar Burke, M.D.**

4. Complete details of the construction and materials used in the pattern — Snow-white hackl... from domestic...

Jungle Cock

"Galline" (Guinea fowl)

Body of flat silver tinsel wrapped with heavy, silver...

Heavi... from... fea...

(1)

Preston Jennings *(Photograph courtesy of The American Museum of Fly Fishing)*

PRESTON JENNINGS

A student of the theory of refraction and reflection of color through a prism, Preston Jennings endeavored to dress his flies as the fish saw them. Jennings's concept of the breaking down of light as it passes through water is exhibited by his innovative use of spectrum colors in his minnow imitations.

UNIDENTIFIED STREAMER

IRIS #1

LORD IRIS

LADY IRIS

PLATE 12

Streamer Flies Originated and Dressed by Preston Jennings

#1

BLACK-NOSED DACE

Austin Hogan at The American Museum of Fly Fishing, circa 1976.
(Photograph courtesy of The American Museum of Fly Fishing)

THE SNOW GOOSE

THE DEPTH RAY #1

UNIDENTIFIED STREAMER #1

UNIDENTIFIED STREAMER #2

UNIDENTIFIED STREAMER #3

THE MILKWEED FLY

THE DEPTH RAY #2

PLATE 13
Streamer Flies Originated and Dressed by Austin Hogan

"Depth Ray" Fluorescent green Wing

SILVERSIDE
Originated and Dressed by Joseph D. Bates

PINK SHRIMP
Dressed by Jimmie Albright

TINKER MACKREL
Originated and Dressed
by Bill Catherwood

GOLDEN PRINCE
Originated and Dressed
by Joseph D. Bates

NEEDLEFISH
Originated and Dressed
by Bill Catherwood

FRANKIE-BELLE
Dressed by Jimmie Albright

GIBBS STRIPER
Originated and Dressed by Harold N. Gibbs

PLATE 14
Salt Water Patterns

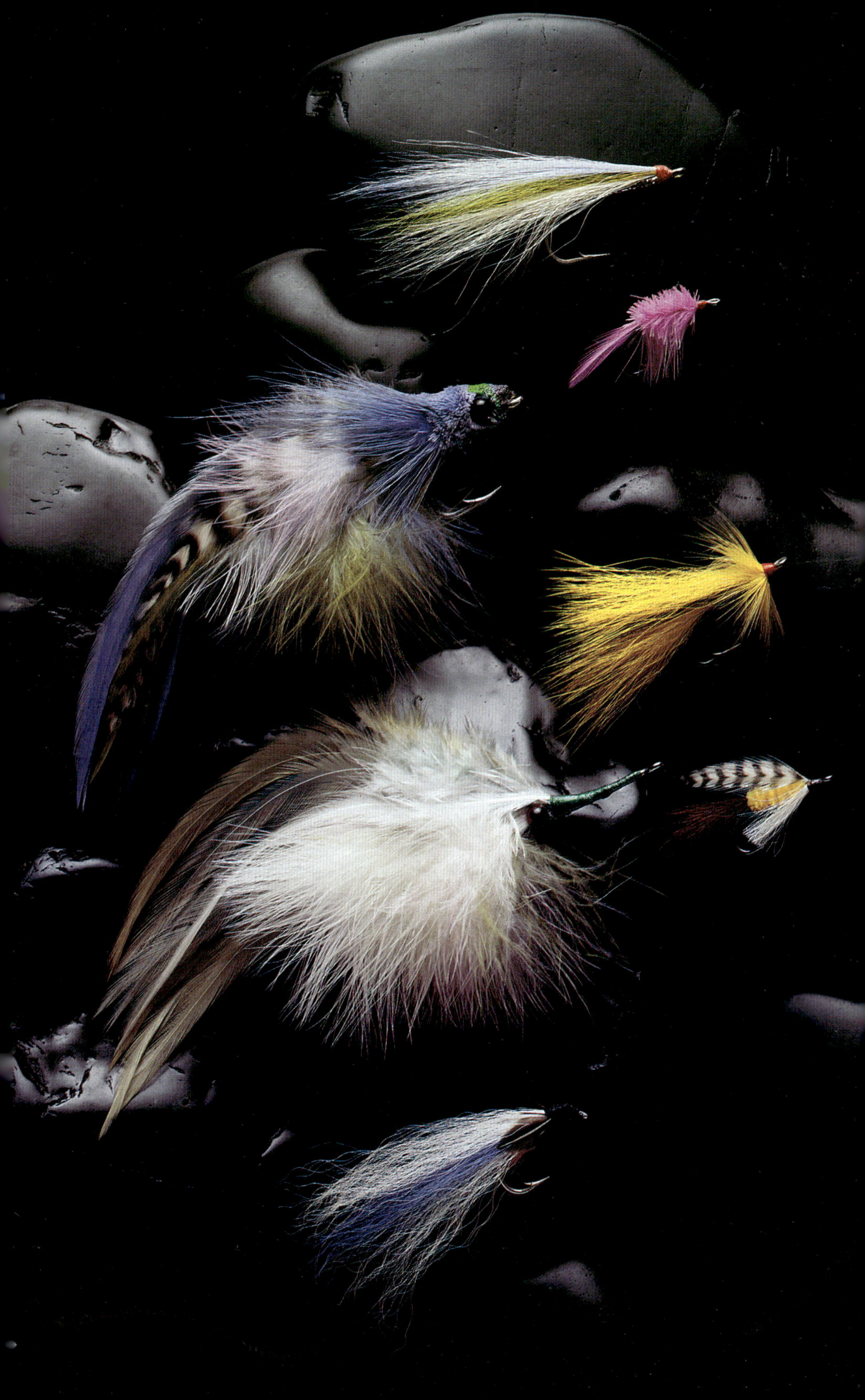

SMELT	SMALLMOUTH BASS	GOLDEN SHINER
SPOTTAIL SHINER	STRIPED JUMPROCK	EMERALD SHINER
STRAWCOLOR SHINER	LARGEMOUTH BASS	SILVER SHINER
STEELCOLOR SHINER	BROOK TROUT	FATHEAD MINNOW
YELLOW PERCH	BLACKNOSE DACE	BROWN TROUT
WEDGESPOT SHINER	SWAMP DARTER	REDLIP SHINER
REDFIN SHINER	RAINBOW TROUT	MARABOU SHINER

PLATE 15
The Thunder Creek Series
Originated and Dressed by Keith Fulsher

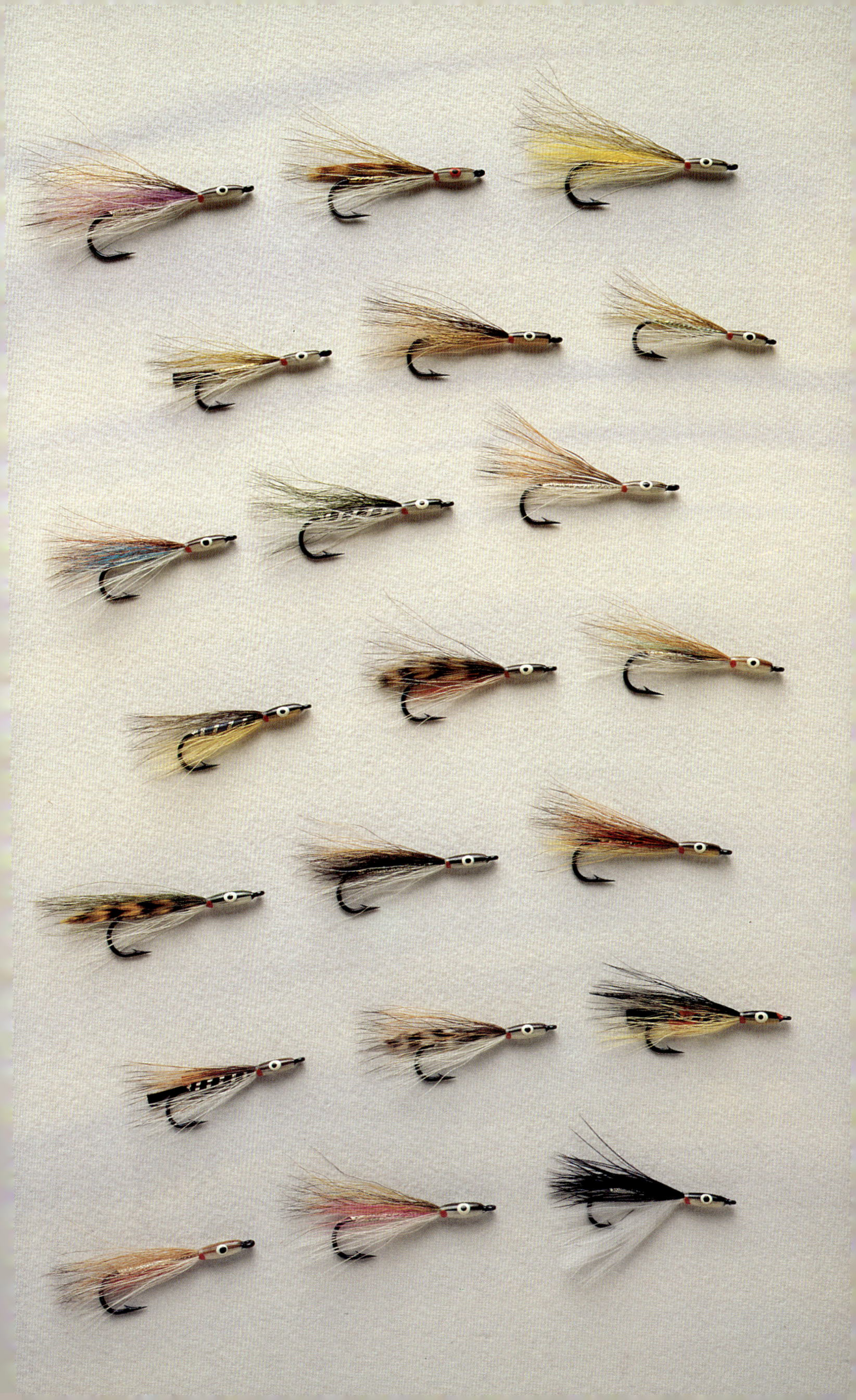

UNIDENTIFIED (TEAL WING) STREAMER
Head: Black
Tag: Flat gold tinsel
Tail: Two slips of red goose
Ribbing: Flat gold tinsel
Body: White wool
Throat: Bunch of brown hackle points
Wing: Two teal feathers, back to back
Cheeks: Gold metal "Edson" cheeks

UNIDENTIFIED (TRI-COLOR) BUCKTAIL
Head: Amber
Tag: Flat silver tinsel
Tail: Two slips of barred wood duck
Throat: Small bunch of light blue bucktail
Wing: White and brown bucktail in two equal bunches
Cheeks: Gold metal "Edson" cheeks

Bill Edson and Chief Needabeh exhibiting the day's catch in Naples, Maine, circa 1932. *(Photograph courtesy of The American Museum of Fly Fishing)*

MANUFACTURER AND DEALER IN FISHING TACKLE AND SPORTING GOODS

BILL EDSON

REGISTERED GUIDE   DENNYSVILLE, MAINE

Dec. 2, 1940

Joe Bates
95 State St.,
Springfield, Mass.

Dear Joe:

      Your letter of recent date received. In answer to your question regarding the originator of the streamer fly, I do not know who first used this style fly in fishing for trout and salmon. I made crude streamers on pickerel hooks long before I ever saw a real good streamer, in fact, I never thought of fishing for trout or salmon with such a lure until I went to the Rangeleys, there, I was given a red and white streamer tied on a small hook by Fred Fowler who told me about the large trout and salmon that were caught at Upper Dam on this style fly. I am inclined to beleive that Mr. & Mrs Stevens who live at Upper Dam were the first ones to make streamer flies for salmon and trout fishing; off hand, I think that was about 19 years ago.

      I doubt if I will go to the Boston show this year, last year I was down country for five weeks and worked with two shows, the expense is too great to make it worth while. I am amking fly-books that take most of my time, last season I was back in my orders.

      Will be looking for you next spring, when you hook your first Atlantic salmon and experience the thrills that go with this fish you will understand why I moved up here.

      Dot joins me with best regards

ATLANTIC SALMON FLY FISHING EQUIPMENT A SPECIALTY

Yours Truly
Bill

Mr. Joe D. Bates Jr
5 Prynwood Road
Longmeadow Mass

Dear Joe:

Glad to receive your letter, as soon as I could get to work I got together six items varied in selection, for landlocked salmon, sea salmon, and square tail trout.

No. 1 is the original pattern of Chief Needahbeh several years ago I was fishing on and front of the dam at Wilson's Camps at East Outlet, Moosehead Lake Maine. There were several fly fishermen casting only standard patterns such as Black Ghost, Grey Ghost, Red and White Bucktails etc. Very few fish were taken and I decided the fish were used to these flies and if presented with something out of the ordinary they would take a bite. So I had my good friend Bert Quimby of South Windham Maine who by the way tied most of my streamers to tie this like "exhibit No. 1. Bert has since taken off the tail and the red hackle feather making it all yellow, perhaps because I used to have some tied with orange instead of red, I liked the orange and yellow combination on dark days. The tail though because the average average fisherman after catching a few fish considered the fly a weak lure after the tail had been chewed off, it is a weakness but a good and better lure with that flag.

best and if of my flies because the Dunleys on only by constant hitting by fish. they hold together tiers in the business. are pulled apart Yes sir, best

Let me hear from you soon. My best to your success. Sincerely yours
    the chief

P.S. This letter with enclosed two pages of descriptive information on the flies and a

Plate 8

Streamer Flies Originated and Dressed by Bert Quimby

WHITE PHEASANT STREAMER

Head: Black
Tag: Flat silver tinsel
Tail: Golden pheasant crest and peacock sword
Butt: Red chenille
Body: Flat silver tinsel
Ribbing: Silver tinsel lace
Throat: A bunch of red hackle fibers under which is a bunch of orange hackle fibers
Wing: Four white neck hackles
Topping: Strands of peacock sword
Shoulders: Golden pheasant tippet

Plate 12

Streamer Flies Originated and Dressed by Preston Jennings

Given below are Preston Jennings's original dressings from the Preston Jennings Collection at the American Museum of Fly Fishing in Manchester, Vermont.

The pattern that appears in the text for the *Iris #1 Bucktail* (page 290) varies only slightly from that in Jennings' personal pattern file; however, the Fur, Fin and Feathers, Ltd. dressing given for the *Lord Iris* (page 298) is considerably different from that of the fly bearing the same name in Plate 12. To qualify these differences, Jennings' dressings for both the *Iris #1* and the *Lord Iris* are included here.

IRIS #1

Head: Black with a red band
Tag: Silver oval tinsel
Tail: None
Body: Flat silver tinsel
Ribbing: Silver oval tinsel
Hackle: None
Wings: Polar bear or bucktail, dyed red, yellow, light green and blue; the yellow should predominate. Colors should follow in order beginning with red at the bottom.
Cheeks: Jungle cock

Appendix

LADY IRIS

Head: Black with a red band
Tail: Golden pheasant crest and Indian crow
Body: Flat silver tinsel
Ribbing: Silver oval tinsel
Hackle: Yellow dyed cock's hackle
Wings: Two yellow dyed cock's hackles, red and yellow swan, four strands of peacock herl, green and blue swan
Sides: Badger cock's hackle
Cheeks: Jungle cock

LORD IRIS

Head: Black with a red band
Tail: Golden pheasant tippets
Body: Embossed silver tinsel
Ribbing: Silver oval tinsel
Hackle: Light orange cock's hackle, dyed
Wing: Two light orange cock's hackles, red and orange swan, four strands of peacock herl, light green and blue swan
Sides: Badger cock's hackle
Cheeks: Jungle cock

UNIDENTIFIED STREAMER

Head: Black
Tag: Silver oval tinsel
Tail: None
Body: Flat silver tinsel
Ribbing: Silver oval tinsel
Hackle: Light purple cock's hackle
Wing: Light purple bucktail underwing, two medium blue cock's hackles
Sides: Badger cock's hackle
Cheeks: Jungle cock

PLATE 13

Streamer Flies Originated and Dressed by Austin Hogan

As an avid scholar and relentless researcher and historian, Austin Hogan contributed greatly to documenting and consolidating fly fishing history. Combining his talents as both fly tier and artist, Hogan's color-blended streamers exhibit meticulous combinations of materials he thought might be tempting to game fish. Although an accomplished tier of all types of flies, Austin is known for patterns of his own design that were often first created as carefully detailed watercolors. During his later years, Austin Hogan served as executive director of The American Museum of Fly Fishing, where his extensive collection of research is held.

DEPTH RAY #1

Head: Black
Tail: Orange polar bear
Butt: Black wool
Body: Flat silver tinsel
Throat: A bunch of yellow hackle fibers
Wing: Fluorescent green depth ray wool, over which is a bunch of natural black squirrel

DEPTH RAY #2

Head: Black
Tail: Lemon wood duck
Butt: Fluorescent orange floss
Body: Flat silver tinsel
Throat: Orange polar bear
Wing: Fluorescent green ray wool, over which is a bunch of black bucktail

MILK WEED FLY

Head: Black
Tail: Lemon wood duck
Body: Orange floss
Ribbing: Flat silver tinsel
Throat: Barred wood duck
Wing: Two slips of milkweed

SNOW GOOSE

Head: Black
Tag: Flat silver tinsel
Tail: Barred wood duck
Butt: Black wool
Body: Three quarters red floss, one quarter black wool
Throat: A bunch of black hackle fibers
Wing: A small bunch of white calf tail, on either side of which is a section of white goose

Appendix

UNIDENTIFIED PATTERN #1
Head: Black
Tail: Barred wood duck
Butt: Black thread
Body: Flat silver tinsel
Throat: Four strands of peacock herl under which is a bunch of white bucktail. Under these is a bunch of white hackle fibers under which is a bunch of brown hackle fibers
Wing: Two light blue saddle hackles on each side of which are three white saddle hackles
Shoulder: Lemon wood duck
Cheeks: Jungle cock

UNIDENTIFIED PATTERN #2
Head: Black
Tail: Yellow hackle fibers
Body: Yellow floss
Ribbing: Flat gold tinsel
Throat: A bunch of yellow hackle fibers
Wing: Two orange saddle hackles on each side of which is one white saddle hackle

UNIDENTIFIED PATTERN #3
Head: Black
Tail: Red hackle fibers
Body: Flat silver tinsel
Throat: Orange hackle fibers under which is a bunch of white bucktail
Shoulders: White duck breast
Cheeks: Jungle cock

PLATE 14

Salt Water Patterns

GOLDEN PRINCE
Thread: Red
Body: Of 00 red nylon wound evenly to the hook point
Tail: A medium-size bunch of golden-yellow polar bear hair with all underfur removed. The bunch should be as long as the hook and the tied-in end should extend nearly to the eye of the hook. After tying, the red thread is wound evenly to the head. The thread should then be tied off and the body lacquered and allowed to dry before completing the fly.

Wing: About fifteen peacock herls tied in at the head and extending to the end of the tail. Above this is a bunch of golden yellow polar bear hair of the same size as the tail and extending to the end of the tail.
Collar: Two bright yellow hackles, wound on as a collar at right angles to the hook.

(Originated by Joseph D. Bates)

NEEDLEFISH

Hook: Long shank
Underwing: White, blue dun, and green marabou
Wing: Eight light olive gray and two very light blue saddle hackles
Eyes: Amber and black
Head (nose): Green

(Originated by Bill Catherwood)

PINK SHRIMP

Thread: Red
Tail: Two pink saddle tips
Body: Flat silver tinsel
Hackle: Pink saddle hackle palmered through body and clipped at top (hackle extends slightly beyond gap width)
Head: Red

(Originated by Joe Brooks)

SILVERSIDE

Thread: Red
Body: Medium oval silver tinsel
Wing: A small bunch of white bucktail, over which is a small bunch of medium green bucktail, with a small bunch of light blue bucktail over this. The wing should be twice as long as the hook.

(Originated by Joseph D. Bates)

TINKER MACKREL

Underwing: White, blue and olive marabou
Wing: Olive and medium blue saddle hackle
Sides: Grizzly hackle
Eyes: Amber and black
Head: Blue and green body hair, trimmed

(Originated by Bill Catherwood)

Originator of the series of flies now known as the Giant Killers, Bill Catherwood's vision and innovation is an integral part of saltwater flyfishing history. Developed in the 1950s, his oversized baitfish imitations are an extraordinary combination of blended marabou, hackle, and hair that have influenced an entire generation of saltwater fly dressers.

Appendix

PLATE 15
The Thunder Creek Series
Originated and Dressed by Keith Fulsher

Keith Fulsher and friend. *(Photograph by Lois Fulsher)*

BLACKNOSE DACE *(Rhinichthys atratulus)*
Hook Shank Covering: Embossed silver tinsel
Lateral Coloring: Black bucktail, with a few strands tied forward on each side of the hook eye, then reversed with the back and belly material
Top of Head and Back: Brown bucktail
Bottom of Head and Belly: White bucktail
Eye: Cream lacquer with black pupil

BROOK TROUT *(Salvelinus fontinalis)*
Hook Shank Covering: Embossed gold tinsel
Lateral Coloring: Well-barred grizzly hackle feathers (two) dyed an olive color on top of the hook shank; a few red or bright orange bucktail hairs underneath the hook shank.
Top of Head and Back: Brown part of a blue dyed bucktail, having a blue-gray color
Bottom of Head and Belly: White bucktail
Eye: Cream lacquer with black pupil

BROWN TROUT *(Salmo trutta)*

Hook Shank Covering: Embossed gold tinsel
Lateral Coloring: A very few strands of red and black bucktail mixed together on top of the hook shank
Top of Head and Back: Brown bucktail
Bottom of Head and Belly: White and yellow bucktail in equal parts, mixed together
Eye: Cream lacquer with black pupil

EMERALD SHINER *(Notropis atherinoides)*

Hook Shank Covering: Pearl mylar tubing
Lateral Coloring: None
Top of Head and Back: Brown part of green dyed bucktail
Bottom of Head and Belly: White bucktail
Eye: Cream lacquer with black pupil

FATHEAD MINNOW *(Pimephales promelas)*

Hook Shank Covering: Embossed silver tinsel
Lateral Coloring: Black hair half the length of the hook shank under bright green bucktail the full length of shank, all on top of the shank
Top of Head and Back: Light brown bucktail
Bottom of Head and Belly: White bucktail
Eye: Cream lacquer with black pupil

GOLDEN SHINER *(Notemigonus crysoleucas)*

Hook Shank Covering: Yellow tinsel
Lateral Coloring: Yellow bucktail
Top of Head and Back: Brown part of a green or blue dyed bucktail
Bottom of Head and Belly: White bucktail
Eye: Cream lacquer with black pupil

LARGEMOUTH BASS *(Micropterus salmoides)*

Hook Shank Covering: Thin black floss ribbed with fine embossed silver tinsel
Lateral Coloring: None
Top of Head and Back: Brown part of a green dyed bucktail, a strong green color should dominate
Bottom of Head and Belly: White bucktail
Eye: Cream lacquer with black pupil

MARABOU SHINER (A General Shiner Pattern—Genus *Notropis*)

Hook Shank Covering: Embossed silver tinsel
Lateral Coloring: None
Top of Head and Back: Silver pheasant crest feather or black marabou
Bottom of Head and Belly: White marabou
Eye: Cream lacquer with black pupil

Appendix

RAINBOW TROUT *(Oncorhynchus mykiss)*

Hook Shank Covering: Embossed silver tinsel
Lateral Coloring: Pink bucktail
Top of Head and Back: Brown part of bucktail dyed green
Bottom of Head and Belly: White bucktail
Eye: Cream lacquer with black pupil

REDFIN SHINER—Male *(Notropis cornutus)*

Hook Shank Covering: Embossed silver tinsel
Lateral Coloring: Red bucktail underneath hook shank
Top of Head and Back: Brown bucktail
Bottom of Head and Belly: White bucktail
Eye: Cream lacquer with black pupil

REDLIP SHINER *(Notropis chiliticus)*

Hook Shank Covering: Black floss tail, black floss with embossed gold tinsel rib, orange floss fins (black floss is used to tie in fins: dorsal fin, one half in on hook shank top; anal fin, one third in on bottom of hook shank)
Lateral Coloring: Pale yellow bucktail
Top of Head and Back: Black bucktail, tip of nose is lacquered red
Bottom of Head and Belly: Pale yellow bucktail
Eye: Cream lacquer with black pupil

SILVER SHINER—Female and Immature *(Notropis cornutus)*

Hook Shank Covering: Embossed silver tinsel
Lateral Coloring: None
Top of Head and Back: Brown bucktail
Bottom of Head and Belly: White bucktail
Eye: Cream lacquer with black pupil

SMALLMOUTH BASS *(Micropterus dolomieui)*

Hook Shank Covering: Embossed gold tinsel
Lateral Coloring: Well-barred natural red grizzly hackle feathers (two) on top of the hook shank
Top of Head and Back: Brown part of a green dyed bucktail (brown should show through the green dye to provide a good bronze coloring)
Bottom of Head and Belly: White bucktail
Eye: Red lacquer with black pupil

SMELT *(Osmerus mordax)*

Hook Shank Covering: Embossed silver tinsel
Lateral Coloring: Orchid bucktail
Top of Head and Back: Brown bucktail
Bottom of Head and Belly: White bucktail
Eye: Cream lacquer with black pupil

SPOTTAIL SHINER *(Notropis hudsonius)*

Hook Shank Covering:	Black floss tail, embossed gold tinsel
Lateral Coloring:	None
Top of Head and Back:	Brown part of bucktail dyed green
Bottom of Head and Belly:	White bucktail
Eye:	Cream lacquer with black pupil

STEELCOLOR SHINER *(Notropis whipplei)*

Hook Shank Covering:	Blue fluorescent floss, embossed silver tinsel rib
Lateral Coloring:	None
Top of Head and Back:	Brown part of bucktail dyed blue
Bottom of Head and Belly:	Pale yellow bucktail
Eye:	Cream lacquer with black pupil

STRAWCOLOR SHINER *(Notropis stramineus)*

Hook Shank Covering:	Embossed silver tinsel
Lateral Coloring:	Blue dyed bucktail
Top of Head and Back:	Brown part of bucktail dyed pink
Botom of Head and Belly:	White bucktail
Eye:	Cream lacquer with black pupil

STRIPED JUMPROCK *(Moxostoma rupiscartes)*

Hook Shank Covering:	Embossed gold tinsel
Lateral Coloring:	Pale orange bucktail
Top of Head and Back:	Dark brown to black bucktail
Bottom of Head and Belly:	Pale orange bucktail
Eye:	Cream lacquer with black pupil

SWAMP DARTER *(Etheostoma fusiforme)*

Hook Shank Covering:	Embossed silver tinsel
Lateral Coloring:	Two grizzly saddle hackles
Top of Head and Back:	Brown bucktail
Bottom of Head and Belly:	White bucktail
Eye:	Cream lacquer with black pupil

WEDGESPOT SHINER *(Notropis greenei)*

Hook Shank Covering:	Black floss tail, black floss, embossed silver tinsel rib
Lateral Coloring:	Two strands of brown floss
Top of Head and Back:	Light brown bucktail
Bottom of Head and Belly:	White bucktail
Eye:	Cream lacquer with black pupil

Appendix

YELLOW PERCH *(Perca flavescens)*

Hook Shank Covering: Embossed gold tinsel
Lateral Coloring: Well-barred grizzly hackle feathers (two) dyed bright yellow on top of the hook shank
Top of Head and Back: Brown part of a green dyed bucktail
Bottom of Head and Belly: White bucktail
Eye: Cream lacquer with black pupil

Note: The back and belly hair is tied on with the tips pointing forward over the hook eye, then reversed to shape the head and body of the flies. White thread should be used, and gill coloring added by placing a touch of red lacquer on each side of the bottom part of the thread collar. Heads are all coated with a thin coat of epoxy and allowed to dry before the eyes and gills are added.

A Brief History of the Thunder Creek Series

The first Thunder Creek patterns were tied in the spring of 1962 and tested in their northern Wisconsin namesake river that same summer. I was searching for a method of tying a minnow fly that would produce an imitation more lifelike in appearance and action than the conventional bucktails and streamers that were in general use. I was familiar with the old procedure of reversing bucktail on a hook to make a small ball head on a fly, but the technique had not been developed to accurately imitate a baitfish in overall proportion or in coloring. Using this reversing technique and two or sometimes three colors of bucktail, I lengthened the head to about one fifth the length of the entire fly, using brown hair for the back, white for the belly, and dyed shades for the flank coloring, if needed. Red tying thread provided a flash of gill coloring. After the head was well coated with lacquer, a yellow base eye with a black pupil was added in about the center of the head.

The first three flies tied in this manner were the *Silver Shiner* and the forerunners of what would eventually become the *Strawcolor Shiner* and the *Smelt* patterns. By 1965, when the Theodore Gordon Flyfishers published THE GORDON GARLAND, there were eight established patterns in the series, although only two of them appeared in the text and sepia plates of that book. In 1966, Joe Bates in his classic STREAMER FLY TYING AND FISHING gave dressing recipes for all eight patterns and provided detailed tying instructions. Four additional patterns were added in July 1968 in connection with a *Field & Stream* article entitled "The *Field & Stream* Match-the-Minnow Streamer Fly Series," written by Al McClane, then fishing editor of the magazine.

Thunder Creek Series

By 1973, when Freshet Press published my book on the flies, TYING AND FISHING THE THUNDER CREEK SERIES, I had increased the number of patterns to fifteen and all were included in the color plates. Since then I have added six new patterns, bringing the total number to twenty-one. I doubt that I, at least, will add any more, although other tiers have used the tying technique to produce their own favorite designs.

Of the original eight patterns listed in the first edition of STREAMER FLY TYING AND FISHING, one, the *Mickey Finn,* has been eliminated and another pattern added in its place, as I wanted to keep the series to copies of actual baitfish. The *Mickey Finn* was originally included simply because its color combination was right for the Thunder Creek style of tying. Another of the original patterns, the *Satin-Fin Minnow,* has been renamed the *Steelcolor Shiner.* Although the two species of baitfish are similar in appearance, especially the males in their breeding colors, I opted to name the pattern after the *Steelcolor Shiner.* Others of the originals have had very modest changes in their makeup as indicated in the pattern listing for all twenty-one flies. This has to do with changes in my thinking on coloring or in the use of new materials as they became available, such as the use of mylar tubing to cover the hook shank of the *Emerald Shiner.*

Over time modest changes have also been made in tying procedures. I now tie the flies with white thread instead of red. This allows them to be tied more sparsely because it eliminates the necessity of using a heavy batch of white bucktail to cover up the red thread wrappings in the throat area. Now if little gaps appear between the strands of reversed white hair in the head area, the white tying thread blends in and the fly looks slim and neat. Gill coloring is added by putting a touch of red lacquer on each side of the bottom part of the white thread wrappings that hold the bucktail in the reversed position. In addition, I now use light cream-colored lacquer instead of yellow for the base eye. This is more in keeping with the true eye colors of most baitfish. There is one exception, the *Smallmouth Bass* pattern, which calls for a red base eye. I also now coat the heads with one very thin layer of epoxy rather than three coats of lacquer. This is a time-saver more than anything else, as the epoxy can eventually chip with use the same as lacquer because of the spongy nature of the bucktail underneath.

All of the Thunder Creek patterns can be tied in marabou by substituting that material in the proper colors for the bucktail initially called for. In weighting a fly, I like to add the weight only to the forward part of the hook shank, primarily under the head. This keeps the fly from riding upside down due to the added weight upsetting the natural hook balance and gives the fly a little diving action as you swim it across the water in a series of darting motions. A 4X to 6X long straight eye hook is the best one to use because the straight eye acts as an extension of the head and the retrieve is not influenced by an up- or down-turned hook eye. In addition, the procedure of reversing the bucktail to shape the head and body of the fly is much easier to accomplish on a straight eye hook than on an up or down eye. Partridge of Redditch makes a beautiful Thunder Creek hook and I highly recommend it.

I do have a favorite out of the twenty-one Thunder Creek patterns and it's the *Emerald Shiner.* It not only imitates that species of baitfish but duplicates the broad range of forage fish that have dark backs, whitish underparts, and bright iridescent flanks.

Good fishing.

KEITH FULSHER

Index

Pages containing particulars of fly dress are noted within parentheses.

Abercrombie and Fitch Co., 28, 235, 327
Adaline Bucktail, 295
Aiken, George D., 277
Alaska, 216, 217
Alaska Mary Ann Bucktail, plate VIII, 21 (215)
Albright, Captain Jimmie, 148
Albright, Frankee, 148
Aleck's Wonder Streamer (Cains River), 243 (245)
Alexander III, A.I., 324
Alexandra Streamer, plate II (217)
Algoma Bucktail, 267
Allagash country (Maine), 29
Allcocks, 137
Allen's First Choice Streamer (Cains River), 243 (245)
Allie's Favorite Streamer, plate IV, 177 (217)
Anglers Cove, Inc., The, 306
Anson Special Bucktail, (218)
Anticosti Island, 259
Argentine Blonde Bucktail, 205
Artula, plate 3 (361)
Ashdown Green Streamer, plate VII (218)
Assassin Bucktail, 303
Atom Bomb Streamer (Gray), 219
Atom Bomb Streamer (Yellow), plate VIII (219)
Aunt Ider Streamer, (219)

Au Sable River (Mich.), 329, 354
Ausable River (N.Y.), 261
Australia, 187

Bacon, Alonzo S., 25, 26
Bailey, Dan, 311
Bair, Fred, 322
Bair's Railbird Streamer, (322)
Bali Duck Streamer, (220)
Ballou, A. W., 26, 220, 221, 229
Ballou Special Streamer, plate VII, 7, 12, 26, 57, 91, 102, 187 (220) 221
Barnegat Inlet (N.J.), 132, 136
Barnes, C. Lowell, 222
Barnes Special Streamer, (221) (222)
barracuda, 154, 155
Barr, Andrew, 261
Bartlett, Arthur, 222, 223
Bartlett, Donald, 264
Bartlett's Special Streamer, plate II (222)
bass, channel, 155–57
bass, fresh water, 62–64, 104, 105
bass, striped, 118–20, 122, 125–29, 134–36
Bates, Arthur, 220
Bates, Jr., Colonel Joseph D., 256
 Streamer Fly Fishing in Fresh and Salt Water, 154, 207
 Trout Waters and How to Fish Them, 55
Bates, Jr., Mrs. Joseph D., 287
Battenkill River (Vt.–N.Y.) 223, 261, 335

385

Index

Battenkill Shiner Streamer, plate VI, 182, 222 (223)
Bauman, Art, 223
Bauman Bucktail, (223)
Becker, Bob, 270
Belknap Bucktail, (223)
Bellamy Bucktail, plate VIII, 57, 189 (224) 225
Bellamy, George B., 194, 224, 225
Bell, Anson, 218, 224
Bell Special Streamer, (224)
Benn, John S., 321
Benn, Martha, 322
Bergman, Ray, 220, 238, 285, 292, 323, 325
  Trout, 224, 263, 292, 299, 354
Beverage, Henry S., 312
Bi-Buck Bucktail, (225) 268
Big Bar Riffle, 252
Big Diamond Streamer, (226)
Bill Special, plate 6 (367)
Binns, J., 226
Binns Streamer, plate II (226)
Biplane Streamer, 103, 185
Bjornberg, Andy, 133
Black and White Streamer, plate II (227)
Blackbird Bucktail, 49, (227)
Black Blonde Bucktail, 205
Black Demon Bucktail, plate VIII (228)
Black Demon Streamer (Cains River), 228, 243 (249) 250
Black flies, 49
Black Ghost Streamer, plate VII, 4, 8, 12, 51, 105, 214, 222 (228) 229, 230, plate 2, plate 6
Black Gordon Bucktail, (230)
Black Leech Streamer, (231)
Black Marabou Streamer, 49, 356
Black Nosed Dace Bucktail, plate I, 35, 40–42, 96, 181 (231) 274 (306) (307), plate 2
Black Optic Bucktail, 195
Blondes, Brooks, 138, 149, 153, 155, 204, 205
Blueback Shiner, (307)
Blue Devil Streamer, plate IV, 177 (232)
bluefish, 129–35
Bluefish Bucktail, 130 (232)
Blue Marabou Streamer, plate III (233)
Bobby Dunn Bucktail, 57 (234)

Bob Wilson Streamer, (233)
Bolshevik Streamer, (234)
Bonbright, G. D. B., 28, 235
Bonbright Streamer, plate V, 28, 29 (235) 314
Bond, Horace P., 339, 342
bonefish, 139–48
books, fly tying, 165
Botty, Kenneth, 256
Brass Hat Bucktail, 57, 190, 193 (236)
Brewster, Al, 274
British Columbia, 42, 338
Brook Trout Streamer, plate VI, 12, 182 (237)
Brook Trout Variation, plate 5
Brooks Blonde Patterns, plate V, 138, 148, 152, 204, 237
Brooks, Joe, 118–120, 151
Brown, Chandler, 118
Brown Falcon Bucktail, (237)
Brown Ghost Streamer, 58 (238)
Brun, Major Theodore, 187
"bucktail" defined, 30, 31
Bucktail Silver Streamer, (238), plate 10
bucktails, making, 32–34, 166–206
Bugbee, Frank, 280
Bumblepuppy, The, plate VII, 22, 23, 26 (239–42) plate 1
Burgess, William, 258
Burke, Dr. Edgar, 263, 269
Burnham, Fred, 243

Cains River (N.B.), 60, 61
Cains River Streamer, 243 (246), plate 9
Cains River Streamers (Series), 242–50, plate 9
California, 36
Campbell River (B.C.), 42
Campeona Streamer, plate II (250) (251)
Canada, 217, 262
candlefish, 106, 111
Candlefish Bucktail, plate V, 113, 114, 116, 117 (251) 258, 288
Cape Cod Trout Club, 295
Carter Fly Bucktail, The, (251) (252) 253
Carter, Harley R., 252, 253
Carter's Dixie Bucktail, plate VIII (252)
casting
  cross stream, 78, 79

Index

downstream, 81, 82
to shore lines, 100–103
upstream, 71–78
Catherwood baitfish imitations, 108, 138
Catherwood, Bill, 138
Cavanagh, Jr., Robert H., 184, 206, 349, 350
Cedar River (N.Y.), 24
Champ's Special Streamer, (253)
channel bass, 155, 156, 157
Chapman, L. Dana, 28, 235
Chappie Streamer, plate VIII, 254
Chesapeake Bay Shad Fly, plate V, 67
Chief Needahbeh Streamer, plate II (255) plate 7
Christian, Herman, 241, 242
Clark, Gregory, 303, 304
Coachman Streamer, 12 (255)
Cock Robin Bucktail, plate III (255) (256)
Cock Robin Optic, 196
Colonel Bates Streamer, plate IV, 12, 57, 173, 177, (256) 257
Colonel Fuller Streamer, 28, 57, 58, (257)
Colonel White Streamer, 28, 29, 235 (258) 314
Colvin, F. D., 351
Colvin's Rogue River Special Bucktail, 351
Complete Fly Fisherman, The, John McDonald, 21, 239
Congdon, Frank, 226, 253
Congdon, Mr. and Mrs. Frank, 219
Connecticut Lakes country, 226
Connecticut River Shad Fly, 67
Connett, Eugene, 10
Conrad, Charles H., 318
Cook, Newton and Smith, Inc., 197
Cooper, Frank, 303
Coos Bay (Oregon), 68, 118, 120
Cooseboom, John C., 259
Cooseboom Special Bucktail, plate III (259)
Coronation Bucktail, plate V, 113 (258)
Coulson, Robert E., 298, 331
Cowee Special Streamer, plate III, 185 (259)
Cowee, Stanley, 259
Cowichan River (B.C.), 219
Craig, Jane, 291, 357
Cranberry Lake, 293
Crandall, Julian, 270
Crane Prairie Special Steamer, (260)
Crosby, Ted, 60

Cupsuptic Stream (Maine), 261
Cupsuptic Streamer, (260), plate 5
Cut Lips Streamer, plate VI, 182 (261)

dace
black nosed, 40
horned, 40
red bellied, 40
Damsel Streamer, (261)
Dana Streamer, 29
Dan Bailey's Fly Shop, 311
Dark Edson Tiger, plate 2
Dark Edson Tiger (Squirrel Wing), plate 6
David, Judge Lee Parsons, 327, 330
Dazzler, plate 3 (362)
Dean, Gordon, 162, 186
Delaware River, 242
Delaware Streamer, 316
Delman, Maury, 338
Demon Streamer, 217, 292
Denby, Lord, 298
Depth Ray #1, plate 13 (374)
Depth Ray #2, plate 13 (374)
Deschutes River (Oregon), 16, 57, 260, 293, 313
Dick's Killer Bucktail, (262) 266
Dillon, Burt, 67
dolphin, 160, 161
Donaldson, Harvey A., 24
Don's Delight Streamer, plate IV, 177, (264)
Dot Edson Streamer, (265), plate 6
Drain, Wesley, 114
Dr. Burke Streamer, plate II (263) 269, plate 11
Dr. Milne Streamer, 263, plate 8
Dr. Oatman Streamer, plate VI, 182 (264)
dri–ki, 4
Dufresne, Frank, 196, 215, 216
Dunk's Special Streamer (Cains River), 243 (246)
Dunn, Bobbie, 194, 234
Dusty Streamer, (265) plate 8

"Eagle-Claw," 137, 207
Eastman, Dick, 262
Edson Dark Tiger Bucktail, plate VII, 90, 91, 262 (265)
Edson Light Tiger Bucktail, plate VII, 16, 91, 262 (266)

Index

Edson Tiger, 3, 4, 12, 15, 16, 30, 57, 91, 195, plate 6 (367)
Edson, William R., 15, 19, 262, 265, 266
Eel River, 250, 290, 321, 322
Elm Sporting Goods Co., 197
Emerald Minnow Bucktail, 42, 181
Emerson Hough Bucktail, (267)
Engells Splaywing Coachman, 204
England, 187, 259
Esopus Bucktail, (268)
Esopus River, 230, 268
eulachon, 111
Evans, Kani, 306

fallfish, 40
Family Secret Streamer, (268) plate 11
Field and Stream (magazine), 135, 147, 188, 196, 254, 280, 322, 343, 347, 348, 351
Fin, Fur and Feather, Ltd., 217, 218, 225, 226, 261, 277, 284, 286, 292, 296, 298, 300, 315, 317, 319, 329, 349
Finland, 259
First Connecticut Lake, 262
Fishes of Massachusetts, The, Dr. Jerome V. C. Smith, 21
Fishing Gazette (magazine), 22
Fish, Leonard F., 24
Flick, Arthur B., 42
Streamside Guide to Naturals and Their Imitations, 40, 231
Florida, 28, 235, 286
Florida Keys, 139–164
fly
  body, 166
  butt, 166, 187
  cheeks, 168
  coloration technique, 184
  diving, wobbling action, 198
  feathers, 172, 173
  head, 169
  hooks, 45, 169–72, 189
  horns, 169
  Matuku Streamers, 187
  optic patterns, 195–97
  radio tube pins, 195
  ribbing, 166, 167
  Schwab methods, 189–95
  shoulders, 168
  Silver Garland body, wrapping, 188
  splayed wings, 185–187
  Stevens methods, 173–78
  tag, 166
  tail, 166
  throat, 167, 168
  Thunder Creek patterns, 180, 181 (377)
  topping, 169
  treating to float, 186
  "Upside down" types, 199
  visibility, 50, 51
  weed–guards, 199
  wings, 168, 172–78, 184–87, 191–95
Fly Patterns and Their Origins, Harold H. Smedley, 22
Fly Tying, William B. Sturgis, 23, 54, 199, 243, 249
Forest and Stream (magazine), 22
Forester, Frank, 21
Fort Wayne Bucktail, 22
Fowler, Fred B., 235, 290
Fox, Charles, 356
Frankee-Belle Streamer, 148, plate 14
Franklin, C. L., 254
Fraser, George, 234, 269, 270, 299
Fraser Streamer, 234 (269)
French, Allie W., 218
F.R.S. Special, plate 3 (362)
Fuller, Colonel Charles E., 257
Fulsher, Keith, 12, 42, 51, 178–81, 222, 223, 324, 332, 333, 340, 348, 377–84
"Fur Grip," 35
Fusco, Arthur W., 201, 301

G.A.B., 60
Galloping Ghost Streamer, (270) plate 8
Gapen, Don, 310, 311, 347
Gapen Fly Company, 310, 347
Gasperaux Bucktail, (270)
Gee, Lacey E., 65
Gees-Beau Streamer, plate IV (270) (271)
Gerlach, Herbert, 288
Ghost Shiner, plate VI, 182, 183 (273) 350
Gibbs, Harold, 130, 232, 273, 274, 300
Gibbs Striper Bucktail, plate V, 125, 126 (273) 274, plate 14
Giradot, Al, 338
G.J. Streamer, 285
Godfrey Badger Hackle Streamer, 343
Godfrey, Mr., 342, 343

Index

Godfrey Special Streamer, 343
God's River, 338
Gold Demon Streamer (Cains River), 243 (249) 250
Gold Sprat #1, plate 6 (368)
Gold Sprat #2, plate 6 (368)
Golden Darter Streamer, plate VI, 182, 183 (274)
Golden Prince, plate 14 (375)
Golden Rogan Bucktail, plate II (275)
golden shiner, 39, 40
Golden Shiner Bucktail, plate VI, 42, 182 (276) 358
Golden Shiner Streamer, 307, 308
Golden Shrimp, 147
Golden Smelt Streamer, plate VI, 182 (276)
Golden Witch Streamer, plate IV, 177 (277)
Gordon, Clarence, 231, 351
Gordon Dean Bead-Head Streamer, 186
Gordon, Theodore, 21, 22, 23, 26, 186, 239–42
Governor Aiken Bucktail, plate III (277)
Governor Brann Streamer, (278) plate 8
Governor fly, 290
Governor Special, 290
Grand Lake (Maine), 25, 26, 27, 29, 279, 349
Grand Lake Streamer, plate III, 58 (278) 279
Grant, Dick, 269
Gray Ghost Streamer, plate IV, 3, 4, 17, 40, 58, 61, 91, 173–75, 177, 213, 256 (279) 280, 281, 283, plate 2, plate 3
Gray Smelt Streamer, plate VI, 12, 182, 183 (281)
Green, Ashdown, 218
Green Beauty Streamer, plate IV, 177 (283)
Green Drake Streamer, (282)
Green Ghost Streamer, 281 (282) (283), plate 2
Green King Streamer, (283)
Green's Pot Streamer, 283
Green Spot Streamer, 283
Greig, Mrs. Elizabeth, 251, 275
Greyhound Streamer, plate IV, 177 (284)
Grey Prince Streamer, plate II (284)
Grey Squirrel Silver Streamer, (284) plate 10
Griswold, Morley, 313
Grizzly King Streamer, (285)
Grizzly Prince Streamer, plate I (285)

Gulf Stream, 160
Gulline, B. A., 284, 286, 349
Gulline Brothers, 185
Gulline, Frier, 217, 219, 226, 292, 296, 300, 319, 349
Gulline, H. L., 218
Gunnison River, 285, 351

Hagen Sands Bonefish Fly, plate V, 149 (286)
Haig-Brown Roderick, 42
Hair Basser Bucktail, 199
Hance, John P., 22
Hardy Brothers, 197, 217, 237, 346
Harger, Don C., 118, 230, 313, 338, 344, 350
Harlequin Streamer, plate II, 35 (286) 349
Helen Bates Streamer, (287)
Herb's Ghost Streamer, (287)
Herman, Raymond E., 243
Herman's Favorite Streamer (Cains River), 243 (246)
Herring Bucktail, plate V, 113, 114, 116, 117, 258 (288)
Herter's, 197
Highlander Streamer (Cains River), 243 (246)
Hoag, Dr., 199
Hobbs, W. H., 197
Hogan, Austin S., 184, 227, 286, 345
"holding water," 56
Homer Rhode, Jr., Tarpon Bucktail, 152, 153
Honey Blonde, 205
hooks
  bonefish flies, 148, 149
  chart, 171
  dolphin, 162
  "Eagle Claw," 137, 207
  for bucktails, 31, 45, 170–72, 190–92
  Limerick, 170, 171
  Model Perfect, 45
  snook, 160
  Sproat, 170, 171
  tarpon, 153
Hornberg, plate 2
Hornberg, Frank, 289
Hornberg Special Streamer, plate I (288) (289)
Horror, The, 147, 149

Index

Hough, Emerson, 267
Houghton, Amory, 342
Houle, Arthur, 358
Howard, Herbert L., 59, 218, 224, 233, 234, 259, 269, 270, 288, 292, 293, 299, 317, 345, 354, 355
Humboldt Railbird Bucktail, 322
Hunting and Fishing (magazine), 304
Hunt, Lynn Bogue, 280
Hurricane Streamer, 222 (289)
Hutcheson, Jim, 322

Iceland, 259
Improved Governor Steelhead Bucktail, plate VIII (290)
Injured Minnow, 44, 45
Iris #1, plate 12 (372)
Iris No. 1 Bucktail, (290) (291)

jack crevalle, 161
Jane Craig Streamer, plate VII, 57 (291) plate 5
Jazz Boa Streamer, 271
Jean Bucktail, (291) (292)
Jennings, Preston J., 291, 299
Jessabou Streamer, 271
Jesse Wood Streamer, plate I, 270 (292) plate 10
Johnson, Lawrence, 66
Jossy Special Bucktail, (293)
Jossy, W. E., 293
Judge, plate 4 (365)

Kahler, Nick, 270
Kandlefish Katie, 114
Kate Bucktail, 322
Kellogg, Al, 343
Kelly, Bill, 293
Kelly Bill Bucktail, (293)
Kennebago Lake (Maine), 359
Kennebago Special, plate 6 (368)
Kennebago Stream (Maine), 23, 263, 269, 294
Kennebago Streamer, (293) (294) plate 5
Kidder Streamer (Cains River), 243 (247)
Klamath River (Calif.) 16, 56, 225, 234, 236, 250, 252, 254, 290, 320, 321, 343, 344, 355
Knight, John Alden, 302–04
Kobuk Hook, 216

Kobuk River, 216
Kotzebue Sound, 216
Kukonen, Paul, 43, 44, 60, 61, 203, 233, 256, 301, 305, 326
Kvitsky, Joseph, 256

LaBranch, George M. L., 317
Lady Doctor Bucktail, plate VII, 12, 57 (294)
ladyfish, 157, 158
Lady Ghost Streamer, plate III, 281, (295) plate 8
Lady Iris, plate 12 (373)
Lady Miller, plate 3 (362)
Lake George Fly, 262
Lambuth, Letcher, 111, 251, 288
Larway, Temple and Cooper Co., 303
Laurentide Park, 262
leaders
 salt water, 140, 149, 154, 163
 with floating line, 81
Learmouth, Alexander, 319
Leech Streamer, plate I, 231 (295)
Leitz Bucktail, (296)
Leitz, Earl, 220, 296, 341
"Life Action" bucktail, 187
Light Edson Tiger, plate 6
line, fast sinking, 49, 92
line guides and salt water, 137
line "mending," 73–76
lines, salt water, 149, 151
Little Brook Trout Bucktail, plate I, 12, 42, 183 (296) (297)
Little Brown Trout Bucktail, plate I, 12, 42, 51, 183, 184 (297)
Little Rainbow Trout Bucktail, plate I, 12, 42, 183 (297) (298)
Lobb, Ginnie, 318
Lohrer's Sport Shop, 110
Lohrer, William, 110, 111
Long Key, 162
Longnose Dace Streamer, (308)
Lord Denby Streamer, (298)
Lord Iris Streamer, plate VII, 291 (298) plate 12 (373)
Lyon and Coulson, Inc., 298, 328, 331
Lyons, Howard, 328

MacArthur, General Douglas, 271
MacGregor Bucktail, (299)

Index

McCafferty, Robert, 49, 356
McClane, Al, 147, 188, 322
McCreadie Special Bucktail, 68, 121
McGinty Bucktail, (302)
McKenney, Ross, 29, 100, 102
McLeod, George, 111, 341
Mad River, 303
madtom, 54
Mad Tom, plate VI, 182, (299)
Magalloway River, 218
Magog Smelt Bucktail, (300)
Maine, 2, 3, 7, 23, 25, 26, 27, 29, 43, 77, 102, 111, 218, 221, 233, 235, 256, 261, 272, 283, 312, 346, 353
Male Dace Streamer, plate VI, 182, (300)
Marabou Perch Streamer, plate I (301)
Maranacook Lake (Maine), 6
Margaree River (N.S.), 259
Mascoma Streamer, plate III (301)
Materne, Edward A., 300
Mathers, Belle, 148
"Matuku" Streamer, 187
Meier and Frank Co., 343, 344
Memphremagog Lake, 277, 300
menhaden, 130
Mickey Finn Bucktail, plate VII, 12, 35, 40, 57 (302) 303, 304, plate 2
Milkweed Fly, plate 13 (374)
Miller's River Special Bucktail, plate III (305)
Mills, Jr., Arthur C., 187
Mills, William and Son, 187, 268, 292, 303
Milne, Dr. Douglas M., 264
Minnow Streamer, (305)
Miracle Marabou Streamers, plate I (306) (307) (308)
Miramichi River (N.B.), 9, 60, 61, 288, 323, 327–29
Miramichi Streamer (Cains River), plate II, 243 (247)
Mohawk River (N.Y.), 24
Montreal Streamer, (309)
Mooney, Frank, 256
Moosehead Lake (Maine), 44, 265, 342
Mooselookmeguntic Lake (Maine), 23, 102, 334
Moose Pond (Maine), 346
Moose River (Maine), 242
Moose River Streamer, (309)

Morning Glory Streamer, plate IV, 26, 177 (310)
Muddler Minnow, plate I, 51, 105, 148 (310) 347, plate 2
mullet, 162–64
Munster, George, 309
Mustad, O. and Son, 195
Myers, Jack, 352
Mylar, 200–03
Mylar Bodied Bucktails, plate I, plate V, plate VIII (311)
Mylar-winged Bucktail, 155

Narragansett Bay (R.I.), 122, 126
National Sportsman (magazine), 25
Needahbeh, Chief, 185, 186
needlefish, 111
Needlefish, plate 14 (376)
Nehalem River (Oregon), 343
Nestucca River (Oregon), 343
New Brunswick, 259
Newfoundland, 259
New Hampshire, 218
Newman, W. A., 286
Newton, Nellie, 228–30
New York, 7, 218, 239, 261, 293, 333
New Zealand, 187
Niagara River (N.Y.), 66
Nimrod Bucktail, (311)
Nine-Three Streamer, plate III, 52, 58, 283 (312) plate 2
Nipigon River, 298, 331
North Umpqua River, 351
Norway, 259
Norwegian Moustache Bucktail, (312) (313)
Nova Scotia, 259

Oatman, Lew, 12, 42, 180, 182–83, 222, 223, 237, 261, 264, 272,274, 276, 277, 281, 299–301, 323–25, 335, 350, 357–58
O'Donnell, Doris, 328
Old Family Recipe, plate 6 (368)
Ontario, 298
Optic Bucktails, 195–97
Orange Optic, 195
Orange Steelheader Bucktail, plate VIII (313)
Ordway, George T., 314
Ordway Streamer, 28, 29, 47, 258 (314)

392 Index

Oregon, 36, 115, 260
Outdoor Life (magazine), 204
Owl Eyed Optic, plate VIII, 118
Ozark Bucktail, 199

Paint Brush Bucktail, 57, 189, 193, 236 (314)
panfish, 66
Parkhurst, Zell, 111, 251, 288
Parmacheene Beau Streamer, plate II (315)
Parmacheene Belle Streamer, plate VII, 12 (315) 316, 351
Patrick Roy A., 111, 113, 165, 251, 258, 288
Paulina Lake, 343
Paul's Fishing Tackle, 35
Peet's Masterpiece Streamer (Cains River), 243 (247)
Percy, Gardner, 28, 29, 219, 222, 230, 237, 257, 258, 271, 282, 283, 285, 295, 309, 332, 340, 358
Percy Tackle Co., 28, 229, 235, 258, 314, 332
Perinchief, Pete, 147
Phair, Charles, 271
Phoenecia Bucktail, 230
pickerel, 64
Pierce's Pond (Maine), 102, 233
pike, 64
Pink Blonde Bucktail, 205
Pink Ghost Streamer, 43
Pink Lady Bucktail, (316) (317)
Pink Shrimp, plate 14 (376)
Platinum Blonde Bucktail, 205
Plymouth Streamer, (317)
Polar Chub Bucktail, plate I, 52 (317)
pollock, 136, 137
pompano, 161, 162
Powder Puff Streamer, 221
Practical Fly Fishing, Charles W. Wetzel, 270
Pray, C. Jim, 118 195–97, 243, 244, 249, 252, 290, 321, 348
Price, Everett, 327
Princess Bucktail, 47, 57, 189 (318)
Puget Sound (Wn.), 106, 110, 258, 288

Quebec, 259, 281
Queen Bee Streamer, (319)

Queen Bess Bucktail, 47, 57, 189, 193, 236 (319) (320)
Queen of Waters Bucktail, (321)
Quimby, Bert, 29, 264, 265, 270, 278, 283, 295, 312, 359

R.A.B., 60
Railbird Steelhead Bucktail, plate VIII (321) 322
Rainbow Streamer (Cains River), (247)
Raritan River (N.J.), 345
Ray Bergman Bucktail, (322), plate 10
Raymond Streamer, (323)
Raymond, Warren G., 323
R. B. Streamer, 323
Reade, Brigadier Philip, 25
Red and Yellow Bucktail, 303
Red Fin Streamer, plate VI, 42, 182 (323)
redfish, 155, 156, 157
Redhead Bucktail, plate III (324)
Red Horse Streamer, plate VI, 182, (324)
Red Optic Bucktail, 195–97
Red Phantom Streamer, plate VIII (325)
Red Spruce Streamer, 343, 344
Red Squirrel Gold Streamer, (325), plate 10
Reed, Fred A., 313, 339
Reliable Streamer, (325) (326)
Restigouche River, 288
Reverse-tied Bucktail, 177, 178
Reynolds, William, 227, 287, 321, 323, 358
Rhode Jr., Homer, 154, 159, 163, 164
Richards, George T., 270
Rifle River, 354
river bait, 307
Roach, Roxy, 328, 329
Roaring Rapids Streamer (Cains River), 243 (248)
rod holder, 92
Rodman, Oliver, H. P., 127
rods, salt water, 137, 140, 148, 151
Rogan, Alex, 275, 327
Rogan, Michael, 275
Rogan Royal Gray Ghost Streamer, plate II, 275 (326)
Rogers, Edward W., 230
Rogers Knight Streamer, 230
Rogue River, 252, 351, 352
Rogue River Special Bucktail, 351

Index

Rooster's Regret Streamer, 26, 27, 29, 258, 278
Rosborough, E. H., 52, 54, 188, 219, 231, 260, 293, 305, 318, 325, 336, 342, 343, 353
Rose of New England Bucktail, (327)
Ross McKenney Streamer, 29, 235
Roxy's Fox Squirreltail Bucktail, (328) (329)
Roxy's Gray Squirreltail Bucktail, (328)
Royal Coachman Bucktail, plate VIII, 55 (329) 351
Royal Coachman Streamer, plate II (329)
Russell, Jack, 60, 288, 330
Russell's Fancy Bucktail, (330)

Saguenay Streamer, 298 (331)
Salminan, Ray, 223
salmon
    Atlantic 58–62
    Chinook, 107, 108, 111
    landlocked, 57, 58
    Pacific, 108
    silver, 108, 114, 115
salt water, drift fishing, 157
salt water fly fishing
    Eastern, 122–38
    Southern, 139–64
    Western, 106–21
Sanborn, Dr. J. Hubert, 312, 319
Sanborn, Fred, 332
Sanborn Streamer, plate II, 57, 58 (331) (332)
Sanders Brothers Store, 332
Sanders Streamer, (332)
sandlaunce, 111
Sands, Hagen R., 286
Sapp, Gene, 348
Satin Fin Streamer, plate III (332)
Savage, Frank, 263
Scaled Shiner Streamer, (333)
Scarborough, Henry, 305
Schwab, Peter J., 15, 16, 19, 30, 47, 57, 189–195, 197, 224, 234, 244, 254, 267, 315, 318, 320, 352, 355
Scotch Lassie Streamer (Cains River), (248)
Scotland, 259
Scripture, Jr., William E., 24
sea trout, 131–35
Sebago Lake (Maine), 221, 222, 229

Second Connecticut Lake (N.H.), 262
Seth Brown Streamer, 316
"Sevenstrand" (leader material), 131, 154, 202, 203
shad, 67–68, 120, 121
Shang's Favorite Streamer, plate IV, 177 (333) (334) plate 4
Shang's Special Streamer, plate IV, 177 (334) plate 4
Shenandoah Fly, 227
Shenandoah River (Va.), 63
Shields, John, 257
Shiner, Don, 333
Shushan Postmaster Bucktail, plate VI, 182 (334) (335)
Silver Admiral Bucktail, 353
Silver and Orange Bucktail, (339)
Silver Darter Streamer, plate VI, 182, 183 (335) 350
Silver Demon Bucktail, 196 (335) (336)
Silver Demon Streamer (Cains River), 243 (249) 250
Silver Doctor Streamer (Cains River), (248)
Silver Garland Marabou Streamer, plate V, 7, 52, 187, 188 (336) (337)
Silver Gray Streamer (Cains River), (248)
Silver Minnow, plate I (337) (338)
Silver Minnow Bucktail, plate V (338)
silver salmon, 108, 114, 115
Silver Salmon Streamer, (339)
Silver Shiner Streamer, (308)
Silver Spruce Badger Bucktail, 343
Silver Spruce Bucktail, 343
Silver Tip Bucktail, plate III (340)
Silverside, plate 14 (376)
Skykomish River, 341
Skykomish Sunrise Bucktail, (340)
Slaymaker II, Samuel R., 12, 42, 51, 183, 184, 297, 298
Slosson, Steward, 28, 235
Smedley, Harold H., 330
smelt, 58
Smelt Bucktails, 116, 117, 237, 277
Smith, Andy, 252
Smith–Ely, Mr. and Mrs., 344
Smith, Harry, 61
Snake Pond (Maine), 100
Snake River (Wyo.), 254
snook, 158–60

Index

Snow Goose, plate 13 (374)
Snow, Sr., Captain Harry, 139–42, 145
Sodersten, Hector, 187
Songo River (Maine), 221, 229
Soo Fly Bucktail, (341)
Spencer Bay Special Streamer, plate III, 233 (342)
spinners, 114
Sports Afield (magazine), 189, 224, 320, 338, 352
spot-tailed minnow, 40, 42
Spruce, plate 2
Spruce Bucktail, 343
Spruce Streamer, plate VIII (342) 343, 344
Square Lake (Maine), 358
St. Ignace Streamer, 298 (331)
St. Mary's River (Mich.), 220, 296, 341
Steelhead Streamer (Cains River), 244 (246)
steelhead, 117, 118
Steenrod, Roy, 22, 23, 239, 241
Stevens, Mrs. Carrie G., 17, 173–78, 218, 232, 256, 264, 271, 277, 279–81, 282, 284, 310, 334, 355
Stevenson, Clive N., 344
Stevenson's Special Bucktail, (344)
Stevens, Wallace, 174, 279
Stewart, Clarence, 345
Stewart's Hawk Streamer, plate III (344) (345)
Stickney, Warden Supervisor Joseph S., 19, 294, 346, 353
stonecat, 54
Stone, Robert J., 357
Strawberry Blonde Bucktail, 205
streamer flies, making, 35, 166–206
"streamer fly" defined, 30, 31
striped bass, 118–20, 122, 125–29, 134–36
Stroud, Paul D., 199
Summers, Dr. Orrin, 345
Summers Gold Bucktail, (345)
Superior, Lake, 296, 341
Supervisor Streamer, plate VII, 57, 213, 233 (345) (346), plate 2

tandem flies, 95, 109, 202, 203
Tapply, H. G., 347
Tap's Tip Bucktail, (347)
tarpon, 149–154
Tay River, Scotland, 269

Terror streamers, 346
Thief, The, plate III, 49, 311 (347)
Thor Bucktail, plate VIII, 55 (347) (348)
Thoreson, Walter, 348
Thunder Creek Bucktail series, plate I, 12, 42, 178–81, plate 15 (377–84)
Tinker Mackrel, plate 14 (376)
Tomahawk, plate 3 (362)
Toronto Star (newspaper), 304
Towne, Captain Sumner, 255
Trask River (Oregon), 343
Treadwell, Benn, 278, 279
trolling, 88–95, 110, 111
trout
  brook, 50
  brown, 51
  cutthroat, 53, 115–117
  Dolly Varden, 54, 55
  lake (Mackinaw), 53
  Marston, 281
  rainbow, 52
  steelhead, 55–57, 117, 118
Trout and Salmon Fishing, John E. Hutton, 61
Trout Fin Series, 287
Trout Fin Streamer, plate III, 35, 184, 287 (348) (349)
Trout Perch Streamer, plate VI, 182 (350)
Trude, A.S., 23
Trueblood, Ted, 52

Umpqua River (Oregon), 231, 313
Umpqua Special Bucktail, plate VIII (305) 351
Unidentified Streamer, plate 12 (373)
Unidentified Streamer #1, plate 13 (375)
Unidentified Streamer #2, plate 13 (375)
Unidentified Streamer #3, plate 13 (375)
Unidentified (Teal Wing) Streamer, plate 6
Unidentified Tri-Color Bucktail, plate 6
United Fly Tyers Club (Boston), 201, 206
Upper Dam Pool (Maine), 173, 218, 232, 279, 280, 334
Upperman, Bill, 132–36
Upperman Bucktail, 136
Upperman, Morrie, 132–36

Vancouver Island (B.C.), 108
Van De Car Bucktail, (351)

Index

Van De Car, Tom, 351
Vanderhoff, Junior, 303
Van Luven Bucktail, 55, 189, 225, 320, 351 (352) 353
Van Luven, Harry, 348, 352
Voss, George and Helen, 219

Wade's Choice Streamer (Cains River), 243 (248) (249)
Wallenschlaeger, Jack, 330
Warden's Worry Bucktail, plate VII (353)
Washington (state), 36, 106–108
water
  clear, 43, 50
  discolored, 43, 47, 49, 50
  fast, 46, 47, 49, 69–87
  high, 43, 47, 50
  low, 43
  slack, 88–105
weakfish, 131, 132, 135, 157
Weber, Oscar, 243, 244
Weber Tackle Co., 42, 184, 217, 222, 223, 226, 243, 244, 253, 289, 297, 304
Welch, Herbert L., 19, 23, 228, 230, 261, 291, 294, 354, 357
Welch Rarebit Streamer, plate VII, 57 (353) (354) plate 5
Wells, Henry P., 316
Wesley Special Bucktail, (354)
Westfield River (Mass.), 262
Wharton Red Bucktail, 351
Wheeler, Hon. Charles E., 334
White Devil Streamer, 177

White Ghost Streamer, 281
White Marabou Streamer, (52) (53)
White Pheasant Streamer, plate 8 (372)
White River (Vt.), 74
White Water Bucktail, (354)
Wilkinson Streamer (Cains River), (249)
Will Ketch, plate 3 (362)
Willowemoc River (N.Y.), 10
Wilson, Robert, 234
Wizard Streamer, plate IV, 177 (355)
Wood, Jesse, 292
Wood Pussy Bucktail, 189, 192 (355)
Wotruba, Edward C., 222, 289
Wright and McGill Co., 137
Wulff, Lee, 59

Yellow and Black Streamer, 177
Yellow Breeches Creek (Penna.), 356
Yellow Breeches Streamer, (356)
Yellow Jane Craig Streamer, 291 (356) plate 5
Yellow May Streamer, (357)
Yellow Perch Streamer, plate VI, 12, 182, 276 (357)
Yellow Sally Streamer, 357
Yellow Squirrel Bucktail, (358)
Yellowstone Park, 254, 343
Yerxa, Bucktail, (358)
Yerxa, Jack, 358
York's Kennebago Streamer, (359) plate 44
York, T. Lewis, 359
Youngquist, Frank, 351

Zwirz, Bob, 306